HARVARD HISTORICAL STUDIES ◆ 190

Published under the auspices
of the Department of History
from the income of the
Paul Revere Frothingham Bequest
Robert Louis Stroock Fund
Henry Warren Torrey Fund

News from Germany

THE COMPETITION TO CONTROL
WORLD COMMUNICATIONS,
1900–1945

Heidi J. S. Tworek

Harvard University Press

Cambridge, Massachusetts
London, England
2019

First printing

Library of Congress Cataloging-in-Publication Data
Names: Tworek, Heidi J. S., author.
Title: News from Germany : the competition to control world communications,
1900–1945 / Heidi J. S. Tworek.
Description: Cambridge, Massachusetts : Harvard University Press, 2019. |
Includes bibliographical references and index.
Identifiers: LCCN 2018033145 | ISBN 9780674988408 (alk. paper)
Subjects: LCSH: Mass media—Germany—History—20th century. |
Mass media and culture—History—20th century. | News agencies—
Germany—History—20th century. | Mass media—Germany—
Influence—History—20th century. | Communication—Political
aspects—Germany—History—20th century.
Classification: LCC P92.G3 T96 2019 | DDC 302.23094309/05—dc23
LC record available at https://lccn.loc.gov/2018033145

CONTENTS

Introduction   1

1. The News Agency Consensus   17

2. A World Wireless Network   45

3. Revolution, Representation, and Reality   70

4. The Father of Radio and Economic News in Europe   99

5. Cultural Diplomacy in Istanbul   121

6. False News and Economic Nationalism   141

7. The Limits of Communications   170

8. The World War of Words   196

Conclusion   224

List of Abbreviations   233

Notes   235

Archives Consulted   305

List of Figures   313

Acknowledgments   315

Index   319

HISTORIANS USING newspapers to research public opinion on any matter, event, or historical personality during a particular time period cannot simply interpret and record the statements of one or more newspapers as public opinion. Historians must check newspapers' opinions against the character and intentions of their creators, search for potential influences, research sources that were used. They must know the size and type of audience at the newspapers as well as how far the newspapers depend internally and externally on that audience. Finally, they must measure any results against competing opinions that fought for similar relevance at the time. Personal opinions, party-political intentions, and external influences obfuscate even ostensibly objective, purely factual reporting. That is even more the case for the judgments, conclusions, and consequences that the press pronounces. This is one task of research on the press, but the other is to ascertain the lay of the land—its silent, slow, and barely noticeable changes, whose emergence the press does not chronicle at first, the silent rising, sinking, and repositioning of the intellectual and material bases of popular life. Only by combining and comparing these results will researchers see a sure and truthful picture emerge of what they seek.

—OTTO GROTH, *Die Zeitung: Ein System der Zeitungskunde* (1928)

INTRODUCTION

"The lie is the law of the world!" screamed a cartoon caption in the German satirical magazine *Kladderadatsch* in March 1917. Unrestricted submarine warfare had broken out in the Atlantic and it was a month before the United States would enter World War I. But German satirists only cared about communications. Poems, articles, and cartoons filled their March special issue attacking British control over global news. That control came from the combination of communications technology and one particular business: Reuters, the British news agency that supplied information from around the world to hundreds of newspapers. The cartoon portrayed Reuters as a gremlin gnawing on a globe with green oceans; his gnarled fingers grasped the world and telegraph cables shot out from his sharpened fingernails (see Figure 1). The "Reuters cable network" made words as central to the world war as weapons.

Information warfare may seem like a new phenomenon, driven by the vastly expanded connectivity of the twenty-first century. In fact, information warfare has long existed and long blurred the lines between war and peace. As the *Kladderadatsch* cartoon implied, information warfare was enabled by the infrastructure of communications technologies, whether submarine cables a century ago or fiber-optic cables today. Patterns that often seem new are actually quite old.

Competition over communications became as central to the first half of the twentieth century as it is today. German elites were not just worried about

Die Lüge ist der Welt Gesetz!
Dies lehrt das Reuter-Kabelnetz

FIGURE I. Cartoon, "Die Lüge ist der Welt Gesetz! / Dies lehrt das Reuter-Kabelnetz." "The lie is the law of the world! Reuters cable network teaches that." *Kladderadatsch* 70, no. 13 (March 31, 1917): 208. Courtesy of Universitäts-bibliothek Heidelberg, http://digi.ub.uni-heidelberg.de/diglit/kla1917/0208.

the British; they also competed with the French, Americans, and later Soviets over global news. This competition would not end with the armistice in 1918. It would continue all around the world until 1945. A British intelligence report in 1936 lamented that Germany was "now daily flooding the whole world with news."[1] The Soviets condemned German news as "a dangerous element for the interests of peace."[2] The Nazis became the leading supplier of news to Japanese-occupied China during World War II. All this, and more, built on German investment in international news networks stretching back to 1900.

News networks have always existed. The Roman and Persian empires both had systems of mounted couriers to transport messages swiftly. The Fuggers, a family of prominent German merchants and bankers in the fifteenth and sixteenth centuries, sent letters to inform a network of bankers and traders. Newspaper-like products emerged in the sixteenth and seventeenth centuries in Europe, though newspapers did not become the primary vehicle to convey news until around 1800.[3]

Press and news agencies are a distinctively modern phenomenon. When lithography was developed in the early nineteenth century, press agencies arose to create articles and syndicated products for distribution to multiple newspapers. These were small-scale specialized companies with limited geographical reach that did not supply news on current topics. Spurred by the swift spread of submarine telegraphy around the world, news agencies like Reuters partially emerged from press agencies in the mid-nineteenth century. News agencies built extensive systems of news collection and became the main bottleneck for creating news from events. They used the telegraph to deliver short messages to as many newspapers as possible. To express the difference in commercial terms, news agencies were "news wholesalers," distributing material to their "retail clients" (newspapers) to repackage into articles for their particular publics.[4] Another way to understand news agencies is to see them as gatekeepers who controlled the flow of information to other news organizations.

News agencies had extraordinary reach. Apart from major papers like the London *Times* or *Vossische Zeitung,* most newspapers could not afford foreign correspondents. Many papers did not even have journalists in their own capital cities. In 1926, 90 percent of all newspapers had no correspondents abroad or in Berlin. They received all their national and international news through news agencies or syndicate services.[5] Today, we worry about whether Facebook or Google hold monopolies over information provision. News agencies exerted an arguably even greater grasp over national and international news in the first half of the twentieth century.

It is thus unsurprising that *Kladderadatsch* polemicized against news agencies as the most powerful media companies. German elites agreed and would turn to news agencies to bolster German political, economic, and military power. Starting around 1900, a news agency consensus emerged among German elites—a belief that these firms were not simply media businesses, but offered a covert means to achieve broader political, economic, and cultural aims. News agencies were the easiest way to influence hundreds, or even thousands, of newspapers around the world. German elites often disagreed about how to control news agencies or what political and economic goals their news should achieve. But they agreed that news now played a central role in public life and international relations. A wide swathe of elites concurred that they could use news agencies to control news and that they could use news to achieve wider geopolitical, geoeconomic, and cultural goals.[6] They also believed that it was more important to control news supply than the daily news cycle.

There were no clear lines between news and information, propaganda, espionage, sensationalism, and opinion. Definitions of "news" have changed over time and space, affected by political, economic, cultural, social, and technological factors.[7] Sports became news in the late nineteenth and early twentieth centuries; human interest stories were de rigeur by the early twentieth century when they had not been a century before. The battles over what is legitimate news still rage today. One person's news is another person's gossip. One person's fact is another person's fake news.

News is sometimes a commodity sold for profit; sometimes it serves social or political purposes. Some see news as a public utility rather than a commodity. Objectivity was only one potential aim or value for news. In contrast to Anglo-American standards of impartiality that developed over the nineteenth and twentieth centuries, the meshing of opinions and facts remained critical to German journalism.[8] German journalists saw their profession as governed by an ethics of conviction or, as Max Weber called it, *Gesinnungsjournalismus*.[9] Their duty was to provide opinions on the facts and interpret them for readers.

News was always about more than novelty. The word "news" in English derives from a contraction of "new things." The German word for news, *Nachrichten,* more accurately reflects the role that news played in German and international history. *Nachricht* emerged from the verb *darnachrichten* and means to direct, orient, or control something (the German term *Neuigkeiten* conveys the idea of "new things" or personal news).[10] During and after World War I, news became enmeshed in debates about cultural diplomacy, economics, propaganda, and international relations. Could news promote foreign trade? Could news create support abroad for German aims? Could the soft power of news bolster hard power? Could the press defend democracy? These debates did not happen in full view of newspaper readers. Instead, competition over world communications happened before news ever reached the readers.

The history of news is often told as a simple tale of inevitable Anglo-American dominance over international media in the modern era, whether through Hollywood, the BBC, or Facebook. The German story is one way to point out the flaws in that tale. Many individuals, groups, and states challenged Anglo-American infrastructures, firms, and approaches to news.[11] Those seeking alternatives did not always succeed, but they contested the global media landscape long before Al Jazeera, Xinhua, or RT (Russia Today). States using news as a form of international power has been the norm since 1900, not the exception.

Beyond understanding that news is a form of power, the more challenging task is to explain why certain groups became interested in news at a particular moment and how they tried to influence it. Germans had not always cared about international news. In the 1860s and 1870s, only a few men like Chancellor Otto von Bismarck and his banker Gerson von Bleichröder had seen news as central to domestic and European politics. It would be the turn of the twentieth century before most German elites would agree. Unlike Bismarck's focus on the European continent, however, Germans now sought to spread news beyond Europe to mirror Germany's new political and economic ambitions. Like the *Kladderadatsch* cartoonist, German elites in the first half of the twentieth century believed that news did more than inform the public. News seemed to affect political decisions, govern trade strategies, and direct public opinion. Communications were not simply soft power.[12] They seemed to support political, economic, and military power at home and abroad.

Germans had integrated into global trends of trade, migration, and missionary activity long before Germany became a unified nation in 1871.[13] Only around 1900, however, would most German elites come to see the world beyond Europe as a vital battleground for their national interests. Their view of the world remained Eurocentric, but it now saw continents like South

America and East Asia as important spaces for German politics, trade, technology, and culture as well as communications.[14] Many Germans became invested in *Weltprojekte* (world projects).[15] Some Germans had been interested in cultural world projects since Johann Wolfgang von Goethe first elaborated the concept of *Weltliteratur* (world literature) in the 1820s and 1830s.[16] By 1900, world projects were political and economic too. Germans developed the concept of a world economy (*Weltwirtschaft*).[17] Politicians discussed world politics (*Weltpolitik*). They wanted Germany to be a world power (*Weltmacht*). Academics debated the question of world traffic (*Weltverkehr*), which at the time meant trade, communications, and transportation.[18] These questions about world power dovetailed with some Germans' increasing investment in building a colonial empire overseas like the French and British. Communications was as critical to these world plans as politics or economics.

At the turn of the twentieth century, many of the elites who turned to world projects also feared that other imperial powers were encircling and constraining Germany. In communications too, elites saw a Germany boxed into second-class international status. As British-German rivalry intensified, Germans became increasingly convinced that the British were using the global submarine cable system to undermine German foreign policy and turn neutral countries against it. World War I seemed to confirm German suspicions. Starting under the semidemocratic/semiauthoritarian constitutional monarchy of Wilhelm II through the democratic interwar Weimar Republic and ending with the Nazis, many Germans believed that they could only escape their second-class status if they created their own international communications networks.[19] This conviction was not just about rivalry with Britain; it was about challenging the entire international communications system of submarine cables and news agencies that had emerged in the nineteenth century.

An astonishing array of German politicians, industrialists, military leaders, and journalists became obsessed with news. International powers needed international communications infrastructures. Conversely, if Germany had a world communications network, the country could assert itself as a world power. Communications and power were tautologically and inextricably intertwined. Everyone from the Weimar Republic's most famous foreign minister Gustav Stresemann and first president Friedrich Ebert to prominent Wilhelmine Grand Admiral Alfred von Tirpitz and Nazi Propaganda Minister Joseph Goebbels used the networks behind the news to try to shape politics and economics at home and abroad.

Because historians so often use newspapers as evidence, they have missed how the networks behind the news molded what newspapers reported. Often, news from Germany was not labeled as such. It was printed in languages other than German, particularly English and Spanish. In 1938–1939, one German news agency broadcast 9.5 hours daily of news in German, 9 hours in English, 2 in French, and 18 in Spanish.[20] It was often disseminated through businesses or technological networks that disguised their German connections. Sometimes, even newspaper editors did not know they were printing news from Germany. Networks behind the news shaped what people read more fundamentally than we have previously acknowledged. Scholars often treat newspapers uncritically as sources of information. In fact, their creation was as complicated and contested as any other historical product.

Understanding news just by looking at newspapers is like trying to understand cotton just by looking at clothes. The commodity of cotton has a violent and complicated history spanning the globe.[21] Though less blood was shed, elites similarly sought to control the creation of news for political and economic purposes. For German elites (bureaucrats, politicians, military leaders, industrialists, journalists, and academics), the field of news became a battlefield over political, economic, and cultural influence. The printed words in the newspaper bore no visible scars from that battle, but it fundamentally shaped them.

One of the central aims of this book is to explore how news was actually created in the past and what it meant. Infrastructures, institutions, and individuals made news. Yet historians have long used newspapers as sources without understanding how news was shaped by the networks of its production. This problem is even greater now that vast troves of digitized newspapers are available. Dissertations on Canadian history, for example, cited the *Toronto Star* ten times more often after that newspaper had been digitized in the early 2000s.[22] But there has been no corresponding cascade of work to explain why we cannot take newspapers at face value. Only by venturing behind the printed newspaper can we learn how information traveled the perilous journey from event to news. News was never neutral. And its production never uncontested.

Snappy newspaper headlines have obscured what often mattered more: the institutions and infrastructure that enabled headlines and articles to appear in the first place. By institutions, I mean not individual newspapers, but rather the political, economic, and technological forces that shaped the press. An institutional and infrastructural history of the press takes content seriously, but it examines how that content emerged from the networks behind the news as much as the individual choices of journalists or editors.

An institutional history of the press operates on a different time scale than news itself. The press moves fast, but behind the headlines lay slow transformations in the underlying landscape and infrastructure that often crystallize in single moments. Counterintuitively, it often makes more sense to study the news by moving away from focusing on daily novelty to focusing on hierarchies and control. Only then can we uncover the "silent, slow, and barely noticeable changes, whose emergence the press does not chronicle at first, the silent rising, sinking, and repositioning of the intellectual and material bases of popular life," as Otto Groth, one of the first German media scholars, put it in 1928.[23]

This book takes inspiration from Groth's approach that emphasized long-term trends and structures. It charts Germans' myriad attempts to change how news worked around the world from 1900 to 1945 and how others reacted. To do so, it uses material from state and business archives in multiple countries and languages. The most important parts of an institutional story were not the famous journalists and newspapers, but bureaucrats or other businesses. News from Germany often seemed to surface suddenly in particular places like Argentina at particular moments like the 1930s. But that could only happen because Germans had spent decades building infrastructure and institutions to change how news networks functioned.

Germans became fascinated with news agencies because they came to see news as tied to power. Sociologist Pierre Bourdieu's concept of symbolic power helps to explain why news could command such authority in the first place. Bourdieu built on linguistic work known as speech act theory about how humans use speech to generate action. Bourdieu suggested that we cannot understand why certain speech creates real-world results without understanding the institutional context in which speech acts occur.[24] Institutions exert "symbolic power" over statements. The words, "I do," for instance, only make you married when you say them in front of a registrar or person licensed to wed couples. That license to marry is in turn embedded within the institution of the state. Institutions, in other words, enable communications to be effective and credible. This is also true for news. Presentation is just one part of influencing people through news.[25] The power of news also stems from the infrastructure, firms, and supply networks behind newspapers.

News agencies partly seemed so powerful because they were hidden from ordinary readers. The groups that assessed news agencies were not readers, but clients, end-users of agency material (such as newspaper editors), and the sources of stories.[26] Newspapers often did not list the origins of news items and many readers were more interested in content than source. Although readers in the past often seemed to exhibit greater media literacy than today, current news consumers are particularly vulnerable to forgetting "source information," or where an article came from.[27] This dynamic was a plus for German elites who sought to control news supply behind the scenes.

The history of news from Germany is not so much a story about how ordinary newspaper consumers read news. It is about how elites used news for political and economic power. It is about why elites believed news could be used for those purposes in the first place. Even though the newspapers they owned reached millions of people, elites were often talking to each other through newspapers. Many believed that published opinion could dictate public opinion. Their fixation on news was as much about what elites believed the public should want as what citizens really desired.[28]

Extant histories of German media focus on the domestic press, comparisons with countries like Britain, or international influences on Germany, showing how journalism came to play a key role in German politics.[29] A vibrant newspaper culture helped residents to navigate cities like Berlin in the late nineteenth century.[30] At the same time, colonial motifs pervaded German advertising and created a widespread imperial consciousness.[31] After World War I, the control of news formed a central arena of contestation in Germany's domestic political struggles.[32] But these struggles were not solely domestic: right-wing news became successful at home and among German minorities abroad in Eastern Europe. Following German news providers outside Germany's borders reveals how public and private services exploited new communications technology to become the main providers of news in regions Germany had never dominated.

The international dimension of news has long flown under the radar because scholars portrayed media as national or imperial.[33] Benedict Anderson famously used newspapers as the example of how print created national communities.[34] The national circulation of newspapers has often obscured the international networks behind the news. Yet the news business and communications infrastructure were and still are international. They helped to create "communication space"—a space of interaction that, as historian Charles Maier has argued, "has never been bordered so rigidly, indeed that challenges the territorial limits that prevail at any moment."[35] German elites intervened in communication space to challenge British, French, American, and other nations' political and economic prowess around the world.

In the first half of the twentieth century, many Germans saw news as both national and international.[36] International flows of information were an essential precondition and facilitator of globalization.[37] As one former German news agency employee put it in 1910, of all types of commerce and transportation, news "acquired first and most often a world character [*Weltcharakter*]."[38] News agencies simultaneously became national institutions. Politically, news agencies relied on the state for access to official news and to information infrastructure. Economically, their frequent inability to turn a profit from subscriptions alone made them susceptible to external influences. News agencies were not simply businesses operating in a free market. They relied fundamentally on institutional support from governments and access to the latest technological infrastructure. More than almost any other media institution, they reveal the tensions between political control, profit, and technology.

German politicians, military leaders, and industrialists chose news agencies to reshape world communications for two main reasons: the political economy of news and wireless telegraphy. Wireless telegraphy was a new communications technology that emerged in the late nineteenth and early twentieth centuries and used Morse code to transmit messages through electromagnetic waves.[39] Historian Richard R. John has defined political economy simply as "the relationship of the state and the market."[40]

The specific features of news agencies led to an unusual combination of state intervention and market forces. News agencies had very high fixed and sunk costs due to the expense of stationing correspondents abroad and the high price of telegrams. This significant barrier to entry meant that only a handful of news agencies existed, making them an easier bottleneck to control than thousands of newspapers. Many news agencies relied on the state to provide content and, if possible, preferential access to communications technology. From the 1860s until well into the Weimar Republic, the main news agency in Germany—Wolff's Telegraphisches Bureau (Wolff or WTB)—was the exclusive provider of government news. Politicians and bureaucrats, meanwhile, saw Wolff as an efficient method to control citizens' reading habits, and by extension, their beliefs and behavior.

The political economy of news operated on both national and international scales. Wolff was one of the "Big Three" modern news agencies founded in the mid-nineteenth century, along with the French Agence Havas and British Reuters Telegram Company. Reuters, Havas, and Wolff built on informal cooperation to create a formal cartel in 1870 (though a contract may have existed as early as 1856). The cartel included the American Associated Press from 1893 to 1933–1934. The three founding agencies divided the international supply of news between them: each reported on an assigned sphere and exchanged this news with the others. The cartel was exceptionally long-lived, lasting until the outbreak of World War II.[41] The cartel's rhetoric of total control belied its constant jostling to fend off or incorporate competitors, especially from Germany. Private business arrangements like this cartel shaped internationalism as much as international organizations.

German interest in the political economy of news intertwined with ambitious plans for new communications technologies. From the mid-nineteenth century onward, communication and transportation infrastructures had become critical factors in creating national, imperial, and international orders.[42] Telegraphy, canals, and railroads were the "sinews of the world economy," transforming how goods, people, and ideas traveled.[43] Starting with optical telegraphy in France in the early eighteenth century and then electrical telegraphy from the 1830s, telegraphy enabled information to move exponentially faster than goods or people for the first time. New technologies created new (or sometimes strengthened old) networks of distribution. They increased international cooperation, or at least interaction, and they fashioned new expectations about the availability, accessibility, and abundance of information.

Up to the late nineteenth century, German participation in global communications networks had been comparatively limited. After that, German politicians, industrialists, generals, and journalists seized upon new wireless technology to undermine the premise of the international news system: telegraph cable networks. "The wireless telegraph is not difficult to understand," Albert Einstein supposedly said. "The ordinary telegraph is like a very long cat. You pull the tail in New York and it meows in Los Angeles. The wireless is the same, only without the cat."[44] Wireless remained important even after the development of spoken radio in the 1920s and stayed crucial for disseminating information into the mid-twentieth century. Today, "wireless" means the method of radio communication, or refers to the internet; "radio" denotes the devices used to receive sound.

Germans actively pursued innovation in wireless technology to support their political and economic ambitions for news. Technological innovation does not happen in a vacuum.[45] It is driven by funding; it is driven by political priorities; it is driven by military priorities. Imagination, use, and innovation of technology are inextricably intertwined.[46] Pushed by German visions, wireless became a point-to-many technology, rather than point-to-point like telegraphy or telephony. Point-to-point technologies transfer information between two fixed points, from one transmitter to one receiver. Point-to-many technologies such as wireless and radio broadcast information from one point, but many people can receive that information simultaneously. Any wireless receiver within range could theoretically pick up broadcasts. Government and business subsidies, political visions, and a strongly developed scientific community made Germans world leaders in wireless.

Successive German governments saw wireless as the "path to freedom," as one news agency editor in chief, Wilhelm Schwedler, put it in 1922.[47] Only months prior to the outbreak of World War I, the German government connected its colonies with wireless to circumvent British cables. World War I shifted German ambitions from a colonial to a world scale. Among Britain's first acts of war was cutting most of the undersea cables to Germany in August 1914. The Allies similarly destroyed wireless towers in colonies that they captured. The German government invested or intended to invest heavily in wireless to bypass cable networks. In 1917, the tallest wireless tower in the world was erected at Nauen, just outside Berlin. After defeat in 1918, many Germans saw wireless as one of the only ways to reach beyond their borders and counter an international system of news that they believed had turned neutral countries against them. Wireless companies and news agencies continued to carve out their own sphere of operation on the seas as well as on continents where German telegraph news had never played a major role such as South America and East Asia. Like radio, wireless infrastructure created a new kind of "sonic geopolitics."[48]

Wireless is often forgotten in the history of communications technology or portrayed as a step on the road to spoken radio.[49] It is mainly remembered because of Guglielmo Marconi, a man who flamboyantly overinflated his own role in creating wireless for marketing purposes.[50] In fact, Marconi shared his Nobel Prize in Physics in 1909 for "contributions to the development of wireless telegraphy" with a German inventor, Karl Ferdinand Braun, whose work fundamentally relied on public-private partnerships in Germany.[51]

The neglect of wireless is curious, because the internet raises many similar issues. Wireless was the first technology to reach vehicles on the move, the first to become an instantaneous point-to-many technology, the first where physical connections were not necessary to reach each receiver. It also presented an opportunity for Germany to exert control over a new international infrastructure. Innovations in wireless technology created novel and overlapping news networks, forming different visions of space, audience, and the meaning of news itself.

German faith in communications to achieve broader goals lasted across several domestic regime changes: from semiauthoritarian constitutional monarchy before 1918 to Weimar democracy to Nazi dictatorship after 1933. Historians of Germany long debated whether the country took a "special path"—*Sonderweg*—to modernity that culminated in the Nazi period. Most scholars now generally reject this idea for many reasons, including because German society contained many democratic elements common to other countries and because the *Sonderweg* idea implied a "normal path" to modernity that never existed.[52] Over the past few decades, the preoccupation with German national history has ceded to exploring continuities between violence and genocide in German colonies or the Eastern Front in World War I and the Holocaust.[53] Taking a more transnational approach has revealed other continuities, such as the role of émigrés from Weimar Germany in shaping the postwar Bonn Republic as well as American foreign and defense policy.[54]

The history of news from Germany adds two other avenues to trace continuity across time and space: businesses and technologies. By taking the firm as their unit of analysis, business historians have long explored how businesses traverse borders or survive political turmoil.[55] To take one of many German examples, Beiersdorf—a personal-care company whose products include Nivea skin cream—managed political risk across multiple political regimes to grow into and remain a major multinational enterprise.[56] The history of German news is a story, not just of how businesses survived, but also of when they did not. We can only understand this by putting these businesses into a broader political, economic, cultural, and social context. German news agencies founded in the Wilhelmine period would last until 1945. After 1945, German governments would no longer support news for political or economic purposes. The continuities from 1900 to 1945 came from German elites' beliefs about Germany's place in the world, rather than domestic circumstances.

The same was true for technology. The British often saw technologies as "instruments to stabilize an international *status quo* favourable to their nation, while Germans viewed products of engineering as tools to transform the international environment that stifled their political ambitions," as historian Bernhard Rieger has put it.[57] Nazis could so successfully send news around the world because they relied on technologies and news agencies supported by German governments and industrialists since the early twentieth century.

The chapters of this book trace the emergence, expansion, and expiration of the news agency consensus—the widely shared belief among German elites that controlling news could fulfill broader geopolitical, geoeconomic, and cultural aims. German politicians, military personnel, and industrialists translated that belief into myriad attempts to build media institutions that would support their ambitions. Some of these attempts were coordinated; some competed with each other. This history is one of experimentation, contingency, and wrangling between public and private institutions over who should control news agencies and news infrastructure. By 1945, some of those experiments would succeed. Others would have little effect. None undermined the widespread faith that news could change people's perceptions of reality.

The first two chapters explore the two elements of the news agency consensus: the political economy of news and wireless technology. Chapter 1 examines how news agencies became the international bottleneck of news as well as why German elites came to believe that they needed news agencies to gain international power. Chapter 2 explores why German political and economic visions for news shaped the development of wireless telegraphy. It traces German attempts to build a world wireless network before and during World War I to subvert and surpass rival communication systems.

The next six chapters trace how news agencies propelled German national and international political and economic strategies. Chapter 3 tells two tales of how news could and could not change the course of history. The real story behind the birth of the Weimar Republic in November 1918 was how a news agency effectively abdicated Kaiser Wilhelm II and helped German politicians to create a democracy. That same news agency could no longer make revolution during the Kapp Putsch in March 1920. In November 1918, a news agency could be a tool of political change; in March 1920, it could not.

Chapter 4 traces how the government tried to use a news agency called Eildienst (Swift Service) as a tool of economic policy in the early 1920s. More than change economics, Eildienst shaped government policy for wireless, and later, spoken radio by enabling state control and supervision. State control had been meant to defend democracy. That liberal impulse had unintended illiberal consequences once the Nazis came to power. Only this longer history of Germany's state-supported radio infrastructure explains how the Nazis could control radio so rapidly. Chapter 5 explores the promise and peril of making news agencies part of cultural diplomacy in the 1920s. The German Foreign Office subsidized the salaries of news agency journalists, including the hapless Hermann von Ritgen in Istanbul. But individuals like Ritgen might abuse their position and not necessarily represent the state as bureaucrats wanted.

Some business magnates were just as interested as politicians in using news agencies to control politics and economics. Chapter 6 tells the tale of how industrialist turned media mogul and nationalist politician, Alfred Hugenberg, used a news agency called Telegraph Union as a tool of economic nationalism in the Weimar Republic. False news and sensational reports along with modern advertising and vertical integration into a media empire ensured Telegraph Union's swift rise to prominence in Germany and among German minorities abroad. Chapter 7 explores the limits of using news agencies as tools of domestic politics in the late Weimar and Nazi periods. Weimar bureaucrats tried increasingly illiberal methods to solve antidemocratic discontent and stop Telegraph Union. These efforts inadvertently laid the groundwork for the Nazis to reshape the media landscape. Although news agencies remained at the center of the Nazis' media strategy, they would discover that controlling news did not mean they controlled the population.

Finally, Chapter 8 examines how Germany fought wars of words in the first half of the twentieth century through one particularly successful state-subsidized news agency, Transocean. From its foundation in 1913 until 1945, Transocean played a key role in German foreign policy. The agency's news was printed all around the United States in World War I, raised hackles with British press baron Lord Northcliffe in the early 1920s, and evoked intense paranoia in J. Edgar Hoover about Nazi infiltration in South America. In East Asia, Transocean became the leading news agency in Japanese-occupied China.

For nearly half a century riven by internal and international conflict, German elites had shared one common assumption: that news agencies could alter political, economic, and cultural circumstances. Their efforts to send news from Germany around the world were surprisingly successful; their efforts to change circumstances less so.

The history of news from Germany is not a story about Germany alone. It is a story that challenges the conventional narrative of Anglo-American dominance of international media in the twentieth century. It is a story of how political and economic visions for news drove technological innovation. It is a story of how political and economic ambitions intertwined with infrastructure and information. Finally, it is a story of how communications did and did not change the course of history.

1

THE NEWS AGENCY CONSENSUS

$\mathcal{I}$t was "crucially important" to control an international news agency, concluded Gottfried Traub, editor in chief of the *München–Augsburger Abendzeitung* from 1921 to 1925. News agencies seemed to provide pure facts. At the same time, agencies "conveyed a value judgment" about facts by selecting, omitting, or shaping particular pieces of information. This "double character of a so-called 'news item' is the secret of every daily newspaper," wrote Traub in his memoirs. News agencies created a network behind the news that molded reports before they even reached newspapers. Germany's problem was that Britain and France "controlled the world" by creating news that bolstered their national priorities. Germany could only forge an independent press if it organized "its own international news service."[1] News agencies were embedded in international structures that constrained domestic room for maneuver. For men like Traub, the national and the international were inextricably intertwined.

Traub had to explain the importance of news agencies because they were unknown to most readers. But he would not have had to explain their importance to most German politicians, industrialists, bureaucrats, military generals, and journalists. These elites had come to see Germany as a global power around 1900. They became convinced that Germany could never become a global power without global media to back it up. The international structure of news seemed to undermine German imperial and great power ambitions. Though they disagreed about the nature of Germany's ambitions, many industrialists, generals, bureaucrats, and politicians came to a consensus on how to change international news provision. It would be through the news agency.

Contemporaries understood that it was both expensive and difficult to gather international news. Very few news agencies existed, making them easier to control than thousands of newspapers. Information from news agencies could appear in political and nonpolitical, local and national newspapers. News agencies formed a source of information that most readers did not see. The invisibility of news agencies increasingly seemed a source of strength to elites, not weakness. It enabled them to shape public opinion secretly and, by extension, mold international politics, economics, and culture.

Beliefs about the effect of news on public opinion were paradoxical. Elites saw newspapers as a mirror of "public opinion" (or as a means to justify their actions based on public opinion). Simultaneously, they sought to shape that public opinion by controlling what newspapers published. If published opinion was the same as public opinion, then influencing published opinion would logically manufacture a different public opinion. News agencies seemed the most efficient method to shape many newspapers simultaneously without readers' knowledge. Though they sought to influence news for different purposes, contemporaries increasingly focused on news agencies to achieve their broader goals.

The Rise of News Agencies

In 1920 the political editor of the *Allgemeine Zeitung* in Chemnitz, Ernst Heerdegen, complained about the triple dependency of Wolff Telegraph Bureau, Germany's main news agency. First, Wolff depended politically on the government. Second, it depended financially on its owners, who were bankers. Finally, it depended internationally on its cartel relationship with the British and French news agencies, Reuters and Havas. Heerdegen disliked Wolff's status as a junior partner in a system that had emerged in the mid-nineteenth century.[2] Complaints like Heerdegen's had started around 1900. It was not a coincidence that they focused on news agencies.

News agencies became the central firms collecting international news from the mid-nineteenth century. The "Big Three" news agencies were all created in this period: Agence Havas in the early 1830s, Wolff's Telegraphisches

Bureau (Wolff) in 1849, and Reuters Telegram Company in 1851. The founders of Reuters and Wolff, Julius Reuter and Bernhard Wolff, had fled to Paris from the German lands during the 1848 revolutions. They worked for Havas and built up a personal relationship with the owner, Charles Havas. The three continued to cooperate when Wolff founded his agency in Berlin and Reuter began his business in Aachen using pigeon post before moving to London in anticipation of the first submarine cable laid between Britain and France in 1851.

Informal cooperation between the three men and their agencies arose for technological as well as personal reasons. The spread of telegraphy meant news from around the world could be collected more swiftly than ever before. Although the development of steamships had accelerated travel in the first half of the nineteenth century, telegraphy was the first technology that allowed information to move far faster across oceans than goods or people.[3] After the first permanent transatlantic cable in 1866, submarine telegraph expanded rapidly to reach India, Australia, Latin America, and Africa by the late 1870s.[4] News sent by telegraph became essential for any serious newspaper.

The news agency business model addressed problems of cost and capacity in telegraphic news gathering, where there were very high fixed and sunk costs.[5] Fixed costs are expenses that stay constant, no matter how much news is produced; sunk costs are expenses that a company has incurred and cannot recover. For international news gathering, these included a large network of correspondents stationed abroad and the expense of sending telegrams. Wolff spent over a million marks gathering news in 1913; Reuters spent four to five times that.[6] Cables also had limited capacity: few providers could gain regular, swift access to send telegrams. These high barriers to entry made news agencies the main supplier of international news for most newspapers, which could not afford such expenses.

As fixed and sunk costs were so high, the Big Three news agencies cooperated to minimize the costs of news collection. The three agencies built on informal cooperation to create an astonishingly durable formal cartel from 1870 until the outbreak of World War II.[7] The cartel divided the world into territories. Each agency reported on its assigned spheres and exchanged that news with the other agencies. Each company stationed agents in the headquarters of other agencies to select news items to telegraph back to their home country. Within their spheres, the Big Three negotiated contracts to exchange news with particular national and imperial news agencies.[8] These arrangements fulfilled two aims simultaneously. They saved costs on news collection abroad and assured a dominant position in news supply at home.

Wolff often seemed like the junior cartel partner. Each agency covered its country's colonial territories and any areas that seemed economically or culturally affiliated with the agency's home country. Beyond Germany's small colonial empire, Wolff only covered continental Europe: the Austro-Hungarian Empire, Scandinavia, and parts of Russia. Meanwhile, Agence Havas covered Spain and South America, while Reuters and Havas jointly administered places like parts of China. Both Wolff and Havas paid extra fees to Reuters, which spent more on telegrams from Britain's far-flung empire. But only Wolff had to cede 25 percent of its annual profits to Reuters and Havas from 1890, as it used so much of their news.[9]

Compared to cartels in other industries, surprisingly few major changes occurred during the cartel's formal existence. In 1893, it added a new signatory—the American Associated Press (AP). The AP began to participate as an equal partner in 1893; it left in 1933–1934 after disagreeing with Reuters about news exchange in Japan (though Reuters and AP cooperated informally into the 1960s). In 1900, Wolff gained the right to disseminate individual news items directly to newspapers in China, Japan, and South America, as long as the items were not sent to news agencies. This enabled Wolff to establish relationships with German-language newspapers in those countries, like *Ostasiatischer Lloyd*. The new arrangement barely dented the reach of Reuters and Havas.

After a hiatus during World War I, Reuters and Havas renegotiated the cartel. They restricted Wolff to Germany, but allowed new national agencies in Central and Eastern Europe to sign contracts with Wolff to exchange German news. In a highly contentious clause, Reuters and Havas gained the same rights as Wolff in the occupied Rhineland, though Reuters soon withdrew and left the field to Havas.[10] Still, Wolff was not useless. In 1930, AP general manager, Kent Cooper, ranked Wolff above Havas as the second most useful foreign agency after Reuters "in the order of their efficiency and importance to us."[11]

Wolff's participation in the cartel was normal practice for German businesses. The German Imperial Court had ruled in 1897 that cartels offered a "particularly appropriate service to the entire national economy" and were justified as long as they did not create monopolies or exploit customers.[12] In 1914 a German economist called the news agency cartel "the most rational" way to save costs.[13] Cartels and similar arrangements regulated between 30 and 50 percent of global trade in the early 1930s; Germans were represented in 60 to 75 percent of cartel agreements in 1932.[14] Regular contractual revisions help to explain the news cartel's exceptional longevity, paralleling practices in German coal and steel cartels.[15] Even the Nazis remained in the news cartel until 1939 (though under Wolff's successor agency).

Contemporaries believed that the cartel agencies possessed "a sort of monopoly on world reporting."[16] As high costs created an effective barrier to entry, German scholars from the early 1900s into the 1930s were skeptical that anyone could ever challenge the cartel's "monopoly" on world news.[17] In 1932 three academics noted that the "Ring Combination," as the cartel was sometimes known, "forms one of the most complex and politically significant structures which affected the everyday life of the reading publics of the world, in the whole realm of international affairs."[18]

A news agency could only secure a place in the cartel by dominance at home. A few Germans had long seen a news agency as a vital part of national politics. Soon after establishing his eponymous agency in London, Julius Reuter tried to expand into mainland Europe. When he attempted to encroach on Prussian territory in the 1860s and compete with Wolff, the Prussian government provided financial, political, and technological backing to retain a news agency for Prussia. With support from Chancellor Otto von Bismarck, Gerson von Bleichröder's bank purchased Wolff in 1865 as part of a four-bank consortium and turned it into a limited partnership called Continental-Telegraphen-Compagnie (CTC). The head of Bleichröder Bank sat on Wolff's board until Wolff was finally sold to the government in 1931. In 1874, Wolff became a stock corporation. In 1903 / 1904, it even paid shareholders a handsome dividend of 11.4 percent.[19]

To combat Reuters's encroachment, the state started to provide political and technological guarantees of Wolff's dominance. Bismarck deemed it essential for Prussia to have access to a news agency based in Berlin and not to cede control over German news to London-based Reuters. The Postal Ministry prioritized Wolff telegrams over private messages. Called the *Amts-Correspondenz Privileg* (Official Correspondence Privilege, or AC privilege for short), this enabled Wolff to corner the market in swift news supply. This system functioned because the Postal Ministry controlled communications technology, particularly after the 1892 Reich Telegraph Law gave the Reich exclusive rights over constructing and operating "telegraph facilities for the dissemination of news."[20] Further revisions in 1908, 1919, and 1928 expanded the law to include wireless and radio.

Wolff was the only news agency to receive government news. In return, from 1869 onward, the agency was required to send political telegrams to be approved for publication to the Prussian government (after German unification in 1871, to the German government). Wolff generally sent political items to the responsible civil servant asking: "Is publication of the following message questionable?"[21] Bismarck himself often intervened to prevent or encourage the distribution of certain reports domestically and abroad.[22] This arrangement made Wolff a semiofficial news agency: financially independent but fundamentally reliant on government news and technological support.

By the early twentieth century, some criticized this agreement as contravening the basic principle of a telegraph agency: to report facts. One academic worried in 1912 that the government could bury unpopular news in two lines so news agencies could "never be wholly truthful."[23] Hermann Diez—a director at Wolff from 1912 and managing director from 1929 to 1933—had claimed in 1910 that polemicists did not understand how news worked. Wolff's news was not censored. In convoluted bureaucratese, Diez noted that the agency merely exercised a "voluntary consideration [of government wishes] characterized by objective [*sachlich*] deliberations."[24] Although politicians and businessmen later attributed Wolff's dominance to its government ties, Wolff's directors always maintained that its efficiency and access to international news were more important. In reality, news agencies and governments were mutually dependent on each other.

News agencies were particularly susceptible to political control because it was hard to turn a profit on the news business alone. News agencies branched out to supplement their incomes. Havas maintained an advertising agency. The agency has operated solely as an advertising company since the liberation of France in 1944, when Agence France-Presse (AFP) became France's major news agency. From 1851 to 1930, Reuters functioned more like "a trading company operating in news," meaning its business operated more like companies importing and exporting goods than like other news and press organizations.[25] It also dabbled in private banking and sent private telegrams using Reuters code to reduce the number of words and thus the cost. None of those measures stopped most news agencies from cooperating with their national governments. Havas needed French government approval of political telegrams. In Germany, Bismarck supported a partially state-regulated news distribution during the highpoint of economic liberalism because he saw news as more than just another business. News was a vital way to reach and influence citizens.

Bismarck's actions to protect German news were successful. Reuters withdrew from German-speaking territory; in the cartel treaty of 1870, Wolff gained the exclusive right to supply news within German-speaking territory, except Hamburg (which Reuters ceded to Wolff in 1900 for an annual payment of 10,000 marks). In the late 1880s, Bismarck even tried to create a Triple Alliance in news to parallel Germany's political alliance with Austria-Hungary and Italy.[26] Still, Bismarck and the Foreign Office focused on influencing individual journalists more than news agencies.

The arrangements of the 1860s set the terms for Wolff-government relations into the Weimar Republic. Wolff was the main supplier of government news and used its semiofficial status to provide the swiftest delivery of news over the telegraph, and later telephone. Although Wolff sent news from federal authorities in Berlin, ministries and local municipalities also supplied official notices directly through local newspapers, whose names often indicated this status, such as *amtlicher Anzeiger* (official advertiser). Some ministries paid for these items and only provided these pieces to government-friendly newspapers. This enabled indirect control of newspapers at the state level.[27]

In the late nineteenth century, most German elites found nothing remarkable or problematic about these arrangements. That would change around 1900. German diplomats, politicians, bureaucrats, generals, and businessmen started to pay more attention to news. They did not like the system that they discovered.

Political and Economic Concerns about News

By the early twentieth century, new geopolitical and geoeconomic concerns led elites to question the news networks that Germany had cocreated. Under Bismarck in the 1870s and 1880s, Germany had acted as a broker within Europe rather than an overseas imperial power like Great Britain or France. Bismarck organized the 1884–1885 Berlin Conference to carve up Africa not because he sought imperial advantages for Germany, but because his role as a negotiator might secure Germany greater prestige within Europe.[28]

At the same time, however, imperialist voices increasingly demanded "a place in the sun."[29] Germany seized colonies in South West and East Africa along with islands in the Pacific Ocean like New Guinea and Samoa as well as concessions in the Chinese port city of Qingdao (Tsingtao). Germany morphed from a continental country into an international competitor with other imperial powers.[30] Kaiser Wilhelm II's *Weltpolitik* (world politics) reoriented German foreign policy toward imperial competition with Britain on a global scale in the 1890s. Wilhelm II forced Bismarck out of office in 1890 and appointed more imperially minded chancellors, though a German Colonial Office only emerged in 1907 when it split from the Foreign Office.

Germany possessed a small physical colonial empire, but Germans began to develop a large colonial imagination. In 1913, German colonies contributed just 2.55 percent of the country's total gross domestic product.[31] But colonialism infused German culture. Colonial motifs saturated advertising.[32] Working-class readers devoured colonial books; colonial products were on sale everywhere.[33] Colonial thinking remained relevant even after Germany lost its colonies in 1918. In the Nazi period, the German Colonial Society had 2.1 million members.[34] Colonial attitudes affected German interactions with Eastern Europe and the Baltics alongside Germany's actual colonies in Africa and the Pacific.[35]

Colonial thinking was not monolithic. Some wanted Germany to be a land-based empire; others wanted to develop it into a sea-based power; others wanted to combine the two. These debates rested on different understandings of how control over certain choke points translated into global power. They also adapted American and British theories about how geography bolstered political and military prowess.

Some were deeply influenced by American naval officer and strategist, Alfred Thayer Mahan, who argued in the 1890s that Britain's naval superiority explained its rise to global dominance. Among many others, Kaiser Wilhelm II and German Admiral Alfred von Tirpitz were deeply influenced by Mahan's idea that whoever ruled the sea ruled the world. Tirpitz would use Mahan's theories to justify increased German expenditure on the navy starting around 1900. East Asia also shaped naval officials' understanding of the world. After the mid-1890s, every chief of admiralty staff but one completed a tour in East Asia. Naval officers dreamed of Germany becoming an "East Asian power," as Tirpitz declared in 1896.[36]

Others saw Germany as a land-based colonial power akin to Russia that should dominate Eastern Europe. This thinking informed the harsh treatment of Poles within the German Empire as well as the punitive terms of the Treaty of Brest-Litovsk in March 1918 that ended war between the Central Powers and Soviet Russia.[37] The emphasis on Eastern Europe strengthened over time, boosted by the German reception of British geographer Halford

Mackinder. In the early 1900s, Mackinder pioneered the idea of using geography to analyze history and imperial power.[38] In particular, Mackinder believed that controlling certain geographical areas—especially the "heartland" in the middle of the Eurasian continent—conferred more power than others. Mackinder developed his "heartland theory" over the next few decades and argued strongly in 1919 for the Versailles conference to pay attention to geopolitics.[39]

Even after defeat in World War I, colonial ideas continued in Germany. In the 1920s, German geographers, particularly Karl Haushofer, seized on ideas from Mackinder and Mahan, mixed with German geographers and historians like Friedrich Ratzel and Oswald Spengler, to develop the German concept and subdiscipline of *Geopolitik*. *Geopolitik* incorporated social Darwinism and eugenicist ideas; it emphasized national autarky and German expansion to achieve more Lebensraum (living space) and control the vital area of Eastern Europe. *Geopolitik* also foresaw a balance between sea and land power, rather than privileging one or the other. Rudolf Hess, a leading Nazi, studied under Haushofer in Munich starting in 1919 and Nazi ideology became infused with ideas of Lebensraum.

News formed part of colonial competition. Imperialists increasingly saw international news arrangements as beholden to a bygone age of a Germany with a continental focus. One colonial enthusiast, Paul Rohrbach, argued in 1912 that "the residue of our former political backwardness" hurt the portrayal of Germany in the foreign press.[40] "The belief that we can carry on our political business without a foreign press vigorously instructed and influenced in the interest of Germany reveals our innocence in matters of foreign policy," fumed Rohrbach. The British, French, and Americans had understood that "almost everyone abroad" used newspapers to form opinions. They had already used that knowledge to influence the foreign press "in an anti-German way—and it does not matter whether the papers are written in English, French, Turkish, Arabic, or Chinese." The only solution was shaping the press to make "moral conquests abroad."[41]

These concerns played out in practice as well as publications. Reuters supplied news to the German colony of Samoa, eliciting complaints to the German government in 1894 that it could not even distribute news to areas under its military and political control.[42] Meanwhile, governors of German colonies grumbled that Wolff's news was irrelevant. It summarized important government news and did not provide the original wording of official announcements that bureaucrats often needed to execute their policies. But

Wolff provided long telegrams about insignificant social events or accidents, like "the general inspector of the cavalry Lieutenant-General Windheim was struck down by a stroke on the court hunt at Döberitz. Lieutenant-General Windheim died immediately." Heinrich Schnee, governor of German East Africa, suggested in 1913 that Wolff could telegraph "Lieutenant-General Windheim dead of stroke," if it had to send such messages at all.[43]

Alongside complaints from colonies, reporting on imperial crises heightened concerns about how Germany's junior place in news undermined its great power ambitions. After Kaiser Wilhelm II had made a speech in Tangier in March 1905 in favor of Moroccan independence from French colonial rule, France mobilized for war. This provoked the first Moroccan crisis. A conference between the major European powers convened at Algeciras in 1906 to resolve the dispute. With tensions running high, the drama of Algeciras filled the pages of European newspapers.

In Germany, that news did not come from German sources: Algeciras was Havas territory under the cartel contract. Wolff distributed French Havas telegrams within Germany under Wolff's label. A scandal broke out when major German newspapers such as the *Frankfurter Zeitung* and the *Berliner Tageblatt* sent their own correspondents to Algeciras and discovered Wolff's absence.[44] Algeciras prompted German officials to worry that British and French reporting could turn the German population against Wilhelm II and the colonial enterprise.

Although the Algeciras conference resolved the political dispute, it exacerbated tensions between Germany and the Entente powers. It helped to convince Russia to sign an alliance with Great Britain in 1907. Mutual suspicion about other governments' motives drove forward the formation of entangled alliances on the European continent that would prove so deadly in 1914. The Algeciras incident exacerbated competition over communications too. It accelerated government beliefs that Germany was competing with France and Britain to influence attitudes in neutral countries like the United States, China, Japan, and the Ottoman Empire, where British and French news agencies dominated information supply. Politicians and academics decried the cartel's restrictions. Some blamed the German public's upset at Germany's diplomatic performance in Algeciras on inadequate reporting. Others asserted it was "well-known that Reuters conspires with Havas to use the monopoly in an anti-German manner."[45]

Wolff's domestic arrangements seemed similarly unreliable after the *Daily Telegraph* affair of 1908. Wilhelm II had granted an interview to the British

Daily Telegraph, published on October 28, 1908. His assertions were practically predesigned to cause outrage. Wilhelm II proclaimed that he belonged to a minority of Anglophile Germans, while claiming that he had supplied the winning battle plan for the Boer War—a provocative statement given that Germany was not involved in the war.

News of the interview quickly spread to Germany: on the day after its publication in England, Chancellor Bernhard von Bülow authorized Wolff to print the interview without any commentary. Chancellor from 1900 to 1909, Bülow cooperated closely with Otto Hammann, chief press officer from 1894 to 1916, to influence the press. Heinrich Mantler, Wolff's managing director from 1891 to 1929, completed the press system trio in the early 1900s. Miscommunication between the three meant that Mantler was forced to allow the publication of the interview without commentary, although he and Hammann had advised against it.[46] The *B.Z. am Mittag* printed the item before Wolff could send out any official explanation, unleashing uproar. This impolitic interview became one of the most famous pre–World War I scandals in Germany.

Scandals over Wolff and the press spurred Bülow to rethink how news might create a pro-German climate abroad and calm dissatisfaction at home. After Algeciras, Bülow submitted a request to Wilhelm II to raise the budget for press abroad, calling it "a piece of national defense."[47] Bülow blamed bad French, Russian, and particularly British press for putting Germany on the media defensive. Wilhelm II agreed willingly, especially as Bülow suggested that most of the money be raised from business circles.

Bülow aimed, however, to bolster Germany's position in Europe more than overseas. In a 1908 draft of a speech for Bülow on the press abroad, Otto Hammann asserted that "Europe meant everything for Germany and overseas as good as nothing."[48] Many elites no longer shared this Bismarckian attitude. Mantler emphasized in private correspondence to Hammann in 1908 that Wolff could only operate successfully "with constant regard to the international political interests of the German Reich."[49] Hammann and Bülow would soon promote a German role in overseas news too.

The funds raised by Bülow financed several new agencies. One was the short-lived Wolff-led Deutsche Kabelgrammgesellschaft (German Cablegram Company), which folded by 1918.[50] Another was Continental Korrespondenz (Continental Correspondence), started in 1903 to counter British influence by sending articles regularly overseas on German politics, economics, and culture. Heavy industry and trade subsidized the enterprise until 1909.[51] Finally, Transatlantisches Bureau (Transatlantic Bureau) was founded in March 1908 to supply telegrams overseas and subvert Reuters and Havas in South America and Australia.

These efforts intensified as wars broke out in the Balkans in the early 1910s. By 1913, the Foreign Office decided to streamline the myriad initiatives into the Syndikat Deutscher Überseedienst (German Overseas Service Syndicate). This comprised many smaller government news organizations and would later become Transocean. The government and industrialists also created Syndikat für die Auslandsnachrichten (Syndicate for Foreign News) in early 1914. The British ambassador in Berlin, Sir Edward Goschen, discovered the plan and reported it to the British government and press. There was such public outcry that the German government dropped the idea before it got beyond the planning stages.[52]

Economic concerns drove increased attention to news just as much as politics. Some contemporary economists saw news as just another commodity that was traded more frequently as the world economy grew. Others thought that news had caused the increase in global trade, because the exchange of economic information had decreased the risks of speculation.[53] Either way, news seemed ever more essential to boosting German exports.

The German share of world exports grew steadily from 9.5 percent in 1872 to 13.1 percent in 1913. Germany's increasing prowess in chemicals, engineering, and products of the Second Industrial Revolution drove its success. Germany overtook the French Empire's share of world exports by the early 1890s and nearly equaled the United Kingdom (without the British Empire) by 1913.[54] German participation in the global economy influenced trade and tariff policies at home.[55]

These developments sparked discussions about how news supply affected German exports. German exporters worried about how British, French, and American news agencies filtered news from the rest of the world before reports reached Germany. Conversely, they grew anxious that target export regions were receiving biased news about Germany. In 1913, the Bund der Industriellen (Association of Industrialists) complained about the "one-sided influencing of foreign press by certain French and English news agencies."[56] Industrialists, led by Alfred Hugenberg, founded their own news company, Ausland, to promote German industry abroad.[57] Comparing Germany to the United States, some academics agreed that reporting by the two countries' news agencies had "not kept pace with how their global trade relations develop[ed]."[58] By 1914, even a Wolff's director admitted that Reuters sup-

plied Wolff with a biased service on East Asia and pleaded for a "good supplementary service from a purely German viewpoint" in East Asia and
South America.[59]

Despite generally supporting cartels, industrialists and businessmen disagreed with academic arguments that high costs made the news agency cartel
essential.[60] They believed, instead, that news could be a loss-making enterprise: it should support German business overall rather than function as a
business in its own right. Exporters believed that news could influence foreign trade; they sought to improve Germany's share of news provision to
mirror its growing power in world trade. On this logic, more news to a region
meant more exports. That was a price worth paying.

Finally, nationalist critics suspected pernicious Jewish influences dating
back to the founders of the Big Three news agencies, all of whom were Jewish.
Dr. Ferdinand Werner—member of the Reichstag and later the first Nazi
state president of Hesse in 1933—denounced Wolff in the Reichstag in January 1914, as "the well-known Jewish telegraph agency." He claimed that
Wolff showed important official telegrams to Bleichröder Bank, implying
nefarious Jewish sway over news (as Bleichröder was Jewish). The Foreign
Office, Interior Ministry, and Chancellery swiftly backed up Wolff, stating
that the government "constantly endeavored through contact with the press
to prevent false or misleading alarming news from upsetting the popular
mood."[61]

Wolff's dominance could only hold as long as it fulfilled its two promises
of broad coverage and international influence. From 1900, it seemed increasingly clear to a broad swathe of German elites that Wolff's junior status was
undermining German political and economic prowess. This concern emerged
at the same time as newspapers were catering to an increasingly mass market.
As the newspaper landscape became ever more varied, controlling the bottleneck of news agencies would seem more important than ever.

The Mass Market in Newspapers

News agencies emerged at the same time as an educated liberal middle class
started to seek international and national news. Several large publishing
companies like Ullstein and Mosse emerged in the late nineteenth century.
Leopold Ullstein bought his first newspaper in 1877; the Ullstein family
founded *B.Z. am Mittag,* the first German tabloid, in the early 1900s and

purchased the prestigious *Vossische Zeitung* just before World War I. Ullstein and Mosse were both Jewish-owned, liberal publishers whose papers
would provide some of the last bastions of democratic support in the Weimar
Republic.[62]

The German newspaper landscape was well-known for its highly political
press. Many German newspapers aligned with a particular political party;
many members of parliament served as journalists or worked as publishers.
In 1929, the Social Democratic Party (SPD) reached a zenith of 203 affiliated
newspapers with a combined circulation of 1.3 million.[63] Religion and politics also intertwined. The newspaper *Germania* was founded in 1871 as a
Catholic newspaper affiliated with the Catholic Center Party; it was meant
to bolster public support for Catholicism during the Kulturkampf of the
1870s and 1880s, when Bismarck tried to put the Catholic Church under
greater state control.[64]

In the 1880s, however, a new type of newspaper emerged called the *Generalanzeiger* (General Advertiser). These papers were neutral in their political
and religious affiliations. They were distributed mostly in one city and designed for the swiftly growing mass urban readership. The *Generalanzeiger*
took advantage of lower production costs due to more efficient printing
presses, better and swifter typesetting machines, the reduced price of paper,
and the end of federal taxes on newspapers and advertisements in the imperial press law of 1874. Subscription was also cheap because advertisements
filled most of the pages. The cost of a newspaper subscription dropped from
2.32 percent of average annual earnings in 1843 to 0.54 percent in 1900.[65] The
newspapers were phenomenally successful: by 1903, the *General-Anzeiger
für Hamburg-Altona* was the fifth largest newspaper in Germany with over
100,000 subscribers.

The early twentieth century seemed like a golden age of newspapers. Many
urban newspapers printed multiple editions a day. Residents of major cities
could pick up a newspaper at almost any time of day.[66] Breaking news could
make it from a newspaper office to city streets within fifteen minutes through
extras. During the Weimar Republic, vivacious journalists like Kurt
Tucholsky and Siegfried Kracauer kept the press filled with entertaining content. Newspapers were everywhere: some cafés in Berlin even had newspaper waiters to bring over papers to customers' tables. Living in Berlin in
the 1920s, Austrian novelist Joseph Roth, famous for his Habsburg nostalgia,
composed *Zeitungsromane*—"newspaper novels" that he structured in short,
staccato sections to mirror his journalistic writing for newspapers like the

Social Democratic *Vorwärts* and prestigious *Frankfurter Zeitung.* Franz Biberkopf, the protagonist of Alfred Döblin's iconic Weimar novel *Berlin Alexanderplatz* (1929), sold newspapers on the streets. Films like *Berlin: Die Sinfonie der Großstadt* (1927) featured images of newspapers with dramatic headlines spinning into the camera. Newspapers drove that cinematic story of the city and were central to navigating urban life.

The Weimar Republic also saw the rise of illustrated "boulevard papers" or tabloids that focused on entertainment like sports and sensational stories like murder trials or exposés of apparent financial machinations by pro-Republican politicians. Often printed in the afternoons or evenings and sold on the streets, these cheap papers became wildly popular on the right and the left. Alfred Hugenberg's *Nachtausgabe* expanded from a circulation of 38,000 in 1925 to 202,000 in 1930. The second largest publisher in Germany, the Communist Willi Münzenberg, published *Welt am Abend* which grew from 12,000 papers in 1925 to 220,000 in 1930.

The success of the tabloids did not necessarily translate into votes for their publishers' political parties (the right-wing German National People's Party [DNVP] for Hugenberg or the Communist Party of Germany [KPD] for Münzenberg). Liberal publishers like Ullstein also created several competitors, including *Tempo,* which sold 145,000 copies a day in 1930.[67] Still, Hugenberg's and Münzenberg's papers helped to undermine the Weimar Republic's legitimacy on a daily basis by suggesting that Weimar democracy was crime-ridden, unstable, and unsustainable.[68] In the world of print, the common shorthand of "good" Weimar culture and "bad" Weimar politics makes little sense: the press was infused with politics.[69]

The speed of urban news contrasted sharply with rural areas, where newspapers might be printed only once or a few times a week. The developments that made urban news so vibrant exacerbated the divide between the urban and the provincial. Germany's newspaper market was particularly decentralized with a large number of newspapers. In what he claimed was the first article to create statistics on German newspapers, Hjalmar Schacht counted 3,405 newspapers in 1898. Later Reichsbank president and economics minister under Hitler from 1934 to 1937, Schacht—whose parents gave him the middle names Horace Greeley to commemorate the famous American founder of the *New York Tribune* and unsuccessful candidate for president in 1872—found that 75 percent of newspapers had print runs less than 3,000 and only 10 percent printed more than 7,000 copies.[70] The number of newspapers reached 4,036 by 1913. German newspapers had far lower circulations than papers in Great Britain or France. While there was one different newspaper for every 15,474 German citizens in 1913, there was one newspaper for every 18,700 citizens in England or every 66,000 in France.[71] Due to their small circulations, most newspapers could not afford correspondents in Berlin, let alone foreign correspondents. Provincial papers relied heavily on news agencies for everything but local news. With so many newspapers to supply, the pre–World War I years were the high point of Wolff's success.[72]

While news agencies supplied international and much national news, smaller and more specialized agencies delivered particular genres of news to the press, such as sports, fashion, or news from a political party. Called *Korrespondenzbüros*, these press agencies or correspondence bureaus proliferated from the mid-nineteenth century. By 1932, there were 590 bureaus in Germany alone. The most extreme version of these syndicated services was the *Materndienst*, a technical term for a matrix or stereotype service that delivered preset printing plates. By 1900, offset printing allowed companies to provide set molds on metal printing plates for newspapers. These molds left space for editors to insert their newspaper's title and local news before printing the newspaper on their own presses. Newspapers like this were also known as *kopflose Zeitungen* (headless newspapers) indicating that editors merely inserted a heading, title, or front and back pages. Nearly one-third of newspapers used molds or stereotypes in some way by 1917.[73] The German government was well aware of this. The Interior Ministry noted in April 1915 that *kopflose Zeitungen* had created a "large standardization" of newspaper content.[74] The sheer number of newspapers in Germany belies the relative uniformity of their news.

In the journey from event to news, editors of newspapers that did not use molds or syndicates played the vital role of gatekeepers. Editors decided which Wolff's items to print. Newspapers adapted their items depending on their audience, circulation, and location. Although many newspapers printed Wolff's news verbatim, they could vary the presentation and placement of their articles to influence readers' interpretations of news.[75] Newspapers could subscribe to particular parts of Wolff's news and choose how often they wished to receive news. As newspapers varied so much, Wolff negotiated its subscription prices and distribution with each newspaper individually. In 1880, Wolff sent around 500–600 lines of telegrams daily. By 1905, this trebled to 1,500–1,600 lines sent to around 2,300 subscribers.[76] By 1932, Wolff disseminated 30–35,000 words of domestic news alone every day.[77]

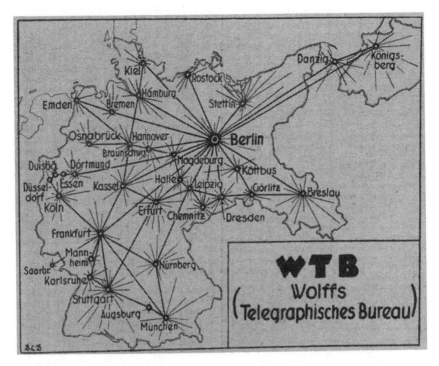

FIGURE 2. Map of Wolff's branches in Germany. *Zeitungswissenschaft* 1, no. 11 (November 15, 1926): 165. Reproduced from a copy held at Staatsbibliothek zu Berlin.

Wolff distributed its news from its central office in Berlin to its branches. The agency created just under forty branches in major German cities by 1900 (see Figure 2). These branches then delivered news to newspapers in their city and surrounding areas by post, courier, train, telegraph, or telephone. By 1912, Berlin newspapers could receive Wolff's news directly from its central office in Berlin via telegraph ticker machines. Wolff paid around 4 million marks annually for telegraph and telephone fees in 1912.[78] From April 1924, Wolff could disseminate its news over radio to any newspapers with the appropriate equipment. By 1926, 400 newspapers participated.[79] Post remained surprisingly important: even in 1934, around 72.2 percent of news in Europe was still sent by post, 26.2 percent through the telephone, and only 1.6 percent by telegram.[80]

Editors also adapted Wolff's news to their political orientation.[81] A Nazi newspaper in the 1920s, the *Hamburger Tageblatt*, provides an extreme example. The journalists felt that agency reports were "not compatible with the goals of a Nazi newspaper." They could not afford their own correspondents so they used "cuts, headlines, and comments" to adapt the news.[82] The same was true for other newspapers with less extreme views. But they could only work with the material that they received.

Cultural beliefs about journalism also influenced how newspapers adapted materials from news agencies. Many leading publishers and journalists of the Weimar Republic, in contrast to the increasingly entrenched Anglo-American commitment to separating facts and opinions, believed that journalists had to interpret news for the reader. One editor purportedly declared that facts were "not fit for the reader when served raw; they had to be cooked, chewed and presented in the correspondent's saliva."[83] An assessment during the Nazi period noted that news in the American sense played a "second-class role" in Europe, where opinion reigned over objectivity.[84]

Still, German journalists had created professional organizations to consolidate their norms and news values around the same time as Americans and Brits. The Verein Deutscher Zeitungs-Verleger (VDZV, Association of German Newspaper Publishers) was founded in 1894 and the Reichsverband der Deutschen Presse (Federal German Press Association) in 1910, while the American Society of Professional Journalists was established in 1909 and the British National Association of Journalists in 1884. The University of Leipzig created Germany's first Institut für Zeitungskunde (Institute for Newspaper Education) in 1916, just eight years after the University of Missouri had founded the first American school of journalism.

German journalists also used different genres and styles of writing. Louis Lochner, the American correspondent for the Associated Press's Berlin bureau from 1924 to 1941, saw "big differences" between German and American reporting. Lochner claimed in 1931 that the American obsession with speed "distinguishes American news services from those in pretty much all other countries." Germans were "more cautious by nature" and provided less "color" in their reporting. American news followed a lede structure and the first paragraph worked as an inverted pyramid, presenting the most important information first. German news was more often presented chronologically. American news consumers, thought Lochner, were far more interested in human accounts of politicians. "I remember," wrote Lochner about his encounter with influential Weimar Foreign Minister Gustav Stresemann, "how heartily Dr. Stresemann laughed when I asked him one evening that for a sketch I was writing about him, I wanted to know if he tinkered with radios, how much sport he played . . . etc." Stresemann answered and was "honestly astonished" when Lochner later told him that "this very simple, human account" had achieved more resonance in the United States than even Lochner had anticipated.[85]

While most German newspapers catered to different political tastes, Wolff remained nonpartisan in order to supply subscribers of all political persuasions. News agencies served newspapers; newspapers served readers. This different customer base gave news agencies a very different mandate from journalists and editors, who molded the news to fit what they believed that their clientele wanted. Arthur Koestler, a journalist for Ullstein in the Weimar Republic and later the famous author of *Darkness at Noon,* caustically noted that reporting news and facts was "contemptuously left to the news agencies," while a journalist used "facts as pretexts for venting his opinions and passing oracular judgments."[86]

This difference continued into the Nazi period. Joachim Rings, who worked for an American news agency, United Press, and then German news agency Eildienst in the mid-1930s, claimed in 1936: "The news agency presents itself with a claim of objectivity, which derives from its economic determination. That makes it basically contradictory to the newspaper, which conveys a more or less pronounced subjective character based on opinion [*Meinungscharakter*]."[87] Of course, the choice of facts was subjective too. Here, news agencies could exercise great influence.

It was often hard to recognize the role of news agencies for the simple reason that newspapers did not always name their sources. Some newspapers labeled Wolff's items with "WTB." Others printed the news without indicating its origin. Even attributions did not necessarily name Wolff, but prefaced items with "by wire," "from Berlin," or "a correspondent reports."[88] Finally, reprinting was rampant everywhere in the nineteenth and early twentieth centuries. Newspapers commonly copied from other newspapers without legal implications or consequences. Despite various attempts to create intellectual property rights in news, no legislation specifically protected news in Germany.[89] These practices meant that the sources of news were often hidden to readers.

Propaganda, Public Opinion, and Reading the News

The last stage from event to news lies with readers, or often elites' beliefs about readers. Media reception is both individual and structural, shaped by factors like race, class, gender, location, and education. Even if someone bought certain newspapers, what articles did they read? Did they believe those articles? How did that change their behavior? These questions are often difficult to answer today, let alone before the age of public opinion polls started in the 1930s. What is certain is that controlling the media did not guarantee controlling readers' minds.

Another approach to understanding whether news matters is to examine how elites *believed* that news worked and how they measured its efficacy. Around 1900, many elites relied on newspapers to tell them what "the people" thought. Communications scholars have described this phenomenon as the "third-person effect." A message may not affect the mass audience it seeks to reach, but it might convince people by invoking "third persons" who supposedly believe in the message.[90] Elites equated published opinion with public opinion. This was not just a German phenomenon. Nor has this tendency disappeared today.

These suspicions would sometimes lead to surveillance. In the Wilhelmine period, some police departments in Hamburg sent undercover officers to eavesdrop on workers discussing their politics in pubs.[91] This was more an attempt to surveil socialists than understand broader public sentiment. In the United States, opinion polls emerged as a new measurement in the 1930s, though they did not reach Germany until after World War II. Only in the Nazi period would government officials start to measure quantitatively, producing reams of statistics about how many words from German news agencies were printed in foreign newspapers. Nazi officials used the volume of German news printed somewhere as a proxy for the success of its news dissemination. At the same time, the SS also tried to measure public sentiment with the same eavesdropping techniques targeting dissenters as the Hamburg police around 1900 (though the Nazis also used far more violent methods in direct interrogations).[92]

What readers *actually* believed was often less important than what elites *thought* that readers believed. Politicians used (and still use) the construct of "public opinion" to justify their actions. The phrase neatly expressed the fiction of a unified public, one where countervailing opinions were elided and counter-publics silenced.[93] In the nineteenth century, the construct of "public opinion" became entrenched in political discourse. William Mackinnon, who became a Tory MP in Britain in 1830, defined public opinion as "that sentiment on any given subject which is entertained by the best informed, most intelligent, and most moral persons in the community, which is gradually spread and adopted by nearly all persons of any education or proper feeling in a civilised state."[94] Public opinion became a powerful rhetorical device and motivating factor for politicians. "Public sentiment is every thing," declared Abraham Lincoln in 1858. "With it, nothing can fail; against it, nothing can succeed."[95] In this telling, "public opinion" was a top-down construct: most of the population would adopt what elites decreed rather than vice versa.

Even when German elites disagreed about everything else, they agreed about the importance of news in creating public opinion (*öffentliche Meinung*). In the confused last days of World War I, the SPD, Kaiser Wilhelm II, Chancellor Prince Max von Baden, and military elites all focused on the press. One cabinet meeting on October 31, 1918, mainly used newspaper articles to discuss Wilhelm II's possible abdication. The Prussian interior minister, Bill Drews, agreed that the flood of newspaper articles on the subject "only mirrored public opinion" and illustrated the vast number of dangerous rumors flying around. The Prussian minister of war, Heinrich Scheüch, concluded that the government's inaction in countering those rumors had led Germans "to believe that the Government is of the same opinion as the Press which makes public opinion."[96]

While Scheüch and Drews thought the press mirrored public opinion, the SPD politician who would proclaim the German Republic from the Reichstag balcony on November 9, Philipp Scheidemann, believed that the press created public opinion. Two days earlier, Scheidemann had stated that "if the masses have become involved in the question of the Kaiser's abdication, the bourgeois press—for instance, the *Frankfurter Zeitung*—has done much to bring this about. The masses can still be kept in check if concessions are made."[97] If the press had made public opinion, reasoned Scheidemann, it could unmake it too.

Finally, some saw the press as the first author of history. A Foreign Office official declared in the heady days of mid-November 1918: "If one is making history, one generally does not have time to write it. It is, however, the task of the press and everyone interested in historical truth to try to establish the real course of events. The government has its head so full that it cannot also establish historiographically what it is doing."[98] The government was supposed to make history; the press was supposed to write the "first rough draft."[99]

Many believed that news could shape international as well as national public opinion. Statesmen from U.S. president Woodrow Wilson to German president Friedrich Ebert felt that the destruction of World War I warranted a new international order. They came to believe in public opinion as the ultimate judge and motivating force of these diplomatic undertakings.[100] The new international organization proposed by Wilson, the League of Nations, saw the press as part of moral disarmament, which paralleled negotiations on material disarmament.[101]

Sweeping assumptions about public opinion started to come under fire from academics, as the new discipline of *Zeitungswissenschaft* (newspaper science) emerged in the late 1910s and 1920s. In 1910, Max Weber had advocated for sociologists to study the press in cooperation with German press associations. In 1912, however, Weber reported to the annual conference of German sociologists that his plan had failed.[102] But *Zeitungswissenschaft* soon blossomed and started to spur debates about "public opinion." One work published just before World War I echoed politicians' position that "the press means, indeed determines public opinion."[103] Others were unconvinced. Wilhelm Bauer noted in April 1914 that newspapers did not represent all public opinion.[104] In 1922 prominent sociologist Ferdinand Tönnies critiqued the idea that the press was the only organ of public opinion.[105]

The founder of the Leipzig Institute for Newspaper Education, economist Karl Bücher, agreed that the press did not form public opinion. Rather, the press reflected public opinion or could shape it, because the publication of an article suggested that collective groups shared certain opinions. For Bücher, the press did not actively create public opinion. Otherwise an event like the Russian Revolution could never have occurred because it had happened without newspaper support. The press was more like "an indicator organ [*Leitorgan*] through which the intellectual current between a people and its leading spirits passes back and forth."[106] In 1928 Otto Groth criticized politicians for seeing newspapers just as a tool of politics.[107] By the late Weimar Republic, sociologists, economists, and newspaper scientists all engaged in sustained research about the role of news in public life.

After World War I, the debate about public sentiment and public opinion broadened to include the concept of propaganda. The term had transformed during the war. Up to 1914, propaganda had been a little-used word, generally associated with the Catholic Church's foundation of the Sacred Office for the Propagation of the Faith (Sacra Congregatio de Propaganda Fide) in 1622. The need to create consent for the increasing scale of war led both sides to establish ministries to produce propaganda in Allied, Central Power, and neutral countries from 1915 onward. The British, and later Americans, sought to associate "propaganda" with "the Hun" and lies, while presenting their own propaganda as "information" for their populations.[108]

Authors on both sides of the ocean conducted a heated discussion about the value of propaganda. In 1919, Paul Rühlmann argued that Germans needed to produce more and better "cultural propaganda" rather than abandoning propaganda altogether.[109] In 1920, internal German Foreign Office documents described one major news agency Transocean as a "propaganda service of an unofficial nature."[110] British writers like Arthur Ponsonby decried propaganda as falsehoods.[111] Some Germans too, like Transocean's editor in chief Wilhelm Schwedler, saw propaganda as a noxious method of falsification that had poisoned foreign attitudes to Germany. In a 1922 book, Schwedler pleaded for an end to the "stain" of propaganda as conducted during the war and advocated for "truthful publishing."[112] An Austrian-American nephew of Sigmund Freud, Edward Bernays, on the other hand, saw propaganda as "simply the establishing of reciprocal understanding between an individual and a group."[113] Propaganda would ensure the consent of the masses to democratic government. This was hardly the mainstream view. Bernays's work would greatly influence the nascent field of public relations. But he could not salvage the concept of propaganda.

Regardless of whether they called government-supplied information "news" or "propaganda," left-wing and right-wing figures alike in Germany were convinced that news affected public sentiment and, in turn, politics. In the 1920s, right-wing industrialist turned politician Alfred Hugenberg had established a media empire, with his news agency Telegraph Union at its heart. By 1926, Walter Aub would declare in the left-wing journal *Die Weltbühne* that Hugenberg's syndicate and news agency services had crowned him "Germany's secret king."[114]

Hugenberg himself was similarly sure that news created political views. He held a less than flattering view of readers' compliance and crowd mentality. He thought that "millions of German newspaper readers run after the big publishing houses like children after the Pied Piper of Hamelin," because these readers failed to realize that the publishers supported "particular Jewish interests and intellectual orientations."[115] The obsession with and inflation of propaganda's effects was a key factor in corroding democracy "not only by nourishing right-wing notions of an authoritarian *Volksgemeinschaft* [people's community], but also by eroding democratic conceptualizations of public opinion across the political spectrum," as historian Corey Ross has put it.[116]

Nazi ideals rejected the very concept of public opinion, which an encyclopedia of 1939 called a "rallying cry of liberalism."[117] Joseph Goebbels, head of the RMVP (Reichsministerium für Volksaufklärung und Propaganda, Ministry of Public Enlightenment and Propaganda), was more interested in the *Stimmung* (mood) and *Haltung* (attitude) of the German population. *Stimmung* was more temporary and changed depending on daily news, thought Goebbels. *Haltung* consisted of a person's long-term attitudes and behaviors that could only alter gradually over time.[118] Propaganda had a dual task of changing and maintaining a Nazi mood and attitude. Goebbels believed that "there is no such thing as absolute objectivity."[119] Instead, he used the vocabulary of truth and lies, noting in June 1941: "Seen in the long run, the best war propaganda is that which exclusively serves the truth."[120] For Goebbels, propaganda created political values to support the Nazi state. During World War II, Goebbels suggested that propaganda to support military interests provided the fastest road to victory. Still, propaganda could not disguise the reality of military defeat on the ground.

At the same time, German Jewish émigrés would fundamentally shape the development of mass communications research.[121] Austrian Jewish sociologist Paul Lazarsfeld stayed in the United States after a Rockefeller Foundation fellowship ended in 1935. He pioneered techniques in mass communications research in the 1930s and 1940s before propounding theories on the two-step flow of communication as well as the deleterious influences of mass media. The Frankfurt School's Theodor Adorno and Max Horkheimer, among others, researched the link between media and authoritarianism during their time in the United States, while also writing *Dialectic of Enlightenment* (1944).

Adorno and Horkheimer's deep skepticism of mass media drew on earlier German concerns. In the early twentieth century, news created controversy about whether it should function as a capitalist business producing public opinion like a factory or as a cultural instrument serving the public outside of preoccupations with profit. Some contemporary researchers like Robert Brunhuber traced the roots of the press's problems to its status as a capitalist enterprise. In 1907, he even compared newspaper production disdainfully to a schnapps distillery: capitalist news intoxicated the population.[122] Some agreed with Brunhuber's pessimistic assessment; scholars up to the present, notably Jürgen Habermas, have drunk from Brunhuber's brew.

A second-generation Frankfurt School scholar, Habermas argued in the 1960s that the late eighteenth century had been a golden age of the "public sphere," or civil discussion about politics in new public spaces like coffeehouses. This "public sphere" had faded in the nineteenth century, according to Habermas, because the interlocking monopolistic structures of technology (like submarine telegraphy) and commercial media companies (like news agencies) stymied the possibility of well-informed public debate.

"Public sphere" became a common term in English after a translation of Habermas's work appeared in 1989.[123] But it is a misnomer. The term is a neologism in English, whereas Habermas used *Öffentlichkeit,* a word in German that means "the public." Habermas's work was an intellectual history of a phenomenon that had emerged in the late eighteenth century; he traced the genealogy of the common German term *Öffentlichkeit* to understand how "the public" developed over time. Only in English has a new term—"public sphere"—emerged to describe what Habermas examined.

In his only specific passage on news agencies, Habermas became rather technologically deterministic. He contended that the news agency cartel homogenized news, because "technological developments in the means of transmission of news . . . in part hastened and in part made possible the organizational unification and economic interlocking of the press."[124] Habermas has since been criticized for idealizing a late eighteenth-century period when women and working classes were generally excluded from public discussions. Habermas himself has acknowledged these critiques as legitimate, though he remained concerned about commercial influences on the press.[125]

Some contemporaries, however, welcomed the development of newspapers as a business, believing that news could promote trade. One economist wrote in April 1914 that the international news cartel had emerged from "natural and economic development tendencies," making news agencies "an extraordinarily important instrument of national and international public opinion."[126] Industrialists and bankers like Alfred Hugenberg and Hjalmar Schacht agreed; they tried to use news to increase German trade abroad and promote economic nationalism at home.

Beyond elite beliefs about readers, it is often hard to find evidence on how readers interpreted the news. Political elites continued to use newspapers as a proxy for public opinion. Kaiser Wilhelm II received daily press clippings, including Wolff's reports, and often annotated them.[127] Next to an item about how the Russian tsar had realized the massive gap between reports on the treasury's riches and his people's poverty, Wilhelm II noted sarcastically "after twenty years' government!"[128] Every chancellor and president in the Weimar Republic attached similar significance to newspapers and to the Press Department, created in 1919. Each chancellor had a daily presentation of news from the chief press officer, though most seem to have read newspapers independently too.[129] Heinrich Brüning, chancellor of the Weimar Republic from 1930 to 1932, met with the chief press officer, Walter Zechlin, every day except Sunday for thirty minutes. The meetings were so regular that Brüning's daily agendas noted when it did not occur.[130] The two presidents

in the Weimar Republic, Friedrich Ebert and Paul von Hindenburg, received a daily morning briefing from the chief press officer too.[131] Ministries
also collected newspaper clippings on certain topics or asked newspaper-
clipping bureaus to do so for them.[132] The press provided officials with what
they saw as public opinion on a daily basis.

Though some leading Nazis rejected the idea of "public opinion," they still
used news agencies to receive information and shape public beliefs. The Nazi
news agency, Deutsches Nachrichtenbüro (DNB, German News Office),
served as the main source for the Nazi party and state. The DNB produced
a daily summary of materials just for Hitler in large "Führer type."[133] Joseph
Goebbels received forty to fifty pages of DNB news daily, along with Transocean news. He used DNB news at daily conferences with ministers from
July 1933 as well as press conferences held straight thereafter in the Propaganda
Ministry. News agencies constituted a central source of information, as-
signing them an extraordinary amount of power to affect decision making.

Despite the rich sources on elite interaction with the press, it remains challenging to understand readers' interpretation of the news before public
opinion polls. Local economic, political, and social contexts informed readers'
interpretations of newspapers. Newspapers remained the most important
mass medium up to the end of the Weimar Republic, particularly as the
government deliberately removed politics from the radio in the 1920s. Newspapers constituted most citizens' only formal means of information about
official events, though they drew on informal sources such as rumors and
conversation with coworkers, family, and friends as well as advertising.

We have quite a lot of evidence about book reading and how censorship
laws often emerged from beliefs about how citizens, particularly "susceptible"
citizens like women and children, read literature.[134] But newspapers were so
quotidian that ordinary readers did not generally annotate or collect them.
Circulation figures alone provide next to no evidence of the quality of reading.
The main remaining traces of reading mostly come from surveillance reports
like police files on how groups of working-class socialists in Hamburg discussed the news in the late nineteenth century.[135] We also know that readers
did not necessarily vote as newspapers instructed them: historian Bernhard
Fulda examined the voting patterns of provincial German towns compared
to what their newspapers supported in the 1920s. Residents often voted in
different ways than their newspaper advised.[136]

Advertising research from the late 1920s provides some broader evidence
on newspaper reading. In 1929, Rudolf Seyffert of Cologne University surveyed 1,732 members of the public to understand their reactions to adver-

tising. The survey divided participants into fifteen professional groups to ana-lyze their habits for daily newspapers and magazines.[137] The survey consisted of 76.8 percent men and 23.2 percent women with an average age of thirty-nine. Of the participants, 65.8 percent lived in a large city, 13.3 percent in a town, 9.5 percent in a small town, and 11.4 percent in the country. Newspapers were essential parts of everyday life: 99.6 percent read daily newspapers.

This survey provides helpful checks on overestimating the importance of any individual newspaper. First, no social group read just one newspaper. Top-level civil servants read an average of 3.4 newspapers, while housewives read an average of 1.35 newspapers daily. Those surveyed read an average of 2.16 newspapers daily. Readers supplemented daily newspapers with maga-zines and trade journals. Of all participants, 88.8 percent read magazines and 73.6 percent read trade publications, with professional groups once again consulting a wider variety of publications.

Second, readers actively read different kinds of newspapers: 52.8 percent read big political daily papers, 58.6 percent read nonpolitical local papers, and 55.3 percent read political local papers. The quality of reading varied. The survey found that 35.2 percent read advertisements regularly, 56.2 percent occasionally, and 8.6 percent not at all. Readers read selectively. It also shows the dissonance between contemporary cutting-edge academic research and what elites believed about the press.

Finally, the type of newspapers enjoyed by different professional groups varied tremendously. Political papers appeared most important to profes-sions at opposite ends of the spectrum: higher-level civil servants and workers. While 93.7 percent of high-level civil servants read large political daily newspapers, only around 50 percent of lower and mid-level bureaucrats did the same. This contrasted strongly with workers' habits: 78 percent read local political newspapers, while only 15.1 percent read big political dailies, a far lower percentage than for any other professional group. Workers were the least likely to read a nonpolitical local newspaper: only 26.3 percent read such newspapers.[138] The types of newspapers enjoyed by workers and top bureaucrats differed not in their politicization, but in their geographical scope of local versus national.

Although the survey does not detail *which* newspapers readers purchased, we can assume that there was significant overlap in newspaper readership. This overlap would have been greater in smaller towns with less choice for professionals who read three newspapers a day. Any study of a single news-paper does not accurately reflect readers' experiences.

Conclusion

Elites were both cynical and naive about news. They cynically thought that controlling news would translate into political and economic control. Even skeptics of the press believed in its international reach and influence: Robert Brunhuber thought that the press was a major factor driving the "world economy" and held great "significance in domestic and foreign politics where the press often forms the finest nerve of the people's psyche."[139]

Many elites naively believed that the "right" news could produce the "right" reactions in a reading public. These ideas relied on a particular set of assumptions about human nature: that people believed what they read, that they interpreted information in predictable ways, and that elites could control public reactions. Readers, in their view, were malleable and could not necessarily form their own judgments. Politicians in the Weimar Republic worried about the manipulability of particular groups of readers like women and children; they promulgated the Law against Filth and Smut (*Schmutz- und Schundgesetz*) of 1926 to protect these groups from "dangerous" reading material. Although these ideas proved flawed, they were surprisingly resilient.

Both cynical and naive interpretations of news assigned it great power. A surprising cross-section of German elites saw news agencies as a vital, but hidden means of influencing readers. Greater control over international communications, they believed, would bolster Germany's geopolitical and economic ambitions on the world stage. It would take the innovation of wireless technology to make those ambitions a reality.

2

A WORLD WIRELESS NETWORK

Infrastructure projects, imperial ambitions, and international status were firmly intertwined for many Germans by 1900. The best-known project of this kind is the Berlin–Baghdad railway, which was meant to cement German ties to the Middle East. The railway relied on an alliance between the German government, explorers, engineers, and a consortium of banks led by Deutsche Bank. Much of the effort was spurred by Wilhelm II, who had visited the Middle East in 1898, was infatuated with Islam, and proclaimed himself "Hajji Wilhelm," the Western guardian of Islam. The Ottoman Empire granted the concession for the railway to Germany in 1903 partly because Germany did not have the same imperial baggage as Britain and France. Secretly, Germany agreed to finish the railway in eight years and to provide all the capital in return for exclusive rights to excavate coal, copper, and archaeological artifacts near the railway. Although it would never be completed, the British, French, and Russians interpreted the Berlin–Baghdad railway as a German attempt to compete with British infrastructure—here the Suez Canal.[1] It was a land-based imperial strategy to counter British naval domination.

Communications were part of this global competition to further imperialism through infrastructure. The development of new wireless communications technology also made air a third dimension of global power alongside land and sea. By 1908, German military officials became increasingly convinced that the British had plans for wireless domination to complement their cable network. General Helmuth von Moltke the Younger, chief of the general staff, devoted multiple memoranda and committee meetings to discussing the British-based Marconi Company's purported plans to erect large wireless stations around the world. Moltke emphasized that the first nation to transmit wireless around the world would gain significant military and political advantages. No doubt remembering the Herero uprising of 1905 in German colonial South West Africa and German troops' subsequent genocidal slaughter of the Herero and Nama people, Moltke wanted to prevent Germany from relying on foreign communications networks in case of unrest.[2] Germany needed its own colonial wireless network. Moltke had played a critical role in securing the concession for the Berlin–Baghdad railway: he folded communications into his wider aims for German infrastructure.

Alongside Moltke's pleas from the military perspective, Wilhelm II and other ministers invested in wireless for geopolitical and technological reasons. The German government intervened in private enterprise to create Telefunken, the main competitor to Marconi. Wireless was a swifter means to counter British submarine cables around the world; it also helped German business to innovate. It was no coincidence that Guglielmo Marconi shared his 1909 Nobel Prize for innovation in wireless telegraphy with the German Karl Ferdinand Braun. Innovation in wireless technology formed part of a long-term German vision for infrastructural and informational independence centered around news agencies.

Fears about other nations constantly accelerated German plans. In July 1911, Moltke reported to the Colonial Office that the French were looking into creating a world wireless network too.[3] More worryingly, multiple sources claimed that Marconi was working with the British postmaster general to erect a British-controlled "all-red line of wireless towers."[4] A British network seemed dangerous for economic as well as political and military reasons. Marconi devices could not communicate with Telefunken devices, because Marconi had originally constructed his wireless as a closed, incompatible system. If Marconi succeeded, he would create a wireless monopoly.

Telefunken saw an opportunity. The company could exploit the German Colonial Office's fears about British use of wireless. On an enormous map, Telefunken officials drew the planned Marconi routes around the world. In a different color on the same map, Telefunken sketched an alternative German route that it could create with government subsidies. The connections could run from Berlin to New York and then Paramaribo in Suriname. Another connection could run from Berlin to the German colonies in Africa and then the German island colonies of Nauru and Samoa in the Pacific.[5] If the British were planning a world wireless network, the Germans just had to preempt them.

Plans for a world wireless network combined state, military, and business interests. They built on German beliefs that infrastructure could achieve political and economic goals. World War I cemented German focus on wireless; it also extended that focus to the world. German ideas about international wireless networks evolved from colonial connections to a global vision of German wireless towers across the world.

The Curse of British Cables and the Promise of Wireless

German officials only began to pay sustained attention to communications infrastructure around 1900. From the first successful transatlantic submarine cable in 1866, an oligopoly of Anglo-American companies dominated the global laying of submarine cables. Submarine telegraphy spread rapidly, reaching Asia, Australia, and South America by the late 1870s. The German government did not even intervene to support the Siemens Brothers when they attempted to compete with the Anglo-American Eastern and Associated Companies in the 1870s.[6] Other nations were similarly acquiescent to a privately run global system. The privately owned Anglo-American submarine cables formed the basis for international cooperation that was regulated from 1865 by the International Telegraph Union (ITU). Crucially, though, the ITU never secured agreement from its members on protocols for communication during war.[7]

From the 1890s, increasing German discontent with the role of news in politics and trade intertwined with growing unease about communications technology. If Germany was an imperial and global power, then it needed the accoutrements like cables. Competition over cables was not just an expression of geopolitical rivalries. Rather, it was a battle over the information flows that undergirded imperial and global exchanges.

States began to intervene in the cable business for economic and political purposes. The American government, for instance, looked to lay cables to South America to foster economic ties.[8] Cables promised to create new markets. It did not work out that way, but states believed it would in the 1890s. Officials also came to see cables as part of statecraft. They sought to control landing rights for political purposes. The British created great consternation in Germany when they denied landing rights to a German-American cable in the late 1890s despite ten years of negotiations. The cable was laid via the Portuguese Azores islands instead. It was the longest submarine cable in the world when it opened in 1900.[9] The German government became deeply suspicious of the apparent British desire to control cables. This suspicion was heightened in 1902 when the British government completed an "All Red Route" of cables around the world that only landed on British imperial soil by laying the final link across the Pacific Ocean to connect Vancouver with New Zealand and Australia.

Although cable companies often had American investors too and did not always operate in the British government's interests, Germans generally classed them as British. German scholars spilled much ink on calculating the exact percentage of "national ownership" of the "world cable network."[10] German studies categorized companies headquartered in London as British and state-influenced. The British government might have controlled the landing rights for cables, but they did not control the cables themselves. Regardless, Germans imagined that the British would put these cables to reprehensible uses.

The tension over British cables combined with concern over British content. Newspapers in German colonial Africa generally still subscribed to Reuters. The Colonial Office became so concerned about Reuters that it subsidized a Wolff's daily service of thirty-word telegrams from Berlin to German South West Africa from January 1910. That service was also subsidized by companies in the colony like the German Afrikabank and mining firms as well as the Foreign Office, the Navy, and the *Deutsche Südwestafrikanische Zeitung*.[11]

But a subsidized service of just thirty words could not counter British influence. Heinrich Schnee, governor of German East Africa, thought Wolff sent irrelevant items rather than what he needed, like information on government policies.[12] Schnee still relied on Reuters, despite its "British color." Schnee called for further state subsidies to send more Wolff news.[13] The subsidies for South West Africa totaled 17,065 marks for 1912. Yet the service cost around 4,000 marks per month.[14] In October 1913, Schnee even agreed to critique Wolff's messages every month to adapt them to colonial needs.[15] As the Colonial Office fretted about potential damage from British content, it needed to find ways to send more news from Berlin for less money.

This had become urgent because British conduct seemed to confirm what many European elites had long feared: Britain used its control over cables to censor the content sent through them. British censorship of information from South Africa during the Second Boer War (1899–1902) ignited German and French concerns.[16] In response, the Germans, French, and Americans began to lay their own cables to bypass the British. The German postal minister in 1900, Victor von Podbielski, initiated plans to lay a "worldwide German cable network" that would use German news agencies to send information around the globe.[17] The Germans established a joint cable company, Deutsch-Niederländische Telegraphengesellschaft, with the Dutch Telegraph Administration to link German and Dutch colonies in the Pacific with the American Pacific cable in 1904.

French officials also aggressively subsidized and supported a strategy to lay cables to connect the French empire and counteract British influence.[18] The German government worked with the French to lay a cable to South America, in return for German help with France's network in West Africa.[19] The Japanese cooperated with Denmark to lay cables from Asia to Europe.[20] In 1898, one German researcher claimed that Britain owned 65.6 percent of global cables; Germany held 1.9 percent; France 8.2 percent. By 1913, Germany possessed 8.3 percent of the world's cables, while Britain still held a mighty 54.3 percent.[21] The Anglo-American oligopoly over cables continued, as cable-laying proved expensive and time-consuming.

At the same time then, Germans turned to wireless technology to bypass the British-dominated network altogether. From its emergence around 1900, perceived political, economic, and military needs shaped the development of wireless. Many did not see the need for wireless on land, because there was such a dense telegraph network already. In Germany, however, wireless promised to undermine the infrastructural premise of the news cartel: a submarine cable network dominated by Great Britain.

German imperial interests fostered wireless. Buttressed by American naval officer and strategist Alfred Mahan's ideas that the navy was the crucial factor in winning wars, Germany challenged Britain's imperial supremacy through a naval arms race from the 1890s; wireless was one technology to provide an added advantage.[22] Many navies alongside the German seized on wireless because it enabled them to coordinate their ships on the sea for the first time.[23] The German Navy, however, also gained vital support from Kaiser Wilhelm II, who was infatuated with new technologies like wireless.

Pushed by Wilhelm II and the German government, two competing firms—Siemens & Halske and AEG—founded a joint subsidiary called Telefunken in 1903 to conduct research and development, manufacture wireless devices, and erect wireless towers. Subsidies through government contracts were key for Telefunken's development. The German Navy outfitted its ninety warships with Telefunken's wireless devices. Government contracts like these provided 70 to 80 percent of Telefunken's revenue in its early years and made Telefunken the most important driver of innovation in German wireless technology before 1918.[24]

Telefunken soon produced an innovation called the quenched spark system that it implemented in 1909. The quenched spark system (or spark gap transmission) created an electrical oscillation through electrical sparks and transmitted information through Morse code. This reduced atmospheric disturbances and enabled communications across thousands of kilometers.[25] The quenched spark system made it technologically feasible to reach Germany's far-flung colonies from Berlin for the first time; it also allowed Telefunken to expand wireless to commercial and fishing vessels. Some German news agencies used Morse code and the quenched spark system until the widespread introduction of shortwave in 1929. Overall, the close private-public relationship made Telefunken a trustworthy partner for the German government's political, economic, and technological aims.

The government had secured the sole legal right to erect telegraph and telephony stations in German colonies in 1906; this enabled the German Colonial Office to invest in wireless to connect German colonies, starting with Africa.[26] While the technological challenges seemed at times insurmountable, the Colonial Office drew inspiration from other empires. The German consulate in Brussels, for instance, sent numerous reports about wireless towers in the Belgian Congo so that German colonial officials could learn from Belgian technical successes.[27] These towers promised to create more seamless communication between colonial officials and Berlin. They would also reduce the Colonial Office's subsidies to Wolff because wireless transmission would be cheaper than using commercial cables. Finally, they would push back against the British plans to dominate international wireless that many German officials feared.

After 1912, these fears receded. Marconi had initially attempted to monopolize the market by making his wireless system incompatible with other receivers. The Titanic disaster, however, pushed governments toward safety regulations. A radiotelegraphic conference in London in 1912 mandated that all ships with over fifty passengers install wireless receivers. The imperative of safety enabled Telefunken to break Marconi's monopoly: all ships were now legally obliged to be able to communicate with each other. By 1912,

Marconi and Telefunken had agreed to exchange patents and only 294 of the 1,554 ship stations did not belong to Telefunken or Marconi.[28] The market looked more like a duopoly than the oligopolistic cable market.[29]

By now, telegraphy and wireless telegraphy had developed into very different technologies. Telegraph cables operated as a point-to-point technology, only enabling communication between two parties. Wireless could send messages from one transmitter to many wireless receivers simultaneously. This made wireless easier to intercept if one owned the right receiver. Towers were very expensive as they used power to disseminate in all directions. Atmospheric disturbances still meant that services were not particularly reliable while Germany was constructing its colonial towers. Moreover, transmission towers only lasted a few years as the technology increasingly improved and required updating. Cables, by contrast, lasted for up to seventy-five years.

Germans, however, turned wireless's disadvantages into advantages. While cables offered more security and reliability, they meant relying on the British far more than many Germans wanted. As a point-to-many technology, wireless enabled the sender to disseminate messages far more widely. Finally, for German military planners, one feature of wireless made it indispensable. Unlike cables, there were no wires that enemies could cut during times of war.

Ironically, the British government had actually fallen out with Marconi over the plans for an "imperial wireless chain" in 1911. The Admiralty had canceled a contract with Marconi in 1913.[30] Marconi disputed the decisions and continued to request compensation for lost revenue well into World War I. This became so acrimonious that Prime Minister Herbert Asquith even had to create a committee in March 1916 to clear up any outstanding questions.[31] Germans did not know the details of these internal disputes and remained wary. They wanted their own wireless connections.

By 1914, the German Colonial Office could look with some satisfaction at its achievements. There had been setbacks such as the collapse of the tower at Nauen in 1912. But now functioning wireless towers stood in all Germany's major Africa colonies along with Qingdao and several Pacific islands.[32] The company had also erected two towers on the East Coast of the United States at Sayville and Tuckerton. These towers allowed Germany direct access to North America. The creation of a German "All Wireless Route" around the world had become an integral part of *Weltpolitik*. But it was a colonial form of *Weltpolitik*. World War I would change that attitude swiftly. Colonial connections no longer sufficed. The Germans needed a world wireless network.

The *Burgfrieden* of Propaganda in World War I

On August 4, 1914, days after declaring war, Wilhelm II gave a powerful speech in the Reichstag that he no longer knew parties, but "only Germans." Known as *Burgfrieden,* this declaration of German solidarity above party politics incorporated even the Social Democrats in an apparent initial euphoria. Just when the "spirit of 1914" seemed to sweep the German nation, however, the British created a more lasting legacy by cutting five of Germany's transatlantic and undersea cables to Spain, the United States, and the German colonies.[33] Britain also forced the neutral Portuguese in December 1914 to forbid Germany from using its only remaining cable to the United States via the Azores. While Wolff controlled news in Germany, wireless enabled other German agencies to send news abroad.

The modern meaning of propaganda emerged during World War I; every belligerent government created new ministries to influence public discourse.[34] The Germans too established censorship and propaganda mechanisms. The government rescinded freedom of the press upon the outbreak of war, as the press law of 1874 foresaw.

Overlapping competencies hindered seamless news supply. Chancellor Theobald von Bethmann Hollweg had unsuccessfully tried to centralize government press offices in 1912. The German Navy and Colonial Office had resisted, believing that they needed their own news organizations to mold the press.[35] Several military and civilian agencies thus handled censorship and propaganda from the beginning of mobilization until the War Press Office (Kriegspresseamt) was established in October 1915. A fully unified government press department only emerged in September 1917.[36]

Wolff remained the central supplier of official news, particularly army reports, to the press. As the censorship rules issued at the start of the war were complex, newspapers tended to reprint Wolff's news verbatim. The War Press Office decided in November 1915 that only Wolff or local censorship offices could provide press conference news to the provincial press.[37] The censorship handbook of 1917 noted that "reprint of WTB messages is desired."[38] Censorship made Wolff more essential than ever.

Much of the press disliked the situation. The Association of German Newspaper Publishers complained in mid-1915 about Wolff's "monopoly position."[39] Smaller newspapers protested that Wolff overcharged for what it knew were indispensable services.[40] Newspapers grumbled that Wolff gave parliamentary reporting short shrift, while other news items were far too long and thus expensive.[41] Some journalists argued that Wolff should be disbanded altogether after the war in favor of a cooperative news agency owned by newspapers for newspapers like the American Associated Press.[42] Rumors and jokes became increasingly important alternative channels of communication.[43]

Politicians joined in the complaints. Count Kuno von Westarp—leader of the Conservative Party in the Reichstag and later head of the right-wing DNVP (Deutschnationale Volkspartei, German National People's Party) in the mid-1920s—questioned whether Wolff was abusing its monopoly in January 1916 in the Reichstag.[44] By 1916, the Foreign Office warned that Wolff's propaganda had wholly failed to prevent enemy attacks in occupied areas.[45]

Behind the question of domestic propaganda lay the question of infrastructure to disseminate propaganda abroad. In German eyes, the British were using their cables and Reuters news agency to spread falsehoods about Germans around the world. A cartoon in the weekly satirical magazine, *Simplicissimus,* depicted a British toad with his classic top hat (see Figure 3). From the "headquarters of lies," the toad vomits green snakes, or cables. The caption read: "As England's cables are still intact, it is still capable of sending its main export article throughout the whole world."[46] Britain's trade, *Simplicissimus* emphasized, was mostly in falsehoods. Wireless seemed the only option to defang the snakes of lies.

Germans had swiftly retaliated in infrastructural warfare by using submarines to cut British cables. From May 1915 to April 1917, the German Navy cut every cable starting from Britain, except those across the Atlantic. In one instance, a Norwegian repair team finally located a rheostat that the Germans had used to emit false electrical signals about where the break in a submarine cable had occurred. The capsule containing the rheostat held a note, reading: "No more Reuter war-lies on this line. From a 'Hun' and a 'Sea-Pirate.'"[47]

At the same time, wireless offered a way to circumvent cables. The German government relied on the Nauen, Eilvese, and Königswusterhausen transmitter stations. Nauen's trial service had started in 1906. Its operator, Transradio, handed all three stations over to the German Army and Navy for use during the war. The German military also invested in supplying wireless devices to army units. Finally, war funds paid for expanding the wireless tower on the American East Coast at Sayville that Telefunken had erected in early 1914. The tower could now more reliably receive signals from Nauen.

FIGURE 3. Cartoon, "The Headquarters of Lies." *Simplicissimus* 25 (September 22, 1914): 372. Courtesy of Simplicissimus.info.

During the initial months of the war, wireless towers were battle sites more than transmission stations. To disrupt German communications, the Entente conquered wireless towers in German colonies as quickly as possible. Australian forces took German New Guinea in September 1914 and attacked the German wireless station there in the battle of Bitapaka. British troops destroyed German wireless on the island of Yap the next month. In early 1915, the British conquered German South West Africa along with its wireless towers. The British were initially skeptical about using wireless for battle communications. But they worried about German wireless infrastructure.

Beyond expanding Sayville, the German military and government initially expended little energy on wireless communications outside the battlefield. Generals and politicians had foreseen a short war characterized by movement on both fronts. There would be no time to erect wireless towers or create comprehensive propaganda strategies. Moreover, wireless was still not wholly reliable and would need significant investment to improve. Atmospheric disturbances could interrupt signals, particularly in the early summer. Approximately 10 percent of transmissions from Nauen did not reach the United States in early 1915.[48] Nor could wireless yet reach further than the East Coast of the United States. Germans could communicate with places like South America and East Asia only via their towers in the United States. This left the transmissions vulnerable to interception and American censorship.

As the war on the Western Front became a stalemate in 1915–1916, the German military became ever more obsessed with wireless. The military began using wireless to keep unreliable allies on board. Along with the military, the Colonial Office, Foreign Office, and Post Office started working with the German consulate in Istanbul in mid-1915 to erect wireless towers in the Ottoman Empire, particularly in Damascus, Baghdad, and Istanbul.[49] This could spread information to try to foment jihad against the British, as German spies and adventurers in the Middle East were trying to do. The towers were also meant to keep the Ottoman Empire allied with Germany by providing news from a German point of view.

By mid-1916, German officials wanted a "world wireless network" (*Welt-Funktelegraphen-Netz*). And they made it part of their longer-term planning beyond the war. One bureaucrat noted in June 1916 that it was better not to think about wireless "from the viewpoint of the current war conditions, but rather to consider it from the viewpoint of the overall plan for a later German world wireless network."[50] It would take several years to improve wireless technology enough to create a reliable global network with less atmospheric disturbances and greater range. Still, military generals were willing to invest millions of marks to improve wireless's range and reception. That long-term vision increasingly guided the government in its technological aspirations.

Many military officials saw a world wireless network as the only method to bypass the British. One lieutenant suggested to state secretary for foreign affairs Arthur Zimmermann in January 1917 that Germany's "lack of cables, which mainly at the beginning of the war made itself so damagingly effective, will be removed in a few years with the progressive [improvement of the] technology of wireless telegraphy."[51] The lieutenant's letter was ironically sent just ten days after Zimmermann had cabled the infamous Zimmermann Telegram to Mexico, which suggested a military alliance between Germany and Mexico if the United States entered World War I on the side of the Entente. In a major intelligence triumph, the British intercepted the telegram; Zimmermann admitted its authenticity in March 1917, which increased American support for entering the war against the Germans.[52] Wireless seemed more important than ever. A captain asserted that German experiences in the war had shown that a world wireless network was "virtually indispensable." Wireless was critical "as a counterweight to a world cable network that mostly lies in enemy hands."[53] A world wireless network controlled by Germany would be a source of military and political strength as well as an insurance policy against informational isolation in the future.

But the Germans had learned two things from their colonial communications strategy. First, there was only one method to ensure that the British would not destroy their towers. They had to erect them on neutral soil. Second, the network could not be colonial. It had to be global. The British and French had long supplied their news to neutral nations. This seemed to prejudice those countries against the Central Powers in German eyes. The only method of retaliation was to supply neutral countries with German news during peacetime too.

German investment in wireless technology also enabled the shift from a colonial to global perspective. In early 1915, the wireless tower at Nauen could broadcast approximately 6,500 kilometers to the East Coast of the United States. Officials knew that they had to invest in improving the range of wireless. It would be cheaper to extend the range of towers so that the Germans could build fewer. There were also often large oceans or belligerent countries lying between Berlin and its target audiences.

Officials planned their world wireless network around neutral countries. They focused specifically on East Asia and Latin America. The planning involved financial and strategic coordination between the Post Office, Colonial Office, Foreign Office, Army, and Navy. The discussions about wireless were uncharacteristically cordial. The Navy too saw these regions as critical for a global Germany, though it had focused on East Asia.[54] Every other ministry concurred about the importance of wireless to circumvent British cables and counteract the nefarious news that the British were sending to neutral nations. Moreover, the Americans were censoring German news to South America and East Asia.[55]

The plan required technological improvements that only Telefunken could execute. By 1916, wireless technology still had many limitations. Some towers only received signals, while others could both send and receive at greater ranges. Officials foresaw fourteen or fifteen receiving stations in Latin America and East Asia with four large stations that could both send and receive information. In November 1916, officials decided to task Telefunken with erecting towers and securing concessions from the relevant governments. Telefunken would operate as a private company to avoid neutral governments' suspicions about German military involvement. But German war funds would pay Telefunken's costs for personnel, materials, and technological improvement to towers.[56]

Telefunken's executives, Hans von Bredow and Georg von Arco, responded favorably and swiftly to the government's overtures. Before the war, Telefunken had erected towers around the world for private and government customers. While Telefunken had handed over control of many of these towers, Hans von Bredow had started to think about creating a world network as early as 1913. Now the company could pursue its goal with government subsidies.

Telefunken suggested dividing the network into four areas: Central America, Eastern South America, Western South America, and East Asia. The company wanted to start with Mexico in Central America and China in East Asia, because these were simplest for technological and political reasons.[57] It was only 9,700 kilometers to Mexico City and 8,400 to Shanghai. These were feasible distances for Telefunken; by November 1915, Nauen had reached Honolulu, which was nearly 14,500 kilometers.[58]

To enact the plan, Telefunken sent a Dutch engineer, van de Woude, to New York in January 1917. The Dutchman had worked for Telefunken for twelve years. As a citizen of a neutral country, he could operate relatively freely in the United States.[59] Van de Woude was supposed to construct machinery in the United States and purchase materials alongside the four receiving stations that Telefunken was already building on American soil. He was also supposed to commence negotiations for concessions with Central and South American governments, though it is unclear how far he progressed.[60]

The German military was willing to put its money where its mouth was. Alongside erecting towers in neutral countries, the government would improve the towers in Germany and on the East Coast of the United States. The War Ministry estimated that the cost would reach 2–3 million marks. But the savings on telegrams and the political benefits would ultimately justify the expense.[61] The German government also believed wireless to be more secure than it actually was: the British had intercepted the Germans' naval code books and were decoding their messages at a new department called Room 40. The German Navy in particular used wireless to try to compensate for its smaller number of ships than the British.[62] Although there were sometimes communications issues between Room 40 and British naval officers, wireless was not as good an alternative as the Germans supposed.

The planned locations and number of the large wireless towers changed constantly in late 1916 and 1917. Suggestions ranged from Mexico, Brazil, Uruguay, and Sumatra to Paramaribo, Beijing, and Bangkok. Because the German government and Telefunken relied on the good graces of neutral states, they had to adapt to changing circumstances. Original plans focused on stations in Mexico, China, and South America. But the German government added Java in early 1917 because the Dutch government proved so amenable to allowing Telefunken to erect a tower there.[63] A trial signal sent from Nauen to Java worked well in March 1917 and Telefunken sent the materials for a provisional receiving tower for Java from Holland in April 1917. Telefunken also gleefully reported that a station in Bandung was receiving well from Nauen. This had shown the Dutch Colonial Office that it did not need to follow the English plan of forcing Holland to use interim stations on English and Italian territory to reach Dutch colonies. After lengthy negotiations with the Dutch, Telefunken had defeated this purported British attempt to influence Dutch communications.[64] Telefunken sent engineers along with equipment to Java in April 1917. Still, the stations never communicated properly with Nauen before the end of the war. There was still too much atmospheric disturbance and interference for wireless to reach reliably across such great distances.

Plans for a world wireless network always overlapped with plans to influence neutral nations through news agencies. These plans too relied on purportedly neutral entities. The government held the majority of shares in an ostensibly independent news bureau, Hollandsch Nieuwsbureau, created in August 1915 to provide Entente news from The Hague to Germany and Austria and to supply the Netherlands with German news beyond Wolff's telegrams.[65] The Foreign Office also cooperated with and subsidized Europapress, founded in 1916 in Frankfurt am Main as a private telegraph agency.[66]

The Foreign Office used its improved wireless connections to the East Coast of the United States to send information from another newly founded news agency: Syndikat Deutscher Überseedienst (German Overseas Service Syndicate), a syndicate jointly owned and founded by the government and leading industrialists in 1913. The syndicate was registered as a limited company in September 1915. Its working party met regularly in Berlin's prestigious Hotel Adlon and included industrialists and later politicians like Alfred Hugenberg, Hugo Stinnes, Gustav Stresemann, and Hjalmar Schacht.

The government and the industrialists did not cooperate for long. By mid-1916, the Syndicate had split. While the government wished to make the news available to all interested parties as a general newspaper service, the industrialists hoped to gain a market advantage from receiving exclusive information. Two companies emerged: Deutscher Überseedienst (German Overseas Service) and Transocean. The industrialists made Deutscher Überseedienst an exclusive service that principally reported on foreign economic news and became a "monopoly of heavy industry" in the German government's eyes.[67]

The government ran and subsidized Transocean to deliver news overseas. The German chancellor appointed the head of Transocean's advisory committee. Theobald von Bethmann Hollweg, chancellor from 1909 to 1917, chose Otto Hammann, who resigned from his post as chief press officer to concentrate on Transocean in 1916. Academic Theodor Schuchart concluded in 1918 that the split between Transocean and Deutscher Überseedienst meant that "the government will be forced to restrict its outgoing express service essentially to the political."[68]

Now that Transocean was more government oriented, its editors even started working in the Foreign Office building in Berlin.[69] Transocean received news and pictures from various government departments engaged in propaganda activities, such as the Zentralstelle für Auslandsdienst (Central Office for Service Abroad) and the War Press Office.[70] Transocean cooperated with the Zentralstelle für Auslandsdienst for its photo books, *The Great War in Pictures*. Some of the photographs were manipulated or faked to show the German point of view. Transocean also worked with German-language newspapers abroad, such as *Ostasiatischer Lloyd* in East Asia, and created new papers, such as *Germania* in Buenos Aires.

In early 1915, the German government started to transmit Transocean's news over wireless to influence American attitudes. Transocean sent news to the two Telefunken stations on the East Coast up to the outbreak of war with the United States in April 1917; it provided news exclusively over wireless from October 1915.[71] The German ambassador to the United States, Count Johann Heinrich von Bernstorff, sent fortnightly letters to Bethmann Hollweg listing the Transocean wireless messages that had arrived. From mid-1916, the German embassy in Washington, DC, served as an intermediary between Sayville and the American news agencies, as Bernstorff believed that the addition of American news would enhance the service.[72]

Historians have long portrayed German propaganda in the United States as haphazard, amateurish, and ineffective.[73] On the surface, British news seemed to dominate American newspaper coverage.[74] Beneath the surface, the picture looked different. Transocean was widely printed throughout the United States, but it was labeled the "Overseas News Agency" or "Berlin (date) by wireless to Sayville" instead.[75] From 1915 to 1917, American newspapers printed around 20,000 articles from Transocean. The newspapers included the *New York Times, Chicago Herald,* and *New York Herald* as well as myriad smaller provincial and rural publications. Some of these newspapers probably printed the news because they leaned pro-German, like the *Chicago Tribune.* Others may have wanted an alternative perspective to the British or news on other fronts and places like Bulgaria. By late 1916, the head of Transocean's advisory committee, Otto Hammann, advised Bethmann Hollweg that Transocean's news spread further and meant it had more impact than other methods such as American journalists' interviews with top German officials or generals. Hammann also thought Transocean would be a key bargaining chip in peace negotiations after the war, because it would demonstrate German political sophistication.[76]

Figure 4 shows a map of all the digitized newspapers that printed Transocean.[77] Although many newspapers are still not digitized, the map shows the ubiquity of Transocean. Newspapers of all political stripes and all sizes printed Transocean, frequently to portray an alternative perspective from British news. German propaganda was not quite as hapless as historians previously believed. In the early years of World War I, the United States was a battleground of news for the British and the Germans; it meant that Americans

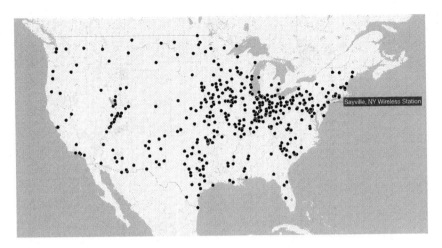

FIGURE 4. U.S. newspapers printing Transocean articles, 1915–1917. Map created in CartoDB. Used by permission of Jonathan Edward Palmer.

would have had very different understandings of the war depending on their newspaper and where they lived. It also alerted American elites to the importance of news. It is no surprise that Americans found communications just as key to World War I as other belligerents.[78]

Transocean also compensated for Wolff's deficiencies. After the war had begun, Wolff had used neutral Switzerland to transfer its news and to receive Reuters and Havas news from a Swiss news agency, Schweizerische Depeschenagentur. The Italian newspaper, *Corriere della Sera,* claimed in November 1915 that three-quarters of small newspapers in Switzerland received news solely from Wolff.[79] Many of Wolff's messages were Tractatus telegrams, meaning that they were paid for by Wolff (or the German government) rather than by the customers.

Wolff's service to German allies like Bulgaria proved inadequate and Transocean stepped into the breach. An important strategic gateway to the Balkans, Bulgaria initially remained neutral, before entering the war on the side of the Central Powers in August 1915. Germany needed the country to stay committed. In October 1917, the German embassy in Sofia denigrated "the absolutely inadequate character of reporting by Wolff and its deficient adaptability to the publishing needs of the day."[80] Wolff had to forward news through Vienna to honor its contract with the Austrian news agency, k. u. k. Korrespondenzbureau. In extreme cases, news reached Sofia forty-eight hours after release in Germany. Because Transocean had no contractual obligations with the Austrian news agency, it could deliver its news directly to the Bulgarian news agency, Agence Bulgare, under the signature "Bulgar."[81] In a letter to German chancellor Georg von Hertling in September 1918, German envoy to Bulgaria Alfred von Oberndorff commented that Wolff's delivery of news would have created an "emergency" if it had not been for Transocean.[82] Transocean offered a "1,000-word service" to European countries where Wolff could not disseminate its news directly.[83]

Transocean received materials directly from multiple German ministries, including the Interior Ministry, Reichsbank, and Foreign Office.[84] A typical day of news in December 1916 included the German army report and telegrams from military offices, news on German submarine successes, press commentary from Scandinavian countries as well as rather more anti-Entente items such as an anti-English movement in Mesopotamia and Dutch press commentary on Romania's guilt. The report also sprinkled in social news such as the death of the Grand Duchess of Mecklenburg-Strelitz.[85]

As the war progressed, officials contemplated how to streamline Transocean's work with Wolff, particularly as the division of labor between the two agencies was often unclear. Although Wolff was semiofficial, Transocean was from 1916 a government-owned and government-operated enterprise. Suggestions for streamlining ranged from a merger to outright competition.[86] In the end, the two agencies signed a contract in April 1918 separating their tasks. Transocean agreed not to disseminate its news within Germany and to refrain from starting any financial news services, as this was Wolff's most profitable service. Wolff gave Transocean the market of news for everywhere overseas except Europe and the United States. Transocean could disseminate Wolff's material overseas for an annual fee of 10,000 marks. Transocean and Wolff updated their contract in February 1919 to include Europapress, which Transocean had secretly purchased, and to remove any remaining overlapping competencies. Later in 1919, Wolff would renew its contract with Reuters and Havas to save costs and thus could not contractually have supplied news to Transocean's overseas clients.[87] Transocean retained a remit to use wireless. This cemented the dynamic for how government ministries would use Wolff and Transocean abroad: Wolff was more important in Europe, Transocean overseas.

The British found Transocean's activities deeply nefarious. In October 1916, the British concluded that Transocean "from the first utilized its large pecuniary resources, not only to obtain the publication of its garbled war telegrams, germanophile articles, and frequently 'faked' photographs, in a large number of newspapers." At the same time, the British believed that Transocean acquired and influenced newspapers. The British had monitored the mail to discover German methods. They were particularly concerned about China as well as newly founded and German-funded papers like *Germania* in San Salvador. Transocean also printed leaflets and operated alongside myriad German efforts to subsidize newspapers in the occupied parts of France. From a British perspective, the German interest in information and in England went beyond the war. It had deep psychological roots in "neurotic jealousy, which is the basis of their hatred of us," noted the British report. But the German attempt "to be all things to all men from the Pope to the Sheik ul-Islam necessitated the production of much that is definitely contradictory" and seemed, to the British, to miss the mark.[88]

Wireless in China

At the same time as Transocean sent news to places like Bulgaria and the United States, the German government and Telefunken pushed forward with plans to counteract British and American influence in China. Germans had focused on China for several decades as one key to global strength. Germany had gained concessions in the Chinese port city of Qingdao; German settlers created Tsingtao beer there in 1903. German travelers like Ferdinand von Richthofen searched for coal in China.[89] Before the war, German engineers constructed dams, and German companies sought contracts to build infrastructure such as railways. A wireless tower in China seemed an obvious choice.

A neutral country in the first years of the war, China was embroiled in internal turmoil after a revolution in 1911 and the fall of the Manchu dynasty in 1912. China's neighbor, Japan, had entered the war on the Entente side in August 1914. In January 1915, Japan sought to take advantage of China's domestic trouble by presenting "21 Demands" to the Chinese government for increased Japanese influence. While the Chinese government managed to rebuff many of the demands, military governors in southern China rebelled against the central authorities. The Japanese supplied the rebels and exploited these divisions within China to advance their own interests until China finally entered the war on the Entente's side in August 1917.[90]

Within the tumultuous situation in China, the German government and
Telefunken sought an intermediary to operate on their behalf—the Danish
engineer Sophus Larsen. Larsen seemed the perfect man for the job. He was
from a neutral country and had connections with Germany and China.
Before the war, Larsen had worked for Telefunken. He then started working
for the Chinese government. In mid-1916, Larsen became severely ill in
China and returned to a European sanatorium. While in Europe, Larsen
traveled to Berlin. He told Telefunken that both the British firm Marconi
and the American Federal Telegraph Company from San Francisco had
proposed wireless projects to the Chinese Department of Transport. The
Chinese government had rejected the offers because both companies had
requested extraterritorial rights for the stations. It was time for Telefunken
to act.

Telefunken proposed to the Post Office that Larsen should offer to erect
a wireless tower as powerful as the German station at Nauen. The Chinese
government would own the tower, but Larsen's company would operate it
under Chinese supervision. The Chinese would repay the cost of the tower
over several decades. Telefunken's plan was only feasible with substantial
German government support.

The firm asked for three forms of subsidy. First, the government would
act as guarantor to Telefunken for the Chinese government's repayments.
Second, the government would reimburse Telefunken for any administrative
or operational costs not covered by the income from the tower. Third, the
government would undertake diplomacy to support Telefunken's actions.[91]
Telefunken and the government would become inextricably linked in a
private-public partnership to create a world wireless network.

In November 1916, Telefunken received permission to begin negotiations
with the Chinese government to erect a large wireless tower that would
become Chinese government property after the tower was operational.[92]
Telefunken and Larsen had signed a contract to work together in February 1917. By March 1917, the German government and Telefunken scaled
down their ambitions for wireless in China because the Chinese political
situation made erecting a large wireless station impossible. They had intended to spend 2 million marks. Instead, they asked Larsen to travel to China
to set up a few receivers that would get news from Nauen. Larsen would use
his own company to negotiate with the Chinese government. He would
follow the same plan of operating the stations himself, but allowing the
Chinese government to own the stations and buy them over the course of

twenty to thirty years. Larsen would sail to China via the United States where he could connect with the Dutch Telefunken engineer, van de Woude, who would help with materials and money.[93]

Officials emphasized to Larsen that he had to avoid written evidence as far as possible. The connection with Germany through Telefunken and government subsidies had to remain covert. Larsen should also ensure that any money he transferred for expenses to van de Woude in New York did not mention the purpose. To sweeten the deal, the German government offered Larsen a 10,000 mark bonus if he succeeded in using the tower to disseminate German-friendly news. This was particularly critical if the German news services already in China—Transocean and the newspaper *Ostasiatischer Lloyd*—were forced to cease operations.[94]

But the war intervened in Telefunken's cunning plan to manufacture towers in the United States. By February 1917, the German Navy's unrestricted submarine warfare had prompted Woodrow Wilson to sever diplomatic ties with Germany. That made manufacturing in the United States impossible. Telefunken turned to Swedish, Swiss, and Spanish possibilities in April 1917. A former Swiss Telefunken engineer declined an invitation to start manufacturing in Spain "for personal reasons." On the Post Office's suggestion, Telefunken found appropriate firms in Sweden to supply raw materials and to construct a few masts, though these were expensive. The Swedish government also took an interest in the delivery and this delayed it by over six months in late 1917.[95]

On April 21, 1917, seventeen days after the United States had declared war on Germany, Larsen left Copenhagen for China via New York. He had already transferred the money from the Landmands-Bank in Copenhagen to National City Bank in New York.[96] Larsen docked in New York on May 4 and made his way across the United States. Communication with Germany became tricky and, besides, officials had advised him against putting much in writing. Larsen telegrammed Telefunken eleven days later in English that he was "leaving via Frisco end of May all relatives ok will cable permanent address soonest possible do not expect to be ready in Peking before autumn because war necessitates making of instruments in China Larsen." Telefunken assumed that by "relatives," Larsen meant German officials and Telefunken employees.[97]

After arriving in China, Larsen mainly communicated with Germany through intermediaries. He sent letters and telegrams to his brother and sister in Denmark. The letters traveled via Russia. Larsen speculated that Russian censors would not stop private letters and telegrams. Sometimes he wrote in English, hoping that this would reduce the chances of censorship.[98] His siblings selected relevant extracts, translated them into German, and sent them to Berlin. In July 1917, he wrote to his brother that political confusion would probably delay negotiations with the Chinese government about erecting a hospital. Everyone in the German ministries knew what Larsen meant.[99]

That same month, Larsen established a company, S. Larsen & Co. Consulting and Contracting Engineers in Shanghai. The "Co." was a Chinese partner, Mr. Pao, who was the director of the Bank of Communications in Shanghai. Pao often lent Larsen money to lubricate proceedings when Larsen ran short.

The Chinese declaration of war on Germany in August 1917 seemed to have little effect on Larsen's progress. Over the next few months, Larsen waited for the raw materials from the United States. In November 1917, Larsen erected a wireless tower that received reports from Nauen. News of the success only reached Telefunken via a letter from Larsen's brother in January 1918.[100] By that point, the entire plan seemed to be in jeopardy. The *Daily Mail* in Britain had reported on December 20, 1917, that the British embassy in Beijing had managed to put an end to the German-Chinese wireless plans. The embassy had instead secured a monopoly for Marconi.[101]

The news was very confusing and incomplete. At the same time as the news from Britain, Larsen seemed to be communicating that he had signed a contract with the Chinese government. His letter via his brother stated that Larsen had already paid a deposit of 10,000 Mexican dollars—a currency on the gold standard since 1905 and long used in China—when he signed the contract with the Chinese government. Telefunken and the German government deduced from Larsen's letters to his siblings and other communication that he needed half a million British pounds to secure a Chinese contract. The Chinese were suspicious and wanted proof that Larsen was operating independently of any German company.

It seemed that Larsen had started to return to Europe on December 22 with two Chinese negotiators. This was just two days after the *Daily Mail* report so German officials speculated that even Larsen might not know the latest situation. Officials did not know what to do. Should they wait to take further steps until Larsen set foot in Europe? Or should they preempt the British by transferring this enormous sum of money?[102]

The German government and Telefunken could only act on highly imperfect information. The situation had become so complicated that Telefunken registered a subsidiary named Drahtloser Überseeverkehr (Wireless

Overseas Traffic) in March 1918 solely to administer the creation of a world wireless network.[103] The company continued to report to the German government and to extrapolate further conditions of Larsen's agreement with the Chinese government. According to Telefunken's information in March 1918, the contract was still valid. But Larsen needed the 500,000 pounds in a Danish, Swedish, or Dutch bank by May 15, 1918, so that the bank could telegraph the National City Bank in New York that Larsen was good for the money. Otherwise the Chinese would renege on the contract and take a different offer, probably from Marconi. Larsen himself was delayed returning to Denmark so Telefunken could not consult with him.[104]

In late April, Telefunken threw caution to the wind. After receiving further information from travelers returning from China that Larsen's contract still stood, the firm sent its executive Hans von Bredow to Copenhagen to transfer the money. Bredow sent Larsen a telegram through neutral intermediaries that he was trying to fulfill Larsen's conditions.[105] Bredow hoped that he was not too late to secure a deal that built on twenty years of German work in wireless.

It was to no avail. Larsen had become jittery and thought that his plan could no longer succeed. He had traveled to Tokyo and transferred the contract to a Chinese-Japanese company that appeared to have relations with Siemens, a parent company of Telefunken. Larsen hoped that the company would give him a subcontract to manufacture the wireless towers. Larsen had telegraphed from Tokyo via Copenhagen informing Telefunken of the developments about a week before Bredow had even set off for Copenhagen.[106] The two men's telegrams to each other practically crossed paths.

The story did not end there. The Marconi Company had almost succeeded in securing a contract for wireless with the Chinese government in April 1914.[107] That had fallen through. As did Telefunken, Marconi often played the nationalist card to secure finances. Starting in 1915, Marconi frequently asked for funds from the British government to fight Telefunken's attempts to obtain wireless contracts or erect wireless towers in China and the United States.[108]

After the war, events took an ironic turn. To counteract Japanese influence in China, the British government decided to subsidize Marconi's contract with the Chinese government in 1919.[109] Marconi replaced the Japanese firm that had taken over Larsen's original contract. The British government financed Marconi to take over an agreement that was originally negotiated by a German-funded intermediary.

Within Germany, the plans for a world wireless network continued un-abated. As late as mid-October 1918, Bredow reported that he had seen French plans for a world wireless network and that the French had set up a governmental commission in December 1917 to investigate the issue.[110] On October 30, 1918, Telefunken also drew up a full draft contract with the Dutch Colonial Office for a concession in the Dutch colonial capital of Par-amaribo in Suriname.[111]

Some connections continued after the war in the new democratic state of the Weimar Republic. By 1918, Nauen's range had increased to 18,000 kilo-meters; Transocean's overseas service could be received in English around the world. Transocean's basic infrastructure and its key personnel were in place, as was its commitment to ambitious dissemination of its news to East Asia and South America. Its top management and editors remained. Wil-helm Schwedler remained editor in chief from 1918 until 1936, while Gustav Stresemann stayed on the board until he became chancellor and foreign min-ister in 1923.

In 1919, Telefunken and the Postal Ministry signed a contract for Tele-funken to deliver three large wireless stations to Java. The two engineers sent by Telefunken to Java in 1917 would erect the stations.[112] Bredow switched to work for the Postal Ministry in early 1919 and became the state secretary for telegraph, telephone, and radio in 1921. He would continue to support using wireless to spread German news abroad through a newly founded news agency of Eildienst. The change from monarchy to democracy and defeat in World War I did not end German dreams of a world wireless network.

Conclusion

Both sides learned lessons from wireless in World War I. The Allies learned to take the new communications technology seriously. Article 197 of the Treaty of Versailles forbade Germany from using its "high-power wireless telegraphy stations at Nauen, Hanover [Eilvese station] and Berlin [König-swusterhausen]" for three months after the treaty went into effect to send "messages concerning naval, military or political questions of interest to Ger-many or any State which has been allied to Germany in the war, without the assent of the Governments of the Principal Allied and Associated Powers." Germany was also forbidden from building high-power wireless stations within Germany, Austria, Hungary, Bulgaria, or Turkey.[113] The

German Foreign Office interpreted the clause literally, allowing broadcasts from Norddeich, which Article 197 had omitted.

Germans drew the lesson that the British and French had long controlled international news supply and infrastructure in order to undermine Germany abroad. The many suggestions to reform the official press apparatus during World War I mostly blamed Germany's problems with propaganda on British control of cables.[114] Some Germans would point to the British cable cutting as the turning point of the war, at least for public opinion on Germany abroad.[115]

Right-wing revisionists in particular believed that the battle had been lost in the minds, not by the military: Germany had lost the war because it had not understood how to counter enemy propaganda.[116] This dovetailed with the stab-in-the-back legend (*Dolchstoßlegende*) promoted by Erich Ludendorff and other generals after November 1918. Ludendorff popularized the myth that civilians on the home front, especially Social Democrats and Jews, had stabbed Germany in the back by surrendering to the Entente. These arguments fit into pre-1914 ideas about Germany's second-tier position in international communications.

Wireless stood out as the only positive development during the war even to skeptics like Paul Eltzbacher, a lawyer who became a Bolshevik supporter after the war. Eltzbacher criticized all other aspects of German propaganda for displaying "a certain unworldliness [*Weltfremdheit*]." But he saw world potential in wireless, stating in 1918 that Germany's wireless service had become "very perfected" since 1914 and was now "our best means to influence countries abroad."[117] The main lesson for Germans of all political persuasions was that wireless offered a way out.

While wireless offered escape, Wolff seemed to box Germany in. Social Democrats too worried about Wolff's role in propagating information. In February 1918, they prepared a question for the Reichstag about the "excessive falsity" of Wolff's news and decried the Foreign Office's "deliberate appetite for suppression" of the truth through Wolff.[118] Those same Social Democrats, however, would find that Wolff was the best way to reach the German population in the revolutionary days of November 1918.

3

REVOLUTION, REPRESENTATION, AND REALITY

𝔄t midday on November 9, 1918, Prince Maximilian von Baden, German chancellor since October 3, committed the first of several illegal acts that would secure his place in history: he announced the abdication of Kaiser Wilhelm II without the Kaiser's knowledge or permission.[1] Prince Max did not pronounce the news from a balcony, as Social Democratic politician Philipp Scheidemann would proclaim a republic from a Reichstag balcony at 2:00 P.M. that day. He did not make a statement at a press conference. Nor did he telephone leading journalists and editors. Instead he used the fastest and securest channel that he knew: the semiofficial news agency, Wolff Telegraph Bureau. He released a short communiqué:

> The Kaiser and King has decided to renounce the throne. The Reich Chancellor will remain in office until the problems connected with the Kaiser's abdication, the renunciation of the throne by the Crown Prince of the German Empire and of Prussia, and the installation of the Regency have been settled. He intends to propose to the Regent that Representative Herr Ebert be appointed Reich Chancellor and a bill be drafted for the holding of immediate general elections for a German National Constituent Assembly which would have the task of giving final form to the future Constitution of the German people, inclusive of those parts of the people who might wish to come within the frontiers of the Reich.[2]

By the end of the day, all the major newspapers had printed the notice (see Figure 5); no one questioned its authenticity. The communiqué set off a

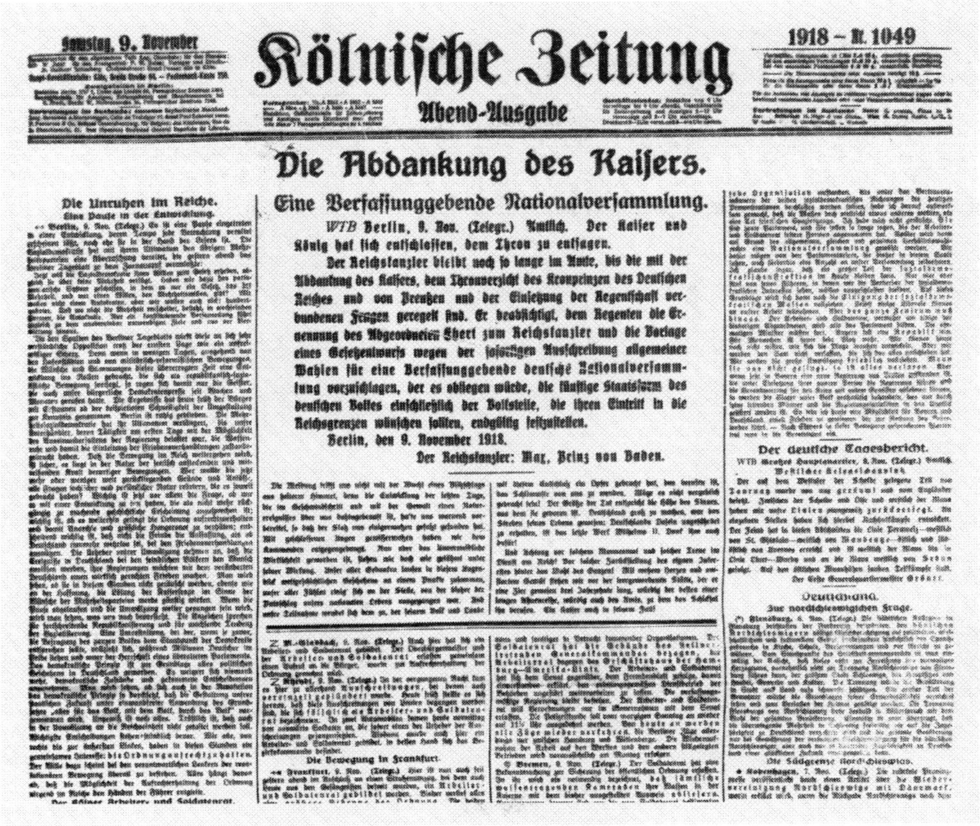

FIGURE 5. The *Kölnische Zeitung* was one of the few major national newspapers. It followed a moderate political course and was associated with Gustav Stresemann during the Weimar Republic. Wolff's notice appears in the top center of the page in the evening edition on November 9. Reproduced from a copy held at Staatsbibliothek zu Berlin.

chain reaction of events that would end World War I and create the new democratic Weimar Republic. The end of the war and domestic regime change were inevitable by this point, but a news agency shaped how they happened. Under certain circumstances, news agencies could be agents of change.

People across the political spectrum believed in Wolff's importance. A mere few hours after von Baden sent his communiqué to Wolff, revolutionaries occupied its central Berlin office to disseminate news of the revolution. Those on the right would also see Wolff as crucial. Right-wing reactionaries occupied Wolff's Berlin office during the Kapp Putsch, an attempt to overthrow the German government in March 1920.

The revolution of 1918–1919 used to excite much scholarship and political passion in West and East Germany, particularly over whether splits on the left doomed the Weimar Republic from the start.[3] After German reunification in 1990, these questions receded so much that 1918–1919 was called the "forgotten revolution" in 2010.[4] This has started to change again with new histories of the everyday experiences of violence as well as transnational comparisons of how women gaining the right to vote for the first time changed electoral politics.[5] The media history remains surprisingly underexplored, especially given that contemporaries constantly referred to news as their sole source of reliable information.[6]

Control over a central node of the media can change the course of political history, as in November 1918. But it only works if broader political circumstances make the messages credible and trustworthy. Despite the general confusion, newspaper editors believed stories from Berlin on November 9, 1918, because they came through Wolff. Wolff's control over domestic news supply had complemented German attempts since 1900 to compete internationally over news. The ubiquitous, though grudging, support for Wolff in 1918 had disintegrated by 1920. In 1918, Wolff was the social institution that lent validity to the declaration of Wilhelm II's abdication.[7] In 1920, it no longer exerted that force. In November 1918, representation became reality; in March 1920, it did not.

Political scientist Brian Klaas has argued that coups succeed when the leaders can, first, generate a bandwagon effect and, second, create an aura of inevitability.[8] The aura of inevitability comes from the media as much as anything else. Sometimes in German history, media coverage helped to accelerate a perfect storm leading to radical political change. Television coverage of Günther Schabowski's bungled press conference on November 9, 1989, sparked the proximate events leading to the fall of the Berlin Wall.[9] Exactly seventy-one years earlier, press coverage had sparked the proximate events that ended World War I and established the Weimar Republic. The difference was that Prince Max von Baden deliberately created news to make Wilhelm II's abdication seem inevitable.

Abdicating the Kaiser and Proclaiming the Revolution

On November 9, all parties worked with imperfect information. Ignoring Prince Max von Baden's pleas to remain in Berlin, Wilhelm II had removed himself and his military entourage to Spa on October 29, a strong indication that the suggested shift to a parliamentary monarchy would not happen smoothly. Telephones became the swiftest and most reliable means of communication between the Kaiser and his chancellor. Wilhelm II had belligerently refused to contemplate abdication, despite numerous discussions after Woodrow Wilson's notes on October 14 and 23 stating that the Allies would only negotiate with a democratic Germany. Wilhelm II declared defiantly on November 3 that he was not thinking of leaving the throne "because of a few hundred Jews and a thousand workers."[10] The Kaiser continued to believe that he had retained control over the army and ordered the commanders of the nearest armies to report to Spa on the morning of November 9. Confidently, he asked them about the troops' views and whether he could reconquer Germany at the head of his army. The reply was overwhelmingly negative. Of the thirty-nine commanders, only one thought his troops would march; twenty-three were certain that theirs would not.[11]

Just before 11:00 A.M., von Baden placed the first crucial telephone call from Berlin. The news was alarming: von Baden thought that the government had to react within minutes not hours, as police battalions were starting to defect to the revolutionaries. He told Spa that there had already been bloodshed, possibly leading to the mistaken impression that Berlin's streets were flowing with blood.[12]

At 11:00 A.M., Wilhelm II mentioned the possibility of abdication for the first time.[13] Two generals suggested a palatable solution: he could remain king of Prussia, but abdicate the imperial crown. This was technically a constitutional impossibility as the two crowns were legally connected. Regardless, the Kaiser asked that this solution be telephoned through to Berlin. Just after 11:00 A.M., a second telephone call connected to Berlin. As von Baden remembered it, the message stated: "The Kaiser has resolved on abdication; you will receive the declaration which is being formulated in half-an-hour's time."[14] Von Baden dutifully waited thirty minutes but no phone call came. He repeatedly tried to contact Spa, but one telephone had been disconnected (probably as workers had occupied the telephone exchanges) and the other line was apparently busy.[15] Prince von Baden felt that he had to fulfill his duty and make the Kaiser's decision known without the Kaiser's explicit consent. Von Baden's memoir of 1928 offers no further clues on why he chose Wolff other than his proclamation that he was "well aware of the seriousness of the responsibility I was taking on myself in sending to the Wolff Telegraph Agency."[16] It is not clear that bloodshed would have occurred if Wilhelm II had remained on the throne. Still, von Baden believed that news of the abdication should circulate while "some good might still come of such publication."[17] For Prince Max, Wolff Telegraph Bureau was the swiftest way to stabilize a precarious situation.

News of the abdication spread fast. Following normal procedure, the central Wolff's office forwarded the message to its branches, which in turn sent the message to newspapers to print as extras immediately and in normal editions later. Theodor Wolff, editor of the liberal *Berliner Tageblatt,* received the message through his newspaper's ticker machine at 12:45 P.M.[18] In the offices of the tabloid *B.Z. am Mittag,* events had moved faster. The Chancellery had rung at noon to ask the paper to stop its presses in advance of "news of the greatest importance." A privy councilor telephoned from the Reich Chancellery shortly after noon to read the Wolff's announcement. Within minutes, the paper's workers had composed the front page, cast it onto the plates, and put it into the foundry before the seven printing presses at the *B.Z. am Mittag* ran overtime to print the news. Fifteen minutes after receiving the phone call from the Chancellery, newspaper vendors were already hawking the extra on the streets.[19] Almost as fast as a smartphone notification today, Max von Baden's announcement reached the people of Berlin.

The news swiftly reached politicians. Just over half an hour after von Baden had sent the message to Wolff, Friedrich Ebert, an SPD (Social Democratic Party) representative in the Reichstag, met with Max von Baden, Philipp Scheidemann, and others in the chancellor's palace in Berlin.[20] Von Baden asked Ebert if he knew that Wilhelm II had abdicated. Ebert replied that he had seen the Wolff publication.

The following exchange led to von Baden's second illegal act of the day: appointing Ebert as chancellor. Von Baden stated that their task now was to solve the question of regency. Ebert, however, had concluded from reading the Wolff's item that it was "too late." The last imperial chancellor, von Baden, suggested that Ebert take over the position. After a moment of contemplation, Ebert answered: "It is a difficult office, but I will take it over."[21] Wilhelm Solf, von Baden's foreign minister, questioned the constitutional procedure of appointing a chancellor now that the Kaiser had abdicated, but suggested dejectedly that the only option was to allow the old chancellor to hand over his role to the new one. Without further ado, von Baden passed on his mantle. No participant in the meeting wished to hear confirmation from the Kaiser himself. All saw the publication sent to Wolff as an act that could not be undone.

Even the Kaiser could not correct the news. His entourage feared for Wilhelm's life: there were rumors that revolutionary soldiers were heading to Spa. As the debate over the Kaiser's next move continued apace, General Friedrich von Gontard brought the Kaiser a sheet of paper with news received over wireless. With shaking hands, chattering teeth, and tears rolling down his cheeks, von Gontard delivered the news: "They have deposed the Kaiser and the Crown Prince!"[22] Unlike his former subjects, Wilhelm II did not read the news from the Wolff's report, but heard about the proclamation from a subordinate. He denounced the act as "treason, shameless outrageous treason!" The Kaiser wrote telegram after telegram in protest.[23] No one sent them, believing that von Baden's message had created an irrevocable reality. Wilhelm soon found himself on a train to Holland into exile from his former subjects, whom he and his generals feared might assassinate him just like his cousin, Tsar Nicholas II of Russia.

After the extras had hit the streets, newspapers continued to print the announcement in normal editions that afternoon, evening, and the next morning. Almost every newspaper in Germany printed Wolff's notice verbatim at the very top of the first page on the evening of November 9 or morning of November 10 (depending on the newspaper's publication schedule).[24] Editors and journalists had retained habits from World War I, when the imperial government had instructed them to name Wolff as the source and to print Wolff news verbatim. Even newspapers abroad like the *New York Times* printed a full translation of the notice and named Wolff as the source.

The newspapers' visual similarity in displaying the item is striking (see Figure 6). The abdication notice consistently appeared at the top of the front page and disrupted the usual format of columns, indicating its extreme

FIGURE 6. The *Berliner Tageblatt* was the most influential liberal newspaper in Berlin with a circulation of around 250,000. It printed the Wolff's notice in the top right-hand corner in its November 9 evening edition. Most newspapers printed the notice with a similar layout. Reproduced from a copy held at Staatsbibliothek zu Berlin.

importance. The telegraphic style of the notice implicitly conveyed the authenticity of the message. Wilhelm II's actual act of abdication relieved civil servants, officers, and soldiers of their monarchical loyalty on November 28, though the document roused hardly a murmur in comparison.[25]

The *Hamburger Echo* commented on November 10 that the population had received the news of the abdication "with the utmost indifference."[26] There were bigger problems. No one knew how or when the war would end. Sailors' protests against a final order to fight on October 24 had morphed into revolution in Kiel by November 4. The creation of workers' and soldiers' councils—soviet-style elected representative bodies—continued apace across the country, reaching Berlin by November 9.

On November 9, von Baden's announcement had failed to calm the competition between SPD and USPD (Unabhängige Sozialdemokratische Partei Deutschlands, Independent Social Democratic Party), a more radical left-wing party that had split from the SPD in 1917. The SPD politician Philipp Scheidemann declared a republic from the balcony of the Reichstag at 2:00 P.M., rising from his lunch of thin watery soup to prevent any "Russian madness" from taking over Berlin and the nation.[27]

Two hours later, the leader of the far-left USPD, Karl Liebknecht, clambered onto the roof of a car in front of the Berlin castle and claimed that the day of revolution had arrived, bringing a free socialist German Republic. The vast majority of Germans heard neither of the competing proclamations. They found out about the Kaiser's abdication, Ebert's assumption of the chancellorship, and the proclamation of a republic from Wolff's items printed in newspapers. Wolff did not remain in Ebert's hands, however. It too was caught up in the turmoil of the revolution.

While Scheidemann and Liebknecht proclaimed republics to gathering crowds, other members of the SPD and USPD had different ideas. The outbreak of revolution in Berlin caught left-wing groups somewhat unprepared. Leaders had planned revolutionary strikes for November 11, but events were moving so fast that they decided to act on November 9. Although they had prepared for the November 1918 strike with leaflets, November 9 unfolded spontaneously. Amid the chaos in Berlin, three main groups set out to control different aspects of the press: the first to occupy a newspaper building; the second to occupy Wolff's headquarters; the third to occupy the wireless station at Nauen.

The first group included many Spartacists, left-wing radicals who later formed the German Communist Party (KPD). They tried, but failed, to occupy the editorial offices of the *8-Uhr-Abendblatt, Deutsche Zeitung,* and *Berliner Tageblatt.* However, one group succeeded. In an occupation that became an important founding myth for the KPD, and later the ruling party in East Germany (SED), the Spartacists seized the editorial offices of the widely read *Berliner Lokal-Anzeiger* in the heart of Berlin's newspaper quarter.[28] The *Berliner Lokal-Anzeiger* was intimately tied to the monarchical establishment: it was the only paper that the Kaiser read in toto. As the newspaper had already been set, the group only had time to change the front page, printing the headline "Berlin under the Red Flag" and producing the first issue of *Die Rote Fahne* on the evening of November 9.[29] The group occupied the office until the evening of November 10, when even Rosa Luxemburg could not convince editorial workers to join the Spartacists.[30] Representatives of the newspaper's publisher, Scherl, complained to the new government. The Spartacists were removed and the *Lokal-Anzeiger* appeared normally on November 11. Simultaneous seizures of newspaper editorial offices occurred in many cities around Germany.[31] Within a few short days, however, newspapers returned to their owners. New papers such as the USPD's *Die Freiheit* emerged. *Die Rote Fahne* appeared again on November 18, once it finally found a willing printer.

The second group to set out on November 9 to control the news was led by twenty-nine-year-old Franz Jung, a left-wing radical whose father had disowned him in 1910 for his disorderly lifestyle. Jung would only return home the next morning, "pale and bleary-eyed," as his wife recalled.[32] An economic journalist and publisher of the first Dadaist journal in Germany, *Die Neue Jugend,* Jung understood how news supply worked. Unlike most revolutionaries' focus on newspapers, Jung saw Wolff as the key to controlling news. Jung wanted to refashion Wolff, keeping the form of the news agency, but changing its agenda. Accompanied by his friend, the writer Georg Fuchs, Jung set out from Potsdamer Platz at the head of a group of soldiers to occupy Wolff's main office. With their IDs from the Berlin Workers' and Soldiers' Council in hand, Jung and Fuchs took control of Wolff's office and immediately set to drawing up a new program of news distribution.

Jung's control lasted just a few hours. Erich Kuttner, SPD politician and a political editor of the SPD's newspaper *Vorwärts* in 1915, arrived with troops to restore order. Thanking Fuchs and Jung for their initiative and fighting spirit, Kuttner promptly substituted their program with his own.[33] He wished to prevent Wolff from disseminating false reports and using its status as an organ of the old regime to escalate the situation further.[34] By the evening of November 9, Kuttner had placed Wolff's main offices in the hands of the Executive Committee of the Workers' and Soldiers' Councils. In Wolff's Berlin branch sat Erich Roßmann, editor of various southwest German newspapers from 1904 to 1915 and later a member of the Reichstag for the SPD from 1924 to 1933. The Wolff office in Frankfurt was in the safe hands of Wilhelm Carlé, who later wrote a sociological dissertation on the press and public opinion.[35] Roßmann and Carlé swiftly disseminated a

Wolff's report that "the revolution has achieved a brilliant, almost wholly bloodless victory. . . . There is complete peace and order in the city."[36] Wolff disseminated items over the next few days emphasizing that the revolution was progressing and there was peace and order. Those in charge hoped that representation would become reality.

Revolutionaries sought to replace newspapers; the news agency Wolff had to retain its name to retain the population's trust in its message. Kuttner was no fan of revolutionary chaos, writing to his mother shortly before the revolution that he aimed to create democracy "and therefore spare Germany from total chaos, Bolshevik anarchy with its terrible decline of all the people's powers and goods."[37] Still the Russian Revolution informed his actions in November 1918. Kuttner declared the following year that he had only believed in the Russian Revolution when a Petersburg telegraph agency reported on it. He believed the same for Germany, stating: "Furthermore, I said to myself: *if one now used Wolff's Telegraph Bureau to distribute a report of the victory of the revolution, then the whole world would believe it [sic]*."[38] The unthinking acceptance of the Kaiser's abdication showed that Kuttner was right.

Kuttner spent less time thinking about the technology of news dissemination, particularly wireless. Over and above controlling newspapers or Wolff, the SPD government sought to regain control of wireless. It was here that interaction with the Soviet Union most damaged the SPD's hopes of peace and domestic order free from potential Spartacist uprisings. The Soviets did not just provide a positive model for men like Jung, but also a worst-case scenario for many Social Democrats and right-wing politicians. A Wolff's news item of November 8 had blamed the whole council movement on Russian influence.[39] Russian wireless stoked fears of Bolshevism after November 9.

Although disrupted on November 10, wireless messages had already reached Berlin from the Soviet government encouraging workers and soldiers to keep their weapons, take over power, and form a government headed by Karl Liebknecht. The message urged workers to fight for bread as well as peace and freedom.[40] Similar messages reached Berlin on November 11, asking councils to communicate with the Moscow and Tsarskoe Selo wireless stations and pledging Russian support.[41] These messages may have played a role in the government's decision in a cabinet meeting on November 18 not to recognize the Soviet Union. At that meeting, a leading theoretician of Marxism and Foreign Office official in 1918–1919, Karl Kautsky, declared that the Soviet government should clarify its position on the radio messages that portrayed the German government so negatively.[42]

Wireless occupied the minds of the third group that set out to control news supply on November 9. They understood that Soviet wireless messages needed German wireless receivers. The group prioritized the wireless station at Nauen, just outside Berlin. The man leading the Nauen operation spoke to Friedrich Ebert and Georg Ledebour, a prominent member of the USPD. He then received orders from the Workers' and Soldiers' Council to occupy Nauen. A troop of eighty armed men drove to Nauen with two tanks and two trucks. After some resistance, they took over the station.[43] By 10:10 P.M. on November 9, Ledebour could send a wireless message from Berlin to all, stating: "Revolution also in Berlin, wholly successfully and thereby in entire country. The authorities have capitulated. The main headquarters recognize Workers' and Soldiers' Councils. Socialist German Republic secured. Ledebour."[44]

Councils took over wireless stations throughout Germany. The Workers' and Soldiers' Councils coordinated through the Central Radio Committee (Zentralfunkleitung), founded on November 9, which intended to create a communications network that could operate independently from the government-controlled postal system.[45] Throughout the day of November 10, despite intermittent signal disturbances, major cities exchanged greetings and assured each other of the victory of the councils.[46]

Nauen even disseminated its daily news service at 3:00 P.M., this time with items from the Workers' and Soldiers' Councils. The station was turned over to a council, elected early in the morning on November 12. Service continued: the station sent a message from Foreign Minister Wilhelm Solf to the United States and received confirmation of receipt within sixteen minutes.[47] By November 12, the government information office declared that press service was "normal everywhere" and mostly under the control of councils or leading parties with almost no censorship.[48]

Despite the proclamation of order, wireless remained a problem. In the long term, fear of uncontrolled airwaves and rogue radio operators, known in German as *Funkerspuk* (phantom radio operators), haunted radio policy into the post–World War II period.[49] In the short term, the dispute over wireless news sparked conflict between the USPD and SPD in early December 1918. On November 10, Ebert had compromised with the USPD: the two socialist parties created a Council of People's Deputies (Rat der Volksbeauftragten), composed of three USPD and three SPD members. The council functioned as a de facto government, supposedly cooperating with the Executive Committee of the Workers' and Soldiers' Council in Berlin (Vollzugsrat) until elections to the Constituent Assembly in February 1919.[50]

Still, tensions ran high. Just four days after the Central Radio Committee had received a broadcast license on November 25, *Berliner Tageblatt* warned foreign and domestic press not to trust German wireless news. The paper had heard that all wireless stations were currently occupied by the USPD and controlled by the Executive Committee of the Berlin Workers' and Soldiers' Council. A week later, on December 2, the reputable *Frankfurter Zeitung* confirmed reports from Berlin that Georg Ledebour and Karl Liebknecht led a group controlling all German radio stations. The article repudiated Wolff's denial of the reports. It even claimed that the United States had broken off radio contact and would not resume service until the German government guaranteed its control of news service.[51]

The matter exploded into a heated discussion at a meeting between the Executive Committee of the Workers' and Soldiers' Council and Council of People's Deputies on December 7, 1918.[52] Ledebour declared that these false reports on wireless, particularly one in *Vorwärts* on December 3, had escalated events in Berlin. Ledebour had refused to participate in the Council of People's Deputies and worried that such rumors fueled suspicions in the press that the Executive Committee was attempting to create "a kind of dictatorship in the name of the Berlin Workers' and Soldiers' Council over the whole country."[53] Ebert protested Ledebour's assertions, trying to deescalate tension between two bodies that had agreed to cooperate.

Yet the damage had been done. The USPD accused government members of entertaining counterrevolutionary thoughts, doing too little to counter attempts to discredit the Executive Committee publicly, and financing reactionary propaganda and movements. The conflict became so heated that one SPD representative of the Soldiers' Council, Max Cohen-Reuß, feared a catastrophic breakup between the Council of People's Deputies and the Executive Committee. The disagreement was deemed so sensitive that the meeting's participants decided not to send a report to Wolff.

Disagreements over wireless and Wolff tore at the heart of the compromise between the councils, the USPD, and the SPD that had enabled a German government to function somewhat in the chaos of late 1918. The USPD and the Executive Committee of the Workers' and Soldiers' Council felt undermined by the SPD's unwillingness to defend their honor against accusations in the press. Ebert too had recognized the gravity of the situation.

On December 4, 1918, he had authorized the creation of a political news office in the Foreign Office to monitor the political content of all incoming wireless items.[54] Ebert also agreed to create a Federal Broadcasting Commission (Reichsrundfunkkommission). Five months later, the commission put all communications networks under the control of the Postal Ministry. This development in April 1919 marked the end of the revolutionary period for German broadcasting.[55] What underlay the whole discussion, though, was the belief that news could change politics. Politicians feared that representation, even if false, could become reality.

The left continued to splinter. The Executive Committee transferred its mandate of oversight over the Council of People's Deputies and provisional governments to the newly elected Central Committee at the first Congress of Workers' and Soldiers' Councils in mid-December 1918. The USPD withdrew its three members from the Council of the People's Deputies on December 29, 1918, in protest at Ebert's domination of the Council and his cooperation with the army. On January 4, 1919, Ebert's dismissal of Berlin's police president, Emil Eichhorn, sparked an uprising and bloodshed.[56]

The next day, workers spontaneously occupied newspaper and press editorial offices, including the Wolff news agency. Franz Jung and Georg Fuchs took part again. They cooperated with Fritz Drach, commander of the workers occupying the buildings of the three major publishers: Mosse, Scherl, and Ullstein. Present when troops stormed on January 16, Jung was taken prisoner but released the same evening.[57] Jung subsequently moved to London under the pseudonym Franz Larsz and tried to establish a correspondence agency.[58] Kuttner too found himself embroiled. He was in the office of the *Politisch-Parlamentarische Nachrichten,* in the same building as *Vorwärts,* when workers occupied the area. Hiding until the next day, he managed to reach the Chancellery building and deliver a speech to loyalist demonstrators, encouraging them to defend the government. Kuttner's escapades had included shooting a drunkard who had threatened to shoot his troop of a dozen soldiers. Kuttner started preliminary proceedings against himself, which concluded that he had shot in self-defense.[59] USPD and Spartacist leaders then organized a general strike in Berlin for January 7. On the morning of January 11, troops stormed the *Vorwärts* building and retook the rest of the major publishing houses along with Wolff.[60]

While November 1918 seemed like a successful revolution, the uprising of January 1919 failed.[61] The councils' occupation of key communications exchanges in November 1918 gave them the initial appearance of control, which was not replicated in January 1919. In both cases, however, government control of Wolff was key. Immediately after regaining use of Wolff's headquarters, the government used it to disseminate news. On January 15, Wolff published a long government report on the deaths of Rosa Luxemburg and Karl Liebknecht, who had been executed by Freikorps soldiers with support from Gustav Noske, the defense minister. Wolff remained the method to plead for order: in an attempt to stop debate about how Liebknecht and Luxemburg died, an official announcement stated on January 17 that the government had investigated the deaths and both sides should regain their composure.[62]

Just two days later, the SPD received 38 percent of the vote in the national elections for a National Constituent Assembly and formed a "Weimar Coalition" with the Catholic Center Party (Zentrum) and German Democratic Party (Deutsche Demokratische Partei). The negotiations for a constitution began in Weimar in February 1919. Simultaneously, bureaucrats and ministers started negotiating new terms with Wolff. After the simple directive to use Wolff during World War I, politicians and bureaucrats needed a new consensus.

Renegotiating News

The revolutionary period of 1918–1919 had shown the unruliness of the press landscape. It was no wonder that the newly elected Weimar coalition wanted to regain control over the central nodes of news distribution. But those months had also prefigured the challenges that the coalition would face in doing so.

Wolff had ended the war in a position of simultaneous strength and weakness. It had proved its capacity to disseminate news and cooperate with any government. It had little choice if it wanted to maintain its unique selling point of exclusive access to official news. Intimately entangled with the old regime, Wolff's fate rested on the new government's attitude to Wilhelmine bureaucrats and elites. Wolff's managing director, Dr. Heinrich Mantler, had led the agency since 1891. He expressed no political views in his correspondence and appeared happy to work for whichever government would have him. Barely any civil servants were removed at the start of the Weimar Republic.[63] Wolff's personnel too hardly changed. Wolff cooperated willingly with the new government after its initial occupation. Newspapers emulated bureaucrats' faith. Despite complaints of slow, inaccurate, or inadequate news, there is no evidence that any newspaper canceled its subscription to Wolff.

Wolff and the German government had a mutually dependent relationship. The government relied on Wolff for its distribution network. Wolff was uniquely placed to save the government substantial costs because its efficient network reached most newspapers at comparatively little expense. Wolff had an electric teleprinter connection with all major Berlin newspapers. Throughout Germany, Wolff had an unbeatable network of thirty-seven branches in 1918. It could reach approximately two hundred–three hundred larger provincial newspapers by telegraph and telephone and served many midsized newspapers by post.[64] Wolff's membership in the news agency cartel provided the government with instant access to an international audience.[65]

In turn, Wolff relied on the government for exclusive access to government news and for unique access to the state's communications infrastructure. Since 1869, the AC (*Amts-Correspondenz*) privilege had enabled Wolff to disseminate official news in exchange for a government commitment to send Wolff's news faster over telegraph than anyone else. Ironically, Wolff's reliance on the state created its main weaknesses. The agency ended the war in a bleak financial state. Wars generally drove up newspaper sales, as more readers were interested in current affairs. German newspaper circulation increased nearly 70 percent from 1913 to 1918, though this did not translate into higher profits due to losses in advertising revenue, paper shortages, and inflation.[66] These problems continued in the immediate postwar years. In April 1920, the chairman of the Association of German Newspaper Publishers desperately wired Konstantin Fehrenbach, president of the National Assembly who would soon become chancellor, that the increased price of paper had brought the German press to "the brink of collapse."[67] Inflation that tipped into hyperinflation in 1922–1923 exacerbated everything.

War also drove Wolff into dreadful deficits. It followed government orders by maintaining the same prices for newspapers that had subscribed before the war. It also did not ask newspapers to cover the full cost of news distribution, as it paid for telephoning news from Berlin to its branches. By December 1916, Wolff's costs had more than doubled and its annual losses mounted as the war progressed. The agency was determined to remain financially independent of the government and retain a modicum of autonomy, even if this meant huge debts. Wolff estimated its losses during the war at

524,330 German marks.[68] Without serious financial aid, Wolff seemed close to bankruptcy.

The SPD's use of Wolff was one of the many compromises that it brokered in the first days of the revolution, akin to the Ebert–Groener pact of November 9 and Stinnes–Legien agreement of November 15. The Ebert–Groener pact was a secret agreement between Friedrich Ebert and army quartermaster general Wilhelm Groener on the evening of November 9. Ebert agreed to allow the army a virtual carte blanche in dealing with Spartacists, if the army supported the new regime and demobilized peacefully. The Stinnes–Legien agreement ended workers' strikes by allowing eight-hour days for workers and creating a committee to mediate between unions and big industry. Working with Wolff was a similar compromise. The SPD had prepared a question for parliament about Wolff's "excessive falsity" in early 1918.[69] Now it sought to work with the agency. Despite the SPD's previous complaints, Wolff remained the only option to reach the entire population as quickly and credibly as possible.

The SPD's interaction with Wolff differed in one crucial aspect: it required no explicit pact. In November 1918, Wolff's "symbolic power" rested on a tacit shared belief in its importance, even by a previously skeptical SPD. As sociologist Pierre Bourdieu has argued, symbolic power succeeds when "those subject to it believe in the legitimacy of power and the legitimacy of those who wield it."[70] Leaders never considered alternative methods of dissemination. Even later, no one condemned the SPD's use of Wolff as a "betrayal." The SPD used Wolff in an ad hoc attempt to establish legitimacy by co-opting an imperial institution.

Nevertheless, complaints resurfaced from early 1919. Officials questioned the tone of Wolff's news and even its obedience to the state. The Foreign Office saw the German press as "an unsuitable instrument" for encouraging public opinion to support the new political enterprise of democracy.[71] Wolff's tone showed that it had "no feel for the modern (except what it is officially taught) and for the personal," wrote one official.[72] The agency had barely mentioned the first speech by a female member of parliament, the Social Democrat Marie Juchacz, when it should have printed her speech in full. Wolff needed modern journalists, thought the Foreign Office official, but he did not suggest where to find them. Similarly, Wolff's status as a government mouthpiece made it a laughing stock after it disseminated an overenthusiastic announcement about Ebert's election as president in February 1919. Foreign correspondents and even sympathetic German journalists poked fun at

Wolff's servility, while questioning its reliability beyond reporting government opinions.[73]

Finally, Wolff signed a new cartel contract with Reuters and Havas in late 1919 that restricted it to reporting solely on Germany. Wolff could enter into direct relations with any agency allied with Reuters or Havas in Europe (except Belgium), but it could only supply German news. Even more painfully, Reuters and Havas acquired the right to distribute their news in occupied areas in Germany.[74] Despite the humiliating reduction of its stature, Wolff saw no choice. The then finance minister (and later chancellor from 1921 to 1922), Joseph Wirth, declared it "a well-known fact" in July 1920 that Wolff's news distribution could not compare with Reuters and Havas, even before 1914.[75] The cartel was the only way to access international news at a reasonable price.

Other news agencies saw the November revolution as their chance to negotiate a more advantageous relationship with the new authorities. After surviving the lean times of World War I, rival agency Telegraph Union sought to break Wolff's stranglehold on official news. In late November 1918, Telegraph Union trumpeted its credentials to the Chancellery, claiming that it had nearly two thousand subscribers, including most of the Social Democratic press, due to Telegraph Union's wartime neutrality. Telegraph Union hoped that the new government would distance itself from "the mistakes and injustices of the old regime," by which it really meant Wolff, and solemnly promised to support the new government.[76] Telegraph Union also appears to have offered a cheaper price to capitalize on dissatisfaction with Wolff.[77] This failed to convince the government: Wolff's pliancy and unique access to international news were too important.

Eager to prove its utility to the new government, Wolff continued to fulfill its wartime functions without requesting reimbursement. Wolff's behavior mirrored the pattern of civil servants' increasing boldness after the defeat of the January 1919 uprising: from February 1919, it demanded government payment for war losses.[78] In April 1919, the agency presented the Chancellery with a bill of 136,733.60 marks for November 1918 through April 1919, blaming the increase in costs mainly on coverage of the Armistice Commission.[79]

Given its own financial straits, the Chancellery was hardly eager to shell out money. It undertook an investigation of how departments used Wolff.[80] Usage varied greatly, as did payment. Some ministries used Wolff as a cheap resource to disseminate information swiftly, while relying on *Korrespondenzen* (correspondence bureaus) for less time-sensitive items that could be summarized in a weekly or monthly publication. For example, the Finance Ministry used Korrespondenz Gelb (Correspondence Yellow) to disseminate weekly reports from the Reichsbank.[81]

Ministries were rather incensed by Wolff's demand for payment. Wolff had also continued to send government news to the cartel agencies through the Tractatus scheme. Tractatus enabled each cartel agency to send government news for the other agencies to disseminate, but the sending agency had to cover the transmission costs. This had cost Wolff 617,554 marks in 1918–1919, though some ministries had reimbursed the cost.[82] Wolff could not afford to continue with current practices.

Both Wolff and government departments needed a new modus vivendi. The Chancellery, Foreign Office, and some other ministries reached a new agreement with Wolff in 1919. During the war, Wolff had taken over duties from the official newsletter, the *Reichsanzeiger*, as well as a government-owned newspaper, the *Norddeutsche Allgemeine Zeitung*. In a Saturday meeting in July 1919 to discuss Wolff's status, Heinrich Mantler presented a spirited defense of his news agency's loyalty to the German government. Mantler asserted that Wolff had eagerly assumed its patriotic duty during the war and absorbed the increased costs of transmitting so many more words. Although Wolff received compensation from the War Ministry for sending more messages, that did not occur with other departments, such as the Foreign Office.

During the revolutionary days of November 1918, claimed Mantler, the Executive Committee of the Workers' and Soldiers' Council had forced Wolff to telegraph news and proclamations that at least 80 percent of Wolff's clients, which were "bourgeois newspapers," did not want in the first place. Mantler argued that Wolff had continued to place the government's requirements above its own financial health. The new government had frequently needed to establish swift and close contact with the press; Wolff was "the victim of that necessity." Mantler declared that some government departments had pressured Wolff with "sweet violence" to print and disseminate items that were "advertisements" more than news. Disseminating government items that were not news had cost Wolff approximately 250,000 marks in telegraph and telephone fees as well as employees' salaries. The financial burden had forced Wolff to take out a loan with a 6 or 7 percent interest rate and the company's financial situation was deteriorating. Mantler feared that his workers would strike in the near future if he did not receive any payment from the government.[83]

Some government officials dismissed Mantler's arguments. One bureaucrat believed that Wolff existed in a symbiotic relationship with the government. Wolff's "entire existence" was based on its exclusive access to government news. Wolff should disseminate that news for free, even if the items had no "news value" for the agency. "One hand washes the other," the bureaucrat declared. He suggested that if Wolff could not cover its costs by raising subscription prices, the government should simply create an official news agency.[84]

Mantler angrily replied that the government had only supplied 3 percent of Wolff's news before the war. Wolff had collected the remaining 97 percent on its own.[85] Mantler portrayed Wolff not as a government mouthpiece, but as a business with a duty to serve its clients. Wolff's status as a business with other sources of news made it an indispensable organization for the government. It saved the government money by transmitting news for free. But it also secured a wide range of clients by supplying a comprehensive news service.

Over the next few weeks, Wolff and various government ministries hammered out a general compromise that acknowledged Wolff's dire financial straits, while accommodating bureaucrats' belief that Wolff benefited financially from access to government news. The newly reformed Press Department agreed in December 1919 to absorb 681,664 marks of Wolff's total debt of 1.5 million marks.[86] Wolff would distribute governmental news for free; the government would cover costs for Wolff's dissemination of official information. Wolff would send official messages for free as long as they were short and of "a purely news character."[87] The Chancellery would pay for items if it chose the form of the article or if the item was a public notice (*Bekanntmachung*), decree (*Verordnung*), order (*Verfügung*), or commentary. The government also agreed to prorate the telegraph and telephone costs.[88]

The agreement held some sticking points. Wolff had to agree to a separate contract with each government department, although most of Wolff's federal business came from the Foreign Office and a few other departments, such as the Economics and War Ministries. The Chancellery still recommended the same agreement, however, redistributing a draft to serve as a basis for negotiations between the Prussian state ministry and Wolff in November 1919.[89]

Unsurprisingly, the definition of "news" proved tricky when money had to change hands. Mantler and government had agreed during negotiations that they intrinsically knew what constituted "news value," that is to say, which items were news and should be covered by Wolff and which items were government information. Even a layman could identify news, claimed then finance minister Matthias Erzberger, who would be assassinated in 1921 by members of the far-right, ultranationalist Organization Consul.[90]

Practice proved all parties wrong. The government often disagreed with Wolff's decisions to categorize items as news or "official messages." Wolff often charged for lengthy messages, but the government would not necessarily agree on how many words were of news value and how many were government information. In February 1920, for instance, Wolff billed the government 4,337.90 marks. The government agreed to pay half the costs on an item it had deemed of news value. Similarly, the two often argued about what messages were news. Wolff complained that the Chancellery had wanted it to disseminate the chancellor's telegram of condolences to the widow of well-known German poet and writer Richard Dehmel for free, when this clearly had no news value and other departments had always paid for similar telegrams. After several weeks of exchanging letters, the government negotiated the bill down by 696 words or 101 lines to 3,101.70 marks, a discount of over 1,200 marks.[91] Every month, bureaucrats and news agency editors debated which items constituted "news" and which were simply "information." These negotiations had serious economic consequences. But economic consequences would seem minor compared to the political consequences of the Kapp Putsch.

The Kapp Putsch

The Kapp Putsch was sparked by attempts to reduce the army to 100,000 men as the Treaty of Versailles had mandated.[92] After General Walther von Lüttwitz refused an order from Defense Minister Gustav Noske to disband his Freikorps unit, Noske relieved him of several duties on March 11, 1920. Lüttwitz resolved to execute a coup on Berlin with a Freikorps unit, Marine brigade Ehrhardt. Lüttwitz decided with its commander that the brigade would march on Berlin the next night from their base near Berlin. The stage was set for a possibly bloody conflict between putschists and government forces: Noske had shown little compunction in quelling the January 1919 uprising and ordering Luxemburg's and Liebknecht's murders. Despite Noske's pleas for help, cabinet ministers decided that escape and a call for a general strike constituted the best course of action. The brigade paraded through Brandenburg Gate at around 7:00 A.M. on March 13, just minutes after the SPD government had interrupted their emergency meeting to flee Berlin for Dresden.

Three men met the brigade: Wolfgang Kapp, cofounder of the Fatherland Party in 1917 and nominal leader of the putsch; Lüttwitz, the highest-ranking commanding general in the Reichswehr; and General Erich Ludendorff, head of the German war effort with Hindenburg from August 1916 and a key proponent of the stab-in-the-back myth that civilians on the home front had betrayed the undefeated German army by signing the armistice in November 1918. The three set to work immediately. Kapp proceeded to the Chancellery and attempted to gain control of the bureaucracy. He failed rather miserably: "technically a Bonaparte, psychologically a Captain of Köpenick," remarked an acquaintance.[93] Only one high military commander joined the operation, while army commander major Hans von Seeckt obstructed, refusing to fire on troops or cooperate with Kapp.

The putschists' nonexistent news organs presented a similarly pressing problem. One of Kapp's first orders sent a military commando to Wolff. By 9:00 A.M., the commando had occupied the office. A little over an hour later, Heinrich Mantler visited the director of the legitimate government press department at the Foreign Office, as the director had not fled Berlin. Mantler later claimed that he promised to forward any government news to another office for distribution.[94] He then informed the Kapp Chancellery that Wolff would send its messages, but would preface them with "Report from the Reich Chancellery" to identify their origins.[95]

Kapp and Lüttwitz wasted no time spreading the word: in its midday edition, Wolff proclaimed their coup and a new "government of order, freedom, and action."[96] That evening, Wolff distributed the putsch government's program, announcing the steps to resurrect strong state authority.[97] The agency disseminated news to its branches throughout Germany by telephone between 5:10 P.M. and 11:45 P.M. Wolff had lost radio contact with parts of Germany, including East Prussia, and telephone disturbances meant that the process took longer than usual.[98]

Kapp had also turned his attention that morning to newspapers, banning the archconservative *Kreuzzeitung* at 10:00 A.M.[99] After reading the morning Berlin papers and realizing their opposition to his cause, Kapp promptly banned evening editions. Claiming that he had banned papers until negotiations with workers' representatives were complete on Monday, March 15, Kapp was forced simply to ban the papers once more when that day dawned.[100]

Kapp did not seem to understand how the press worked: banning news-
papers meant that there was nowhere to print Wolff's items. Still, Kapp used
Wolff throughout his five-day tenure. It had the personnel and capacity that
Kapp could not recruit himself.

Kapp's only other means of reaching the populace consisted of leaflets and
two conservative newspapers. As printers were almost all on strike, barely any
leaflets appeared. One newspaper that had played a rather significant role in
November 1918, the *Berliner Lokal-Anzeiger*, again proved central. Its editor,
Johannes Harnisch, became Kapp's chief press officer on March 15 and printed
a *Berliner Lokal-Anzeiger* extra the same day, claiming that three-quarters of
Germans supported the new order and that the Entente would not intervene.[101]
The conservative *Deutsche Tageszeitung* also declared for Kapp on March 15.

This time, however, representation did not become reality. First, Wolff had
already instructed its branches not to take its messages from Berlin seriously.
The provinces were not informed of a successful regime change, but rather a
flailing and isolated putsch in Berlin. Second, the political landscape had polarized so severely in the intervening two years that much of the population
was unwilling to support a rightist putsch that had escalated mostly because
of the legitimate government's swift departure from Berlin.

Outside Berlin, the putsch called forth massive efforts by the legitimate
government and trade unions to spur workers to a general strike. The General
German Trade Union (ADGB) played the leading role in calling the general strike.[102] Not only was the government without its base in Berlin after
fleeing to Dresden, and then Stuttgart on March 15, but it also could not use
Wolff to reach the population swiftly. Both the ADGB and the government
called for the strike through hastily printed leaflets on March 13. The trade
union had greater experience in using them, as it had not relied on Wolff or
a party paper beforehand.[103] The ADGB would be so strong after the putsch
that it could force the resignation of Noske and the cabinet of Chancellor
Gustav Bauer.

The strike began in Berlin on March 14 and spread quickly. Although
Mantler neglected to mention it in his later version of events, Wolff's
messages had also not achieved wide circulation because bureaucrats had
committed to strike on March 14. This included post and telegraph operators, who were federal employees, which prevented Wolff's telegrams
from reaching any area on strike outside Berlin.[104]

Still, Wolff's branches did not lay idle. Wolff's Berlin headquarters had
allowed them to communicate freely with each other from March 13 to

ensure that Kapp did not wholly control the agency. Over the next few days, various Wolff branches battled through a series of mishaps in their attempts to report on events on the ground. Wolff's office in Berlin had sent a special representative to Dresden on March 13, but he got nowhere close because of the rail workers' strike. Wolff's branch in Stuttgart took up the slack, established a connection with the Weimar government, and labeled its notices as "official" from March 16. The same day, branches in Breslau and Görlitz published denials of news from the Kapp government; they were subsequently occupied by military censors. Mantler claimed later that these maneuvers showed Wolff had done everything in its power to support the constitutional government.[105]

Most accounts deem the Kapp regime dead after two or three days. Kapp and Lüttwitz of course did not think so. They continued to use Wolff to disseminate orders to end the strike on March 15 and order the death penalty for strike leaders on the morning of March 16.[106] Wolff's pliancy contrasted strikingly with journalists' reactions to Kapp's final press conference. In a last-ditch scare tactic, the new press office decried the Bolshevik danger in Berlin and claimed that the USPD's Ernst Däumig would be made chancellor. The journalists jovially shook their heads in disbelief.[107] Wolff still disseminated the item in its midday edition.[108] Kapp even announced his resignation in Wolff's emergency afternoon edition on March 17, when Wolff was hardly acting under duress.[109] Claiming that Kapp had defended Germany from the acutest dangers of Bolshevism, Wolff's notice stated that Kapp believed his mission to be complete now that the Bauer government had conceded to his demands.[110] Kapp fled Berlin unpunished, escaping by plane to Sweden. He returned in 1922 to garner publicity from a trial, but died in prison in June 1922 before the trial could begin.

Almost immediately after the Kapp Putsch, Wolff sought to retrieve its reputation. It published a notice in response to Kapp's resignation: "Even at the collapse of his ignominious adventure, Kapp is still trying to mislead public opinion with falsehoods. Now that he has been forced to resign without conditions, he would like to create the impression that the government accepted his conditions. Let it therefore be emphatically emphasized once more that the government has rejected any form of negotiation with the mutineers and has not accepted any type of condition."[111] The very next morning, Wolff sent out reports as usual, this time under the auspices of the legitimate vice-chancellor. It informed the public of the putsch's defeat and the return to constitutional rule. The government thanked the German people for their "courageous and unshakable determination," asking them to return to work to prevent economic collapse.[112]

The uproar did not subside when the right-wing reactionaries fled Berlin. The general strike not only mobilized general resistance to Kapp but also led to the formation of a Red Army in the Ruhr.[113] In desperation, the SPD turned to the very Freikorps troops that the general strike had just defeated. The Freikorps marched on the Ruhr, easily defeating the uprising by April 6.

The putsch taught significant publicity lessons to all involved: protagonists, trade unions, politicians, and the press. The trouble was that those lessons varied tremendously. Ludendorff agreed with the world's harsh judgment of the putsch because "all propaganda preparation was missing [and] piece-meal."[114] Another right-wing supporter, Prussian colonel Max Bauer, blamed Kapp's propaganda, rather than the will of the "true Germans" who had supported Kapp. Kapp had used Wolff to send counterpropaganda against the strikes so late on March 14 that it did not reach the general public in time. That had allowed the other side, particularly the "Jewish press," to execute what Bauer decried as their "campaign of lies and distortion."[115]

While the putsch showed right-wing factions that Wolff was not suited to their needs, it showed trade unions their strength. They could bypass Wolff by reaching their base through leaflets. Meanwhile, it confirmed to civil servants and politicians that Wolff was simultaneously unreliable and indispensable. Complaints about payment grew, particularly from the Finance Ministry, which increasingly used the services of Korrespondenz Gelb to disseminate weekly Reichsbank reports for free.[116] Nothing could beat Wolff's domestic network, replied the Foreign Office time after time, although it too looked to other news agencies to disseminate German news abroad.[117]

In November 1920, representatives asked in the Reichstag if the government would clarify how much it paid Wolff to distribute news. While the question could have been posed prior to the putsch, the answer revealed the state's continued vehement support for Wolff. The reply asserted that every government needed a bureau to disseminate official and semiofficial news and that news agencies would not send these items for free. Wolff did not receive substantial sums for disseminating news of public importance, but cost the government approximately 100,000 marks annually. The government defended its sole distribution to Wolff as practical: if the government gave its official dispatches to all news agencies simultaneously, it would overload telegraph and telephone networks.[118]

Wolff learned just how much it relied on the government, while the government found itself in a temporary position of power over an agency keen to prove its reliability. In July 1920, Wolff agreed to numerous concessions: it granted the Foreign Office authoritative influence over choosing Wolff's editors; it agreed to send all important reports that it received to the Press Department, even prior to publication; it agreed that any contracts signed with foreign agencies would be designed to ensure as wide a dissemination of German news as possible.[119]

Economic dependence had made Wolff more politically dependent than ever. Prior to World War I, Wolff had maintained its status as a semiofficial agency by remaining financially independent of the German government. Now, it could not escape its massive debts through increased sales. The Foreign Office consolidated its influence by subsidizing the salaries of Wolff's workers to the tune of 190,000 marks.[120] Government subsidies pulled Wolff further toward the status of official mouthpiece.

Finally, and perhaps most important in the long term, the press on both the right and the left grew more skeptical of Wolff. Already a key figure in the news landscape, Alfred Hugenberg very nearly supported the Kapp Putsch. On March 15, a rather late date, he was in the midst of composing a letter to the chairman of the right-wing party DNVP to ask the party to declare openly for Kapp, when the head of the Pan-German League, Heinrich Claß, interrupted him. By this point, Claß wished to distance the ultranationalist Pan-Germans from the Kapp Putsch.[121] Claß persuaded Hugenberg that the putsch attempt would fail; the letter was never sent.[122] Hugenberg had left himself and his news agency, Telegraph Union, free to exploit the growing distrust of Wolff.

The left publicly condemned Wolff as an unsuitable instrument of news distribution. Famous Weimar author Kurt Tucholsky wrote:

> Kapp's childish dalliance at government showed what Germany could have expected from a Ludendorff. . . . The little old yellowed aids were fetched: the WTB had to disseminate lies, hardly a difficult task for it—there had never been a democratic cleansing in that office either—and the WTB disseminated that Kapp wanted to pay back all the war bonds; . . . and an order likewise wasn't lacking: "Whoever [. . .], will be shot." In short: Prussian General Staff.[123]

Tucholsky's was the most caustic of many complaints about Wolff's failure to reform and its authoritarian tendencies. A range of newspapers attacked

Wolff's behavior during the Kapp Putsch in early April 1920. The *Frankfurter Zeitung* accused Wolff of acting as a "willing tool [of] the only functioning department of the Kapp 'government'—the Press Department."[124] Wolff's numerous reports had led those outside Berlin to conclude that the Kapp government was functional. The press on the left concentrated its attacks on Heinrich Mantler in particular.[125]

Wolff felt sufficiently threatened that on April 4, it published a denial of the *Frankfurter Zeitung* version of events.[126] Given the military presence in its offices, Wolff had pursued the only reasonable course of action, wrote Mantler and fellow director, Hermann Diez. Wolff had wished to preserve its apparatus. After all, when the constitutional government returned, it would not have wanted the news agency in ruins. Mantler later claimed that a government representative had stayed on duty in Wolff's office throughout the coup, while the Kapp government was apparently unaware of his existence.[127]

Wolff's main defense rested on how it had labeled the news items. Mantler and Diez justified their distribution of some patently false items by noting that the reports labeled their origin as "from the Reich Chancellery."[128] Yet a correct interpretation of that label would have required knowledge of events in Berlin that newspapers elsewhere could garner from precious few sources. Mantler and Diez believed that Wolff's job was to distribute, not to interpret. Truth and falsity were not the agency's primary concern: it was the responsibility of newspaper journalists and editors to use items as they saw fit. Furthermore, an item meant nothing without its label, a lesson that Wolff had learned well from its payment negotiations with the government over the past few months.

The Press Department and Chancellery launched their own investigation in mid-1920, though this regurgitated Mantler's version of events.[129] Mantler declared in September 1921 that Wolff had acted cautiously "not just on its own [behalf], but also for higher interests."[130] The government did not want to believe that Wolff could turn so swiftly. After all, if the press created public opinion, how would the government have combated wider dissemination of Wolff's news? Could the German nation turn on the government just as quickly, as a cartoon in the satirical magazine *Kladderadatsch* had implied (see Figure 7)? The German Michel—an allegorical figure representing Germany just like Uncle Sam does for the United States—sat in bed, staring dumbfounded at the mirror. The caption told the reader his thoughts: "Hey, what sort of Kapp' did I get there overnight?" Kapp' refers

FIGURE 7. Cartoon, "On March 13th," *Kladderadatsch 73*, no. 12/13 (March 28, 1920): 177. Courtesy of Universitätsbibliothek Heidelberg, http://digi.ub.uni -heidelberg.de/diglit/kla1920/0177/image.

both to Wolfgang Kapp and *Kappe,* the German word for cap, hood, or jester's cap. It also plays on the phrase, "das geht auf meine Kappe," meaning "that's my responsibility."[131]

In the following months, numerous government memoranda circulated and called for a far closer relationship with the press.[132] While most suggestions gathered dust in the archive, their very existence bears witness to government fears that the obvious choice for news collection and dissemination had lost its reliability. Disillusion with Wolff at home would spur efforts to create other agencies to disseminate news from Germany abroad. The national and the international were intimately entangled.

Conclusion

The Weimar state's proponents and opponents knew from the start the importance of conveying news as swiftly as possible. Weimar bureaucrats also recognized the essential importance of maintaining close relations with Wolff. They needed the news agency's established networks to reach the vastly expanded voter base created by universal male and female suffrage, to garner citizens' trust, and to inform them of critical new regulations. Elites in the early Weimar Republic at least agreed on one thing: news agencies significantly shaped politics. The key difference lay in the type of politics: revolutionary, reactionary, or moderate.

Wolff and the new Weimar state needed each other. The state needed Wolff's distribution network. Wolff needed financial support from the Press Department and the renegotiated exclusive contracts with various government departments in 1919–1920 to keep bankruptcy at the door. Hyperinflation in 1922–1923 and mounting costs would make government subsidies ever more important as the 1920s progressed.

Other elites were increasingly unsure about Wolff. Technology had not changed; politics had. Wolff's behavior during the Kapp Putsch had laid bare its apparent obsequiousness to any political master, calling its central role into question. By 1920, Wolff came to symbolize the flaws of the compromise between the imperial regime and the Weimar state. Wolff presented a beacon of imperial bureaucratic obedience that was not adapting adequately to democracy.

The prominent German historian Heinrich August Winkler has argued that "there was even less of a 'zero hour' in spring 1920 than in fall 1918."[133]

Yet there was a rather significant new beginning for oppositional forces, one that has long passed under the radar. Spring 1920 represented the end of the Wolff news agency consensus. Detractors still saw news agencies as the best means to control the population. But the shared belief that Wolff could and must play a central role in any future government's news distribution had faded.

This had domestic and foreign ramifications. After the Kapp Putsch, different political persuasions no longer wished to share a common wellspring of news in Wolff. Newspapers' increasing reliance on other sources of news such as Telegraph Union represented a hidden, but critical, split in information and perspective among the Weimar population. Left- and right-wing anti-Weimar forces put their energies into alternative news networks. So did multiple government ministries.

THE FATHER OF RADIO AND
ECONOMIC NEWS IN EUROPE

"Our way of taking power and using it would have been inconceivable without the radio and the airplane," Nazi propaganda minister Joseph Goebbels claimed in August 1933.[1] Airplanes played a vital role in Nazi electoral strategy in the last years of the Weimar Republic: when Adolf Hitler campaigned to be president in 1932, he had flown to multiple locations a day to give speeches to roaring crowds. Although he lost that campaign to General Paul von Hindenburg, Hitler had still capitalized on German admiration for aviation.[2] Radio could only become central to Nazi aims after Hitler became chancellor in January 1933. But Goebbels could quickly exercise power over radio, because the state already controlled its infrastructure and content. State control over wireless, and then radio, had been intended to defend democracy. It unintentionally laid the groundwork for Goebbels.

The story of how this happened was one of institutions and bureaucracies, as Goebbels himself well knew. Goebbels derided "the art of organization," which he called the "disease of the age." It had infected radio stations and left them spiritually lifeless, he thought. "The more committees, supervisory committees, directors, and managers intervened in the organization of German radio," he polemicized, "the less valuable its positive achievements became."[3] What Goebbels did not mention was that these committees traced their roots back to news agencies—and one economic news agency in particular.

After the debacle of the Kapp Putsch, various government ministries sought to create more reliable news networks. One strategy was to integrate news agencies into foreign and domestic economic policy through a new economic news agency—Eildienst (Swift Service)—that supplied market data and exchange rate news to German and Central European businesses. The success of this strategy rested on one man: Hans von Bredow. Bredow did not own the news agency. Rather, he controlled its access to wireless technology as state secretary for telegraph, telephone, and radio in the Postal Ministry.

Hans von Bredow was one of the most influential figures in German wireless and radio before World War II. As a Telefunken executive, he had nearly facilitated the German world wireless network in 1918 (see Chapter 2). After World War I, he carried into his new position at the Postal Ministry his belief that wireless could solve political problems. Bredow used Eildienst as a springboard to control policy for wireless, and later, spoken radio. Bredow, and other bureaucrats, created the radio committees that Goebbels so reviled. As Weimar democracy became ever shakier, Bredow's committees exerted ever more control over radio content. They believed that depoliticized content would deescalate political tensions. It would not work.

Bredow's beliefs about news, and its place in politics, would fundamentally shape radio content and technological infrastructure. Bredow optimistically thought economic news supplied to businesses would create legitimacy for the Weimar state among industrialists who tended to be antidemocratic. He pessimistically believed that the general population was not trustworthy enough to receive political news directly over the radio.

Bredow's strategy was both national and international. Domestically, Bredow hoped that Eildienst's apparently neutral numbers would halt hyperinflation and stabilize the economy by preventing speculation. Historians of the German economy have concentrated on inflation and corporate power in the 1920s, while generally eliding the role of communications in economic life.[4] But the government attempted to tie firms to the state by controlling their information supply.

In foreign policy, Bredow cooperated with the Foreign Office on its new strategy of economic diplomacy. After the punitive terms of the Treaty of Versailles and hyperinflation in 1922–1923, the Foreign Office started to use German economic prowess deliberately as a tool of foreign policy.[5] Economic news formed another aspect of that foreign policy. Eildienst was part of reestablishing what historian Stephen Gross has called an "export empire" to the Balkans and *Mitteleuropa* (central Europe).[6] If Eildienst could supply standardized economic information, ran the logic, it would boost German trade. Information played a key role in geoeconomic strategy.

Bredow's political and economic vision of news shaped technological development more than anything. Eildienst mattered not so much because it solved the Weimar Republic's economic and political issues. It mattered because it helped to create the technological and regulatory infrastructure for spoken radio. The Nazis could only remake radio content so quickly because they found state-controlled structures when they came to power. The longer history of state-supported wireless and radio infrastructure explains how the Nazis took over radio so rapidly, something often ignored in histories and popular portrayals of how Nazis like Joseph Goebbels understood radio. The "sudden" co-option of radio had a long backstory.

Eildienst at Home

Eildienst emerged from a combination of the Postal Ministry's control over wireless technology and the Foreign Office's personnel and capital. In 1919, the Foreign Office created the Außenhandelsstelle (Foreign Trade Office) to help German businesses revive export contacts abroad.[7] Legation Councilor Dr. Ernst Ludwig Voss worked in the Foreign Trade Office and helped to establish a new section: Eildienst des Auswärtigen Amtes (Swift Service of the Foreign Office). Voss had received his doctorate from Rostock University in 1905 and written several books on South American weather.[8] He then served as a trade representative and diplomat in Brazil and Spain, before working in the Foreign Trade Office after World War I and helping to create Eildienst.

The Eildienst section received economic reports by telegraph or dispatch from abroad and distributed them to around four thousand companies deemed trustworthy by the Federal Chambers of Commerce.[9] The service proved highly popular so the Foreign Office decided to send Voss on leave to establish Eildienst as a private company. Voss recruited many of the 250 Eildienst employees from the Foreign Trade Office when it was dissolved in October 1921.

As with Transocean, the Foreign Office wanted Eildienst to be a private company with capital investment from businessmen to disguise any official character. The Foreign Office brought Voss together with Ludwig Roselius, a Bremen businessman who had invented decaffeinated coffee in 1906. Roselius provided much of the initial capital for Eildienst. Together with Roselius, Voss set up Eildienst GmbH with capital stock of 50,000 marks on July 13, 1920.[10] Its full name was Eildienst für amtliche und private Handelsnachrichten (Swift Service for Official and Private Trade News). Eildienst also cooperated with a small private company that had distributed stock exchange and price news called Ina-Nachrichtendienst. The two companies merged in 1921.[11] The profits from Eildienst's service were to be given to the government and used to subsidize other methods to disseminate economic news, such as newsletters and regional news offices.[12]

Although the Foreign Office was the incubator for Eildienst, its success relied on the Postal Ministry. As Eildienst aimed to use wireless to disseminate its news more quickly than anyone else, it needed to cooperate with the ministry that controlled wireless apparatus. The man who now controlled wireless within that ministry was Hans von Bredow.

Intimately involved in wireless almost from the start, Bredow had worked for Telefunken when it was founded in 1904. He subsequently founded several wireless companies, including the Atlantic Communication Company in 1911 in New York that would participate in transatlantic radio communications between Sayville and Nauen from 1913. Bredow represented German radio companies at the 1912 International Radio Conference in London and negotiated in 1913 for the exchange of British and German radio patents. During the war, he pushed for Nauen's expansion to a global transmission station as part of the government's effort to create a world wireless network. Bredow even headed Transradio, the Telefunken subsidiary that operated Nauen.[13]

Bredow's involvement with wireless soon extended to government service. Shortly after the end of World War I, Bredow argued that German submarine cables should be swiftly reconnected to facilitate peace. He blamed news networks for preventing Germany's rehabilitation into the global community, declaring in December 1918 that "foreign news connections are influencing the world more than ever in an imperialist sense and preventing the dissemination of the general policy of peace that the new Germany is trying to achieve."[14] On April 1, 1921, Bredow became state secretary for Telegraph, Telephone, and Radio within the Postal Ministry. He would use the position to control access to wireless and to steer the development of spoken radio. Bredow supported Voss's Eildienst initiative from the start. The two men cooperated to cement Eildienst's control over economic news and the Postal Ministry's control over wireless infrastructure.

Bredow's wireless strategy contrasted with his approach to submarine telegraph cables. Under Bredow's guidance, the German government subsidized private companies to build cables, such as a new connection from Germany to New York via the Azores.[15] Radio and wireless would be different. Using the 1892 Federal Telegraph Act as a precedent, the Chancellery had assigned the Postal Ministry the duty of regulating the wireless and radio industry in 1919.[16] The Postal Ministry retained more power than over the cable business by controlling both the airwaves and the licensing of wireless receivers. In a provisional agreement of June 1921 with the Postal Ministry, Eildienst assumed the costs for a central broadcast station and guaranteed at least one thousand subscribers. In the final contract between Eildienst and the Postal Ministry in December 1922, the Telegraph Administration agreed not to provide better conditions for other economic broadcast services. This implicitly gave Eildienst an exclusive license to transmit economic news over wireless.[17]

Telegraphy was point-to-point and could not reach private individuals without passing through telegraph offices first. By contrast, wireless could reach many businesses simultaneously. It allowed Bredow to control how and when many more people would receive information. Initially, federal telegraph offices received the news on their wireless apparatus and distributed it to individual subscribers. This changed when technological innovations enabled Eildienst to send its news to individual wireless receivers from September 1922.

Those technological innovations stemmed from the Postal Ministry's negotiations with radio manufacturers. Before any negotiations could happen, the Postal Ministry had to assuage military fears about unsupervised wireless, because private wireless had been forbidden during the war. To sidestep the issue, the Postal Ministry initially classified Eildienst customers as telephone subscribers. It then created an exclusive agreement with the three main German radio manufacturers—Lorenz, Telefunken, and Huth—to create a prototype of a wireless receiver. The three companies agreed to deliver one thousand receivers by summer 1921. Due to various delays, the apparatus only became available a year later.

Simultaneously, Bredow cracked down on amateurs and nonlicensed receivers. In April 1922, Bredow complained about the multiple private press publishers, such as Scherl, that owned radio apparatus along with larger newspapers like the *Tägliche Rundschau*. While most agreed to hand over their illegal wireless receivers to the government, one provincial news agency, Dammert, resisted so strongly that the police were called to confiscate the equipment.[18] Eildienst enabled Bredow to claim that other private services were illegal and unnecessary.

All three radio manufacturers benefited greatly from the exclusive arrangement with the German government to create wireless sets. The arrangement did not just enable them to provide sets to Germany; it also enabled them to manufacture inexpensive radio sets that soon made their way to Great Britain. Even that most British of institutions, the BBC, emerged partly from fears about cheap, German-made radio sets. In 1922–1923, British radio manufacturers negotiated with the British Post Office to create the British Broadcasting Company, a private enterprise owned by radio manufacturers who held the exclusive right over broadcasting. The Post Office granted the company a licensed monopoly and the exclusive right to sell radio sets. This enabled the radio manufacturers to fend off competition from German sets. Foreign radio sets were permitted, though only the BBC could collect license fees. Radio owners paid an annual license fee. Half went to the Post Office and half to the BBC, making the BBC initially a public-private enterprise.[19]

Back in Germany, Eildienst also helped Bredow to justify expenditure on wireless and radio infrastructure, particularly a wireless station at Königswusterhausen. Bredow argued that Eildienst needed Königswusterhausen to disseminate longwave wireless throughout Germany.[20] Eildienst's wireless service began on September 1, 1922. Recipients paid to lease the receivers and paid a monthly subscription fee.[21] Alongside leasing the equipment, the Postal Ministry used lead to seal the dials on the receivers to a certain wavelength; this prevented users from illegally tuning into military or other traffic.[22] Such measures enabled the Postal Ministry to control access to financial information and, theoretically, to refuse a license to businesses it found untrustworthy.

Eildienst swiftly provided financial revenue to the Postal Ministry and justified the initial expense of Königswusterhausen. By June 1923, there were over a thousand participants, and wireless receiver rental had brought in 2.5 million marks. The participants had also paid over 4.5 million marks in installation costs, which proved a handy cash injection for the Postal Ministry.[23]

News flowed to subscribers almost continuously. Eildienst broadcast its news every day except Sunday, with different services every five to fifteen minutes. Some broadcasts for particular commodity prices happened once or twice a week. Other services sent news from various stock exchanges upon

receipt, rather than waiting to send an omnibus edition. Eildienst only supplied numbers, mainly foreign currency and commodity prices.[24] The numer-
ical content allowed Eildienst to prevent *Schwarzhörer* (illegal listeners) by
sending a code for those numbers to subscribers. Even if pirates heard the
content, they would be unable to decode it.

The company had representatives abroad who informed Berlin of the
numbers through telephone, cable, or wireless.[25] News on foreign currency
exchanges came from ten locations multiple times daily, but mainly from
New York, London, Paris, and Amsterdam.[26] Eildienst received news from
New York eleven times daily from 9:30 A.M. to 5:00 P.M. eastern standard
time. The news arrived at Eildienst offices fifteen minutes after announcement in New York and was disseminated wirelessly as soon as possible
after verifying the transmission's accuracy. Subscribers received numbers
from London and Amsterdam eight times daily, from Zurich and Geneva
seven times, from Paris five times, and from Vienna once daily. Commodity
news items were incredibly varied and detailed, ranging from overall reports on crops to prices of American short ribs, international cotton, and
metals.

Eildienst's success hardly went unnoticed by newspaper publishers, journalists, and Wolff. All condemned how Eildienst seemed to bypass the press
and how the Postal Ministry seemed to sanction a private company's monopoly over economic news. The newspaper publishers' journal, *Zeitungs-Verlag*,
declared in November 1921 that the state influenced the private company of
Eildienst to prevent business from harming the general health of the German
economy.[27] The Association of German Newspaper Publishers expressed
concern to the Press Department (located in the Foreign Office) in August 1922 that Eildienst's wireless service competed with Wolff. It asked the
Foreign Office to eliminate competition between two semiofficial bureaus.
This would reduce costs, as newspapers would not need to subscribe to two
services.[28]

Certain newspapers became irate that Eildienst bypassed the press. The
liberal *Berliner Tageblatt* berated Eildienst for supplying businesses directly
and initially not allowing newspapers to subscribe. One article rebuked
Eildienst for creating a threefold monopoly through Foreign Office support,
state-enabled exclusive access to wireless telegraphy, and high subscription
fees.[29] The paper estimated in another article of January 17, 1924, that Eildienst
had approximately seven thousand subscribers but that most companies
could not afford the subscription price. The paper believed that businesses

happily paid the higher subscription fees to exclude smaller firms. Receiving one foreign exchange report from New York several hours before competitors could easily compensate for the high fees. The paper regretted the Foreign Office's complicity in bolstering big business.

Other newspapers of different political persuasions soon joined in. The antirepublican *Deutsche Tageszeitung* claimed in May 1924 that Eildienst demanded a far higher subscription rate than necessary. It was "a concession of a hidden monopoly position [to Eildienst] within the post monopoly." Even worse, Eildienst was duping officials to serve private interests and Voss's pocket. The paper believed that Bredow would not accept an Eildienst monopoly, unaware of his integral role in creating it. As far as technically feasible, the principles of press freedom and freedom of competition should be preserved for wireless too. "At any rate," the article concluded, "using the post monopoly to create a hidden monopoly in favor of private interests is completely unacceptable."[30]

The government's response was muddled. It claimed in 1925 that Eildienst was a private company and the only state interest came from Eildienst's use of government subsidies to promote economic news services.[31] Yet a press conference of June 1924 had previously clarified that Eildienst shares were administered by fiduciaries in the interest of the Foreign Office.[32] Government representatives claimed that the Postal Ministry retained the right to award the concession to disseminate wireless news to other companies (though it had conspicuously failed to do so). What was clear was that the Postal Ministry controlled access to wireless technology and apparatus. Despite a board ostensibly composed of reputable representatives from trade and industry, Eildienst and Voss relied on remaining in Bredow's good graces.

Bredow was convinced that a uniform service for all businesses would solve problems of asymmetric information. He hoped that wireless could standardize economic knowledge and combat inflation. Prior to Eildienst, businesses had waited twelve hours to receive New York stock exchange reports via telegraph. Afterward, Eildienst delivered the news within half an hour. Rather than waiting several more hours or until the end of the day for commodity prices or foreign exchange news, businesses could now adjust prices almost hourly.

In a June 1921 speech, Bredow had polemicized against the few Berlin and Cologne banks that received wireless foreign exchange news from abroad. He believed that they were using this news to destabilize the German economy. If more businesses could receive this news at the same time, it would reduce speculation in foreign currencies and return the German economy to normal.[33] Bredow believed that speed and simultaneity would increase stability, particularly as many Eildienst subscribers were banks and import/export firms. There would be no time for speculation before others received the news, eliminating some market fluctuations.[34] This echoed hopes for telegraphy in the mid-nineteenth century.[35] Telegraphy did not eliminate speculation, as the Panic of 1873 had already made clear.[36] Wireless telegraphy would not either. Postwar inflation still tipped into disastrous hyperinflation in 1922–1923.

Bredow and the Foreign Office now justified Eildienst because it helped them to produce accurate statistics on business activity and currency fluctuation. Once Eildienst sent stock exchange news to subscribers, they used *Blitzfunktelegramme* (radio telegrams) to conduct business quickly. Radio telegrams were faster but far more expensive, than normal telegrams. 61,300 radio telegrams were sent in 1922, the first year of operation. Soon, 5,000–12,000 were sent daily. By June 1923, bureaucrats believed that Eildienst and radio telegrams "complement each other and are no longer imaginable without each other."[37] The number of radio telegrams was the "best measure for the fluctuations of the mark" during hyperinflation.[38] This was a modest aim compared to Bredow's hopes of stymieing inflation.

Others, like the Economics Ministry, held similarly high hopes that Eildienst could stabilize the economy by making businesses depend on the government for economic news. Together with Deutscher Überseedienst (DÜD, German Overseas Service), a news agency owned by industrialists like Alfred Hugenberg, Eildienst's fiduciary committee jointly created Deutscher Wirtschaftsdienst (German Economic Service) in March 1922.[39] Deutscher Wirtschaftsdienst was supposed to inform businesses about export opportunities, whether through newsletters or providing addresses for potential export clients.[40]

While some praised Deutscher Wirtschaftsdienst, others saw another scattered government attempt to provide economic information. Constant reforms were meant to improve the situation whether it was closing the Foreign Trade Office in 1921 or creating myriad periodical publications. At some point before 1926, Eildienst and Deutscher Überseedienst conceded their stakes in Deutscher Wirtschaftsdienst to the Foreign Office.[41] The various ministries' somewhat unstructured information strategy seemed insufficient to the German Association of Trade and Industry (DIHT,

Deutscher Industrie- und Handelstag).[42] The DIHT suggested reforms to the system almost constantly. Nothing seemed to do the trick.

By 1926, government optimism in the power of news to heal the German economy had faded. Experience had shown the Foreign Office "that the delivery of news alone has not helped the business world that is interested in foreign trade. For it, many news items only gain practical value if they are accompanied by disclosure of specific details."[43] The multipronged strategy of Eildienst, periodicals, and news offices to promote German business proved less effective than Bredow had hoped in 1921.

German firms like Beiersdorf did rebuild international connections in the interwar period.[44] While German trade increased with its neighbors to the East and in the Balkans, Eildienst's direct influence would be nearly impossible to measure. No one even tried. Still, Eildienst mattered for other reasons. It might not have singlehandedly revived German business, but it did change the status of news from Germany.

Eildienst Abroad

Bredow had always hoped that Eildienst would also enable Germany to overcome its problems with foreign trade. The Treaty of Versailles had stripped Germany of its patents, a particularly crushing blow for an engineering and chemical industries dynamo. The Allied governments expropriated German-owned affiliates in foreign countries, cutting German foreign direct investment to nothing. Hyperinflation in 1923 compounded the defeat in World War I. Exports were a particular concern. The Treaty of Versailles had stipulated that Germany was obliged to guarantee the victorious powers a one-sided most-favored-nation treatment until 1925. Information provision was one way to prepare for the transition in 1925.

Eildienst formed part of the government's domestic and foreign strategy. It would inform German businesses about export opportunities to prepare for 1925.[45] Conversely, it would inform businesses abroad about opportunities in Germany. From March 1922, Eildienst provided an economic news service from Nauen to neighboring countries under the name Europradiodienst, also known as Europradio. It started in Austria, Hungary, Norway, and Czechoslovakia.[46] Europradio expanded to Poland through a contract with Maison Wdowinski, a commercial and financial news agency in Warsaw that competed with the cartel agency, Polska Agencja Telegraficzna (PAT,

Polish Telegraph Agency).[47] Europradio strove to reintegrate neighboring countries into German economic circles and create a Central European economic information realm.[48] The German Interior Ministry called Europradio's inroads in international economic news very important for foreign policy.[49]

Eildienst also helped the German government to retain links with Austria. In December 1920, Eildienst reported that Viennese banking and press circles were eager to receive New York stock exchange news directly and asked the Foreign Office if it could combine the wireless press service to Austria with the German service, meaning that Austrian businesses would receive Eildienst news rather than Europradio. Although the Allies had forbidden a political union with Austria in Article 88 of the Treaty of Saint-Germain (signed in September 1919), the Foreign Office nourished secret dreams of unification. Happy to promote any connection, the Foreign Office declared the inclusion of Vienna in the Eildienst service "extremely desirable."[50]

This service extended to news agencies as well as private customers. After the Austrian Chancellery incorporated the Austrian news agency as a department in January 1922, Europradio and the Austrian news agency (ANA) signed their first contract in April 1922.[51] In May 1924, the two signed a more exclusive contract, as ANA worried that the first Austrian radio company (Radio-Vekehrs-AG, RAVAG) would gain government permission to disseminate economic news.

The new contract protected Europradio somewhat from Reuters and Havas, both of which had started economic news services to compete with Europradio.[52] Europradio and ANA guaranteed each other exclusivity and Europradio provided a decoded version of its news compiled by its employees in Vienna. In return, ANA paid 7,000 gold kronen monthly.[53] This proved highly profitable for Europradio. Its gross earnings in April 1924 from its Vienna office alone hit 165 million Austrian kronen. Its outgoings were 68 million kronen, 28 million of which it spent on its ANA service. That left profits of nearly 100 million kronen.

The ties with Austria proved binding: Eildienst employees worked in ANA's office until the Nazi annexation of Austria in 1938 subsumed ANA into the Nazi news agency, the DNB. The direct impact of financial news in maintaining Austrian ties to Germany or in preparing the groundwork for the failed customs union of 1931 is impossible to quantify, though it cemented the importance of news in dreams of creating a German *Mitteleuropa*.[54]

Eildienst's success caused major concern for Wolff and the European cartel news agencies, because economic news was the most lucrative type of information. Wolff had begun with commercial news and only expanded into political items six years later in 1855. Approximately 74 percent of Wolff's telegrams printed in newspapers between 1849 and 1919 were stock exchange or financial numbers.[55] Although Eildienst initially only served big business and no newspapers, it created an industry broadcast in January 1924 for companies that could not afford its initial service.[56] The service disseminated world market prices for particular branches, such as metallurgy or cotton.[57] Wolff was under attack.

Wolff tried multiple solutions. First, it tried in January 1923 to persuade Eildienst to allow Wolff to disseminate exchange rate news.[58] It then tried to scoop Eildienst by paying higher rates for American commercial services, but this had little effect.[59] Wolff believed that Eildienst had taken advantage of Wolff's dire financial situation from 1919 to 1921; Eildienst had organized wireless services from London, Paris, and New York and cooperated with wireless manufacturers when Wolff had no funds.

Ultimately, Wolff had to go abroad to combat the threat of Eildienst at home. Wolff blamed the other cartel agencies for taking no interest in Eildienst/Europradio's wireless exploits until it was almost too late.[60] Reuters and Havas started to organize a conference to coordinate European cartel agencies in the mid-1920s, because the emergence of new nation-states in Central and Eastern Europe meant that there were now many more agencies to coordinate. At the first general conference of the European cartel agencies—collectively known as Agences Alliées—in Berne in June 1924, Wolff's managing director, Heinrich Mantler, called Eildienst an "important competitor" at home and abroad.[61] He reprimanded the Hungarian news agency for signing a treaty with Europradio without consulting Wolff.

Fellow allied agencies chimed in. Agence Télégraphique Suisse concluded that Wolff was "exposing itself to the danger of losing its commercial service" because Europradio was far faster.[62] The Swedish news agency, Tidningarnas Telegrambyra, had warned Havas in September 1923 that Eildienst was already operating in Sweden. Tidningarnas Telegrambyra worried that it would be beaten out of economic news unless the Agences Alliées cooperated to combat such competition.[63]

By the end of 1924, French newspapers and journals took these concerns public. Le Matin reported that Eildienst had become one of the largest international organizations sending economic news.[64] A French journal on wireless telegraphy warned that Eildienst/Europradio was "a unique organization" that had "the most complete network of agencies in the whole world" to report on financial news.[65]

Reuters had reacted rather earlier to the threat of Eildienst. Like the British Post Office's reaction to cheap German radio sets, Reuters and the Post Office had monitored Eildienst since it began its wireless services in September 1922.[66] Despite initial reluctance to use wireless, Eildienst's success swiftly persuaded Reuters management to establish a wireless news service.[67] It created a service called Reuterian to disseminate commercial news and broadcast exchange rates in Morse code seven times daily from Northolt, a Post Office wireless station in London. Europradio's increasing success continued to threaten Reuters, particularly Europradio's American service that competed with Reuterian in countries such as Denmark.[68] Reuters relied on its financial services for profit: after 1924, its commercial news services generated more revenue abroad for Reuters than contracts with newspapers.[69] By 1925, Reuters concluded that only the cartel agencies could stop Eildienst.

The Agences Alliées used the same strategy that had always worked in the past: folding the competitor into the cartel. The absorption of innovative firms into cartel structures was common practice. As business historian Jeffrey Fear has put it, "The bottom line paradox [for cartels] is that competition may stimulate innovation but effectively hinder firms from carrying it out."[70] Reuters and Havas called an emergency meeting in Vienna in May 1925, which concluded that Europradio posed a "grave danger."[71] While the renegotiated cartel treaty after World War I had reduced Wolff to reporting solely on Germany, Wolff now found itself in a more powerful position. It could broker the settlement between the largest economic news supplier, Europradio, and the Agences Alliées. Havas and Reuters needed Wolff's permission for Europradio to begin cooperation with them on economic news. While most agencies wanted to incorporate Europradio fully into Agences Alliées, Wolff prevailed with its vision of an information-sharing agreement with Eildienst. The agreement reached at the Vienna meeting paved the way for Europradio to cooperate with Reuters and Havas. Europradio began receiving Havasian, the French economic news service, from December 1925. The cartel increasingly integrated Europradio: as director of Europradio, Arthur Rawitzki participated in Agences Alliées meetings from early 1926.[72]

The cartel reconfirmed the agreement in a contract signed in Berlin in November 1928. Article 4 stated that Europradio would not compete with the Agences Alliées or it would pay a fine of 10,000 gold marks. Article 5 stipulated that Europradio would only distribute financial and commercial news.[73] Altering the structure of the cartel to Germany's advantage, Europradio became the key point of contact with other agencies in Eastern Europe and the Balkans.[74] Eildienst director Arthur Rawitzki negotiated with agencies like Polska Agencja Telegraficzna to sign up for Reuterian, Havasian, or Europradio, though he noted despairingly in 1928 that "many agencies appeared not to understand financial news services."[75] By this point, Europradio was so integrated into the Agences Alliées cooperative structure that Rawitzki suggested a central office to combat competition through a joint service.[76]

Domestically, Wolff took the same approach as the Agences Alliées and merged Eildienst's activities with its own. Eildienst may have agreed because its profits had fallen dramatically from 753,000 Reichsmarks in 1924 to 115,000 Reichsmarks in 1926.[77] This was largely due to greater expenditure on procuring prices and stock exchange news. Eildienst could not rely on the cartel network's far cheaper supply of economic news, but had to gather all its material by itself. Eildienst had to cooperate with Wolff to safeguard its new place in the cartel agency network, ensuring a massive saving in collection costs. There was no domestic solution for Eildienst without an international solution, and vice versa.

Eildienst and Wolff created a subsidiary firm, Deutscher Kursfunk, in 1926 to send trade, stock, and price news to newspapers and private customers.[78] Eildienst shed another part of its exclusive character, when it agreed to send individual radio companies its news for five hundred marks a month.[79] The Kursfunk service was available to both press and private industry, answering newspapers' calls to open up the service in 1923–1924. By 1929, Wolff and Eildienst had such close connections that the executive director of Eildienst, Arthur Rawitzki, became a Wolff director.[80]

Nevertheless, Eildienst retained important concessions within Kursfunk. Both Wolff and Eildienst contributed economic news, but Eildienst still possessed the right to broadcast from the Postal Ministry. Kursfunk paid Eildienst a lump sum for using the broadcast rights. The Federal News Offices' administrative council continued to administer Eildienst and received 12.5 percent of its gross income. The administrative council used that money to subsidize companies specializing in export news services. One bureaucrat who worked on news in the Economics Ministry claimed later that these payments prevented Eildienst from developing into a more successful agency.[81]

Eildienst was one way that Germany tried to use economic news to consolidate its position within Central Europe despite Allied strictures in the Treaty of Versailles. It is not clear whether this succeeded, because no ministry tried to measure the correlation between increased provision of economic news and increased German exports. Technical innovation in wireless, however, certainly increased German leverage within cartel arrangements. It also started the Postal Ministry and Hans von Bredow on the path to designing German radio and creating the organizational committees that Goebbels so despised.

Eildienst and the Future of Radio

Alongside negotiating wireless economic news, Bredow had consistently worked to bring spoken radio to the population at large. In his memoirs published in 1960, Bredow reflected that anyone who had not experienced the emergence of radio would "consider the earlier economic broadcasting compared to the enormous importance of later broadcasting as an incidental occurrence hardly worth mentioning." But Eildienst was the "forerunner of general radio."[82]

Eildienst was instrumental in creating the structure of German radio. The Postal Ministry exerted legal and economic control, while the Interior Ministry supervised decentralized content created by regional radio companies. Bredow fostered these structures, believing he could defend democracy by allowing the state to supervise radio. Ironically, however, Bredow's attempts to protect German democratic politics enabled the Nazis to control radio far faster when they come to power.

From the start, Bredow believed that radio could create a unified democratic citizenry out of war-weary Germans who were downtrodden with "political fatigue."[83] The only method, thought Bredow, was for radio to be neutral and distribute as little news as possible. Content should concentrate on education and entertainment. This was similar to Sir John Reith's initial aims for the BBC in Britain.[84]

Unlike in Britain, Bredow the bureaucrat would use government control over wireless to impose a particular vision of which news should reach whom. Bredow also drew lessons directly from his work on Eildienst. Eildienst showed Bredow how to balance government control of technology and content as well as how to cooperate with private radio manufacturers to shape the development of new technology. But in the end, those lessons would not lead to robust radio. They led to unexpected consequences and mistaken beliefs about how communications technology might help to sustain democracy.

Bredow again cooperated with Ernst Ludwig Voss to shape radio. As with Eildienst, Voss created content, while Bredow controlled infrastructure. Voss applied in May 1922 for a broadcasting license to the Postal Ministry. Voss's initial idea was to erect loudspeakers in halls and to charge an entrance fee. Known as *Saalfunk,* the plan foundered on the poor quality of loudspeakers and problems with the transmission tower at Königswusterhausen. Most importantly, the Postal Ministry was determined to retain control over radio, and here, Bredow contradicted Voss very explicitly.[85] With this plan quashed, Voss founded a company, Deutsche Stunde für drahtlose Belehrung und Unterhaltung (German Hour for Wireless Education and Entertainment), as a subsidiary of Eildienst. This company was to provide the musical and literary programs for radio.

Bredow also shaped how private firms fit into the development of radio. Although Bredow had negotiated with the main private manufacturers of radios (Telefunken, Lorenz, and Huth) to create wireless receivers for Eildienst, he denied them a radio license. Bredow feared the potential for a private monopoly; he also did not want a centralized radio system.[86] This contrasted with the initial public-private BBC model that gave radio manufacturers an exclusive monopoly over broadcasting. Bredow also did not want Germany to follow the American model, which he deemed overly chaotic and not in the public interest.[87] Bredow's anti-American sentiments also emerged in his (relatively) successful campaign to call radio *Rundfunk* in German, rather than the American terms "radio" or "broadcasting."

After the initial scuffle over *Saalfunk,* Voss fit right into Bredow's vision for radio. Bredow thought radio should be regional, politically neutral, and focus on education and entertainment. Voss and Bredow agreed in early 1922 that the founders of regional companies should be responsible persons "who were not primarily thinking of a capital investment, but rather wished for idealistic reasons to participate in the introduction of radio," as Bredow later put it.[88]

From 1922 onward, Voss negotiated with backers in Bavaria to create a regional Deutsche Stunde. Broadcasts started from Munich on March 30,

1924. This was the first regional radio company and spurred the foundation of the other eight regional firms in 1924–1925, producing what radio historian Kate Lacey has called a "system of public transmissions of privately produced programs."[89] Eight other regional companies soon emerged. Voss sat on the boards of seven of the eight other regional companies as representative for Deutsche Stunde.[90]

By 1925, Bredow and state governments used political leverage to ensure Voss's compliance. The Postal Ministry and Bavarian state government pressured Voss to sell his shares to them; the state now held a controlling stake of 51 percent.[91] The Postal Ministry coordinated the nine regional companies within the Reichsrundfunkgesellschaft (Federal Radio Company) that began operations on January 1, 1926.[92] In the regional companies and the Federal Radio Company, Bredow ensured that the Postal Ministry always controlled a 51 percent share of any station.[93]

Meanwhile, the Postal Ministry followed the same model as with Eildienst by retaining control over the apparatus and technical infrastructure of spoken radio.[94] The ministry cooperated with various companies to sell receivers and stamped each legitimate radio before sale. Radios promised big business, and the Postal Ministry hoped to use the money from sales to subsidize its other activities.[95] The technical experience of disseminating Eildienst news from Königswusterhausen had also helped with establishing the radio network in 1923.[96] Königswusterhausen itself was decommissioned in January 1926 after the national broadcaster Deutsche Welle was created and a German broadcasting tower erected in Zeesen.[97]

In content, Eildienst's existence justified retaining public radio almost exclusively for entertainment and education. Bredow argued that only businesses needed swift economic information, while the population was so restive that radio's main task was to ensure support for the Weimar state. Given the various uprisings in 1923, Postal Minister Anton Höfle believed that radio could occasionally serve to spread official news to a wider public in order to bolster state security.[98] One bureaucrat in the Interior Ministry, Kurt Häntzschel, regretted that radio had not existed in 1920 to avoid the "unnecessary fighting and confusion" after the Kapp Putsch.[99]

Various ministries agreed that radio should be nonpolitical, meaning that no party politics would be broadcast. The Interior Ministry hoped that radio would strengthen support for the democratic state by disseminating "propaganda for the neutral conception of the state and the awareness of national interests."[100] Bredow believed that this was too political. Still, all sides agreed that radio should create Weimar citizens out of a population where many still questioned the value of democracy.

Of course, using state-regulated radio to create citizens could never be as apolitical as Bredow and other bureaucrats claimed. It meant very political censorship of content. At the time, state censorship of programming was not deemed political, but rather a guarantee that radio would promote national culture. This followed the logic applied to another new communications technology—cinema. Article 118 of the Weimar Constitution forbade press censorship except for cinema. Cinema seemed to exert such psychological power that the state had to curb it; the Weimar coalition promulgated a censorship law for cinema in 1920. Bredow argued that radio was analogous to cinema. He used that analogy to justify state observation and censorship of programming to ensure its nonpolitical nature.[101]

Bredow did not succeed in banishing news completely from radio. Instead, he restricted supply to news agencies. Initially, the Federal Radio Commission planned that Eildienst would provide news for spoken radio, as its close alliance with the Foreign Office would ensure its reliability.[102] Eildienst's news, however, was too narrow and other news agencies too persistent. From early 1924, news agencies, publishers, and newspapers petitioned for permission to use radio to disseminate press news.[103] All ministries agreed with Bredow's principle of impartial news and only allowed stations to use items from news agencies.[104] The ministries assumed that news agencies were neutral and less subject to commercial influences and editorializing than newspapers. This might seem a naive assumption; it may have rested more on bureaucrats' knowledge that they could exert greater influence over news agencies than newspapers.

In 1926, Wolff and Telegraph Union acquired 12.25 percent each of Dradag (Drahtloser Dienst, Wireless Service), the company responsible for political programming, along with smaller shares for the Federal German Press Association and the Association of German Publishers. The remaining 51 percent belonged to the state.[105] Wolff and Telegraph Union were instructed to supply news that "basically restricts itself to the reproduction of facts [Tatsachen]."[106] From December 1926, Dradag supplied all regional radio companies with news. This unified the news that the companies received, though not what they chose to broadcast.[107]

Both state control over radio content and cooperation with news agencies were not unusual. Reuters led a consortium of news agencies that supplied most of the BBC's news well into the 1930s. The Sykes Committee convened by the British government in 1923 to discuss the British Broadcasting Company was clear that "the control of such a potential power over public opinion and the life of the nation ought to remain with the State."[108] Only in 1927 did the company become the British Broadcasting Corporation—a public-interest corporation with a royal charter and a royally appointed Board of Governors. The charter gave the BBC editorial independence, although it operated under a government license.

A radio reform of 1926 started to take Germany down a different path of more direct state supervision of content. The radio reform of 1926 reinforced the separation of spoken radio from the press.[109] It insisted on political neutrality for radio: this meant no party politics in broadcasts. The Postal Ministry set up committees for each regional radio company to supervise programming. News could only come from official agencies, which had acquired stakes in Dradag. Only the printed press would provide the public with political news; this aligned with Bredow's vision of using radio for entertainment and education. The 1926 legislation allocated responsibility for news to the Interior Ministry, while the Postal Ministry held a controlling stake in the Federal Radio Company and coordinated the supervisory committees. Radio programming retained the "character of an aesthetic educational dictatorship," as one media historian has put it.[110] A further reform in 1932 solidified the state's control over radio, allowing the Nazis easy access when they came to power in 1933.[111]

The Postal and Interior Ministries thus built on experience with Eildienst to create a decentralized system of regional radio companies. They continued to allow the Postal Ministry to license and control the technical instrument of the radio receiver itself. The Interior Ministry held the major say in political news over the radio. The concept of "neutral" news dominated the German state's attitude to radio right up to the radio reform of 1932. The initial role of Eildienst in German spoken radio faded quickly from even contemporaries' memory. But it had helped to determine the structure and logic of German radio.

When the Nazis came to power in 1933, they would find a radio system that they could instantly control. For all his political differences with a man like Bredow, German constitutional law professor and political theorist Carl Schmitt was similarly convinced that "no state can afford to relinquish to others the new technical media for the transmission of news."[112] He concurred that new media technologies like cinema could be used to unify, or even homogenize, the population. He disagreed with Bredow that new communications technologies could avoid the political.[113] For Schmitt—who would join the Nazi Party in May 1933 and become known as the Nazis' "crown jurist" for his central contributions to the regime—it was clear by February 1933 that "the total state" now held "new means and possibilities of tremendous power, the range and consequences of which we hardly suspect, whereas our vocabulary and our imagination are still deeply rooted in the nineteenth century."[114] Schmitt's thinking dovetailed with leading Nazi propagandists like Goebbels. Goebbels believed that it was impossible to explain nineteenth-century political events "without the powerful influence of journalism." Now, radio held similar "revolutionary significance." It was quite clear that "the radio will be for the twentieth century what the press was for the nineteenth."[115]

Much Nazi policy pushed in that direction. The Nazis produced as many cheap radios, *Volksempfänger* (people's receivers), as possible. They believed in the power of the spoken word and the cinematic to convince, often much more than the written. Goebbels intended to replace the organizational structure of committees he despised with the "leadership principle." Radio transformed the soundscape of cities and became an enduring symbol of the Nazi era.[116]

Still, radio did not become primarily a source of news. Radio was meant to entertain with games, jokes, and popular music (though not jazz, which was decried as an African American phenomenon). Nazi radio continued to broadcast far more entertainment than news, though this entertainment was often meant to lure listeners to stay tuned for Nazi communiqués or speeches.[117]

Bredow's shaping of wireless and radio policy in the Weimar Republic never resulted in his vision of an apolitical, harmonious society. Still, he remained a staunch opponent of extremist politics, resigning his post shortly after Hitler became chancellor. After the first of his colleagues was arrested, Bredow telegrammed President Hindenburg to request either that his colleague be released or that he be arrested as well. Bredow was thereupon imprisoned for sixteen months. After the war, Bredow became a key figure in radio, serving as head of the administrative council of Hessian radio from 1949 to 1951. There is now a media institute in Hamburg named after him.

Conclusion

The radio that Bredow helped to create looked very different in 1933 than he could possibly have imagined in the early 1920s. The bureaucratic structures, cooperation with technology companies, and state control over content would culminate in a regime that valued radio. But the Nazi regime would propagate politics that Bredow abhorred.

At the opening of a radio exhibition in August 1933, Goebbels spent most of his speech deriding Weimar radio policy and ridiculing Weimar politicians for failing to understand the political possibilities of radio. "They left radio and its development essentially to technical and organizational administrators," sneered Goebbels.[118] He heaped particular scorn upon a subset of experts. "Some participants today call themselves 'the fathers of radio.' One can only counter that they did not invent radio, but rather that they sensed how to earn a wholly disproportionate amount of money from it in troubled times and exploited that without any scruples whatsoever."[119] For those in the know, this was a none-too-subtle reference to Bredow, who was at that very moment languishing in prison.

The "fathers of radio" were just as much bureaucrats as inventors or innovators. Wireless technology enabled men like Bredow to reconfigure government control over news. Bredow used the Postal Ministry's jurisdiction over wireless to grant preferential access to Eildienst. Radio did not simply succeed wireless; wireless shaped how radio would develop and the two technologies existed simultaneously to provide news to different groups in different ways.

Like many, Bredow held overinflated expectations of what news could achieve. Eildienst's apparently neutral numbers were supposed to stop hyperinflation, reassure German big business, and revive German exports. In the end, better economic information could not prevent the hyperinflation of 1923. Nor did it solve problems with German foreign trade. Controlling political news on the radio was similarly ineffective. Ultimately, Eildienst had less effect on geoeconomic strategy than on the organizational structure of radio. The history of spoken radio is not just a history of technological developments. It is also a political history of how beliefs about news shaped the development of domestic radio. The details of interagency wrangling may be intricate, but they show how politics and bureaucracy shape new technology as much as scientists and businesses.

The new technology of wireless offered possibilities abroad as much as at home. For foreign news, different ministries (and different parts of the same ministries) pursued overlapping policies. The Foreign Office and Postal Ministry used wireless economic news to promote German trade in Central and Eastern Europe. Eildienst was part of the Foreign Office's plan to integrate economics into foreign policy. Other parts of the Foreign Office subsidized Wolff to integrate culture into diplomacy. But this could prove disastrous for individual journalists caught in the crossfire between Wolff and the state.

5

CULTURAL DIPLOMACY
IN ISTANBUL

In August 1926, a young woman responded to a job advertisement. The advertisement was placed by Hermann von Ritgen, who was looking for a secretary in Istanbul. Ritgen and the young woman, Käte Witt, met briefly in a public building on Berlin's Wilhelmstraße. Ritgen informed Witt that he both represented the Wolff news agency and held a Foreign Office position in Constantinople (as Germans still called Istanbul in the mid-1920s). Witt also knew that Ritgen edited a German-language newspaper in Istanbul connected to the Foreign Office. After their meeting, Ritgen wrote to inform Witt that there was currently no position available, but that a spot might open up in the future.

The following summer of 1927, Witt contacted Ritgen again to inquire about a temporary position in Istanbul. The reply was anything but professional. Ritgen wrote that he remembered her name, but not her appearance. He hoped that Witt would provide further information:

How old are you? How tall? Hair color, figure? I have no doubt about your social skills. But I only enjoy working with people whom I like. That includes a good eye and a healthy female body. I'm not a fan of the modern, overly slim figure. If you somewhat correspond to my wishes, then I'll find a way for you to spend your holidays here with employment that appeals to you and also enough free time to get to know everything here and, if you like, a little love and pleasure. So write to me at your earliest convenience when you wish to come (not before July 10). Send me <u>a photo, preferably in a swimsuit.</u>[1]

Shocked by the letter's content, Witt promptly contacted the Foreign Office to demand redress.

Witt believed that "the shocking insolence and insulting impudence of this letter crosses the boundary of a personal, private insult" because Ritgen was employed by the Foreign Office. Ritgen had even sent his letter in a prewar envelope giving his address as Kaiserlich Deutsche Botschaft (Imperial German Embassy) in Constantinople. "In Turkish circles," Witt continued, "he is seen as an official personality and belongs to those circles that claim to promote Germandom abroad [*Auslandsdeutschtum*] particularly strongly." Finally, Witt presented her demands. If the Foreign Office failed to address her complaint or bore no responsibility for Ritgen, she would have no compunction in going public. Witt did "not care at all, whether the [Foreign] Office arranges for Mr. v. Ritgen to apologize." She had written "to clarify whether this type of personality is suitable in the eyes of the Foreign Office to represent German interests more or less publicly and with support from the Reich (even if the support might be only moral)."[2] It was not a matter of a personal apology. It was a matter of German honor.

Witt, it turned out, was wrong about Ritgen's employment status. He was not technically employed by the Foreign Office. He was a Wolff employee whose salary was subsidized by the Foreign Office. That simple distinction would seal his fate when Witt complained. Ritgen's career would be particularly scandalous. But it also shows how news agency employees operated abroad and how the Foreign Office tried to use Wolff's foreign correspondents as cultural diplomats.

Over the past few decades, historians have become increasingly attuned to the importance of culture within "hard" diplomacy and foreign relations. They have also paid greater attention to culture as a form of diplomacy or "soft power."[3] Historian Michael David-Fox defines cultural diplomacy as "the systematic inclusion of a cultural dimension to foreign relations, or the formal allocation of attention and resources to culture within foreign policy."[4] News too played its part.

The rise of cultural diplomacy within foreign policy was a transnational phenomenon. The Soviet Union courted foreign visitors to change their worldviews. Many private American philanthropic organizations conducted cultural activities abroad; the State Department established the Division of

Cultural Relations in 1938. Both the British and French Foreign Offices created organizations like Service des oeuvres françaises à l'étranger.[5] The diplomatic crises of the 1930s intensified efforts to coordinate cultural activities through international organizations such as the League of Nations International Committee on Intellectual Cooperation as well as national institutions like the British Council, established in 1934.[6]

Germany was particularly invested in cultural diplomacy after 1918. When excluded from the negotiations at Versailles, the Foreign Office tried to use cultural diplomacy to influence the final treaty. It established the Kriegsschuldreferat (War Guilt Section) to publish diplomatic documents that would convince the international public and by extension, their governments, of Germany's innocence. The Treaty of Versailles created another unique aspect of German cultural diplomacy: the promotion of German language and culture among ethnic Germans abroad. Weimar politicians wanted both to protect those minorities' rights and to regain some economic and political regional dominance in Central and Eastern Europe as well as the Balkans.

Cultural diplomacy complemented Hans von Bredow's strategy to use Eildienst for economic diplomacy. Bredow and other bureaucrats believed that sending Eildienst's economic news abroad could boost foreign trade. Men like Gustav Stresemann saw increased foreign trade as a key tool to reassert German political prowess on the world stage. Another method to boost political prowess was to use news as cultural diplomacy. Germany had pursued press policy as part of diplomatic relations since the late nineteenth century.[7] Politicians and practitioners of press politics thought that secrecy was paramount. As a Press Department official put it in 1930, "a press policy whose methods could be presented publicly is no longer press policy."[8] What made the German version of cultural diplomacy unique was its secret use of news agencies like Wolff (though Japan would follow a similar policy after the Manchurian Incident in 1931).[9]

Another feature of Germany's idiosyncratic bureaucracy was that the Press Department was located in the Foreign Office. This made the department particularly attuned to how news could support cultural diplomacy. The Press Department provided significant financial and logistical support to Wolff's foreign correspondents, whose tasks soon expanded beyond working for Wolff itself. In Istanbul, that support was supposed to be technological too: Ritgen was sent there partially to take advantage of a new wireless station in Turkey. Most foreign correspondents had good relations with their respective embassies and would receive information or exchange contacts. German support went further and drew Wolff's employees into quasi-state positions. The Foreign Office came to see these journalists as almost identical to diplomats. But they were not identical, as Ritgen would soon find out.

Akin to a Diplomat in Istanbul

A few weeks after the Foreign Office had received Käte Witt's indignant letter, the German ambassador to Turkey, Rudolf Nadolny, wrote to the Foreign Office from Tarabaya (Therapia), a district in Istanbul that had traditionally housed the German ambassador to the Ottoman Empire and where Nadolny maintained his summer residence until the German embassy moved to Ankara in 1930.[10] Nadolny had spoken to Ritgen, who had immediately admitted authoring the offending letter. Ritgen had claimed that Witt's original letter had rather encouraged his reply, though conveniently he no longer held that letter in his possession. Ritgen had played the gentleman, offering to send a formal apology (*Ehrenerklärung*) to Witt and declaring himself ready to face any consequences. Nadolny wanted the relevant authorities to take into account Ritgen's "skill and productivity," though he realized that a recall from Istanbul was probably unavoidable.[11] Although everyone recognized that Ritgen had to go, finding a replacement delayed his return to Berlin for several months. The Foreign Office hoped that deferring his return would "ensure the best possible conditions for him with the Wolff management."[12] Even before the Witt scandal, though, Ritgen had struggled to use news to revive German-Turkish political and economic interactions.

Imperial Germany had cultivated a close commercial and political relationship with the Ottoman Empire prior to 1918. Although Bismarck had paid little attention to the region, Wilhelm II found Islam fascinating. His visit to the Middle East in 1898 deepened that fascination. The Kaiser saw close relations with the Ottoman Empire as a way to counter British, French, and Russian influence in the region. This combined with economic interests and infrastructural ambitions like the Berlin–Baghdad railway.

Journalists also played an important diplomatic role. The German press in Constantinople also helped to cement German-Ottoman relations through the German-language newspaper *Osmanischer Lloyd*.[13] Many German foreign correspondents and German newspapers were sympathetic to the Ottoman Empire and engaged in what contemporaries termed "turcophilism."[14] Foreign correspondents of prominent newspapers like the *Times* and

Frankfurter Zeitung were "politically more influential than the ambassadors of their countries" in Constantinople prior to 1914, one former Wolff correspondent claimed in retrospect.[15] This was part of a broader trend: the rise of the mass circulation newspaper at the end of the nineteenth century had made foreign correspondents important diplomatic figures.[16]

Up to World War I, the Turkish part of the Ottoman Empire had been shared ground between Agence Havas and the Austrian news agency, k. u. k. Korrespondenzbüro, through a joint bureau named Agence de Constantinople.[17] During World War I, the Ottoman Empire mainly received German news from k. u. k. Korrespondenzbüro, though the German government also disseminated propaganda through the Nachrichtenstelle für den Orient (News Office for the Orient).[18]

German government propaganda in the Middle East was part of a broader German plan during World War I to foment jihad against the British and French. The German government sent envoys to instigate holy war all around the Middle East. They simultaneously planned wireless towers to disseminate news from Germany more efficiently. Technical difficulties stymied these plans, just as they did the Berlin–Baghdad railway. The end of the war meant the end of such infrastructural ambitions. But Weimar governments and German elites would still see news as the first useful step to reestablish connections with what would become Turkey.

Violent population exchanges and war with Greece in 1921–1922 convulsed the area until Mustafa Kemal Atatürk established a secular Turkish republic in October 1923. During the turbulence, Reuters and Havas had operated a joint bureau in Istanbul. Thereafter, Reuters and Havas began to work on reintegrating a Turkish news agency into the cartel.[19] Under the renegotiated cartel contract after the war, Reuters and Havas gained the right to negotiate contracts with areas formerly covered by Wolff and the Austrian news agency. Those territories could, if they wished, sign separate contracts with Wolff to receive news from Germany. If an agency did not conclude an agreement with Wolff, it could receive German news from Reuters and Havas.

After the reestablishment of German-Turkish diplomatic relations in March 1924, Wolff sought to create a close connection between German and Turkish news as part of rekindling commercial and political ties. Wolff suggested exchanging 150 words daily to Agence d'Anatolie—the new national, government-subsidized Turkish news agency—to encourage the Turkish agency to bypass the cartel system. The Turkish agency was only willing to agree if Wolff provided substantial subsidies that it could not afford.[20] Siemens had given Agence d'Anatolie trial apparatus to receive Eildienst's telephone service, but the reception was too poor. Instead, Agence d'Anatolie consolidated its relationship with Havas. Wolff lamented that the Turkish news agency's workers did not even recognize the bias in reports from Paris.[21] In January 1925, Agence d'Anatolie signed a contract with Havas and Reuters that resembled those signed with new Central and Eastern European nations. The contract allowed the Turkish news agency to conclude an agreement with a German news agency, but stipulated that it could only work with Wolff.[22]

Wolff's financial concerns clashed with bureaucrats' belief that Wolff mainly served the Foreign Office's political interests. In 1919–1920, the Press Department had paid off 681,664 marks of Wolff's total debt of 1.5 million marks, to prevent the agency's bankruptcy.[23] As Wolff's financial straits worsened with (hyper)inflation, the government provided a loan to the company in May 1923. But it came with stipulations. The Press Department reserved the right to suggest a suitable person as Wolff's editor in chief for foreign politics as well as to stipulate the conditions of that person's appointment.[24] The Foreign Office agreed to subsidize Wolff's telegrams to Agence d'Anatolie in September 1924 after Wolff refused to pay.

The German ambassador to Turkey, Rudolf Nadolny, condemned Wolff's concern with finances. He saw Wolff as "one of the most important instruments of our politics."[25] For Nadolny, the first imperative of foreign policy was to create a news service because news was "by far the most essential means of propaganda." Nadolny thought news far more effective than pictures or articles. While pictures wore their tendentious nature on their sleeves, news could function as almost pure propaganda because it was "in general taken as fact" and not even seen as propaganda at all.[26]

Like Hans von Bredow, Nadolny saw a strong connection between news and communications technology. Nadolny hoped that Wolff could send news to the new wireless station Osmaje, as the telegraph connection between Istanbul and Berlin was still being repaired.[27] Wolff's radio service from Nauen had operated in Germany since November 1924 and the agency intended to extend the service abroad in 1925. Wolff wanted to use the same wireless strategies as other agencies like Eildienst to undermine British, French, and American news agencies abroad. Wolff hoped that the German embassy would soon set up a wireless receiver in its building to receive Wolff's news directly.[28] Into the breach stepped Hermann von Ritgen, apparently the perfect man to boost Wolff's share of news and act as Germany's cultural diplomat in Istanbul.

Hermann Paul Arno von Ritgen was born in 1895 in Wetzlar, a small town in Hesse famous for being the seat of the Imperial Supreme Court of the Holy Roman Empire. After leaving school in 1913, Ritgen studied law for three semesters before serving in World War I. He left the army in 1918 with the rank of first lieutenant and continued his studies, afterward working for the Federal Coal Commissar and in a commercial company. Ritgen began his journalistic career working for the Press Department in May 1922, editing press reports. He worked there until October 1922 and then again from January to September 1923, when government cuts meant that these reports were no longer produced. A recommendation noted that he completed his tasks with "hard work and aptitude."[29] He joined Wolff in April 1924 on the Press Department's recommendation and embarked on his first foreign commission as Wolff's representative to Istanbul for three months in March 1925.

Ritgen's appointment was the counterpart abroad of Berlin's new focus on foreign correspondents stationed in Germany. Although Bismarck had already distinguished between foreign and domestic press within Germany, the Press Department began to cultivate closer relationships with foreign correspondents in Berlin after World War I, particularly after Stresemann became foreign minister in August 1923.[30] As part of a broader move toward modern opinion management, the Press Department organized press teas, weekly press conferences, and interviews with various ministers and high officials. Domestically, the Press Department sanctioned interviews by foreign papers with German ministers, but it did not control domestic journalists' access to ministers. The Press Department thus concentrated on the foreign press both at home and abroad.

The reorganization of the Press Department after World War I had created a newly centralized, and theoretically streamlined, body. Officials wished to unify press policy after disastrous decentralization in World War I.[31] The Edmund Schüler reforms of 1918–1919 extensively reorganized the Foreign Office: departments were now divided by geographical areas, rather than subject.[32] The reforms also encompassed the Press Department. The Vereinigte Presseabteilung der Reichsregierung und des Auswärtigen Amtes (Unified Press Department of the Federal Government and Foreign Office) emerged on October 1, 1919, as Foreign Office Department P from the former Nachrichtenabteilung (News Department) in the Foreign Office and the Press Office in the Chancellery. This bureaucratic structure intertwined domestic and foreign press policy. The national and the international were organizationally inseparable.

Centralization produced new problems. No one wished to relinquish control over the press; the resulting compromise created an "idiosyncratic" structure of overlapping competencies, as one chief press officer put it.[33] Although the Press Department was part of the Foreign Office, the chief press officer reported directly to the chancellor. While the chancellor suggested the candidate for chief press officer, the Foreign Office appointed all other Press Department employees. This made the chief press officer simultaneously responsible to the chancellor and the foreign minister.

While these interwoven responsibilities meant navigating internal rivalries within the government, they also gave the chief press officer considerable room to influence German politics through the president, chancellor, and the Foreign Office. The chancellor and president both received a daily oral presentation from the chief press officer, who also received orders from weekly cabinet meetings and participated in the Foreign Office's Board of Directors meetings. The Press Department often held more consistent policies than other parts of the Weimar government. Chief press officers generally supported using news to promote German interests abroad in places like Turkey. Chief press officers also tended to outlast cabinets and chancellors. There were only nine chief press officers during the Weimar Republic as opposed to twenty-two cabinets and thirteen chancellors. This could create problems: Dr. Otto Kiep, chief press officer in 1925–1926, complained that the constantly changing cabinets pushed for "propagandistic transmission of party-political points of view" which fundamentally contradicted the "objective working method" of bureaucracy.[34]

After just a few months in Istanbul, Nadolny reported happily to the Press Department that Ritgen had achieved close to a miracle. Only a year before, there had been relatively few articles on Germany in Istanbul newspapers and most had described Germans in pejorative terms like the French term *boches*. Ritgen had achieved a "visible success" and placed many positive articles on Germany in newspapers.[35] For Nadolny, it vindicated the strategy of concealing Ritgen's work for the German embassy and presenting him to the public solely as a Wolff correspondent. Nadolny pleaded with the Foreign Office for Ritgen to stay, even though it was relatively expensive and Wolff was less than enthusiastic. While he characterized the Turkish press as "the purest gutter press," Nadolny hoped that it would soon become more civilized. Then the embassy would find methods to save costs. Until that time, Ritgen was vitally important.[36]

The Foreign Office agreed with Nadolny. Wolff did not. It refused to pay Ritgen's salary after his initial three-month contract. The issue was particularly complex, because Ritgen only held a contractual relationship with Wolff as his employee. The Press Department acknowledged that Wolff was Ritgen's formal employer, not the Foreign Office or the Press Department. Yet the Press Department believed that Ritgen provided service to the embassy, giving him some form of employment status. Despite his contract with Wolff, the Press Department actually paid Ritgen's salary, allowing it the greater say.[37] This fact would prove decisive for his fate after the Käte Witt affair.

After the Press Department had determined that Ritgen was too valuable to lose, Ritgen traveled to Berlin in September 1925 to regulate his status. He would now be paid through the German embassy in Istanbul, rather than Wolff. Ritgen never actually received any contracts stating his rights and duties. Nor did he manage to clarify precisely *who* his employer was. Ritgen believed eighteen months later that he was "on leave" from Wolff and working for the embassy, though he had no confirmation on paper. "The WTB [Wolff Telegraph Bureau] has no real interest in the fact that I am here," Ritgen surmised, "but it agrees to my holding the title of WTB representative here."[38]

The Foreign Office made clear to Ritgen that he was not simply a foreign correspondent or journalist. Because he worked on the German press abroad and received pay from Foreign Office funds, his position was "not dissimilar to that of a diplomat abroad."[39] Ritgen himself agreed, but disliked the tasks that entailed. By 1927, he complained that his work in Istanbul had become "purely organizational, diplomatic, and also commercial."[40] Like any other embassy employee, Ritgen combated anti-German sentiment and worked to increase pro-German public opinion abroad for political and economic purposes.

Other Wolff representatives abroad also understood that their relationship with German embassies was closer than other journalists. The Wolff representative in Paris refused in October 1926 to accept an honorary post in the newly founded Association of German Journalists because of his proximity to the German embassy.[41] For the Foreign Office, the press functioned as a cultural cog in the diplomatic wheel.

Although the Foreign Office compared Ritgen to a diplomat, the journalistic profession was less well regarded than diplomacy in social circles. In

Warsaw, Count Hans von Huyn switched from diplomatic service for Austria to working for Wolff in 1924 and remained until 1934.[42] Huyn later remembered that the "good society" of Warsaw and Vienna found it incomprehensible that he "could give up the respected profession of a diplomat for the far less gentlemanly career of a newspaperman. Their imagined journalist must be a little Jew with a greasy coat-collar covered with dandruff, who is admitted to receptions where he and his like blockade the buffet—an equivocal personage who is anything but pleasing in manners or appearance."[43] Opinions about foreign correspondents were often condescending, pejorative, and mixed with a dose of anti-Semitism.

The vast majority of diplomats had no journalistic experience. In fact, until the Schüler reforms of 1918–1919, it was effectively impossible for journalists to join the foreign service. The reforms opened consular and diplomatic positions to men other than those trained within the Foreign Office for the first time. Relatively few took advantage of the new policy. The German ambassador in Warsaw from 1922 to 1930, Ulrich Rauscher, was an exception: he had been a foreign correspondent for the *Frankfurter Zeitung*.[44] Diplomats still mainly came from aristocratic backgrounds. They often had little understanding and appreciation for the work of journalists, though ironically diplomats used newspapers as one of their main sources of information. This mismatch often led to overinflated conclusions about the power of the press.

While few German diplomats had been journalists, many parliamentarians at home had a background in newspapers. This was particularly true for the SPD. Nearly a quarter of Social Democratic members of parliament in Imperial Germany and the Weimar Republic were involved in party journalism at some point.[45] Some parliamentarians and bureaucrats displayed a strong interest in and knowledge of the workings of the press. Diplomats, by contrast, were often willfully ignorant of networks behind the news.

Ritgen never discussed problems of social prestige with his employer, the Foreign Office, although he was hardly content with his daily journalistic work. Despite the ambassador's and Foreign Office's satisfaction, Ritgen felt that he was overworked and underpaid. He complained that he worked remarkably little for Wolff: he only produced a short weekly report for its Außenpolitische Korrespondenz (Foreign Political Correspondence), sent telegrams about important news, and conducted occasional meetings with Agence d'Anatolie. Wolff also refused Ritgen's pleas to spend more on telegrams to counteract French news in December 1926.[46] Ritgen mostly worked for the embassy, producing daily summaries of press materials from various news sources.[47] At his own cost, he employed a secretary to copy originals and a translator to translate the items into French or Turkish. He supplied the press in Istanbul with these summaries and other news items, often visiting newspapers personally with his translator while maintaining and building friendly relations with journalists and editors.

These tasks sounded more like press attachés' work for European embassies: press attachés and officers in embassies commonly informed their own countries of events abroad by summarizing and translating from newspapers and journals. Like Ritgen, they often did not speak the language of their country of residence if it was outside Western or Central Europe. Hans von Huyn was a noteworthy exception, who learned Polish.[48] A more typical example was Hans Tröbst, who worked in China in the 1930s for the Nazi news agency (DNB, Deutsches Nachrichtenbüro) without speaking Chinese or Japanese.[49] Journalists like Tröbst used translators as well as any English, French, or German newspapers that might exist. The Foreign Office thus believed that news supply did not just influence citizens of a country abroad, but also diplomats stationed there and politicians who read press summaries from abroad. News agencies like Wolff and men like Ritgen offered an efficient amplification of news from Germany to citizens, diplomats, and politicians.

Ritgen also acted as publisher of the German newspaper in Istanbul, the *Türkische Post*, founded in 1925 to promote German industry in Turkey and to counter French dominance of the foreign-language newspaper market in Istanbul.[50] There were commonly English, French, and German newspapers in major trading cities around the world, which exerted considerable influence on expat communities and diplomats. They became battlegrounds for the Foreign Office to increase German influence abroad both by maintaining ties to Germans in that city and by countering other foreign-language papers.

The German embassy owned the *Türkische Post* and its printing press. The *Türkische Post* was the only German daily paper in the Middle East and expanded to include representatives in other Middle Eastern cities by mid-1927. Its finances were constantly precarious; Nadolny even once massively subsidized the paper when the Foreign Office did not have the funds to pay.[51] While the paper reached the German community in the Middle East, it was a constant "problem child" for Ritgen.[52] Its other employees, such as Dr. Schmidt-Dumont, appeared not to care about the paper's economic sustainability. Ritgen was also concerned about its journalistic integrity and worried about dependence on Reuters because the cartel contracts required Wolff to take its reports on the English-speaking world from Reuters.

Ritgen tried unsuccessfully to interest Wolff in supplying international news directly to the *Türkische Post* and in creating a correspondence for the Balkans and Middle East as it had for Warsaw. Ritgen suggested that Wolff could send its material through reporters for the *Türkische Post* stationed in Berlin. This would disguise the origins of the news and avoid contravening Wolff's contract with Reuters and Havas, which only allowed it to supply news on Germany to Agence d'Anatolie. In exchange, Wolff would receive news from *Türkische Post* reporters in the Middle East to gain independence from Reuters.[53] This did not materialize, rather unsurprisingly given Wolff's difficult financial circumstances and reluctance to pay for further journalists' salaries.

Finally, Ritgen fulfilled several other posts. He was the official representative in Turkey of Pressa, the international press exhibition in Cologne scheduled for 1928.[54] He worked as the speaker of the Association of German Press Representatives in Istanbul and started to improve German press relations with other countries in the region, traveling to Alexandria in February 1926 and laying the groundwork for a news office in Cairo in April 1927.[55]

Alongside his unclear employment status and huge list of tasks, Ritgen also complained about undercompensation. He believed that he spent too much of his salary on professional expenses, such as a translator and typist. In June 1925, Ritgen asked for his salary in pounds instead of Reichsmarks, because the Turkish lira was pegged to the British pound and the pound had just been put back onto the gold standard. The exchange rate with the German currency of the Reichsmark constantly fluctuated, making his existence in Turkey more precarious. The request was not granted. His annual salary remained 5,040 Reichsmarks, which was lower than the starting salary of 6,000 Reichsmarks for some newspapers' foreign correspondents.[56]

Circumstances changed just over a year later. In July 1926, the Foreign Office decided to treat Ritgen more like a diplomat and set his salary in pounds like other civil servants. His salary was set in relation to positions at the Foreign Office, earning him just over 84 pounds a month. This was the same as a legation secretary and approximately 71,000 U.S. dollars a year in today's money.[57] Ritgen found this highly unfair, complaining that he worked harder than a legation secretary and incurred more professional expenses. He estimated that he spent £30 of his monthly salary on expenses (around

35 percent of his total salary). For instance, he rented his own offices, as he could not work in the embassy without attracting unnecessary suspicion. He needed translators and interpreters, as he did not speak Turkish. Turkish journalists were also high maintenance and Ritgen claimed that he had to entertain them frequently to keep them satisfied. Because even Ritgen was not clear about who really paid him, Ritgen believed that Wolff could cover a salary increase, although he had previously complained that he spent far less time working for Wolff than he would like.[58]

In fact, Wolff covered none of his salary. Ritgen was one of twelve Wolff representatives abroad whose salaries were paid in full or partially by the Press Department. The subsidies gave Wolff an outward appearance of an agency powerful enough to operate globally. The Press Department, on the other hand, thought that these correspondents served as excellent cover agents for government work and German news dissemination abroad. Most correspondents were based in European capital cities except correspondents in Istanbul, Moscow, and Washington, DC.[59] At 249,300 Reichsmarks in 1928, the correspondents' salaries comprised well over half of the government's total annual subsidy of approximately 400,000 Reichsmarks to Wolff.

The 400,000 Reichsmarks in turn comprised 20 percent of the 2 million Reichsmark budget for the fund for "Promotion of German News Abroad."[60] This fund had been created in 1911 in response to a Reichstag request that the Foreign Office provide a clearer overview of its budget for the press. There were two other funds: one for promoting German news domestically and one for secret expenditure, such as purchasing the *Deutsche Allgemeine Zeitung* in 1926, paying secret agents, or financing particular political campaigns.[61] The foreign news fund formed a substantial portion of the budget available to the Press Department.

To govern its subsidies to Wolff, the Press Department rejected the provision of general subsidies and preferred to provide payment for specific services rendered. This was intended to increase the department's influence on the agency itself. Most of the other subsidies covered transmission costs of news abroad as well as half the salary of the editor in chief for foreign politics (whose appointment the Foreign Office suggested).

The Foreign Office soon suggested an editor in chief for foreign politics who agreed with its emphasis on cultural diplomacy. Wolff's editor in chief for foreign politics from 1925 to 1929, Dr. Edgar Stern-Rubarth, had written one of the most influential books on propaganda "as a political instrument" after World War I. Stern-Rubarth argued that Germany needed to provide positive propaganda abroad "if it seriously wishes to maintain its claim to world significance [*Weltgeltung*] and execute it in the foreseeable future."[62] Stern-Rubarth worked as editor in chief at Ullstein before becoming editor in chief for foreign politics at Wolff. From 1929, he served on Wolff's board, but was sent on leave in March 1933 due to his ties to Stresemann. The Nazis dismissed him in March 1934. He emigrated to England and became London correspondent for various German newspapers after World War II.[63]

The subsidies seemed like a win-win situation for Wolff. It gained more correspondents that it could not afford to employ; it sacrificed no integrity because the arrangement was secret. Chief Press Officer Walter Zechlin found it an "absurdity" (*Unding*) in 1929 that the Foreign Office paid Wolff 400,000 Reichsmarks annually without having specific influence.[64] Yet the financial relationship made Wolff dependent on the Foreign Office. In 1930, Wolff had twenty-seven correspondents abroad, while the newspaper with the largest number of foreign correspondents, the *Kölnische Zeitung*, had twenty-four correspondents.[65] Wolff's semiofficial relationship with the government also obliged its correspondents to cooperate closely with German embassies and legations abroad, creating two masters who disagreed about the correspondents' priorities.

The Press Department had not originally intended to rely so heavily on Wolff's correspondents. In 1923, it had tried but failed to influence independent bureaus, such as Ullstein's service. Ullstein had founded the service during World War I to create a network of correspondents to supply its newspapers, akin to the *Times*. The service became so successful that it was offered to newspapers not published by Ullstein and became an independent editorial and commercial enterprise in 1923, named Ullstein-Nachrichtendienst (Ullstein News Service). At its height, Ullstein employed fifty main correspondents in Germany and over forty abroad. Still, only fifteen German and ten foreign papers subscribed to the Ullstein service in 1927.[66] The Foreign Office continued to support the successful news agency enterprises of Transocean and Eildienst, though these services did not have a substantial corps of correspondents abroad. The Press Department brought in Stern-Rubarth from Ullstein in 1925 to learn from his experiences. But the department's inability to co-opt the Ullstein service made men like Ritgen more important than ever.

Payment from the Foreign Office did not provide Ritgen with any diplomatic or financial advantages. It resulted in the very opposite. Ritgen's final and perhaps bitterest complaint concerned his taxes. As a journalist working abroad, Ritgen had initially not been obliged to pay Turkish income tax and had only paid 4 percent income tax in Germany. However, on June 1, 1926, Turkish income tax reforms meant that he was obliged to pay full income tax in Turkey too. This double taxation in Turkey and Germany meant that Ritgen's salary barely covered his living and professional expenses. Taking pity on him, Nadolny agreed to raise his salary in October 1926, but refused to release him from German taxes. Ritgen had to pay German taxes to disguise that the embassy paid his salary and to maintain his appearance as a private journalist working for Wolff.[67] Covert operations meant effective cultural diplomacy in the eyes of the Foreign Office.

Ironically, in June 1927, the very month when Käte Witt informed the Foreign Office of Ritgen's inappropriate behavior, Wolff and the Foreign Office had finally drawn up a provisional contract to regulate Ritgen's employment. It took several years for Wolff and the Foreign Office to reach an agreement because Ritgen had originally only been expected to stay in Istanbul for three months. The contract foresaw that Ritgen would work with the press in Turkey for the Foreign Office and consult closely with the embassy. Subterfuge even became explicit. Ritgen would present himself externally as a Wolff representative and would not even count as a member of the German embassy. This would obscure his actual employment for government purposes.[68] This was a common arrangement between Wolff and the Press Department: a similar arrangement existed for Dr. Wilhelm Röllinghoff, Wolff's representative from September 1926 in the Soviet Union.[69]

Ritgen's status as a quasi-diplomat for the Foreign Office meant different expectations for his behavior. In this instance, his dishonorable letter to Witt resulted in his dismissal. Although officials and Nadolny were highly satisfied with Ritgen's work, they saw his behavior as unacceptable for a representative of the German state. Ritgen's return to Berlin in September 1927 would not lead to further employment within Wolff. He would instead experience a long series of disappointments.

From Pillar to Post after Istanbul

At the end of his time in Istanbul, Ritgen looked back with both satisfaction and disappointment at his achievements. Despite Ritgen's best efforts, Agence d'Anatolie still mainly used Havas news. It remained anti-German, while maintaining minimal contact with Wolff. Wolff's reports were simply too detailed, often disseminating entire parliamentary speeches verbatim (at the German government's behest).

Simultaneously, Ritgen's work was undermined by the German government's own duplication of efforts. The Foreign Office used some of its other funds for news to subsidize Transocean, the news agency that sent news abroad over wireless. Agence d'Anatolie received wireless news from Transocean for free, saving it telegram costs for Wolff's news.[70] The Foreign Office was subsidizing telegrams whose content had already reached Turkey over wireless, while Wolff did not even know what Transocean had sent.[71] Wolff had tried to persuade Agence d'Anatolie to take its telephone service, but the reception was too poor. Wolff even admitted in December 1926 that Transocean's wireless service often beat its telegraph service hands down.[72] Finally, Agence d'Anatolie had changed into private hands in June 1925, but it retained close ties to the government and generally reflected the Turkish government's pro-French views.[73] The Foreign Office's efforts could have been an efficient multipronged approach to press policy. Instead, they overlapped and wasted resources.

These issues continued after Ritgen's departure. In February 1928, the German ambassador to Bulgaria, Eugen Rümelin, expressed puzzlement to the Foreign Office that it bothered to spend any money on Istanbul at all, disparaging the city as "a politically wholly dispossessed place, whose barren land is only still fertilized by international bureaucracy."[74] Nadolny pleaded in 1931 for Wolff to send material in French so that journalists could use it more easily and asked Wolff to start a joint wireless service with Transocean to save costs.[75] It also proved difficult to find a replacement of Ritgen's caliber. His scatterbrained subordinate at the *Türkische Post*, Dr. Schmidt-Dumont, eventually replaced Ritgen and continued in the post intermittently until September 1932.[76]

Meanwhile, Wolff and the Foreign Office could never see eye-to-eye about the potential of wireless. One original reason to send Ritgen to Istanbul in 1925 was to take advantage of a new wireless station in Turkey. That had never really worked. Wolff did deliver news over wireless, but Turkish newspapers complained that it was slower than the French service from the Eiffel Tower. By 1931, Wolff thought that wireless was not worth the money.[77]

Despite the Foreign Office's successful support for wireless through Transocean and Eildienst, Wolff retained a more conservative attitude to technology. Although Nadolny believed in wireless, Wolff thought that news sent by telegraph remained "the backbone of any political propaganda."[78] Finally, in mid-1932—after the German government had acquired a majority financial stake in Wolff in 1931—the Press Department took more concerted action against the increasing complaints that Agence Havas ruled the roost in Turkey. It asked Wolff to send news to the Balkans and Turkey by wireless and to concentrate on news provision rather than collection.[79]

None of these efforts revived German-Turkish connections to their pre–World War I level. Even after the Nazis came to power, technical problems continued to plague news dissemination. The Nazi news agency, DNB, could not send news swiftly to Turkey until the late 1930s, because the new technological innovation of the Siemens Hellschreiber (wireless ticker machine) did not function fully in Turkey.[80]

Ritgen himself bounced from pillar to post searching for a job. Initially, he agreed with the German embassy in Turkey that he would still be listed as a publisher of the *Türkische Post* and would work on the paper's advertising and subscriptions in Berlin. He would report for the Turkish government press from Berlin and represent Turkey at Pressa, an international conference on the press in Cologne in 1928. Ritgen assumed that he would stay working for Wolff, though he hoped to report for the Turkish press on the side to supplement his "probably very small salary" from the news agency.[81]

After arriving home in January 1928, Ritgen found to his dismay that Wolff did not welcome him back with open arms. Wolff agreed to pay him until April 1, but Wolff's directors declared categorically that Ritgen's continued employment was out of the question. Ritgen had proved himself unfit to represent Wolff as a quasi-diplomat abroad. He could not work for Wolff domestically, because his brother Otto worked for Wolff's right-wing rival, Telegraph Union.[82]

Ritgen turned time and again to the Press Department over the next few years, pleading for employment. On May 3, 1928, Wolff paid Ritgen a settlement of 1,500 Reichsmarks. Ritgen in return signed a declaration that he had no outstanding demands on either the German Republic or Wolff. Ritgen still felt aggrieved. He claimed that despite his constant pleas for written confirmation of his employer and status, the German embassy had refused, telling him that he was "as good as a civil servant of the Foreign Office."[83] A civil servant had a guaranteed position for life. Ritgen found himself unemployed, because the Foreign Office had paid him, while never employing him officially.

Furthermore, Ritgen had had to resign from membership in the Federal German Press Association (Reichsverband der Deutschen Presse), because he was acting as the publisher of *Türkische Post* and thus was considered a publisher rather than a journalist. This had meant losing his health and pension insurance. Ritgen felt that the Press Department had "a moral obligation" to find or create a suitable post for him.[84] The Press Department continued to use Ritgen's skills, paying him a subsistence wage to write weekly articles for various Turkish and Egyptian newspapers and to report on Egyptian King Fuad I's visit to Berlin in June 1929.[85]

Ritgen retained political conviction even under financial duress. He refused an offer in June 1928 from his brother's employer, Telegraph Union, because his politics did not align with the agency's nationalist bent. Ritgen tried unsuccessfully to found a press service on the Balkans and Near East, named Balkan-Orient-Dienst (Balkan Orient Service), in July 1928. It failed after barely a month when just one newspaper asked for a trial subscription and only the Bulgarian embassy expressed interest in subsidizing the venture.

Ritgen wrote countless letters to newspapers and private companies asking for employment and extolling the virtues of cultural propaganda as the key to political and economic prowess. In July 1929, he wrote to a company specializing in placing articles about Germany in foreign newspapers that "cultural propaganda must be the first. Economic and political propaganda come afterward and last comes special propaganda, i.e., advertising for particular German products."[86] The sentiment garnered him no success.

Ritgen's concerns grew particularly acute with the outbreak of the Great Depression. The Press Department emphasized that there were simply no jobs given the department's massive reduction in personnel from 1929. Three long years after his letter to Käte Witt, Ritgen found steadier employment as the executive director and president of the Association of Foreign Press Representatives (Verband ausländischer Pressevertreter) in Berlin in 1930. The Foreign Office thwarted even this position, refusing Ritgen entry into official press teas for foreign newspaper correspondents, as Ritgen did not work full-time for foreign newspapers.[87] Ritgen pleaded otherwise, stating that he now reported on foreign news for the very company whose offer of employment he had refused in 1928—Telegraph Union. Although Ritgen had turned down permanent employment for political reasons, his financial situation had left him no choice but to freelance for an agency whose politics he abhorred.

By 1934, Ritgen's integration into nationalist news reporting was complete: he had become a full-time employee of the Nazi news agency, the DNB. He rose swiftly to a position of prominence, becoming DNB representative in Vienna by October 1934.[88] Upon arrival in Vienna, Ritgen proclaimed that he had received orders from the DNB's central office in Berlin to present the Austrian news agency with only "strictly objective reports of facts and to avoid every polemic and artificial tendency in his reports."[89] In the end, the security of employment outweighed political convictions.

Even in Vienna, Ritgen stirred up trouble. This time, it was at the highest level. General Franz von Papen, chancellor in 1932 and German ambassador to Austria from August 1934 until the *Anschluss* in 1938, demanded that Ritgen be recalled in August 1936, and preferably fired from the DNB.[90] It is unclear why. This time, Ritgen got lucky. In late 1936, he was sent to Bucharest.[91]

In November 1939, shortly after the outbreak of World War II, Ritgen was transferred into the service of the consulate in Bucharest. The post was supposed to be temporary, but by 1944, Ritgen was still working in the Romanian capital. At some point before 1941, Ritgen married a woman eighteen years his junior. His first daughter, Barbara, was born in November 1941 and a second, Kristine, arrived two years later in November 1943. Ritgen was recalled from Bucharest in May 1944, showed up for service in Berlin on June 13, and was deemed to have left the service of the Foreign Office as of June 23, 1944. The archives do not reveal the circumstances of his departure. His wife was provided a cost of living supplement for up to two months between her husband's departure and her own. Ritgen passed away in 1952, though the files leave no further trace of what happened to his family.[92]

Conclusion

After World War I, broad swathes of German elites became convinced that cultural diplomacy could achieve revisionist political and economic goals. News played a crucial role in these efforts. Still, the Foreign Office's cooperation with Wolff had less effect than the technologically innovative Eildienst on the international structures of news. German-Turkish trade resumed unexpectedly successfully during the Weimar Republic with German banks taking on railway projects, among others.[93] But German news barely bothered the French in Turkey and British in the Middle East. Writing about his long career as chief press officer from 1926 to 1932 and chief press officer for the minister-president of Lower Saxony from 1946 to 1954, Walter Zechlin reflected in 1956 that influencing public opinion was "more important and also more difficult" for interwar Germany, because "we were always the claimants, while the other major powers did not need to expend as much effort."[94]

Regardless of demonstrable results, diplomats like Rudolf Nadolny saw the press as an indispensable instrument of cultural diplomacy. German embassies and legations employed qualified men as press attachés or government press officers in Wolff's clothing. The bureaucratic placement of the Press Department in the Foreign Office underscored the inseparability of news and foreign policy. The Foreign Office came to see the journalist as similar to the diplomat, if not almost identical. One senior officer in the Press Department, Walther Heide, declared that there was "no good journalist without diplomatic sensibility."[95] Although it often obscured its role, the Press Department paid in full or subsidized the salaries of journalists who worked abroad to achieve government aims through soft power.

Wolff's correspondents often found themselves caught in the middle between the agency and the Press Department. Both wanted to spread German news abroad, yet neither wished to take full responsibility for the correspondents undertaking that task. After his dismissal, a bitter Hermann von Ritgen noted that the Foreign Office's use of Wolff's name as a "figurehead" for its press relations officers abroad harmed Wolff's reputation and caused resentment among its employees.[96]

In successive contracts with Reuters, Havas, and the Associated Press, Wolff never regained a semblance of its former status. Even in February 1932, Reuters and Havas declined to allow Wolff back into the "family circle" of the top cartel agencies.[97] Other news agencies complained about Wolff's content. The Havas correspondent in Berlin commented in 1927 that the service was only usable when it contained official communications or urgent official notices before they were printed in newspapers. The correspondent generally supplemented his service with the morning editions of the *Vossische Zeitung* and *Berliner Tageblatt* as well as smaller items from other newspapers.[98] It is no wonder that the Foreign Office turned simultaneously to rival agencies like Transocean and Eildienst to achieve its goals.

Wolff's troubles were even worse at home. The 1920s saw the rise of a nationalist news agency, named Telegraph Union. Owned by industrialist turned right-wing politician Alfred Hugenberg, Telegraph Union would not just challenge Wolff's control, but also succeed with new business structures and very different news values.

6

FALSE NEWS AND ECONOMIC
NATIONALISM

𝕸any Germans opened their newspapers on April 9, 1926, to read of an assassination attempt in the Soviet Union. A young student had shot Aleksandr Grigorievich Beloborodov, the interior minister of Soviet Russia. Beloborodov was infamous for supposedly cosigning the execution order for Tsar Nicholas II and the royal family in July 1918 during the Russian Revolution. The identity of Beloborodov's would-be assassin was unknown but he was apparently the son of a former employee at an imperial palace and possibly still enraged by the death of the tsar. He had shot Beloborodov in the shoulder, seriously wounding him. The right-wing news agency Telegraph Union (known in German as Telegraphen-Union) reported the story. It claimed the Soviet government was keeping the incident secret but would release an official declaration the next day.

There was just one problem with the sensational story: the Soviets claimed it was not true. The Soviet embassy in Berlin was incensed. It believed that Telegraph Union's falsified and biased reports were producing a "systematic poisoning of German public opinion."[1] The incident spiraled into denunciations and recriminations among politicians, diplomats, and journalists. It nearly derailed a German-Soviet trade treaty. It also revealed Wolff's impotence to stop right-wing rumor. When one news agency valued speed and sensationalism over reliability, the other was hard-pressed to compete.

In one respect, at least, the Soviets were right. Telegraph Union did more than supply news: it supported nationalist political and economic aims as part of industrialist and right-wing politician Alfred Hugenberg's media empire. Telegraph Union relied on a very different model of style and content from Wolff: it prioritized speed over accuracy, nationalist rumor over fact, politics over purported neutrality. Telegraph Union also had a different business model. Its main purpose was not to turn a profit, but to enable Hugenberg and his circle of industrialist friends to influence politics and the economy. This influence would come both from the agency's content and its place in Hugenberg's innovative business structure of vertical integration.

The vertical integration of Hugenberg's media empire meant that he controlled all aspects of news from paper production to news collection to advertisements. Vertical integration guaranteed customers. It also enabled Hugenberg to subsidize Telegraph Union, which specifically targeted provincial papers. News agencies were a priori not profitable businesses.[2] The cost of collecting and disseminating news generally outstripped revenue from subscribers. Wolff relied on the state for subsidies; Telegraph Union received cross-subsidies from Hugenberg's more profitable companies, like the Scherl publishing house. Telegraph Union required the largest subsidies of all Hugenberg's companies, as it operated at an annual loss of 200,000–300,000 Reichsmarks by 1929.[3]

Outside Germany, Hugenberg and fellow industrialists worried greatly that the absence of German influence on the press abroad harmed exports and undermined German minorities. Telegraph Union created alternative news networks to reach German minorities in Central and Eastern Europe as well as the Baltic states. This upset governments in the region, who worried that Telegraph Union might disrupt the fragile balance within their borders. Internationally, Telegraph Union joined an attempt by second-tier news agencies to cooperate globally. In exchanging news with the American United Press and British Exchange Telegraph Company, Telegraph Union provided a nationalist perspective on European news.

These news structures served economic as well as political purposes, although the two were intertwined in Hugenberg's eyes. Hugenberg believed that Germany needed a nationalist party to enable the "rebirth of the German people" through their rediscovery of a "Volksgemeinschaft."[4] For Hugenberg, this party had to provide a vision of economic nationalism, focusing on autarky and rebuilding German economic strength. He laid his hopes on the DNVP (Deutschnationale Volkspartei, German National People's Party), a party mainly of industrialists that Hugenberg would lead from 1928 to 1933.[5]

Hugenberg's approach to politics and the press was new in German conservatism. Rather than just try to influence the public during election years, Hugenberg facilitated "greater coordination in systematically shaping political opinion through the media," as political scientist Daniel Ziblatt has put it.[6] Hugenberg shaped his media empire as a right-wing enterprise with no party affiliation, believing that readers would desert newspapers representing particular groups or one-sided business interests. Instead, Hugenberg's media enterprises supported antisocialist and nationalist politics *outside* of party affiliations. From 1920 onward, every editor working for Telegraph Union was contractually obliged to "campaign for the route of political and economic reconstruction of Germany without party-political or other ties on a national basis."[7] This directly impacted content. Telegraph Union reported accurately on the German Reichstag and state parliaments but almost exclusively covered speeches by German conservative parties such as the DVP (Deutsche Volkspartei, German People's Party) or DNVP.[8]

Hugenberg's strategy did not pay off as he had hoped. He greatly increased his influence over the media; he did not increase voter support for the DNVP, whose share of votes halved from 14.3 percent in May 1928 to 7 percent in September 1930. Instead, Hugenberg's media laid the groundwork for Nazi government by increasing votes further on the right. The rapid rise of scandal sheets and the widespread coverage of political scandals further deepened the population's skepticism of "the system" overall.[9] The Nazi share of the vote rose swiftly from 2.6 percent in 1928 to 18.3 percent in 1930, a peak of 37.3 percent in the July 1932 election, and then a slight decline to 33.1 percent in the last election of November 1932 before Hitler became chancellor in January 1933.

Within this dynamic, Telegraph Union played an important, but neglected role. It took time to build a network that could spread false news of an assassination so fast and so far. As newspapers came under increasing financial strain in the 1920s, ever more of them relied on news agencies. Even ostensibly nonpartisan papers often unwittingly presented a nationalist take by printing Telegraph Union, particularly in the provinces. Telegraph Union's increasing success divorced much of the German population from direct contact with the Weimar government and polarized the supply of information. Telegraph Union exerted tremendous power in the arena of symbolic politics by framing events and setting news agendas. That power would not translate into direct political success. But it would undermine the shared space for news within the increasingly fragile Weimar Republic.

Nationalist News from the East

Many newspapers printed the article on Beloborodov, though some added notes of caution about its veracity.[10] By 1926, contemporaries estimated that 1,600 German newspapers subscribed to Telegraph Union. The prestigious *Vossische Zeitung* claimed that many larger papers, like the *Leipziger Neueste Nachrichten,* were ashamed of the source, but that only the *Frankfurter Zeitung, Berliner Tageblatt,* and *Vossische Zeitung* appeared not to take the agency.[11] It is difficult to provide exact numbers, as most newspapers, especially provincial ones, did not name their sources and no Telegraph Union subscriber lists survive. Starting in 1931, Telegraph Union contracts stipulated that newspapers had to name the agency as a source, but not all newspapers complied.

Telegraph Union had emerged from a merger of four smaller news agencies in 1913.[12] Hugenberg became the majority shareholder in 1916 after a failed bid to gain control over Wolff. After purchasing 47 percent of Wolff's shares in 1916, he found them to be useless: Paul von Schwabach, owner of Bleichröder Bank and majority shareholder in Wolff, had quickly bought any remaining shares to retain an absolute majority.[13] Hugenberg became the full owner of Telegraph Union in 1921. The agency vastly increased its number of subscribers and talented personnel by buying the provincial publisher and news agency Dammert in March 1921. Liberal newspapers dated the boom in Hugenberg's media empire to that merger, which gave Telegraph Union greater access to provincial papers.[14]

The purchase of Dammert built on a decade of mergers and acquisitions. Starting just before World War I, Hugenberg and his circle of industrialists had used trusts and holding companies to purchase myriad media companies. The companies' complicated financial structures were designed to obfuscate the owners: Hugenberg and his close friends. Hugenberg had been involved in the Allgemeiner Deutscher Verband (Pan-German League), worked from 1894 to 1903 for the Prussian Settlement Commission in Posen (Poznań), from 1903 to 1908 for the Prussian Finance Ministry on Eastern Questions, before leaving state service and swiftly becoming the chairman or board member of various industrial companies, such as Krupp, and associations such as the Centralverband Deutscher Industrieller (Central Association of German Industrialists).

At the same time, Hugenberg became interested in using media to influence economic and political views. Prior to World War I, he and other industrialists had subsidized multiple newspapers like the liberal *Münchner Neueste Nachrichten* and sought to change their political direction. These industrialists tried to dictate everything from personnel to the politics of individual articles. This clumsy direct intervention reduced the circulation of one previously liberal newspaper, *München-Augsburger Abendzeitung*, from selling 50,000 copies a day before World War I to 13,000 by 1927. The newspaper needed direct subsidies to stay afloat.[15] After these disastrous attempts to dictate journalistic practices to individual newspapers, Hugenberg and his fellow industrialists no longer tried to micromanage media, but sought personnel whose political orientation matched their own.

Hugenberg became interested in media in midcareer, but he has come to symbolize the German equivalent of magnates like William Randolph Hearst, Lord Beaverbrook, and Lord Northcliffe.[16] Unlike those magnates, much of Hugenberg's success came from importing techniques of vertical integration from heavy industry like steel. Companies like Thyssen and Krupp had thrived by incorporating vertical integration after 1900.[17] These techniques were less common elsewhere, until Hugenberg used his experience at Krupp to introduce them into the media sector.

Hugenberg followed the idea of vertical integration to incorporate all aspects of the newspaper business from paper to advertising. By the end of World War I, he owned or had founded the basic companies to complete his suite of media products. In 1916, he purchased the ailing publishing house, August Scherl, which published many leading newspapers, like the *Berliner Lokal-Anzeiger* and *Der Tag*, and popular magazines like *Die Gartenlaube*, *Die Woche*, and *Berliner Illustrierte Nachtausgabe*. Hugenberg founded the advertising agency, Allgemeine Anzeigen (ALA), in 1917 and owned numerous paper companies. Hugenberg's biggest expansion came with his takeover of Universum-Film AG (UFA) in 1927, which produced and distributed films and cinema news reels called *Wochenschauen*. Hugenberg cooperated with a range of industrialists like Hugo Stinnes and Theodor Reismann-Grone to build his companies. Stinnes too embarked on creating a vertically integrated media empire in the Weimar Republic, but this was cut short by his death in 1924.

Only after the early 1920s would Hugenberg's media empire become an instrument of political power. That power came substantially from the provincial press. By the mid-1920s, many of the smaller newspapers printing the Beloborodov article had little choice. Local newspapers that claimed to be nonpartisan thus generally cleaved closer to nationalist and conservative values.[18]

Hugenberg had increased control over provincial papers in the early 1920s by supplying financial aid in exchange for loyalty. Hugenberg provided consulting and financial aid to failing newspapers with Vera-Verlagsanstalt, founded in October 1917. He used hyperinflation in 1922–1923 to subsidize and indirectly influence more papers. In 1922, he created Mutuum and Alterum to help right-wing newspapers in financial trouble and he held partial ownership of at least fourteen provincial papers.[19] The help came with conditions attached. If a publisher received a loan, he had to allow Vera to take over his accounting and he had to subscribe to Telegraph Union. Stinnes commented to Hugenberg in October 1920 that Vera could "not be an instrument for North German party politics." Rather it had to function as an "economic consultancy for the press on a national footing that has no other party political ambitions."[20]

Simultaneously, Hugenberg and Stinnes used a paper supply crisis in the early 1920s to purchase newspapers and create larger media conglomerates than Germany had ever seen. The phenomenon was so closely associated with Stinnes that contemporary journalists often called this the "Stinnesierung" of the press.[21] Even after Stinnes's death in 1924, left-wing academics like Paul Baumert worried that the magnate had only bought newspapers to boost the profits of his paper factories. Instead of paper facilitating news, news and "public opinion" only served to increase demand for coal, cellulose, and paper.[22]

Beyond direct financial control, Hugenberg created Telegraph Union services specifically for provincial newspapers. Provincial subscribers could choose among four services with different political orientations ranging from "neutral" to Catholic nationalist or German nationalist. Telegraph Union's differentiated political services enabled Hugenberg to attract a greater number of customers in the splintered newspaper landscape of Weimar Germany and to cater to more market sectors than Wolff, which never divided its services by political orientation.

Telegraph Union also provided news to Wipro (Wirtschaftsstelle der Provinzpresse, Provincial Press Economic Bureau), which was founded in September 1922 to produce syndicated columns and a stereotype service for smaller provincial newspapers more cheaply than the two market leaders. Until the end of 1924, the three largest syndication companies explicitly agreed not to engage in competition, but this lapsed in 1925. From January 1925, Wipro supplied two services to accommodate more newspapers: one for papers not affiliated with a political party and one for right-wing newspapers. Wipro worked in tandem with Hugenberg's advertising agency to provide newspapers with advertisements.[23] Some of those provincial newspapers were kept financially afloat by one of Hugenberg's loan companies, Mutuum or Alterum.

Subscribing to syndicate services cut personnel costs and remained the most common answer to financial problems for newspapers. Approximately 1,200 of the 3,200 newspapers in Germany relied wholly on syndicated services by 1926.[24] Wipro controlled about a third of the syndication market: around 350 newspapers used only Wipro by the early 1930s. Newspapers' financial troubles never really dissipated in the Weimar Republic, as some fixed costs of salaries, taxes, and production never decreased after inflation. In 1927, publishers' costs were four to five times higher than in 1913.[25] On top of that, advertising revenue effectively halved from 1928 to 1931.[26] No wonder many newspapers felt that Telegraph Union and Hugenberg's syndicated services were the only choice.

Larger newspapers, of course, still engaged in fact-checking and investigative work. They would uncover the apparent lack of veracity behind the Beloborodov article. After receiving the shocking news, various newspapers rang the Soviet embassy in Berlin to verify the item. Surprised by the very inquiry, the embassy vigorously denied the report.[27] The embassy asked the newspapers for the origin of the report and was told that it had come from Warsaw. A Telegraph Union editor had even rung the Soviet embassy to check the news' authenticity, but had trusted his own source despite the embassy's denials. The news item was printed in Telegraph Union's political and economic news service on the Soviet Union, named Asia Eastern Europe Service (Asien-Osteuropa-Dienst, AOD). Its reports on the Soviet Union always listed the origin of the news as Moscow. Yet the news often came from Soviet newspapers. Other items seemed wholly fabricated to the Soviet embassy in Berlin. The German left-wing press also condemned Telegraph Union's Asia Eastern Europe Service as biased against the Soviet Union.[28] Telegraph Union's use of newspapers as sources was common to all correspondents abroad and their foreign correspondents received a daily hectographed service with information about other countries. Telegraph Union representatives took this principle further by using newspapers in a well-connected city to report on news from other countries like the Soviet Union and China.[29]

Determined to counter this potentially damaging rumor, the Soviet official news agency (Telegrafnoe agentstvo Sovetskogo Soiuza, TASS) asked

Wolff's representative in Moscow, Dr. Wilhelm Röllinghoff, to issue a denial in Germany. Wolff had reestablished relations with TASS in 1925, sending Röllinghoff—whose salary was paid by the Foreign Office—as a representative to Moscow. Wolff issued its denial that same day of April 9, labeling the item's origin as Moscow. In a brief statement, it noted that "the WTB representative is authorized to deny the news of an attack on Commissar of the Interior Beloborodov."[30] The language indicated a cautious distance from the denial, though it also advertised Wolff's access to official sources in the Soviet Union unavailable to Telegraph Union.

According to convention, Wolff generally labeled the origins of items that it received from foreign agencies in parentheses after the title, date, and place of the item. This was intended to indicate that Wolff had a correspondent in that area or to show when a foreign news agency partner was involved in procuring a news item. Complaints continued to surface over the next few years, however, that labeling alone did not indicate sufficient distance from what one official at the German embassy in Moscow called TASS's "pure propaganda dispatches."[31] The official provided an example from November 1929, where Wolff had reprinted an item about a trial in Moscow against what the item described as "42 members of an antirevolutionary organization, which had conducted its activities under the cover of a religious sect." The item did not describe the trial as an investigation and the defendants as innocent until proven guilty, but summarized their crimes as follows: "Over several years, the accused carried on antirevolutionary monarchist agitation and conducted terrorist acts and arsons."[32] Wolff's director Hermann Diez defended Wolff's dissemination of the item for diplomatic reasons: TASS had complained about the general censorship of its news. This was not the diplomacy that the Press Department had intended: it did not want Wolff to prove too accommodating to the Soviet Union.

In the case of Beloborodov, Wolff's denial failed to prevent the incident from escalating. Telegraph Union responded by releasing further details of the attack the same day. An item titled "Soviet Russian Denials" in its Asia Eastern Europe Service revealed that Beloborodov was under police protection in a hospital in the Kremlin and was being treated for his severe wounds by the commissar for health, Professor Nikolai Semashko. Beloborodov had been shot by a twenty-five-year-old student, Porfiri Alekseev, whose father had worked at the former residence of the imperial family in Tsarskoe Selo located just outside St. Petersburg (known at the time as Leningrad). The item used the opportunity to decry the Soviet government's methods of disseminating information. In a blend of editorializing and reporting, the item claimed that readers could only really believe 5 percent of the news that the Soviets disseminated. All the other denials simply stemmed from Soviet paranoia about the "alleged contamination" of German public opinion, officialdom, and economic organizations by "Balts" who were "satanically furious" with the Soviet Union.[33]

Social Democratic papers found Wolff's denial odd too. Writing the next day, *Vorwärts* contrasted Telegraph Union's new details with Wolff's denial in an item headlined: "What is truth? TU: Beloborodov is shot.—WTB: I am allowed to issue a denial." The paper reprinted some of the details released by Telegraph Union and compared this with the one-sentence Wolff denial. It found the denial "strange," as the Soviets could have issued a denial through their own news agency. Why, then, had Wolff taken on the work of the Soviet news agency, asked *Vorwärts*.[34] The newspaper was frustrated with Wolff's gullibility.

Unlike the universally accepted Wolff notice of the Kaiser's abdication in November 1918, no newspaper appears to have accepted Wolff's denial wholesale, except the Communist Party newspaper, *Die Rote Fahne*. The paper used the incident to attack Telegraph Union. Echoing claims by the Soviet embassy in Berlin, an item on April 11 called Telegraph Union an "agency of lies" that received its news from White Russian spies in Warsaw, who were in the service of English imperialism. The paper attacked *Vorwärts* for printing and defending the item. Finally, it noted that Telegraph Union's service on the Soviet Union was "a mere repository of anti-Bolshevik lies" and that it was beneath the dignity of *Die Rote Fahne* even to respond to such "sham products" ever again.[35]

The refusal to discuss Telegraph Union in the future represented more than just rhetorical posturing. It crystallized an increasing divide of silence between Left and Right. Wolff's news reached a smaller number of newspapers. Even its denials had lost resonance, as they were barely believed. Similarly, the Far Left's wholesale rejection of engaging with Telegraph Union relied on the public's ability to identify and differentiate news items in a way that mostly exceeded their knowledge and abilities, as so many newspapers did not even label when their news came from a news agency.

This dispute came at a sensitive moment in German-Soviet relations. As foreign minister since 1923, Gustav Stresemann had pursued further treaties with the Soviet Union to create a balance between East and West and to foster increased economic relations between the two countries. Trade relations lay at the heart of Weimar Germany's Eastern policy. The Germans and Soviets had signed a trade treaty on October 12, 1925, at the same time that Germany was negotiating two other treaties: an extension of the Treaty of Rapallo of 1922 that had normalized diplomatic relations between the Germany and the Soviet Union as well as the Locarno treaties to solidify Germany's borders.[36] An updated neutrality treaty was due to be signed in Berlin just a few weeks after the Beloborodov news.

The Foreign Office wanted to avoid any potential disruption to its delicate balance of East-West treaties. The Beloborodov incident was proving vexing. The Soviet embassy turned to the Press Department a week after the first article on Beloborodov, noting that Telegraph Union reached "almost all the German press," and particularly importantly, "the entire provincial press, which our denials either do not reach or reach very belatedly." "Due to its systematic instigation" of false news, the Soviet embassy continued, Telegraph Union was "poisoning" German public opinion and "starting to become a real danger to the further development of friendly German-Russian relations."[37] Telegraph Union had upset the applecart.

It seemed more than a coincidence that Telegraph Union news was undermining German-Soviet economic relations at such a critical moment. Telegraph Union was particularly invested in economic news, just like Alfred Hugenberg. In 1925, Hugenberg claimed that he had entered the media from "the economy and [saw] things first from economic points of view."[38] While he thought that Germany's economic woes stemmed from political causes like losing the war, he saw the economy as the key to rebuilding political prowess. Economic autarky would enable "political freedom" from foreign countries.[39] While Hugenberg supported trade and export as "pillars of the economy," he drew the lesson from World War I that Germany had to prioritize the domestic market. He believed that the greatest danger lay in the "internationalization" of the German economy, which would undermine German self-sufficiency in agriculture and reproduction, threatening its national culture.[40] His media empire was meant to support these autarkic ideas: Hugenberg thought that "a truly great German press can only find its crystallization point in an *idea* or in a personality."[41]

In 1921, Hugenberg's conglomerate had used a merger with Westdeutscher Handelsdienst (West German Trade Service) to create an economic news service for Telegraph Union: Deutscher Handelsdienst (DHD, German Trade Service). DHD's economic service generated considerable surpluses that subsidized Telegraph Union's political service (although the company generated losses overall). Telegraph Union had poured energy into DHD "to balance out the increasing shortfall of the political service and to keep earning."[42] By the mid-1920s, this also meant fighting with the government for the same access to wireless as Wolff.

Competition with Wolff had grown particularly fierce over economic news by 1926 and government protectionism was riling Telegraph Union. Wolff created its new economic radio service, Deutscher Kursfunk, by establishing a subsidiary company with Eildienst. When the Postal Ministry had renewed its contract with Eildienst in 1925, Telegraph Union had protested the Postal Ministry's exclusive grant of radio privileges to Eildienst for supplying economic news to private customers.[43] Despite Telegraph Union's repeated appeals, the Postal Ministry continually rejected its application for an economic radio service to private customers.

Political and general economic considerations outweighed legal arguments. Multiple government ministries supported the Postal Ministry for reasons ranging from protecting the governmental monopoly on wireless content to worries about political effects, as ministers made clear in a meeting in October 1927. The Postal Ministry and Hans von Bredow believed in controlling access to information by controlling access to radio waves and privileging the pliable Eildienst. The Foreign Office agreed that the government's ownership of Eildienst provided "the best censorship" of economic news. Politically, the Foreign Office worried about the international and domestic ramifications of allowing Telegraph Union's economic service access to radio. It believed that Telegraph Union's probable bias and unreliability would destroy foreign countries' trust in German economic news, undermining the international connections that Eildienst had created. This was hardly a surprising conclusion after problems like the Beloborodov incident. Domestically, the Foreign Office thought that an economic news service outside government control could be "catastrophic" for the economy. The problem was not just that stock market news would arrive faster. The problem lay in the very nature of radio. Radio broadcasts might provoke "sudden mass action" that "no one can quickly contain, particularly in smaller towns or in the country."[44] Fear of the crowd justified control over conduit and content.

Other ministries expressed concern that Telegraph Union might abuse the service for profits. The Economics Ministry worried about intermingling political and economic news, arguing that a radio service for stock exchange prices had to remain "neutralized" like Eildienst.[45] First, a news agency like Telegraph Union could manipulate its economic service for private gains.

The service could disseminate false share prices, for instance, with no means of government control. Second, it might not encode stock exchange news like Eildienst, allowing anyone with a radio to obtain the news for free. Third, Telegraph Union might create a precedent for other private organizations to request wavelengths for their own economic news services. The Chancellery agreed. It even argued that falsified or biased political news was "less harmful" than falsified or biased economic news directed at private persons, which could directly hurt the economy. The government feared that Telegraph Union was pursuing its own policy of economic nationalism and was less interested in "earning money than influencing the economy."[46]

The Postal Ministry concurred that the government needed to exert greater control over economic news than political news. In 1924, the Postal Ministry had even given Wolff and Telegraph Union permission at the same time to disseminate their political news services over radio to newspapers. This was the first time that the German government had publicly treated the two news agencies equally. Telegraph Union had celebrated that victory with a barrage of advertisements bombarding newspaper publishers in their weekly trade journal *Zeitungs-Verlag (Newspaper Publisher)*. Almost every week between late August and October, full front-page advertisements pushed one relentless message: subscribe to Telegraph Union.[47] The vast array of Telegraph Union advertisements contrasted strongly with Wolff's sheer invisibility in trade journals. Unlike Wolff's (and liberals') distrust of commercial advertising techniques and photography, Telegraph Union advertisements embraced visuality just as right-wing political parties did.[48] Telegraph Union presented itself as a magnetic force of nature, drawing newspapers to its services irresistibly (see Figure 8).

The Postal Ministry's control over Telegraph Union's technological access contrasted strongly with the Foreign Office's inability to control Telegraph Union's content. In its initial investigation of the Beloborodov incident, the Press Department downplayed its inability to subdue Telegraph Union. On April 19, just days before the German-Soviet treaty was to be signed, it dismissed Telegraph Union's Asia Eastern Europe Service as "interesting, strongly sensational, and comprehensive, but superficial." Claiming that the Beloborodov news was "politically not of the importance that it could justify action by the Soviet embassy," it still noted that Telegraph Union's attack on Soviet news could create tension.[49] Furthermore, the report criticized the Soviet press's hostile attitude toward Germany and its reliance on *Die Rote Fahne,* rather than Wolff, for its news on Germany. Still, good

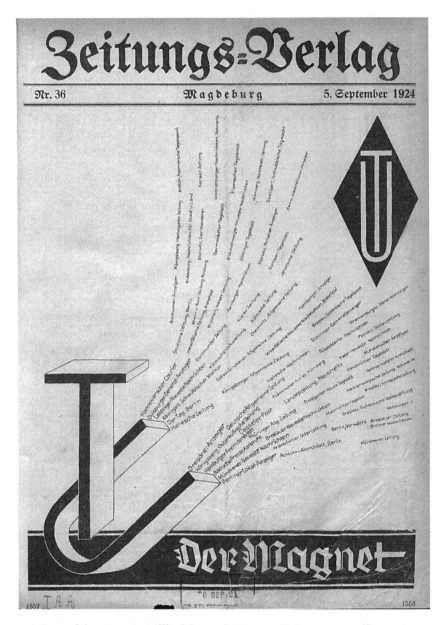

FIGURE 8. Advertisement, "The Magnet," *Zeitungs-Verlag* 25, no. 36 (September 5, 1924): col. 1557–1558. Reproduced from a copy held at Staatsbibliothek zu Berlin.

relations with the Soviets remained the highest priority. The Press Department swallowed its concerns about the Soviet press and continued quietly to research the Beloborodov incident.

Telegraph Union retaliated by denigrating Soviet news as a whole in its general service on April 21. It was easier to dismiss everything as false than repudiate specific details. The hostility toward the Soviets was hardly surprising given nationalists' consistent anti-Bolshevism. The item implied that the Soviet government used denials as a political tool and that Wolff continually fell into the trap. It gave the example of a "typical denial." Telegraph Union had reported a few weeks earlier that the Soviet Union would decline the League of Nations' invitation to a disarmament conference. The Soviet Union had issued a denial the next day through Wolff, but an official Soviet note to the League a mere week later confirmed the Telegraph Union report. The Telegraph Union item called for readers to translate this triumph of truth into trust for its report on Beloborodov. Naturally, the item's author concluded, Telegraph Union would continue "its independent and objective reporting from Russia in the interests of the German press."[50] The cartel alliance system with TASS had left Wolff issuing denials for the Soviets, while Telegraph Union attacked Wolff as a gullible stooge for Communist politics.

Meanwhile, the Soviet embassy had found another reason that Telegraph Union's report simply could not be true: it did not have a representative in Moscow. While leading German and English-language newspapers, like the London *Times,* employed their own journalists in Moscow, the embassy claimed that Telegraph Union received its reports from White Russian emigrant circles that were naturally biased against the Soviet Union.[51] Telegraph Union claimed that it had two representatives in Moscow but could not reveal the names for security reasons. News items were often anonymous and Telegraph Union did not allow its foreign correspondents to use their real names, for fear that their news reports might result in their expulsion from Eastern European countries or prosecution at home. Labeling the news' origin as Warsaw also helped to guard its representatives.

Despite extensive inquiries over the next ten days, German diplomats were unable to verify this information and it is unclear whether these representatives existed or not. Telegraph Union had tried to set up a central office in Moscow and had negotiated in vain with the Soviet Union to create a Russian-German news service in 1922–1923.[52] By 1926, Telegraph Union still had failed to procure an entry visa for a representative. In 1928, Telegraph

Union appeared to receive its Russian service in Riga, where it could listen to Russian radio broadcasting.[53] This may well have been a source in 1926. Furthermore, if Telegraph Union had received the news from Warsaw, it might have trickled out through secret news networks and smuggled letters from the Soviet Union.[54]

Such confusion over the identity of Telegraph Union representatives was surprisingly common. In Warsaw in 1925, for example, the German embassy initially could not discover if a Telegraph Union representative existed. When it did verify the presence of a correspondent, Telegraph Union refused to reveal his name, stating that it "did not think it wise after earlier experiences with the Press Department etc."[55] Nevertheless, it confirmed one important detail for a nationalist agency: the representative was definitely *not* a Pole.

Over and above whether the Moscow representatives even existed, the problems of verifying the item remained. The Press Department realized that it could not ascertain the veracity of Telegraph Union reports. A report concluded that Telegraph Union's reports appeared to be truthful, though the denials by the Soviet embassy, TASS, and Wolff cast much doubt.[56] Despite a request from the Soviet embassy, the Press Department refused to intervene with Telegraph Union's reporting, stating that it could not be "the referee in an argument about news."[57] The Department felt that it could only regret Telegraph Union's polemical tone and note the Soviet embassy's point of view, acknowledging the limits of its domestic power to control news from abroad. Significantly, the Press Department no longer accepted Wolff news items as fact, beginning instead to doubt the power of its own semiofficial news agency to judge the truth. No newspapers abroad reported on the alleged assassination attempt on Beloborodov. Telegraph Union skillfully turned rumor into fact, at least for some German readers.

Ironically, the false reporting presaged the violence of Beloborodov's eventual demise. After Leon Trotsky was expelled from the Kremlin in November 1927, he stayed briefly with Beloborodov. The next month, Beloborodov himself was expelled from the Communist Party and exiled to Siberia. By the early 1930s, he was readmitted to the party and working in Rostov-on-Don. In 1937, his final fate was sealed when he was named in the show trial of former *Izvestia* editor Karl Radek as an alleged coconspirator with the now exiled Leon Trotsky; that news made it into the *New York Herald Tribune*.[58] In February 1938, Beloborodov was shot, though he would be rehabilitated posthumously twenty years later.

Still, Telegraph Union news did not undermine German-Soviet political relations this time. Right-wing political parties, the civil service, and the military saw the treaties with the Soviet Union as a necessary evil to regain German territories and to unite two anti-Polish countries. Nationalism triumphed over anti-Communism.[59] The Press Department's de-escalation worked and politicians signed the German-Soviet Neutrality and Nonaggression Pact in Berlin on April 24, 1926.[60]

German-Soviet official press relations did not run quite so smoothly, however. Despite Wolff's assiduous dissemination of Soviet denials, the Soviet government remained unhappy about Wolff's service, complaining that it only sent thirty-word telegrams of TASS news back to Germany. This limit was stipulated in the Wolff representative's contract, signed in 1925. He sent less important news by post to Königsberg.[61] The Soviet Press Department claimed that this left the door open for enemy reports from the French news agency Havas and Telegraph Union in Germany. Although the German Press Department suspected that these complaints were partially a ploy to secure all reporting on the Soviet Union for TASS, Chief Press Officer Walter Zechlin recognized that thirty words were too little and asked Wolff to expand its service.[62] Costs were the major problem as usual. Wolff retained its system of short telegrams and longer letters, leaving space for Telegraph Union's swifter, but less reliable reporting. German newspapers began to reach outside of the cartel and to make contracts with rival American news agencies, such as United Press and International News Service, for their news supply as early as 1924.[63]

The Beloborodov incident was only the most egregious and potentially damaging misrepresentation in Telegraph Union reporting on the Soviet Union. The Soviet embassy continued to contact the Press Department about Telegraph Union's "hostile campaign" against it.[64] The Soviet newspaper of record Izvestia even devoted space on its front page to deny a Telegraph Union report of a high-level Soviet bureaucrat's speech about possible Soviet bankruptcy if farmers did not save the situation.[65] Other reports alleged mutinies in the Black Sea fleet in September 1926, eager to provide an impression of Communist chaos.

Falsified assassination attempts appeared to be a particular specialty. In September 1927, the agency reported an attempted attack on the king of Spain. Many German newspapers printed the item and Wolff issued a correction the next day.[66] This placed Wolff in a dilemma. Disseminating the denial of the incident drew attention to Telegraph Union. A vicious circle now provided Telegraph Union with a perverse incentive to report false news. It was free advertising: Wolff would issue a correction, as it felt morally and politically obliged to do so.

The ramifications of Telegraph Union's false news practices were potentially enormous. Research in psychology and political science has reached mixed conclusions about the effect of denials and retractions. It is also important to be careful about reading contemporary findings backward, though they provide some sense of the dynamics of denials. Psychological studies have shown that denials have surprisingly little effect. Readers remember the story, particularly if they read about it twice—once as a news item and once in a denial. They do not remember that the story is false.[67] Political scientist Brendan Nyhan found that presenting readers with facts that contradict their opinions could create a "backfire effect," where readers double down on their erroneous beliefs.[68] Nyhan has subsequently revised his own beliefs after a study on voters in the 2016 American presidential election showed that facts could change people's minds about policies. The new facts did not change people's overall belief systems, however, nor their propensity to vote for a certain political candidate.[69]

Telegraph Union did not just falsify. It also changed rumors to facts. In July 1928, the Press Department received a worrying report that a Telegraph Union item could damage German-Polish political relations.[70] Telegraph Union had disseminated a report based on an item from a German-language newspaper in Kaunas, Lithuania. Telegraph Union claimed that the newspaper *Jüdische Stimme* had published a suggestion by Józef Piłsudski to the Lithuanian government that Lithuania should cede its claims on Vilnius and allow it to remain part of Poland.[71] In return, according to the report, Piłsudski—chief of state from 1918 to 1922 and leader of the Second Polish Republic from 1926— had offered Lithuania a few border districts and the "Lithuanian part of East Prussia," if Poland could retain the city of Königsberg. Piłsudski had purportedly stated that he would march into Kaunas in September and would then remove those troops, if the Lithuanian government agreed to his suggestion. Stating this interpretation as fact, the report expressed only two suppositions. First, Piłsudski thought that the Entente states would not oppose the plan. Second, Polish foreign minister August Zaleski's latest trip to Belgium and France "is supposed to have some connection to this plan."[72] A number of mostly right-wing German newspapers ran the story.[73]

A few days later, however, the evening edition of the Social Democratic *Vorwärts* revealed the truth about Telegraph Union's sensational story.[74] The newspaper had secured a copy of the original report from the Lithuanian paper and it read quite differently. Printing the two items one after the other on its front page, *Vorwärts* titled the piece "How to Bait Peoples against Each Other: Poland Promises East Prussia to the Lithuanians—View into the Factory of Lies." Noting that the Telegraph Union report was merely designed to create new bitterness between Germany and Poland, *Vorwärts* revealed that the original story had been based wholly on rumor. The original item had started by casting doubt on its own veracity, putting a question mark behind its headline: "Poland to give three districts to Lithuania?" Question marks had become full stops in the Telegraph Union item. The *Jüdische Stimme* had heavily emphasized the suppositional quality, revealing that it was a rumor started in Berlin. "As reported from Berlin, circles close to Lithuanian-Polish negotiations announce that rumors are supposed to have been spread in Berlin, according to which a prominent Polish politician close to Piłsudski is supposed to have made the following suggestion to settle the Lithuanian-Polish conflict: Lithuania renounces [claims to] Vilnius and recognizes the current demarcation line as a border with certain corrections in Lithuania's favor."[75] The contrast to the start of Telegraph Union's item was striking. Berlin no longer featured nor did the word "rumor."

Telegraph Union reporting turned rumors into facts. The item in the *Jüdische Stimme* mentioned that the Poles saw a "possibility in the future that the Lithuanians might receive the Lithuanian parts of East Prussia." Telegraph Union claimed that Piłsudski had offered to return those parts immediately. Telegraph Union added an extra dose of militarism by claiming that Piłsudski was prepared to march into Lithuania. The only aspect that remained almost entirely unchanged was the two suppositions about the attitude of the West: the reaction of Entente governments and Zaleski's trip to France and Belgium.

Vorwärts printed the item just below a large photo on what was the main story of August 1928, the signature of the Kellogg–Briand Pact, officially known as the General Treaty for Renunciation of War as an Instrument of National Policy. The juxtaposition implied that the Telegraph Union had not disseminated the item coincidentally just a few weeks prior to the signature of the Kellogg–Briand Pact, designed to create peace among all. The manipulated article suggested that Poland could simply not be trusted. By extension, a Kellogg–Briand Pact could hardly rein in Polish aggression.

The news item bolstered prevalent right-wing views about a militarist and revanchist Poland. One newspaper editor in the right-liberal *Tägliche Rund-*

schau commented a few months after Józef Piłsudski's coup in May 1926 that Poland was afflicted by a "Chinese state of affairs" that had plunged the country into "a crisis of state culture." The article characterized Poland as torn between an external appearance of a European, Latin state with a constitution, parliament, democracy, and free speech, and an underlying Byzantine character of anarchism, brutality, and despotism. Unsurprisingly, the geographical boundaries of Poland's Latin state lay on the old German-Russian border.[76] Tendentious items such as the Kaunas report were "typical" for Telegraph Union's reporting on Eastern Europe and simply seemed designed "to cause harm," noted one German editor of a press bureau specializing in Eastern Europe.[77] Telegraph Union saved considerable sums by extracting reports from newspapers in the local area and transforming them to fit its general outlook. Telegraph Union, like other right-wing reports, cast the East as a wild space with indeterminate borders and calculating leaders.

In response, the Press Department started to observe Telegraph Union more closely. The Press Department instructed the German embassy in Warsaw to keep a close eye on Telegraph Union's new representative from November 1928. A Press Department representative even met with the new correspondent, Ernst von Mensenkampff, prior to his departure for Warsaw to encourage him to stay in close contact with the German legation in Warsaw as a precaution against further falsifications. German embassies and legations had been required to send the Foreign Office regular reports on correspondents for German newspapers since February 1924, though diplomats were reluctant to engage with Telegraph Union representatives. In contrast to Wolff's involvement in governmental cultural diplomacy, German diplomats found Telegraph Union correspondents uncooperative and ignorant of conditions on the ground.[78]

The Press Department and German embassies made little impact on Telegraph Union's conduct. Mensenkampff did not consult the embassy and reports continued to surface with false claims. In 1930, the German ambassador to Warsaw, Ulrich Rauscher, complained that news items on the Soviet Union and Poland were designed to stir up trouble. Rauscher wrote to the Press Department to ask that Mensenkampff consult with the embassy to avoid news that was "100 percent false and so obviously biased and thus highly capable of discrediting German news services abroad."[79] There is no evidence that Mensenkampff ever did. The German ambassador to London complained similarly about the Telegraph Union representative there in 1932.[80] Given that there were only around eight correspondents for German newspapers in Warsaw from 1925 to 1933, Mensenkampff held tremendous power.[81] Rauscher and his fellow diplomats found themselves unable to influence that power in any meaningful way.

Telegraph Union and Scherl representatives also compared themselves to diplomats, but in a different way than the German government had with Wolff employees. The Foreign Office saw Wolff correspondents like Hermann von Ritgen almost as diplomats (see Chapter 5). By contrast, one representative in Paris for Scherl, the Hugenberg-owned publisher, reflected that the diplomat was in "a similar, but not the same position" as a newspaper correspondent. Unlike the reporter, who had to know the boundaries of discretion, the diplomat "will communicate everything to his government that he finds politically significant, regardless of whether he found out about it for that purpose or not."[82] The reporter decided what to communicate, while the diplomat was not supposed to make those types of judgment calls.

For Telegraph Union correspondents, speed was the first, last, and only commandment. Now the main Telegraph Union correspondent in Paris, Mensenkampff wrote in 1932 that "precisely for me as an agency representative, speed of reporting is the first and most important duty and it is unacceptable for me to lag behind the official WTB in this regard."[83] Many correspondents for papers published by Scherl also worked for Telegraph Union or vice versa; they did not have to search for extra work to supplement their incomes as did Hermann von Ritgen and other Wolff employees.

Telegraph Union's mantra was speed over accuracy. Despite the false reports, Telegraph Union sold its products as beating Wolff.[84] Many newspapers found the sales pitch convincing. It is obvious that Telegraph Union could often beat Wolff on certain news items. Wolff was required to show the Press Department potentially critical news items before publication and this could slow down dissemination substantially. The Press Department insisted on this at the expense of speed: it reprimanded Wolff in 1932 for not sending all items about the sensitive subject of Memel—a part of East Prussia under German rule prior to 1918 that became an autonomous region of Lithuania called Klaipėda in 1923—to the Press Department for approval prior to publication.[85] Wolff always waited diligently for permission from the relevant state secretary or the Press Department before disseminating an item; Telegraph Union sometimes contravened those directives.

Telegraph Union's advertisements disguised the reality for subscribers abroad. An assessment by the Czechoslovak news agency, Československá tisková kancelář, compared the two agencies' radio services to Czechoslovakia in May 1927. The report concluded that Wolff provided a better service in terms of speed and quality, attributing any differences to the two agencies' different regular transmission times. Both agencies seemed to provide similar domestic political news, though Wolff provided more information on sessions of the Prussian parliament and the Reichstag that barely interested foreign customers. Wolff provided more information relevant for foreign customers, such as detailed news on Czechoslovak politics, which Telegraph Union omitted. Telegraph Union's bias stemmed not just from what it included in its services, but what it left out. Technically, Wolff's transmitters functioned better. Their announcers read more clearly and consistently, while Telegraph Union employees dictated monotonously and changed encryption codes too often, leading to misunderstandings. Finally, the Czechoslovaks found that Wolff's service contained no obvious tendentious reporting, unlike Telegraph Union.[86] The German legation in Beijing echoed the Czechoslovak agency's assessment, stating that Telegraph Union news from Beijing, then known as Peking, displayed "unreliability, inaccuracy, sensational tinge."[87]

It is hardly surprising that the agency fell under suspicion of excess German nationalism and unreliable reporting abroad too. Telegraph Union had expanded rapidly in the early 1920s, starting a telephone service to Spain in February 1923 and sending its own representative to London at the start of 1924. It had established contracts with agencies such as the American United Press and British Exchange Telegraph Company. Permission to radio to newspapers abroad from 1926 greatly enhanced Telegraph Union's range. Telegraph Union swiftly set up branches abroad. It expanded its services to newspapers in Austria, Hungary, Bulgaria, Romania, Turkey, Czechoslovakia, Yugoslavia, and the Baltics by 1928. German newspapers in Central and Eastern Europe comprised 15 percent of Telegraph Union's subscribers.[88]

Telegraph Union's advertisements emphasized that these subscribers formed an integral part of the German nation. In one of a flood of advertisements in 1924, Telegraph Union emphasized its community of radio subscribers (see Figure 9). Circles radiated outward from the Telegraph Union headquarters and radio tower in Berlin, transgressing contemporary political boundaries. Although the map indicated that East Prussia was somehow separate from Germany, it resolutely refused to admit or represent demarcations or borders of the postwar German state.[89] The caption portrayed those receiving Telegraph Union services as part of a collective. "We all have the radio service of Telegraph Union," it declared. Unlike most representations

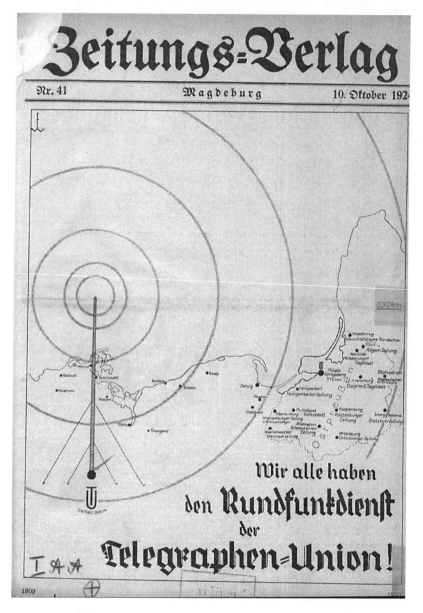

FIGURE 9. Advertisement, "We all have the radio service of Telegraph Union!" *Zeitungs-Verlag* 25, no. 41 (October 10, 1924): col. 1809–1810. Reproduced from a copy held at Staatsbibliothek zu Berlin.

of radio, including Telegraph Union's economic news service, half the circles were incomplete. The center of the circle, Berlin, was not the center of the advertisement, but sat quite far off-center to the left. Telegraph Union's radio service did not seem concerned with those inside Germany's borders, but rather those in-between or cut off from the "mainland." Telegraph Union could undermine national boundaries, using news to encompass those excluded politically from the Weimar Republic toward the east, but also toward the south in Austria.

Telegraph Union Abroad

On July 26, 1927, a highly distressed letter from Wolff landed on the desk of the official Austrian news agency, Amtliche Nachrichtenstelle (ANA, Official News Office).[90] ANA's reporting on the strikes of July 15 had been "an almost total failure" and had put Wolff's directors "into the most embarrassing situation in which we have ever found ourselves."[91] On July 15, workers had started to demonstrate in Vienna after the acquittal of three right-wing youths who were accused of murdering a Social Democrat and an eight-year-old boy. The police were underprepared; heated exchanges between the police and protestors swiftly escalated into violence. The police shot at the crowds, killing eighty-five workers and injuring many more. July 15 illustrated the Austrian Social Democrats' weak control over the police in the city that they supposedly governed. Moreover, it showed their inability to control the course of political events: Chancellor Ignaz Seipel refused to resign after the leader of the Social Democrats, Otto Bauer, insisted on it. The day displayed the Social Democrats' weakness to right-wing opponents like Seipel and caused internal dissent within the party itself. July 15 was the first deep calamity for interwar Austrian socialism.[92] And Wolff's reporting had not lived up to expectations.

On July 15, Wolff had suffered a series of unfortunate setbacks: its usual representative, Wilhelm von dem Hagen, was on holiday, so it was forced to rely more than usual on its Austrian partner, ANA.[93] As an official news agency that was government-controlled since the mid-1920s, ANA had waited for permission before disseminating any news on the workers' strikes raging throughout Vienna. In an attempt not to escalate the situation, it seems that the Austrian chancellor himself ordered ANA not to report too many details on the burning of the Palace of Justice, mass arrests, or police clashes with demonstrators. ANA felt beholden to downplay reports to stop demonstrations from escalating into full-scale revolution. Wolff had received bitter complaints from German newspapers as well as news agencies in neighboring countries like Denmark about the poor and slow reporting on July 15. One of its biggest newspaper customers that had previously relied solely on Wolff was so disappointed that it subscribed to an additional news service.[94]

On a day that would prove a turning point in the young Austrian republic's history, Wolff had been beaten to the punch by its archrival: Telegraph Union. Unencumbered by ties to official news agencies, Telegraph Union had reported news on the strikes two hours before Wolff. Defending itself, ANA stated that in a moment of state crisis, it was "impossible" for an official or semi-official agency's most important task to be competing with private reporters.[95] Despite several exaggerated and false reports, Telegraph Union's speed advertised its worth for German and Austrian newspapers alike. Its overinflated reporting also contributed to the impression of a country roiled by anarchy, which might prosper through annexation.

Changes in German radio policy enabled Hugenberg's companies to expand their reach to Austria. The German Postal Ministry had allowed news agencies other than Wolff to broadcast their news through radiotelephony from early 1926, apparently as it no longer felt that it could answer to the public about restricting foreign newspapers from receiving German news.[96] The issue was particularly acute in Austria, where successive German governments still harbored hopes of unification to create a *Großdeutschland* (Greater Germany).[97] Proximity also simplified radio reception.

Hugenberg's companies began their typical multipronged approach to influencing the press. In Austria, Hugenberg purchased at least one newspaper (*Deutsch-Österreichische Tageszeitung* in Graz) and attempted to gain some control over the *Wiener Neueste Nachrichten* in 1926. To counteract this, Austrian Chancellor Ignaz Seipel turned to the German Foreign Minister Gustav Stresemann. Well aware of the dangers of Hugenberg's companies, Stresemann agreed to send several thousand Reichsmarks monthly through Concordia, a company that the government often used to buy up ailing newspapers, particularly in border regions.[98]

Furthermore, Telegraph Union looked to open a branch in Vienna in early 1927, headed by a former editor of the *Vossische Zeitung,* Dr. Alexander Redlich. Telegraph Union then provided a trial service to Viennese newspapers.[99] Redlich needed a concession from the Austrian government to set up an official branch. It appears that Hugenberg used his industrialist connections to the Austrian envoy in Berlin to persuade the Austrian trade minister, Dr. Hans Schürff, to consider the request.

ANA worried about Telegraph Union's encroachment upon its territory, but Wolff remained surprisingly unconcerned. Director Heinrich Mantler noted that a branch in Vienna would require massive subsidies. However, he did worry about "grave political disadvantages" for Germany if Telegraph Union's actions encouraged other nations' news agencies to set up shop.[100] Mantler's obsession with finances and Germany's international political reputation misunderstood Telegraph Union's business strategy. Profit from individual branches was irrelevant. Rather, a branch in Vienna would expand Telegraph Union's reach, allowing it to use news to tie more German speakers abroad to Germany. As industrialists believed that press exposure led to favorable public opinion, an expansion of Telegraph Union must have seemed to facilitate greater access to the Austrian market.

Within Vienna itself, Telegraph Union received the long-anticipated concession in mid-1928. Despite complaints about the reporting of July 15 and the Social Democratic control of the office responsible, the office granted the concession both on principle and because it hoped to create the precedent to establish a Social Democratic news agency. ANA also failed to understand the danger fully, dismissing Telegraph Union news as "mainly *faits divers* presented as sensationally as possible," which ANA would never stoop to send anyway.[101] Some Austrian newspapers clearly found Telegraph Union's service more useful. The *Salzburger Volksblatt*, for instance, received wireless material from both Wolff and Telegraph Union, but wrote to ANA that Telegraph Union was sufficient, especially for news from the Balkans, Eastern Europe, and Russia.[102] It suggested that ANA might cancel its wireless and telephone services from Wolff, saving it 100 schillings a month. While ANA maintained ties with Wolff, Telegraph Union's increasing power did not bode well for the continuing dominance of the Central and European news agencies allied with Reuters, Havas, and Wolff. Indeed, the three agencies had partially established annual conferences for the Agences Alliées in 1924 in response to competition from German news agencies abroad such as Eildienst.[103]

Similarly, Eastern European and Baltic states grew fearful of Telegraph Union's ability to affect their German-speaking populations. A German academic noted in 1926 that Telegraph Union had "gained particular importance for German press abroad" because of its radio service.[104] Representatives of Eastern European and Baltic countries with large German-speaking minorities had noticed too. At the Agences Alliées annual conference in 1927, the Latvian news agency (Latvijas telegrafa agentūra, LETA) complained that Wolff had been too slow in responding to newspapers' requests that Wolff establish a radiotelephony service in Latvia. Meanwhile, Telegraph Union had swiftly installed a receiver and offered its services for free or at extremely low prices. LETA's director believed that Telegraph Union gave newspapers the sensational news items that they preferred over the cartel's "objective but short news."[105] Although LETA's director pleaded with Wolff to create a service for Latvia, Mantler merely replied that Wolff's radiotelephony service was meant for small subscribers in Germany, rather than abroad, and that the Latvians should develop their own service, as Latvian needs differed from German ones.

The Polish government too monitored Telegraph Union with an eagle eye, particularly worried about news supply to the German minority within its borders.[106] The official Polska Agencja Telegraficzna had signed a contract with Reuters and Havas in 1921 providing it with Havas and Reuters news from everywhere, except Poland and Germany. The Polish agency retained the right to negotiate with Wolff on the supply of German news.[107] This had stabilized news supply somewhat in Polish eyes, although officials continually offered suggestions for improving reporting on Poland both in Germany and elsewhere.

Telegraph Union disseminated news from Poland into Germany from the early 1920s. As with reporting on the Soviet Union, the German embassy in Warsaw complained bitterly about the news items' errors and tendentious bias.[108] Once Telegraph Union could disseminate its news via radio in 1926, however, the agency began to make inroads into the Polish market. The Polish government was happy to have a Telegraph Union representative reporting on Poland in the country, but worried about its news reaching the Polish population. Concerned about potential nationalist rhetoric, the Polish consulate in Berlin asked the Polish government to investigate how to refuse or remove permission for receiving wireless from Telegraph Union under Poland's July 1927 press law. The Post and Telegraph Ministry abrogated the right of Polish newspapers to receive Telegraph Union news over wireless in December 1928 in an attempt to remove Telegraph Union from the Polish newspaper market.[109]

Telegraph Union continued to exploit the invisibility of radio waves and found new ways to supply the Polish market. In Łódź, for example, Telegraph Union appointed a local twenty-eight-year-old Polish man, Heinrich

Berman, as its representative in late 1929. His Judaism proved no hindrance and he appears to have worked as a correspondent for Telegraph Union's economic service too. The Polish Foreign Ministry found the development worrying and asked a Polish news agency, Agencja Telegraficzna Express, to monitor Berman as well as Telegraph Union's economic news from Poland. The German Foreign Office insisted on representatives with clean slates and stellar reputations, firing Ritgen when he transgressed a moral rather than legal norm. By contrast, Telegraph Union did not fire Berman when it turned out that he hardly had a distinguished past: he had been arrested in 1925 and 1929 for forgery and embezzlement.[110] The Polish Post and Telegraph Ministry soon began to investigate Berman for unregistered use of a radio to receive Telegraph Union news. Telegraph Union then dropped its relationship with Berman. Regardless, the Polish Ministry forbade any reception of Telegraph Union's news over radio in Łódź.

The very nature of radio makes it impossible to tell whether anyone still listened illegally and printed the news in Polish papers, perhaps without naming the source. What is certain, however, is that the Polish government worried about how Telegraph Union's extraterritorial propaganda might affect the country's German minority. The Polish Foreign Ministry hoped to stop widespread dissemination within Poland. In a final attempt to prevent Telegraph Union from unilaterally disseminating over radio in Poland, Agencja Telegraficzna Express entered into a contract with Telegraph Union with the Polish Foreign Ministry's explicit permission and support in 1931. Agencja Telegraficzna Express took responsibility for forwarding Telegraph Union news to the press. Nevertheless, Telegraph Union continued to evade detection and to disseminate its news within Poland, presumably aiming primarily at German speakers. By late 1933, it still had radio receivers in at least Warsaw, Łódź, Kraków, Katowice, and Vilnius.[111]

For political and economic reasons, Telegraph Union did not experience unmitigated success in Austria and Eastern Europe. As the Depression continued, finances finally outweighed other considerations. In early 1931, expenses pushed Telegraph Union to downgrade its branch in Vienna to just one reporter, who would sometimes forward news from the Balkans.[112] The agency could also use wireless transmission from Berlin to supply newspapers abroad and perhaps found that more cost-effective. Some countries like Poland attempted to restrict the agency's activities, aided by increasingly authoritarian governments in the region that controlled press policy. German-language papers in Prague had taken Telegraph Union since 1926.[113] The Czechoslovak government watched over the developments closely. Finally, with rising tensions, the Czechoslovak Postal Ministry used its control over permission to install radios and receive certain services to ban newspapers from receiving Telegraph Union service in August 1933.[114]

Conclusion

There was no inherent reason that competition could not have improved news supply within Germany. The problem was that Telegraph Union was not just interested in news. It formed part of a political project to espouse economic nationalism. It catered to newspapers, particularly in the provinces, that were "not at all in the position to judge with certainty the meaning of every 'bald fact' reported by a news bureau," as Hugenberg's close friend Ludwig Bernhard put it in 1928. Bernhard claimed that provincial newspapers actually wanted to print editorialized content over facts.[115] Telegraph Union provided that service by selecting and interpreting the news. Its point of view did not explicitly support any particular party. Rather, it laid the groundwork for nationalist politics in general.

Telegraph Union's paradigm of economic nationalism contrasted strongly with Wolff's and the Foreign Office's belief in using cultural diplomacy to achieve economic and political ends. Cultural diplomacy, they hoped, could provide a counterpart to political treaties such as Locarno, Rapallo, or the Kellogg–Briand Pact. Telegraph Union's economic nationalism, on the other hand, antagonized not just German diplomats but also Central and Eastern European governments. Despite different content and aims, both the Foreign Office and Hugenberg agreed on method—news agencies that would filter reports before they reached newspapers. A consensus remained that news agencies could achieve broader political and economic goals.

Unlike the Foreign Office, Telegraph Union thrived on politicizing news supply. Ludwig Bernhard thought that news could never be apolitical, writing that "every international news bureau claims to be nonpartisan, but in fact conducts some form of news politics." Bernhard believed that Telegraph Union's "main political achievement" had been to destroy Wolff's monopoly on news, particularly official news.[116] It was a battle that Wolff could not win. Telegraph Union could portray Wolff as biased because it relied on a democratic government and supported "the system" that right-wing nationalists wished to overthrow.

Hugenberg's indirect influence on political and journalistic elites far out-weighed his direct influence on electoral politics.[117] Telegraph Union shaped information provision; many who opposed Hugenberg feared that his agency was fatally undermining Weimar democracy's legitimacy by cutting off much of the population from centrist and left-wing news. Regardless of whether that was true, Weimar governments would try myriad methods to combat and co-opt Telegraph Union. They would increasingly see full control over Wolff as the only way to control the news that Germans read. Many of these efforts would not shore up the Weimar Republic. Instead, politicians and bu-reaucrats would inadvertently enable the Nazis to seize swift control over a key tool of domestic politics.

THE LIMITS OF
COMMUNICATIONS

On January 2, 1934, the Nazi news agency, Deutsches Nachrichtenbüro (DNB, German News Office), published its first news sheet. The DNB's editor in chief, Peter Theodor Koch, laid out his philosophy of news. News was meant to be "truthful." But truth was not objective. It was political, just like news. Politics and news were linked by "magic connections" that were "perhaps better intuited" than defined.[1] Koch hoped that the DNB would revive the German people's trust in politicians by producing truthful news after the lies of the Weimar Republic. The DNB would help to create the *Volksgemeinschaft* that the Nazis asserted so enthusiastically.

During their first years in power, the Nazis transformed the news landscape of Germany. They promulgated laws to constrain journalists, restricted newspaper ownership, and took control of news supply. They created the DNB from a merger of two Weimar rivals: the semiofficial news agency, Wolff, and right-wing news agency, Telegraph Union. They radically changed the content of much DNB news. They also used the DNB to inform state officials as much as newspapers.

Despite radical changes in 1933–1934, there were significant continuities from the Wilhelmine and Weimar periods. Koch may have condemned the content of Weimar news. Nazi politicians may have disparaged journalists as liars, Jews, and Marxists. They may have cried *Lügenpresse* (lying press) and *Systempresse* (system press) to denounce the media in the Weimar Republic. They may have rejected "liberal" concepts like public opinion. They may have come to power without significant newspaper support. But once in power, the Nazis swiftly saw the utility of news agencies.

The Nazis could only assert control over news so quickly because they found so much already under state supervision. As ever more newspapers subscribed to Telegraph Union, politicians and bureaucrats had panicked about their increasing inability to reach vast swathes of the population. Telegraph Union's paradigm of economic nationalism had challenged Wolff's and the Foreign Office's belief in news as cultural diplomacy. These conflicts had not just taken place in a capitalist marketplace of news. They had played out within Weimar ministries.

The mid-1920s created a pattern that would only intensify with the Great Depression. The late 1920s and early 1930s saw Weimar bureaucrats and politicians trying to solve broader problems like unemployment and reparations payments by asserting greater control over communications. As trust in social institutions like the press faded, successive Weimar governments tried multiple solutions ranging from new technologies to new laws to new agencies. Most significantly, the government would purchase financial control of Wolff in 1931. In reaction to Telegraph Union's apparent power, Weimar governments renegotiated agreements that had stood since Bismarck. Instead of preserving democracy, however, Weimar politicians' attempts to counter antidemocratic right-wing news inadvertently enabled the Nazis to undermine the free press far more swiftly.

Weimar, and then Nazi, politicians saw news agencies as vital tools of domestic politics. Despite very different political beliefs, both Weimar and Nazi officials shared the conviction that controlling news agencies enabled them to control communications and, in turn, the domestic German population. The business of the news agency remained, even if the product—news—had changed dramatically.

Competition and Control in the Late Weimar Republic

In 1929, Telegraph Union launched an aggressive advertising campaign.

The first advertisement in the series (see Figure 10) celebrated the fat-cat newspaper magnate. Three men sat around a table playing cards. One smoked a cigar, one a cigarette, and one abstained. Before the other players even had a chance, the cigar-smoker played the TU (Telegraph Union) as his trump card. The cigar-smoker discarded his other cards face down on the table: they

FIGURE 10. Advertisement, "TU is trump!" *Zeitungs-Verlag* 30, no. 7 (February 16, 1929): col. 341–342. Reproduced from a copy held at Staatsbibliothek zu Berlin.

were worthless in the face of Telegraph Union's power. The other two players' hands were on show: their card-playing / news-gathering strategies were too obvious. They had to follow Telegraph Union's trump and smilingly acknowledged that they had lost.

Over the next year, further ads emphasized Telegraph Union's wide range of services, its close cooperation with German newspapers, and its speed. By 1930, Telegraph Union reached out beyond newspaper publishers. In *Deutsche Presse,* the journal for the Federal German Press Association, an advertisement triumphantly claimed: "TU controls the modern newspaper business!" A small man dwarfed by machinery and rolls of paper stood motionless with his arms glued to his side, gazing out toward the reader (see Figure 11). An even more dominant force sat astride the machinery: the initials "TU." The only other human figure, barely detectable, worked at one of the factory lines of paper production, but appeared almost crushed by the letter "U." Telegraph Union's modern machinery purportedly dominated the newspaper business.

By 1930, many in the publishing industry and government concurred that Telegraph Union had achieved a "monopoly position." One former director of an agency purchased by Alfred Hugenberg in 1921, Dr. Rudolf Dammert, believed that Telegraph Union's financial strength made its system unbeatable.[2] Others blamed the monopoly on Telegraph Union's vertical integration into Hugenberg's media empire, ensuring its cooperation with Hugenberg's syndicate services. One rival company in August 1930 estimated that two-thirds of Germany's 3,000 newspapers now used some form of syndicated material, while 1,600 solely subscribed to Hugenberg services.[3]

In reality, newspaper subscriptions were divided fairly evenly between Wolff and Telegraph Union. One survey of seventy-five newspapers in July 1928 found that nineteen papers took only Wolff, eleven only subscribed to Telegraph Union, and nineteen to both. The remaining twenty-six papers took printing plates preset with content (*Materndienste*), had their own cable and radio services, or used smaller news agencies like Sozialdemokratischer Pressedienst (Social Democratic Press Service). Newspapers of all political leanings took Wolff.[4] In some regions, such as East Hanover, the percentage of newspapers printing Telegraph Union sources rose slightly from 73 percent to 81 percent in 1932. The proportion taking Wolff fell dramatically from 88 percent in 1920 to only 34 percent in 1932.[5] Such statistics were possibly not representative for the rest of Germany. In 1932, Wolff still had around

FIGURE 11. Advertisement, "TU controls the modern newspaper business!" *Deutsche Presse* 20, no. 21 (May 24, 1930): 2. Reproduced from a copy held at Staatsbibliothek zu Berlin.

2,000 newspaper subscribers and Telegraph Union 1,350; both had 350 subscribers to their radio services.[6]

Despite the reality, many agreed with the assessment presented by Telegraph Union's advertisements. They believed that Telegraph Union's increasing dominance conferred unprecedented political power on Hugenberg. By 1929, the journalist Erich Schairer was convinced that "to conduct news politics at the level Hugenberg does it—that means to rule over the people." Schairer anointed Hugenberg the "uncrowned king of Germany."[7]

Weimar officials agreed by this point that Telegraph Union was too important to ignore. By the mid-1920s, the government had realized that it was caught between a rock and a hard place. Should it only use a semiofficial news agency whose contents it could control? That meant ignoring the increasing number of newspapers that did not subscribe to Wolff. Or should the government cooperate with a right-wing news agency, Telegraph Union, that despised the Weimar state's existence? Different ministries offered different answers, undermining the possibility of a unified official press policy and diluting efforts to defend democracy.

Over the course of the 1920s, various ministries and officials dealing with the press subverted the government's deal to supply Wolff first with official news. Although the Press Department was technically the central department responsible for news distribution, there continued to be overlapping competencies and interdepartmental tussles. Individual ministries or leaders of Foreign Office departments also maintained personal relationships with journalists from larger newspapers like the *Frankfurter Zeitung, Hamburger Fremdenblatt,* or *Kölnische Zeitung.*[8]

Telegraph Union's increasing strength exacerbated the problems of coordinating press policy. From the start of the Weimar Republic, Telegraph Union had persistently asked the Press Department to provide it with official news simultaneously to Wolff. The government experimented with supplying news to Telegraph Union in June 1923, but stopped swiftly when the agency released the material prior to receiving permission.[9] Telegraph Union's requests heightened the government's increasing dissatisfaction with Wolff. In the early 1920s, some newspapers complained to the Press Department that Telegraph Union subscribers had an advantage because Wolff's service was slower and less detailed.[10] Telegraph Union's self-promotion hardly helped the situation: it erroneously claimed that it received all the same official news as Wolff (this was only true for some news by the late 1920s).

The Press Department tried two tactics in the mid-1920s, though neither solved the dilemma. First, the department sought direct contact with journalists. While foreign minister in the 1920s, Gustav Stresemann held special conferences for particular editors in chief or political correspondents to test out sensitive material, rather than consulting with Wolff. From November 1926, the Press Department created a monthly evening gathering to increase informal contact with journalists.[11] The department also offered to provide official notices to journalists for free that Wolff distributed as part of its paid subscription service.[12] The Press Department had begun to undermine one of Wolff's key selling points: its exclusive access to official news.

Second, the Press Department started to supply Telegraph Union with news at the same time as Wolff. By 1925, the government supplied Telegraph Union with transcripts of government speeches before the actual speech. Despite admonitions to wait until the relevant state secretary had granted permission to disseminate the speeches, Telegraph Union and its branches kept forwarding the news straight to newspapers and expecting them to wait. In a bid to beat competition, newspapers often printed the news earlier than allowed. Wolff complained that it could do nothing about its competition if Telegraph Union refused to play by the rules. Rather despondently, Wolff's director Heinrich Mantler merely pleaded for the Press Department to allow Wolff to disseminate the speeches to its branches ahead of time so that its newspapers would not receive the texts so much later.[13] Wolff remained bound to its beliefs about proper process and the purpose of a news agency: to disseminate government news at the appointed time in the appointed manner. Wolff stuck to convention over combating competition.

Wolff lost further support when the Press Department discovered that it did not even control the government's supply of news to the press. The Foreign Office lost control over the budget for "Promotion of German News Domestically" in 1926. This budget had mostly comprised payments to press agencies and for publications by the Reichszentrale für Heimatdienst, a government office set up to support "political education" in the Weimar Republic.[14] While the Foreign Office retained control over funds for German news abroad and subsidizing Wolff, losing the domestic budget decreased the Press Department's power at home.

These problems were exacerbated once other ministries acted unilaterally to solve their problems of news supply, in particular the Economics Ministry and Statistical Office. Economic news provided Wolff's main source of profit; it needed its monopoly of government statistics and economic data. The Statistical Office did not care. It began to supply Telegraph Union in May 1926, believing that it should disseminate indexes of wholesale prices, cost of living statistics, and monthly bankruptcy data as widely as possible. In November 1926, the Statistical Office jettisoned the last aspect of Wolff's monopoly: export statistics. The Statistical Office emphasized that widespread dissemination lay "in the general interest of the public."[15] Though the Statistical Office initially acted alone, the Press Department soon cooperated by printing the Statistical Office's exports statistics as an addendum to the Press Department's economic news bulletin.

The Economics Ministry partially followed the Statistical Office's lead by putting Telegraph Union in second place after Wolff. Although it worried about Telegraph Union's potential power over economic wireless services and had denied its Deutscher Handelsdienst (DHD) access to radio, the Economics Ministry still believed that Telegraph Union was vital for informing the public about economic policies. In mid-1928, the ministry did not supply export statistics to Telegraph Union's economic service, DHD, at the same time as Wolff. However, it gave DHD these statistics two hours earlier than they reached the rest of the press through the government publication *Wirtschaftsnachrichten (Economic News)*.[16]

Ostensibly, the Press Department remained committed to privileging Wolff "in the interests of the government as well as the WTB [Wolff's Telegraph Bureau]."[17] Reality was a different story. In May 1927, the Press Department allowed individual ministries the latitude to disseminate "news of a purely departmental character" directly to other news agencies simultaneous to Wolff. The Press Department only explicitly named Telegraph Union as an acceptable alternative news agency.[18]

After years of debating whether to supply Telegraph Union with news, the Press Department finally agreed in January 1928 to treat Telegraph Union "on equal terms" with Wolff "as far as possible." Department officials retained the right to judge based on "political expediency alone" whether it was appropriate for both agencies to receive an item simultaneously.[19] Chief Press Officer Walter Zechlin emphasized that the Press Department was under no obligation to treat the two organizations equally. But Telegraph Union complained when equality was not practiced, such as with the emergency decrees of 1932.[20] By agreeing to treat the two agencies equally, the government dissolved its own control over news supply.

At the same time, Weimar bureaucrats sought broader solutions to regain control over news. Four main options presented themselves: technological, legal, business, and political. The state could double down on the new technological innovation of wireless ticker services. It could return to the old legal tactic of banning official notices from certain newspapers. Officials could create a new agency to compete with Hugenberg's media empire. Or officials could increase political control over Wolff to remake its news more to their liking. Each option revealed the limits of state-media relations in a flawed democracy.

The technological solution was a wireless automatic ticker service. Ticker services had existed since the nineteenth century and were mainly used to print financial data. In the late 1920s, an American innovation had created wireless tickers that could print over three hundred characters a minute automatically. This could eliminate stenographers and increase accuracy. By 1929, over ten thousand machines had been sold in the United States. The German Postal Ministry had already licensed a machine (Springschreiber T28) and regulated the fees. In 1929, the ticker company only disseminated economic news, supplied by Eildienst. But the ticker machines still needed a cable connection, which was pricier, because wireless remained too unreliable in summer atmospheric conditions.

Nevertheless, the Foreign Office hoped that the wireless ticker service could counteract Telegraph Union. In early 1928, it commissioned studies on wireless dissemination over long- and shortwaves. Meanwhile, the Postal Ministry set certain conditions for operating tickers with Lorenz, a company that manufactured radio sets and that held the ticker patent in Germany. The agreement with Lorenz enabled the Foreign Office to counter Telegraph Union's intention to begin a ticker service in fall 1928. Soon after, Lorenz signed an agreement with Siemens & Halske to create a joint ticker production company, Deutscher Tickerdienst.[21] As the ticker expanded to forty-eight participants by mid-1930, Wolff started to cooperate with the new ticker company to supply big cities. Although the unreliability of wireless prevented grand plans to supply provincial newspapers, the government still hoped that ticker connections to major industrial companies in western Germany could counter Telegraph Union's "very one-sided political" influence.[22]

Ministerial infighting stymied the proposal. Most ministries found the technical setup too expensive; they also suspected that large industrialists and party papers would refuse the service. Some officials wondered why the

Foreign Office was involved in "a purely technical matter."[23] The Foreign Office claimed that it wanted to prevent a Hugenberg monopoly. The Chancellery, now run under Heinrich Brüning, disparaged the Foreign Office's "anxiety psychosis" about Hugenberg's potential use of the ticker, as the patent system ensured that this was impossible.[24] Still, the Foreign Office remained deeply enmeshed in domestic news, partially because it overinflated the fear of Hugenberg's media tentacles.

The second approach to combat Hugenberg came from law. Weimar press laws had restricted various freedoms of the press since the early 1920s, but they had concentrated on banning entire editions of a newspaper for seditious content or postprint censorship, rather than preprint restrictions to information.[25] This changed in 1929, when Hugenberg's campaign against the Young Plan for restructuring German debt sparked the concern of Social Democratic interior minister Carl Severing. In cooperation with other nationalists, particularly Hitler, Hugenberg's newspapers and Telegraph Union agitated for a referendum on a "Law against the Enslavement of the German People" that would renounce the Treaty of Versailles and criminalize collecting reparations. The campaign gained sufficient signatures for a referendum in December 1929. The vote itself only garnered 14.9 percent turnout, far below the 50 percent threshold. Still, Severing was spooked. He decided that the best approach to Hugenberg's antirepublican newspapers, particularly the *Berliner Lokal-Anzeiger* and *Der Tag,* was cutting them off from official publications. Severing drew on tactics that had worked in the Kaiserreich: removing official news from newspapers had often pulled them into line. After consulting the government from the largest German state of Prussia, the federal government released "Guidelines for Selecting Newspapers for the Notification of Official Publications," stating that ministries should no longer supply antirepublican newspapers. In December 1929, the same month as the referendum on the Young Plan, the Prussian Interior Ministry stopped supplying the three major Scherl newspapers due to their "invidious and extremely provocative way" of attacking the democratic state.[26]

Severing's almost unilateral decision exposed deep fault lines in government press policy. The Press Department was barely consulted, although it technically still held the mandate of supplying government news to the press. Meanwhile, certain ministries found the decree unacceptable. The Finance Ministry argued that its official publications had to reach as many people as possible, regardless of a newspaper's political orientation. The Finance Ministry believed that the government's duty was to follow readers, rather than to dictate press policy, stating that "if an official notice is not announced in the newspapers which the main crowd of defaulting payers read, then it falls short of its purpose."[27]

At base, the Finance Ministry and Severing disagreed about the nature of newspaper readers and their habits. The Finance Ministry found it "improbable" that readers of Scherl papers would choose papers of different political orientations, just because they carried official notices.[28] Severing—who later served as the last Prussian interior minister from 1930 to the "Prussian coup" of July 1932—believed the opposite. "A large part of the anti-state press retains its readership precisely through official notices," Severing argued, before concluding that "a removal of official notices and entrusting other newspapers with official notices would lead without further ado to a corresponding reorientation of the reading public."[29] Severing saw the press as stenographers to power. If they lost their access to official information, they would lose their readership.

It turned out that the stenographic part of journalism was less important than Severing believed. By 1932, it was obvious that the Finance Ministry had judged readers' habits more accurately. The Prussian Justice Ministry removed the ban on official publications in Scherl newspapers on June 24, 1932, possibly because the Scherl publisher had launched a court case against the ban in February.[30] Two days later, Wilhelm von Gayl—interior minister from June to December 1932 and member of Hugenberg's DNVP—decreed that ministries should decide the matter themselves, as there had never been a uniform opinion on the guidelines for choosing newspapers to supply with official publications.[31] Ministerial machinations prevented coordinated action to combat antirepublican sentiment.

The third approach against Hugenberg was to create a competing agency. Heinrich Brüning's government subsidized new syndicate services to compete with Hugenberg, such as an agrarian press agency (Landwirtschaftliche Korrespondenz) in early 1931.[32] Brüning himself did not have the backing of a majority in the Reichstag and had been appointed chancellor by President Hindenburg in 1930. Brüning saw news as a vital means to increase public support for his policies. He suggested measures like pamphlets, interviews with journalists, and disseminating their own newspaper notices and articles.[33] He also intervened directly in some Wolff notices, rewriting them himself.

The new syndicate services proved the most successful initiative. Subsidized by Brüning's government, Kristian Kraus used Wolff's news for a syndicate service for the provinces (Provinzial-Landesdienst). Kraus's service swiftly supplied Wolff's news to between eight hundred and nine hundred provincial newspapers and gained the lead over Hugenberg's Wipro.[34] Although Kraus appears to have raised Hugenberg's hackles, Wipro claimed that it had survived the Kraus service "unscathed."[35] These battles exacerbated the division in news supply to the German population. Germans receiving provincial newspapers read syndicated versions of Wolff or Wipro/Telegraph Union news with the comfort of their own newspaper's title and local news, unaware of the machinations behind their news.

Despite their success with syndicate services, Wolff's directors embraced defeatism. Hermann Diez declared in January 1930 that Wolff was on an inexorable slide into second place far behind Telegraph Union, unless it managed to become "more journalistic" and pay more attention to "what newspapers really wish to have." Even in Wolff's specialty of official news, "Telegraph Union boasts and can unfortunately boast about receiving all interesting official German information just about as early as the WTB." At the same time, Telegraph Union's lack of official connections gave it "the fullest journalistic room for maneuver" because it did not have to worry about offending German politicians. Telegraph Union could "feed its newspapers with sensations." Diez finished with the gloomy appraisal that "this is a situation that is becoming not only morally unbearable, but also is gradually threatening our business interests in the gravest fashion."[36] Some of this was a self-fulfilling prophecy. As government officials and Wolff's own directors believed that Wolff was weak, they acted like it.

Increasingly, government officials turned to the fourth option of exerting full control over news supply. The government came to believe that the only solution was to control financially the providers of both content and technology. In 1931, Wolff became a fully official news agency, though the transaction occurred in relative secrecy. The Bleichröder Bank—partial owner of Wolff since 1865—still held the majority of shares in Wolff's holding company, Continental-Telegraphen-Compagnie (CTC). Wolff's financial issues had grown acute during World War I, when the government had forced it to disseminate more news without raising subscription costs for newspapers. The government had injected cash in 1919 and 1920 to prevent insolvency and provided a final loan in May 1923, as the company suffered greatly under inflation. By the end of 1927, Wolff requested the cancellation of its remaining debt. In early 1929, the Finance Ministry had yet to decide and so Wolff had simply not paid interest on the loan since the start of 1928.[37] The economic crisis from 1929 compounded the increasing loss of newspaper subscriptions to Telegraph Union. Many newspapers that had subscribed to both services canceled one or the other. The head of Bleichröder Bank since the turn of the century, Paul von Schwabach, decided to sell in 1931. The Foreign Office held the right of first refusal. Upon purchase, the Foreign Office erased any remaining debt, but simultaneously reduced subsidies by approximately one-third to save costs.[38]

The Foreign Office's financial takeover of Wolff's holding company paralleled the Postal Ministry's takeover in January 1931 of news distribution technology through Transradio, a Telefunken subsidiary founded in January 1918 that owned Nauen. A government contract of February 1921 had regulated Transradio's use of the Nauen and Eilvese towers to disseminate wireless news overseas. It had given the government the right to purchase the company's equipment on January 1, 1932, at the price of at least 140 percent of the initial costs. If the government and Transradio failed to reach an agreement, the government was obliged to purchase the equipment at that price.[39] Transradio had suggested abrogating the treaty, as the development of shortwave had devalued the equipment. The Postal Ministry still decided to purchase Transradio. It saw the company as a useful addition to its fifteen radio lines, which would allow it to take over radio and wireless broadcasting overseas. Furthermore, the Postal Ministry wanted to secure Germany's position in overseas communication. The takeover also reinforced the long-standing cooperation between the Foreign Office and Postal Ministry to control news supply.

Despite industry opposition advocating for German cable companies to enter a consortium with foreign companies, the Postal Ministry believed that government ownership provided the best protection from the "danger of foreign infiltration."[40] Furthermore, the Postal Ministry differentiated wireless and radio from cables after its experiences in 1914: radio had no lines for enemies to cut in times of war. Financially, the Postal Ministry found it unfair that the German government currently carried the risks for Transradio, while the private Deutsch-Atlantische Telegraphengesellschaft reaped the dividends. The purchase of Transradio removed the need for subsidies, which had reached 10.8 million Reichsmarks over the previous six years. Operations would also become cheaper, thought the Postal Ministry, because it would amalgamate overseas cables and radio into one.[41] This mirrored the British approach that culminated in the creation of Cable & Wireless in 1932.

With Wolff and technical equipment in its hands, the government controlled much of the news supply system by 1932. This paralleled the 1932
radio reforms giving the government complete control over spoken radio content (see Chapter 4). All these moves were meant to shore up the Brüning
government and, in the long run, protect Weimar democracy. They had the
opposite effect. In the early months after gaining power in January 1933, the
Nazis could take advantage of the key news institutions that already lay in
government hands. Before 1933, the Nazis had relied on local organization,
rallies, and Hitler's personal charisma.[42] While the Nazis had previously not
used news agencies to increase votes or gain power, they too would create
their own domestic news agency to propagate their ideological and cultural
goals.

The Creation of the Deutsches Nachrichtenbüro

For the Nazis, the DNB represented a key method to create and maintain a
new *Volksgemeinschaft*. Ideas of national reawakening (palingenesis) to create
a new, modern community pervaded Nazi ideology.[43] News, and particularly
propaganda, played a key role in disseminating a quasi-religious faith in Nazi
ideals. Even the seemingly anodyne choice of the DNB's name emphasized
a German community. The name Wolff had to be removed, as the agency's
founder, Bernhard Wolff, had been Jewish.[44] The name Telegraph Union
emphasized the technology of the telegraph rather than the product of
news. Deutsches Nachrichtenbüro—German News Office—underscored
the national community that the agency served as well as its product.

Despite the new name, the DNB kept a combination of strengths from
the Telegraph Union and Wolff. It remained a member of the news agency
cartel; it kept significant numbers of personnel; it kept technological infrastructures from both agencies. While the DNB had new philosophical
underpinnings, it did not represent a clean break from the Weimar Republic.
Nazis could be pragmatic as well as dogmatic.

Although the Nazi Party had gained power without a specific news agency
to back it up, officials recognized the value of Wolff. As the agency was majority government-owned, the Nazis changed personnel after establishing
the RMVP (Reichsministerium für Volksaufklärung und Propaganda,
Federal Ministry for Public Enlightenment and Propaganda) on March 13,
1933. The Press Department was incorporated as Department IV, although

a small Press Office remained in the Foreign Office under Otto Dietrich, the chief press officer.[45] The RMVP, or Propaganda Ministry, gained full financial control over Wolff in July 1933 by forcing Delbrück, Schickler & Co. to sell their 49 percent stake in Wolff to Herold Verlagsanstalt, which belonged to the Nazi Eher publishing house.[46]

Choosing personnel was more complicated. The most important criterion was not journalistic skills, but rather support for the Nazis. Jettisoning most of Wolff's upper echelons seemed the clearest and swiftest route to ensure a new direction. Seventy of Wolff's foreign representatives changed at the start of the Nazi period.[47] Of the six board members, Hermann Diez retired in May 1933, while two others were sent on leave and fired. Only Peter The-odor Koch and one other remained. Arthur Rawitzki suffered the cruelest fate. He had worked as the director of Eildienst and conducted major negotiations with European cartel agencies (Agences Alliées) in the mid-1920s. When Wolff's managing director, Heinrich Mantler, had retired in October 1929, he was replaced by commercial director, Hermann Diez. Rawitzki moved from his position as managing director at Eildienst to fill Diez's vacant position as director.

At the start of the Nazi period, Rawitzki surprisingly remained a director, despite being Jewish. Notwithstanding universal appreciation of Rawitzki's skills and efforts, he soon found himself imprisoned and unemployed. In mid-1933, Rawitzki was about to undertake a long-planned journey to England to discuss Wolff's relationship with Reuters. After embarking on the boat to Southampton, Rawitzki was arrested and returned to Germany. He was imprisoned at the police prefecture in inhumane conditions. Crammed into a large communal room with two hundred other prisoners and no beds, Rawitzki had fallen from a position of power into squalor.[48] The reason was simple: the Nazi regime accused him of introducing too many Jews into Wolff.

As so often under the Nazi regime, an opportunistic personal denounce-ment was key. The young new editor for domestic politics, Alfred-Ingemar Berndt, had fought with Rawitzki in the past and seized the moment to rise up the ranks and rid himself of Rawitzki. Berndt was a twenty-eight-year-old stormtrooper (*Sturmführer*) and longtime Nazi Party member who had worked at Wolff for four years. He accused Rawitzki of allying with for-eigners and producing false declarations of imports. Finally, he accused Rawitzki of corresponding with former Jewish editors for Wolff, who were now refugees in Holland, and of conspiring with them on an anti-German campaign. Rawitzki's lawyer had no opportunity to receive any precise information about the accusations. Rawitzki was forced to quit Wolff after his arrest and Wolff sent out an official notice on August 15, 1933, stating that Rawitzki had "retired" from the board.[49] The records provide no trace of his eventual fate.

Personal networks and loyalty to the Nazi Party helped others to climb the career ladder quickly. Rawitzki's accuser, Berndt, became Wolff's domestic editor in chief. Goebbels also entrusted the remaking of Wolff to Berndt. Berndt proved politically reliable, but journalistically incompetent. By 1938, he had aroused such enmity among journalists that Chief Press Officer Otto Dietrich stopped him from leading government press conferences.[50] Wolff's managing director, Hermann Diez, was replaced by Dr. Gustav Albrecht, previously editor of the *Rheinisch-Westfälische Zeitung*, a newspaper once owned by a Nazi supporter Theodor Reismann-Grone, whose son-in-law was Otto Dietrich. Albrecht would become managing director of the DNB in 1939. Adulatory adherence to Nazism ensured meteoric promotion.

Anything less than adulation was insufficient, as Telegraph Union quickly discovered. Although Telegraph Union toned down criticism, it did not produce wholly conformist news and was faster than Wolff. This made it a valuable source of information in the initial months of the Nazi regime.[51] Multiple Nazi press directives forbade newspapers from printing Telegraph Union's version of a particular event or a Hitler speech in September and October 1933.[52] The nationalist sentiment of Telegraph Union was not nationalist enough for the Nazis.

Telegraph Union found itself in increasingly dire financial straits and Hugenberg swiftly lost any political clout to keep the company afloat. Hugenberg and Hitler had long had a tumultuous relationship. From 1929 to 1933, Hugenberg had sometimes tried to coopt Hitler, but Hugenberg had refused to endorse Hitler in the presidential campaign of 1932 that Hitler eventually lost to Hindenburg. In 1933, Hitler coopted Hugenberg. Hitler appointed Hugenberg as minister of agriculture and of economics. This only lasted a few months: Hugenberg was forced to resign in June 1933, after suggesting at the London World Economic Conference that German colonial expansion in Eastern Europe and Africa could end the Great Depression.

Legal measures compounded Hugenberg's political isolation. The promulgation of the Editors Law in October 1933 ruined Hugenberg's vertical integration. The law allowed an individual to own only one newspaper, forcing Hugenberg and powerful provincial press owners to sell off papers. A ban on Telegraph Union's branches in Czechoslovakia and Austria did not help.[53] Political pressure and the promise of retaining Scherl publishing house finally convinced Hugenberg to sell Telegraph Union in October 1933 to the Cautio Trust, which functioned as a cover-up for Nazi ownership. The Nazis had eliminated political dissent in news supply, however negligible.

Hugenberg later lost the rest of his media empire to Nazi holding companies. Wipro was merged with other syndicate services into a DNB department in 1938. Hugenberg held on to Scherl until forced to sell to the Nazi Eher publishing house in 1944. After the war, the Allies' denazification process placed Hugenberg in Category III (less incriminated) for his work in the initial Nazi government and his right-wing control of the press. Following multiple appeals, Hugenberg's status was downgraded to Category V (exonerated) in 1950 due to his advanced age of eighty-five.

The merger between Wolff and Telegraph Union was about business as much as beliefs. It proved the most cost-effective solution for news supply. It would streamline news agency operations as well as lower personnel and distribution costs.[54] As with other newspapers and publishing companies, the Nazis used a holding company to cover their ownership. Cautio Trust—already the holding company for Wolff—merged its 800,000 marks in shares with Telegraph Union shares to create a holding company for the DNB. The contract to create the DNB on December 5, 1933 provided the company with capital stock of 2 million Reichsmarks from seven backers, including Cautio.[55] Of the three editors in chief, the DNB retained just one Wolff employee: the conservative Peter Theodor Koch. Otto Mejer, director of Telegraph Union since 1921, headed the company. As the Nazi Propaganda Ministry wished to retain Wolff's international ties, Koch became responsible for foreign news and relations with foreign agencies. The other two editors in chief were Berndt and Hermann von Ritgen's brother from Telegraph Union, Otto von Ritgen. Meanwhile, the three service editors in chief—Gerike, Hesse, and Frederic von La Trobe—had worked for Telegraph Union.

The merger also enabled the Nazis to purge more employees. The DNB dismissed 240 Wolff employees, while only 120 were forced out of Telegraph Union.[56] A detailed survey examined 168 DNB employees within Germany in May 1934, all of whom had at least one relative working for the DNB. Some 105 had worked for Wolff, 56 for Telegraph Union, 2 had joined the

DNB since it emerged, and 5 were unknown. There were 19 women: stenographers, cleaners, typists, and secretaries. A total of 29 were members of the Nazi Party, SS, SA, or Hitler Youth. The others had obviously fallen into line.[57]

From 1935, prospective employees had to prove that their wives were Aryan to receive a post at the DNB.[58] An investigation in February 1939 found seven employees whose spouses had a Jewish parent or grandparent. Everyone agreed that they had to fire one employee whose wife was fully Jewish. The DNB was allowed to keep five of the seven because they possessed vital skills like speaking Polish or Russian.[59] Personnel choices were partially pragmatic.

Beyond retaining significant numbers of employees, the Nazis merged the infrastructural strengths of Telegraph Union and Wolff. The DNB retained Telegraph Union's branches in Eastern Europe, as it had a far better network of branches there. Meanwhile, the DNB maintained Wolff's superior domestic branch structure of forty-two offices. By 1939, there were forty-five branches, as Germany had annexed the Saar, Austria, and Bohemia / Moravia.[60] The DNB symbolically took over Wolff's infrastructure by establishing its headquarters in Wolff's main office in Berlin's newspaper quarter.

Similarly, the DNB decided to fulfill Wolff's international treaties, rather than Telegraph Union's, though either would theoretically have been possible. The DNB declared itself the legal successor to Wolff's holding company. The DNB thus honored all Wolff's legal contracts.[61] The DNB dissolved Telegraph Union contracts with the reasoning that Telegraph Union had entered liquidation. This caused consternation among the agency's old contractual partners, such as United Press, an American news agency. United Press had hoped that the DNB would honor Telegraph Union's contract, leaving the Reuters-Havas-Associated Press group without a German news agency.[62] The DNB initially tried to deceive Reuters and Havas by continuing to deliver a service to United Press. Nevertheless, Havas and Reuters prevailed, forcing the DNB to honor Wolff's contracts and to stop exchanging news with United Press in 1934.[63] Reuters and Havas had often represented the oppressive system of news that restricted Wolff to the European continent and incurred Germans' wrath for apparently biasing foreign countries against Germany. Yet they remained the obvious international partners, as they and the Agences Alliées continued to supply a far greater number of newspapers.

The Nazis also retained Wolff's international connections in economic news. The Wolff/Eildienst subsidiary, Deutscher Kursfunk, was dissolved on December 31, 1933. The DNB took over commercial services for German papers, leaving Eildienst to supply private customers. The DNB supplied news to the press; Eildienst delivered news to industry.[64] Eildienst continued to run the "Eildienst for Foreign Trade and Foreign Economy," which was affiliated with the Federal Office for Foreign Trade (Reichsstelle für den Außenhandel). A government trustee had purchased Eildienst's shares in 1928, making Nazi control over the agency automatic upon their assumption of power. The DNB soon took over many of Eildienst's main services. From May 1937, the DNB forced Eildienst to stop delivering foreign trade news to newspapers, eliminating its main task. In 1944, the Foreign Office and Economics Ministry took over all Eildienst shares. The company was dissolved in 1951.[65]

To secure their relationship, Havas, Reuters, and the DNB signed a revised contract in March 1934. International arrangements had fundamentally changed with Associated Press's departure in 1933–1934, but European agencies continued to cooperate closely. The three-party treaty between Reuters, Havas, and the DNB mostly replicated the treaty of 1932, though now each news agency was free to exchange news with any European agency in the cartel. This left more space for the DNB to create its own contracts.[66] One of the most important revisions allowed foreign newspaper representatives in Berlin to receive the DNB service and most appear to have taken advantage of the new regulation.[67] Retaining the cartel arrangement gave the Nazis a broad international audience.

Darf Nichts Bringen: DNB at Home

In October 1934, the Agence Havas representative in Berlin, Paul Ravoux, wrote to headquarters in Paris complaining about the DNB service. Ravoux informed Havas that his news reports from Germany could not be as comprehensive as before because the DNB seemed to be withholding vast amounts of information. Its censorship was so tight that only ten months after its establishment, it had acquired its infamous nickname: "Darf Nichts Bringen"—"Not Allowed to Deliver Anything."[68] By 1937, Ravoux could no longer observe the DNB firsthand. The Nazis expelled him from Germany for allegedly false reporting on an influenza epidemic.[69] The DNB abandoned the two guiding principles of news agencies—speed and accuracy—in favor of control and censorship.

The DNB's moniker hinted to the Nazis' transformative understanding of a news agency. Unlike prior news agencies, the DNB both conveyed information to newspapers and collected exclusive information for the state. News agencies had previously functioned as the bottleneck between an event on the ground and its publication as news. The DNB consistently served the government with information that never became news, as censors and constant press directives banned the DNB from forwarding items to the press. The press unknowingly subsidized government intelligence through their subscription to DNB services. The DNB served as the main source for the Nazi party and state, including daily summaries for Hitler and Goebbels.

As an organ of the Nazi state, the DNB displayed many of the classic symptoms of Nazi polycracy. The supply of news was a constant source of contention between Goebbels as head of the Propaganda Ministry, Otto Dietrich as Hitler's chief press officer, Max Amann as head of the Reich Press Chamber, and Joachim von Ribbentrop as foreign minister.[70] The Wehrmacht and Alfred Rosenberg also asserted their claims on news as World War II progressed. These overlapping and competing agencies and leaders alongside diffuse propaganda goals made Nazi propaganda "a tangle of threads, guidelines, discourses and initiatives that were bound together only by vague objectives" such as Nazi hegemony, cementing Hitler's charismatic leadership, and winning the war.[71]

The Propaganda Ministry controlled the DNB with an iron fist, though Goebbels and Dietrich often competed over who could direct news supply within the news agency.[72] By the end of 1937, Goebbels had appointed three "special editors" who censored incoming political news. The "special editors" frequently removed items that appeared damaging to the Nazi reputation or, as World War II progressed, the population's morale. While the volume of news was too high to check all items, the government had never before inspected such a significant portion of news for political content.

Because it provided vital information to the government, the DNB's personnel and budget grew constantly. The Propaganda Ministry explicitly aimed for the DNB to achieve financial solvency through subscriptions from newspapers and private customers. As it had no competitors, it could raise subscription prices and rest assured that newspapers would stay customers, though some smaller newspapers would struggle financially. Wolff and Telegraph Union had always negotiated prices with each newspaper. By contrast, the DNB created standard pricing for subscriptions for the first time from January 1935. From 1936 to 1939, the DNB became financially solvent and claimed that it required no official subsidies. The fiction of financial independence belied the Propaganda Ministry's constant control over its news. Like Wolff during World War I, the DNB could not raise prices once war began, despite increased costs of news collection. It slipped into the red from 1940, particularly because the Nazis demanded far more news from occupied areas.[73] Its only profitable services remained financial and sports news. From 1938, the DNB relied increasingly on the state for subsidies. Goebbels never skimped on these, as Hitler had drawn the lesson from World War I that flagging morale at home had lost the war. To avoid this fate, propaganda remained a budgetary priority.

The increased budget meant that the DNB could expand significantly. Goebbels had the final say in new hires and ensured that DNB employees held Nazi views. At its peak in 1940, there were 856 editors in Berlin, 687 working in branches within the newly expanded Germany; by 1942, there were 261 foreign correspondents. In 1939, the DNB had 31 European and 23 overseas branches.[74] This expansion meant that the DNB used a decreasing amount of news from its news agency partners. Advised by men like Paul Ravoux, these agencies used less and less DNB news, as its propagandistic bent became clear. Reuters and Havas canceled their contract with the DNB on the outbreak of World War II in September 1939. The Associated Press officially broke off relations once Germany declared war on the United States in December 1941. The AP did, however, secretly continue to exchange photographs with Nazi Germany via intermediaries.[75]

The DNB embraced innovative technology to increase its independence. It was the first news agency to use a wireless teleprinter, the Hellschreiber, to eliminate both the technological middleman of cables and the organizational middleman of other agencies. Rudolf Hell invented the Hellschreiber during the 1920s, receiving a patent in 1929.[76] It improved upon cable ticker services that automatically printed words. The Hellschreiber used wireless to transmit around sixty words per minute. This vastly reduced costs, as there was no need to lay cables. It circumvented problems of cut cables that the Germans had experienced during World War I and proved more reliable than speech, which could be distorted and result in mistaken transcriptions.

The Nazis seized on the Hellschreiber to disseminate news directly throughout Germany and Europe. By 1935, all DNB branches abroad used a Hellschreiber to exchange news with Berlin. Domestically, the service was so successful that the Nazis eliminated press news over radio in 1944, though they still collected and disseminated news through telephones, express letters, and telegraphy.[77]

By March 1938, the Hellschreiber sent news abroad to many European news agencies, offering services in German, English, Spanish, and French. Compared to the year before, the share of DNB news increased in eleven of sixteen countries; some changes were astoundingly large. Although Havas still supplied the most news of any agency (with 44.2 percent in 1938), DNB came a close second with 33.6 percent in 1938. Reuters lagged far behind with 18.5 percent in 1938, while the Italian agency, Stefani, supplied a small 3.7 percent.[78] Geographical proximity seems not to have mattered. There was a general increase in the reception of German news throughout the European continent just when Hitler began to expand Germany territorially with the *Anschluss,* or annexation, of Austria in March 1938.

The Nazis believed that the Hellschreiber system was more secure than other methods, because only those with the receiver could see the news. They did not know, however, that the British had gained possession of a Hellschreiber. During the war, the Hellschreiber would help the British at Bletchley Park to learn about German systems for encoding. The Allies' use of the Hellschreiber also greatly aided their own propaganda efforts by enabling them to receive German news at the same time as German newspapers and news agency clients.[79] The device proved as significant for propagandists as the far more famous Enigma was for intelligence.[80]

The DNB not only changed the technology of news dissemination; it also established a highly regulated system of access to news content. Following its dual role as informer of the press and party, the DNB created a color-coded system of news.[81] The press could publish green items verbatim, for example, while white information was for top Nazi leaders only. Prior to 1939, the press received only 33 percent of the DNB's political news; that dropped to 18 percent after 1939.[82] Meticulous control of content gave the DNB a far greater monopoly on government news than Wolff ever had. The other two-thirds of DNB news was for Nazi Party members exclusively. Goebbels also issued daily press directives, ordering journalists what *not* to print as well as which sources to use. Around 40 percent of Nazi press directives up to 1937 forbade journalists from printing particular items.[83] The DNB thus filtered information to fit Nazi Party needs more than inform the population.

The DNB also molded all official items emanating from the government. It soon began to distribute so-called *Auflagenachrichten,* probably best translated as "requirement news," though *Auflage* also means "circulation" or "edition." Newspapers were required to print these items as given. Newspapers often had to reserve their first two pages for *Auflagenachrichten*, removing the freedom of news arrangement from editors. Speeches had to be printed in the form that the DNB forwarded to editorial offices, even if journalists had been present and taken notes. This allowed the DNB to smooth over any infelicitous statements or ineloquent phrasing. It also meant that the DNB easily adapted to any new demands of Nazi propaganda, whether that was imbuing the population with National Socialism during the 1930s or keeping up morale during World War II. Radio also relied on the DNB for news. These policies created "staggeringly comprehensive, but unwieldy, press directives," as one historian has put it.[84]

Like other news agencies, the DNB produced many different services. This increased to 150 services by 1936. It included services that explicitly directed editorial offices on the style and tone of their content, building on the Telegraph Union's provision of commentary to the provinces. The DNB's most important service was its general political news service (Politischer Nachrichtendienst), which sent around 25,000 words daily to customers by 1944.[85] In the mid-1930s, 89 percent of all newspapers printed used the general political news service, an incredible market dominance.[86]

DNB news became the major source for almost all German newspapers.[87] The Nazis had swiftly established tight control over news supply for radio and the press. The Editors Law, Goebbels's constant directives to editors, and daily press conferences left newspapers little room to maneuver, especially on political topics. The vast majority of newspapers, 84 percent in 1934, had a circulation of less than ten thousand.[88] As they could not afford their own correspondents in Berlin, they relied on the DNB for everything except local reporting. By 1939, the Nazis had also purchased two-thirds of German newspapers and magazines through Eher Verlag, run by Max Amann. Newspapers rarely indicated the origins of their news, if at all.[89] They often printed DNB news verbatim to avoid the wrath of the Nazi state, leaving readers with no means to trace the creation of their news.

While most newspapers and editors received only DNB news and followed Nazi press directives assiduously, one newspaper subtly informed readers of machinations behind the scenes. Although newspapers had listed Wolff as a source since the mid-nineteenth century, this practice died down somewhat after 1900. The *Frankfurter Zeitung* consciously listed the DNB as its news source to indicate bias.[90] An exception to the general rule of Nazi control over ownership and content, the *Frankfurter Zeitung* was still independently owned by I. G. Farben until 1938 and could exert relative autonomy during the first years of the Nazi regime, ironically because of I. G. Farben's close relationship with the Nazi government. Other newspapers did not have such leeway.

Readers did not react positively to Nazi measures and complained bitterly about the monotony of their news. Gestapo reports as early as March 1935 noted that "the uniformity of the press is felt to be unbearable by the people and also in particular by those who are National Socialist in their views."[91] Circulation numbers provide one proxy measure of the population's reaction to Nazi control of news. Newspaper circulation stagnated and the share of the Nazi press declined after mid-1934. Larger newspapers became more important, growing from 8 percent to 44 percent of the market. Smaller, local newspapers declined, ensuring greater uniformity of the press landscape and reducing the amount of local news.[92] Around two hundred newspapers had disappeared as early as 1936.[93]

The stagnation indicated a turn away from German newspapers as the main guides to the world. Germans increasingly saw Nazi entertainment as escapism. The Nazis found that entertainment programs were more popular and increased musical broadcasts from 61.6 percent of airtime in 1935 to 69.3 percent in 1937.[94] News constituted only 9.9 percent of radio programming in 1938.[95] Some citizens purchased foreign newspapers, especially German-language newspapers from Switzerland. The Nazis countered this by banning newspaper sellers from distributing foreign papers in the mid-1930s, only creating more suspicion among the population. Others illegally listened to foreign radio in numbers running into the millions.[96] Particularly after 1941 and the invasion of the Soviet Union, Nazi propaganda failed to resonate with the German civilian population's lives.[97]

Citizens constantly sought news. But they sought it from unofficial sources like gossip and rumor. In French-occupied territory, the DNB was known as "derniers nouveaux bobards" (our latest fibs) or "diffusez nos bobards" (spread our fibs).[98] This only increased as World War II progressed and the tide of war turned against the Axis powers. From 1943, the Allies airdropped leaflets over Germany, providing an alternative source of information. The British also operated a radio station in German from 1943 to April 1945. The station received DNB news through a Hellschreiber that no one in Germany knew the British possessed. Programs mixed DNB news with lies to try to convert Germans to the Allied cause.[99] Finally, the reality of destruction around Germans and the increasing number of soldiers' deaths created a stark dissonance between official propaganda and lived experience.

From October 1944, the DNB swiftly declined, canceling thirty-two of its news services and losing domestic branches as the Allies advanced through Germany. On February 3, 1945, the DNB headquarters in the center of Berlin burned to the ground after an Allied bomb, destroying all the archival documents housed there except a few files left in the cellar. The DNB operated briefly from a suburb in southeast Berlin. A dozen loyal servants worked for the DNB even after the Soviets occupied the suburban headquarters on April 24. The DNB office in Hamburg disseminated the agency's last report on May 2, though there were no German newspapers left to print it. After the German surrender on May 9, the Allies quickly confiscated the DNB's assets. As DNB employees were deemed state officials, the Allies conducted denazification investigations, classifying them as category IV or V (fellow travelers or exonerated).[100] The DNB was officially dissolved in 1956.

Conclusion

Nazis and Weimar elites disagreed about the concept of public opinion. But they agreed on the mechanisms to control it. Bureaucrats and politicians alike were convinced of the "persuasive power of the press" and devoted considerable energy to influencing it.[101] The Nazis' hyperactive grip over content reflected their overestimation of the effects of the media and their underestimation of the population's ability to think for itself.

As in other arenas, the Nazis did not step into a "power vacuum" (*Machtvakuum*), but rather into an "order vacuum" (*Ordnungsvakuum*), as one German historian has put it.[102] Ministerial infighting at the end of the Weimar Republic had undermined any coherent response to challenges from right-wing news sources. This infighting was based on an erroneous belief that German citizens acted as their newspapers directed. Heinrich Brüning's government purchased the majority of Wolff's shares in 1931 to control news more tightly. That, Brüning believed, might shore up citizens' support for government policies. Social Democrats like Carl Severing similarly overestimated the government's importance in determining how citizens chose their sources of information and how they interpreted news. What became clear in the early 1930s was not the power of Wolff, but rather the state's inability to dictate opinions to newspaper readers through news agencies.

The Nazis may not have needed the support of a specific news agency or many newspapers to come to power. Once in power, however, they too saw the benefits of controlling a central node of communication. Control over news agencies enabled the Nazis to reach the entire population far more efficiently than by influencing individual journalists or newspapers. This control could begin with Wolff because the government already held financial control over the agency. The Nazis soon extended this to Telegraph Union. The merger between Wolff and Telegraph Union to create the DNB amalgamated the two news agencies' approaches and infrastructure. It retained the idea that a news agency was the key bottleneck in news provision.

After 1933, the DNB became the behemoth in domestic reporting, removing the competition in news that had characterized the later Weimar Republic. But it became more of an informer to the Nazi state than an information service for the German population. Despite these sweeping domestic changes, the Nazis accelerated Weimar policies for disseminating news abroad. In contrast to domestic reform, the Nazi regime kept geographical and technological strategies and priorities from the Weimar Republic. News agencies like Transocean would reach audiences around the world through networks behind the newspapers.

THE WORLD WAR OF WORDS

ust after midnight on June 6, 1944, came "the first true word of invasion." The Allies were landing on French beaches to open up another front in the war. A few days earlier, the Associated Press (AP) and American radio networks had mistakenly announced the landing after someone in London had transmitted what should have been a practice flash bulletin. Now, the AP could report the real D-day landings. But the news "came from the enemy."[1] The first AP bulletin breaking the news of D-day reported that "the German news agency Transocean said today in a broadcast that the Allied invasion has begun."[2] American radio stations proceeded with caution, but still interrupted their programs to bring their listeners the story. Journalists soon confirmed the report with Allied sources. A Nazi news agency had informed Americans about the beginning of the end of World War II.

Transocean's prominence did not come from nowhere. It built on thirty years of German investment in news agencies. The agency had been founded just before World War I to transmit news from Germany around the world. Ever since, it had tried to operate as a private company, disguising its government backers. Transocean's news had reached the United States before 1917; it stoked anger from British press baron Lord Northcliffe in the 1920s. In the late 1930s, Federal Bureau of Investigation (FBI) director J. Edgar Hoover pursued it for espionage and infiltrating Latin America. Journalists, politicians, and spies fretted about Transocean's increasing success in China. Transocean's news reached places where Nazis had no boots on the ground. It was a critical tool of foreign policy.

Nazi investment in Transocean meant doubling down on communications as a tool of foreign policy. This was hardly surprising. The Nazis saw themselves as a "propagandistic state."[3] Marketing for the Nazi brand lay at the heart of their political and economic strategies. Alongside propaganda films by directors like Leni Riefenstahl, parades, and posters, news agencies played a more hidden role. Nazis hoped that Transocean could achieve two main goals. First, it would undermine British, French, and American news on the world stage. This would bestow a *political* advantage. Second, wireless would enable Germans to reach vital export markets directly, garnering them *economic* advantages.

These beliefs made news from Germany central to Nazi ambitions; measuring those ambitions became central too. By the late 1930s, the Foreign Office created reports on the number of items, words, or characters printed. As news agencies paid for transmission by the word, measuring output in words seemed the most logical test of efficiency and impact. Table after table compared monthly increases and decreases in the percentage of German news printed in cities and countries across the world. No report examined the placement of news or investigated why particular newspapers printed which stories. The more Transocean news printed, ran the underlying logic, the more readers would be convinced of the Nazi cause. French, American, and British journalists, politicians, and spies held similar views. Quantity mattered over quality.

Transocean's quantity depended fundamentally on wireless and radio. The centrality of wireless was also clear to foreign elites, inspiring Britain and France in particular to improve their technological capabilities. By the time World War II broke out, Transocean was widespread in regions from the Middle East to South Africa, South America, and East Asia. Most observers could not see the world war of words. But there was no escaping news from Germany.

Paranoia and Propaganda

In 1936, a report by MI5, Britain's domestic intelligence service, concluded that Transocean was "now daily flooding the whole world with news." The Germans had "carefully considered their limitations on the field of propaganda during the Great War and have taken steps to remedy this defect." Transocean's very purpose was "to develop in peace-time a comprehensive service of reliable news mingled with propaganda, so that its recipients would continue in war-time to accept it."[4] The British were convinced of continuities from World War I: they even dug out a report on Transocean from 1916 to inform their policy in May 1939.[5]

The British were not completely wrong about continuities. From the start, Transocean's success relied on government subsidies of communications technology to create a German wireless route around the world. Transocean was founded in 1913 as a coalition between German industrialists and politicians like Gustav Stresemann and Hjalmar Schacht. After disputes over what news and places to prioritize, the industrialists had split from the government in 1916 to found their own news organization, Deutscher Überseedienst. Transocean became a government operation. Its news had been printed in hundreds of American newspapers until the United States entered the war in April 1917. By 1918, Transocean's service could be received in English around the world. Transocean and Wolff agreed by the end of the war that Transocean could send wireless news anywhere in the world except the United States and Europe (see Chapter 2).

After the war, technology was Transocean's unique selling point. Wireless meant that "we are more or less standing in the middle of a revolution in world news," wrote Transocean's editor in chief Wilhelm Schwedler in 1922.[6] Wireless would provide "the path to freedom" from British and French dominance of news and, by extension, international politics.[7] By 1922, Schwedler had already seen how wireless had worked. Even British ships took Transocean, causing a scandal that reached all the way to the House of Commons.

In late 1921, Lord Alfred Northcliffe sailed from Great Britain to Asia as part of a round-the-world tour. A press baron akin to William Randolph Hearst and Alfred Hugenberg, Northcliffe had founded the *Daily Mail* in 1896, the *Daily Mirror* seven years later, and bought the London *Times* in 1908. Northcliffe combined innovative features, like social gossip and women's columns, to create immensely successful papers. In 1917–1918, the politically conservative Northcliffe served as the British government's director for propaganda.[8] Germans saw him as the embodiment of Allied propaganda.

Northcliffe's journey to Asia convinced him that Germany was still fighting a world war of words. Northcliffe had traveled on a British liner, the P&O Nellore. But the Nellore's wireless operators picked up and printed news from Transocean for their passengers. Since its inception, German wireless had focused on the sea. The Imperial Post Office had established press news for ships from the Norddeich wireless station in 1907. Wolff had sent this news until World War I. Transocean resumed the service in November 1918, sending five hundred words daily in English by 1921 as well as one daily service in French and one in German. State subsidies enabled Transocean to offer its news for free.[9] British services cost money.

A free daily five-hundred-word news service seemed an added bonus for ships, no matter the news' origins. Lord Northcliffe disagreed. When he landed in Colombo, Sri Lanka on January 2, 1922, Northcliffe complained to a foreign correspondent from his London *Times* that Germany "may not have money for reparations, but she is expending immense resources in propaganda in the Far East by daily wireless from Berlin." Northcliffe claimed that the daily wireless service was "hungrily absorbed by vernacular writers in all Far Eastern countries, where countless wireless stations now exist." There was no evidence for these claims, but Northcliffe extrapolated from one ship to the entire region. Northcliffe had been "a close student of the notorious Berlin wireless during the war" and believed "that the same minds are writing the present mischievous dispatches." He was not wrong: Transocean's staff remained mostly the same. Northcliffe was irate that the Nellore had used news from Germany that "consists largely of misleading statements, and actual lies, about Egypt, India, the Washington Conference, Ireland, Japan, China, the responsibility for the Great War, and the gloomy condition of British trade."[10]

Northcliffe's views appeared in the *Times* and *Daily Mail* the next day. The Northcliffe-owned *Times* investigated thoroughly: it subscribed to Transocean for one week in mid-January and one in mid-February 1922. The *Times* criticized Transocean for bad English and using so much jargon that the *Times* writers had to read some parts four or five times to understand them: "The chances seem to be that Nauen would be unable to recognize its own children if it saw them in their last transformation in print."[11] A German envoy to Beijing agreed a few years later, giving these examples of sentences from a Transocean bulletin: "Even the communists confinded [*sic*] themselves within order" and "the Hitlerites have filed protest to the Ministry of the Interior and threaten to proclaim the election guilty."[12] Transocean's news was not always high quality. The service was also an omnibus and not adapted for regional differences.

Still, articles on Transocean appeared in places as far-flung as Italy, Japan, and China.[13] Newspapers barely reported the comments in France, but politicians worried about the spread of false German news, especially in the occupied Rhineland and the Ruhr. In late February 1922, the notoriously anti-German French prime minister Raymond Poincaré ordered the French radio station at Bordeaux to keep a constant watch on news from Nauen and to correct any news that could be detrimental to France.[14]

British politicians also voiced their concerns. On March 6, 1922, Percy Angier Hurd, the first of four generations of Hurds to sit in the House of Commons, asked if Prime Minister David Lloyd George "knew that the German wireless Press service from Nauen was spreading anti-British and anti-French propaganda around the globe."[15] Hurd had anxiously asked the postmaster general the previous year if Britain was making progress in wireless compared to Germany, France, and the United States.[16] In 1922, Hurd posed his question on Transocean to Austen Chamberlain, at that time leader of the Conservatives in the House of Commons and head of the Office of the Lord Privy Seal. Chamberlain replied that Lloyd George did know about Nauen and that the Foreign Office News Department broadcast three wireless messages daily from the General Post Office wireless station at Leafield. Chamberlain claimed that these messages were "reproduced in most European countries and by ships at sea" and that they would hopefully reach East Asia once the wireless station at Cairo was complete.[17]

The Germans' apparent advantage spurred Britain's urgency. Unlike multiple British strategic cable committees' energetic efforts to establish an "All-Red Route" of submarine cables around the world in the early twentieth century, the wireless subcommittee moved lethargically.[18] German efforts pushed Reuters to cooperate with the Post Office to begin wireless transmissions in 1922, though these mainly broadcast commercial news under the name Reuterian.[19]

The British remained wary of German wireless. In 1924, the British Embassy in Berlin asked for information on government or government-subsidized wireless services transmitted from Germany for foreign consumption. Obscuring its involvement, the German Foreign Office merely sent the calendar for German radio traffic from the private transmission towers of Nauen and Eilvese.[20] The Foreign Office encouraged ships to take Transocean news for free, noting in 1928 that it was in Germany's political interests for Transocean news to be disseminated as widely as possible.[21] The government also guaranteed Transocean the best times to radio its services.

Transocean's news already spread far beyond the sea. Transocean broadcast directly to Japan until the Japanese government forbade Transocean from transmitting to its wireless station in the mid-1920s. The major newspaper in Buenos Aires, *La Prensa,* started taking Transocean as early as 1925. Ships still subscribed to the Transocean service.

"Continuity was as important as change" for the Nazis, as historian Richard Evans has noted.[22] The Nazis overhauled domestic communications by creating the DNB. There was more continuity in news sent abroad, where Transocean's structures, personnel, and technology stayed similar. Nazi groups abroad reported that the main Nazi newspaper, the *Völkischer Beobachter,* was unsuitable for daily propaganda outside Germany.[23] Transocean worked better, particularly as it seemed to be independent. While Jewish employees were removed, almost all other personnel stayed. Karl Schulte remained managing director until 1943. Wilhelm Schwedler continued as editor in chief until his death in 1936. The Nazis also kept Transocean's geographical priorities: South America, East Asia, the Middle East, parts of Africa, and the seas (see Figure 12).

Where the Nazis intervened heavily was in news production and financing. Between 1933 and 1936, government subsidies to Transocean doubled and then skyrocketed.[24] The share of Transocean's outgoings covered by its own incomings sank from one-third in 1933 to under 5 percent by 1941.[25] Just as Eher Verlag disguised Nazi ownership of most media, the state kept Transocean's government ownership a secret.

The *appearance* of financial and political independence remained important. A report in March 1933 noted that "the basis for successes in the dissemination of news abroad is the trust of consumers (news bureaus and newspapers) in the deliverers of news."[26] The report argued that Transocean could only infiltrate foreign markets and compete with Reuters, Havas, and American news agencies if it seemed financially independent. Schwedler's successor, Friedrich von Homeyer, called it a "foreign political necessity" to have another news agency besides the official DNB, "which is technically in the position to operate worldwide, but is still available as a propaganda organ for Reich politics in every way."[27] Even after World War II, some Americans believed that Transocean was only semiofficial.[28]

The British were less naive. Transocean reached Tehran, Tiflis, Jerusalem, and Cairo from the 1930s as part of an effort to spur local resistance to the British.[29] In Africa, Transocean focused on former German colonies. It sent news to South-West Africa as well as South Africa (which had taken over administration of former German colony South-West Africa as a League of Nations mandate territory after World War I). The British foreign secretary and later prime minister, Anthony Eden, was appalled to discover in late 1937 that Reuters distributed Transocean in South Africa.[30] The items were not labeled "Transocean" and South African authorities were ignorant of the German connection.[31] In a secret memo to the British cabinet, Eden

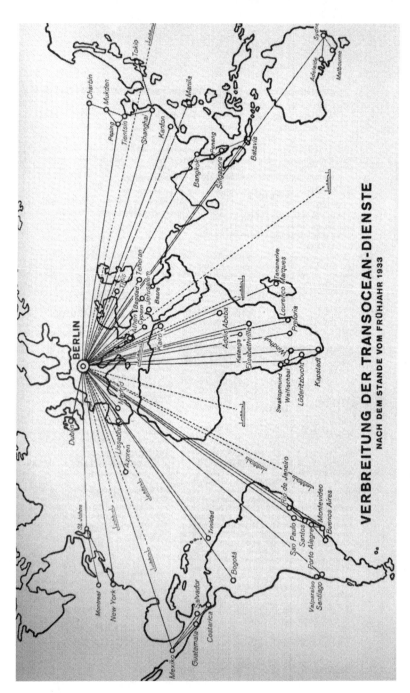

FIGURE 12. Map of Transocean services, 1933. Courtesy of Bundesarchiv Berlin, BArch R901/60792.

noted that Reuters amplified British news abroad. But Reuters's service was often "not news seen through British eyes at all, but actually news seen through the eyes of foreign Governments." The most troubling example for Eden was Reuters's supply to South Africa of the "Government controlled and propagandist" Transocean. Eden recognized that "this system of news exchange, on which all modern international news agencies depend, cannot be changed." Still, the British government needed to "mitigate, so far as possible, the unfavourable results" through better coordination with Reuters and better wireless stations to disseminate news abroad.[32]

Nazi governance of the press mirrored other areas of policy: it was plagued by polycracy, or overlapping and competing competencies between departments. After the Propaganda Ministry was created in March 1933, most of the Press Department, including Transocean, was transferred from the Foreign Office to the Propaganda Ministry as Department IV. The Foreign Office (re)gained power over international news supply after Joachim von Ribbentrop became foreign minister in 1938. Until then, the Foreign Office had retained considerable autonomy, despite Hitler's view that it was an "intellectual garbage dump."[33] After 1938, Ribbentrop rebuilt the decimated Press Department within the Foreign Office, putting him in direct conflict with Goebbels regarding who would inform Hitler about foreign affairs. Ribbentrop increased his influence by paying for Transocean correspondents from the budgets for embassies. Hitler solidified these overlapping competencies at the outbreak of World War II, when he ordered the Foreign Office to deal with propaganda in neutral and enemy countries.[34]

Press policy intertwined continuously with infrastructure. Even the outbreak of World War II relied on radio infrastructure: the director of the Gestapo, Reinhard Heydrich, ordered SS troops to pretend to be Poles and attack the German radio tower at Gleiwitz as a pretext for invading Poland. The false flag attack on August 31, 1939, became known as the Gleiwitz Incident. The organizer of the Gleiwitz Incident, Alfred Naujoks, recalled at the Nuremberg trials that Heydrich had emphasized publicity: "Actual proof of these attacks of the Poles is needed for the foreign press, as well as for German propaganda purposes."[35] Nazi news agencies would be key to spreading propaganda throughout the war.

The polycracy in Nazi propaganda made it less effective. Initially, the DNB tried to muscle into the Chinese market. Transocean's head of operations in East Asia in the mid-1930s, Edmund Fürholzer, called the DNB "an expensive waste of energy."[36] The DNB regarded Transocean as "competition."[37] Goebbels explicitly encouraged that competition, calling it in July 1940 "the securest guarantee that they [the two agencies] do not flag in their efforts." He implied that Transocean was more effective, noting that the DNB often "largely failed" in its reporting.[38] The DNB operated in Europe, though its correspondents overseas gathered news in places like China. By 1935, the DNB persuaded the government to forbid Transocean to conduct activities in Europe, though Transocean's secret subsidiary in Europe since 1919, Europapress, helped with news gathering.[39] Transocean also maintained a successful photo service in Europe.[40] The DNB's attempts to disseminate its news in China never achieved real success.[41] Transocean's attempts would.

Although the division of labor between the DNB and Transocean was purposefully unclear, the two agencies developed a modus vivendi to supply different news at home and abroad. Schwedler insisted that Transocean had to adapt news from Nazi newspapers for foreign audiences because "outside [of Germany] other principles simply apply."[42] More pliable editors in chief, Friedrich von Homeyer (1936–1942) and Erich Schneyder (1942–1945), increasingly followed Goebbels's ideas of news as propaganda presenting the Nazi cause. The DNB could not conceal major events, but tried to put its own spin on them for foreign publics. The DNB reported for foreign publics on the fall of Norway in April 1940 and Rudolf Hess's landing in England in May 1941; editors in Germany were not allowed to print these reports because they were explicitly meant for foreign consumption.[43] Foreign consumption of Transocean in South America and East Asia would cause particular concern for Germany's competitors.

Pro-Axis Propaganda: Transocean in South America

In July 1941, a trial began in the United States of America, but there were no human defendants. On the stand was a news agency, or "espionage agency"—Transocean.[44] The trial was the culmination of three years of dogged investigation spearheaded by J. Edgar Hoover. The notorious first and longest-serving director of the FBI, founded in 1935, had started to worry about Transocean as soon as it had reopened an office in New York in 1938. Hoover instructed his agents to draw network diagrams of Transocean agents' acquaintances and even to infiltrate Transocean bureaus in Latin America.[45] Letters flew back and forth between Hoover and Attorney General Robert H. Jackson, as Hoover pushed to prosecute the Transocean agents in the United States.[46] Hoover did not see Transocean just as a news agency; he saw it as a cover-up for Nazi espionage in Latin America.

Previous accounts of American involvement in South America have generally dismissed American fears of Nazi infiltration.[47] But understanding how men like Hoover read the news explains American concerns. Though they fought on different sides, Americans like Hoover shared German assumptions about news. They equated published opinion with public opinion; they concluded that more Nazi news inevitably meant more Nazi influence. As the spread of a country's news was often linked to political, economic, and military prowess, Transocean's encroachment into South America seemed very serious indeed.

By 1941, Hoover got his prosecutions. The Foreign Agents Registration Act (FARA) of 1938 provided the means. FARA was enacted in 1938 after multiple Nazi-inspired or Nazi-encouraged groups had emerged in the United States in the 1930s. One group, the German American Bund founded in 1936, attracted tens of thousands of members, leading Congress to worry that the Nazis were encouraging Germans in the United States or Americans of German descent to undermine American democracy. In response, Congress passed legislation establishing FARA.

FARA decreed that agents of a foreign principal register with the State Department. An agent of a foreign principal was "any person who acts or engages or agrees to act as a public-relations counsel, publicity agent, or as agent, servant, representative, or attorney for a foreign principal or for any domestic organization subsidized directly or indirectly in whole or in part by a foreign principal."[48] The German embassy in the United States criticized the act as targeting Nazis—which it did, along with Communists. The embassy interpreted the act to mean that foreign reporters only needed to register under the act if they disseminated news articles in the United States, whether paid or unpaid. Men like Sir Willmott Lewis, Washington correspondent of the London *Times*, had registered. The German embassy thought that Agence Havas should register too because it had disseminated free articles in the United States for some time. The German Railroads Information Office and North German Lloyd shipping company registered. Transocean's manager in North America, Manfred Zapp, and Transocean representative Günther Tonn did not.[49]

Hoover was convinced that Transocean had contravened FARA. His concerns sparked an investigation by the House Un-American Activities

Committee (HUAC) into Transocean's activities in North and South America.[50] Alongside FARA, HUAC was created in 1938 to investigate subversive communist or fascist activity. Transocean was one of its first targets. In 1940, HUAC's conclusion seemed to vindicate Hoover: "When Hitler took over the Government of Germany, he transformed the Transocean News Service into an agency for the dissemination of propaganda in foreign countries and also utilized it as an organization that could, with a minimum of suspicion, engage in espionage activities."[51]

In March 1941, the Federal Grand Jury of the District of Columbia approved an arrest warrant for Zapp and Tonn, indicting them for failing to fulfill the Foreign Agents Registration Act.[52] After the indictment, Zapp and Tonn were required to testify before an investigative committee. Zapp claimed Transocean was a normal business that received no government subsidies. He was an ordinary businessman who did not need to register under FARA: businesspeople were exempt as long as they were engaged in "bona fide trade or commerce."[53] This was a lie: Zapp had been a member of the Nazi Party since May 1933 and Transocean was very much government-subsidized.

The case proceeded to trial. But Zapp and Tonn never took the stand. Soon after their arrest, they were released and returned to Germany. This was probably in a prisoner swap with two United Press (UP) agents, whom the Gestapo had arrested in Berlin several weeks after the Grand Jury indictment.[54] The trial continued in July 1941 even without live defendants.[55] The court found that the German Foreign Office controlled Transocean and subsidized 93 percent of its activities. One witness, a Swedish correspondent in New York, testified that Transocean aimed to transmit news to South America that might be "harmful to the United States."[56] The trial even formed a central piece of evidence of Nazi cunning in a book published in 1942 in the United States, *The Nazi Underground in South America*.[57] (Ironically, the American Associated Press at the same time made a secret deal to exchange photographs with Nazi Germany; the deal was approved by a U.S. censorship office.)[58]

Transocean's main impact in the United States came not from its news. Zapp had never intended to distribute much news there; he mainly wished to compete with Associated Press and United Press services to South America by sending breaking stories from North America.[59] Along with other organizations like the Foreign Organization of the Nazi Party, leaders such as Joseph Goebbels hoped that more Nazi news in the South American press would increase sympathy for the Nazi cause. Transocean's news was supposed to provide a service that no self-respecting South American newspaper could do without.

Transocean's main impact in the United States was to spur American intervention in Latin America out of fear that governments there might maintain neutrality or even become pro-Axis. The U.S. government had established an Office of the Coordinator of Inter-American Affairs (CIAA) in 1940 to block German attempts at subversive radio propaganda and underhand news activities. Alongside Transocean, the Nazis had invested in shortwave music and entertainment programs since 1933, increasing the number of people working on foreign radio to 150 by 1939; they only started to push Nazi ideology from 1938. In October 1939, these Nazi radio programs were available in eighteen languages; by summer 1940, it was thirty-one.[60]

In 1941, the U.S. government ramped up its response: it created the Office of the Coordinator of Information to start the government's first international direct radio programming with Voice of America (VOA). VOA was meant to counter German propaganda and support British efforts through the BBC. By 1945, VOA was sending programs in forty languages, though half its services stopped after the war. British, German, and American radio secretly competed to reach populations around the world and to counteract each other's news in what is often called the "black radio" war.[61]

Once Zapp returned to Germany, he stayed in the news agency business, but switched to work for the DNB until he was seconded to the Foreign Office in June 1944 to work for Nazi propagandist Colin Ross.[62] Ross was no stranger to HUAC either. Ross had registered as a Nazi propagandist in 1938 when he toured the United States, giving speeches at think tanks in Chicago, New York, and San Francisco. A HUAC investigation in 1939, however, indicated that Ross had not reported the full scope of his activities: he had traveled in a chauffeured Mercedes with motion picture cameras and far more money than his reported earnings.[63] HUAC found Ross liable for prosecution as he had tried to influence American citizens against democracy. The German embassy in Washington, DC, called the HUAC report an "invented product" solely meant to justify the extension of HUAC into 1940.[64] Ross remained safely outside the United States and the reach of American law.

Transocean's interest in Latin America had started long before the Nazi period. The Nazis built on prior infrastructure to infiltrate the South American news market far more than German economic, political, or emigrant connections might suggest. Although South America was the second most popular choice for German immigrants in the nineteenth century after the United States, only thousands rather than millions journeyed there. German investments similarly lagged behind Britain and America.[65] In news, however, South America became a battleground between German challenges to the international communications order, French fears about losing news territory, and American aspirations for controlling their "backyard."

News dissemination to South America had long occupied the German Foreign Office. Alfred Hugenberg had discussed with Wolff's Director Heinrich Mantler in 1912 whether Krupp could provide subsidies to influence the South American press.[66] While the continent remained a "sideshow" in Weimar Germany's trade policies, the Foreign Office pursued cultural diplomacy, recruiting private travelers.[67] Colin Ross had in fact traveled to Latin America in the 1920s as a semiofficial representative to Germans living there.

Considered neutral until 1876 in cartel contracts, South America was thereafter designated Havas territory (though Reuters kept branch offices in Latin America).[68] During World War I, the two major American news agencies, Associated Press and United Press, began to encroach on South America. In November 1918, Havas agreed to allow AP what the new cartel contract termed a "free hand" in South America.[69] Havas quickly found itself at a disadvantage due to the AP's better financing and American government support for cable construction. By the early 1930s, however, Havas and AP could not afford to compete: Transocean and United Press provided stiff competition. In 1933, Havas and AP signed a confidential agreement to supply South American newspapers with a joint service; in 1935, they signed a contract to coordinate their action.[70]

It took concerted efforts over the 1920s and 1930s for Transocean to enter South America. At first, it had little representation and financing as well as technical problems with longwave wireless. Transocean continued its wartime cooperation with the private German company, Telefunken. Transocean's sole representative in South America after World War I, Dr. Albert Haas, concentrated on Argentina and Brazil. In 1921, Transocean passed distribution duties to Hermann Tjarks, the owner of several German newspapers in Buenos Aires.[71] After Telefunken had built Station Monte Grande for radio transmission near Buenos Aires in May 1924, Telefunken's subsidiary responsible for radio, Transradio, signed a contract to exchange radio telegrams with its Argentine equivalent, Transradio Internacional Compañia Radiotelegrafica Argentina.[72]

In 1925, Transocean achieved its first great success, persuading *La Prensa* in Buenos Aires to take its service.[73] *La Prensa* had over 200,000 subscribers and was considered one of the most important newspapers in South America, if not the world. In 1927, one German journalist praised *La Prensa*'s interest in German affairs as "a fruit of the Transocean service."[74] By 1931, Transocean was sufficiently well known in South America that a representative landed an interview with Sir Eric Drummond, Secretary-General of the League of Nations. Drummond warmly thanked Transocean for the publicity raised by the interview, which he had witnessed during his visit to South America. Drummond even offered to repeat "the experiment" again, as the interview had proved "of real use in clearing up certain misunderstandings" about the League in Latin America.[75]

Transocean's cooperation with Telefunken fostered technological innovation. A history of Transradio noted in 1928 that sending Transocean's messages overseas had "necessitated the creation and introduction of measures . . . which greatly contributed to developing wireless overseas traffic into an excellent and reliable branch of communications [*Nachrichtenwesen*]."[76] Transradio's innovations included erecting another transmitter in Nauen to reach South America and increasing the strength of transmitters as well as the speed and reliability of radio telegrams. This built on Telefunken's construction of forty-eight of the ninety radio towers in Latin America by 1918.[77] Nauen created the longest ever radio-telephonic connection in 1927 between Berlin and Buenos Aires. Nauen was also the first European wireless station to transmit over shortwave, spurred by the incentive to reach South America.

Transocean broadcast via shortwave from 1929. Shortwave was more reliable and less affected by atmospheric disturbances. More reliability meant more Transocean news. German-language papers took the service. So did newspapers like *La Razón* in Buenos Aires, which got the news over a shortwave wireless receiver provided by Transocean.[78] By 1930, Transocean sent out multiple shortwave services: a German service for ships and one for German newspapers abroad, three English services, two in French, and one in Spanish for Spain and South America. A total of 110 newspapers from 20 countries subscribed.[79]

The specter of Transocean spurred French technological innovation too. Over the late 1920s, Havas subsidized cable costs for South American

FIGURE 13. French wireless towers in Buenos Aires, 1933. Courtesy of
Archives Nationales, France, AN 5AR/208.

companies and increased the volume of its news to combat AP, United Press,
and Transocean.[80] But it became clear that wireless was needed. Havas correspondents in South America pushed for French wireless receivers to counteract "German propaganda."[81] They argued that radio was "an incomparable
organ of French propaganda" because Havas could avoid paying foreign cable
companies. The matter became acute with the Great Depression, as the
French worried about retaining gold within France. By 1930, Havas used
shortwave too. French wireless towers soared above the relatively flat Buenos
Aires skyline; they were easy to spot from anywhere in the city (see Figure 13).
Yet the wireless remained below par: correspondents complained in 1931 that
Havas in Buenos Aires had "amateur equipment, pure and simple" operated
by men with "amateur mentality."[82]

The Nazis maintained interest in Argentina for trade and propaganda.
Transocean's director, Friedrich von Homeyer, visited South America in 1938 to
negotiate directly with newspapers and the Argentine news agency, ANDI
(Agencia Noticiosa Argentina). Accompanied by Hermann Tjarks, the long-

time owner of the German-language *La Plata Zeitung,* Homeyer tried unsuccessfully to woo the AP's main newspaper in Buenos Aires, *La Nacion.*[83]
Homeyer did create cooperation with ANDI, although the agency was far
less used in Argentina than United Press.[84] Transocean swiftly expanded its
office in Buenos Aires to thirty-one workers and increased its branches in
South America from four to twelve by 1940.

Transocean's approach varied in each South American country. In some,
like Honduras, the German embassy or consul distributed the news to newspapers. In others, Transocean adopted a different strategy, probably because
it could not find a local contact to forward its items to newspapers. In Brazil,
Transocean created and subsidized a local news agency to distribute its
news. Telefunken had erected a radio tower near Rio de Janeiro. As in Argentina, its subsidiary, Transradio, signed a contract to exchange radio telegrams in July 1926 with Companhia Radiotelegrafica Brasileira.[85] Founded
in 1928, Agencia Brasileira functioned as a cover agency for Transocean,
which owned 60 percent of its shares. Agencia Brasileira mainly distributed
local news; the German newspaper in Brazil, which received Transocean's
wireless news, supplied foreign news to Agencia Brasileira. The German legation subsidized the wireless receiver and the subscription.[86] The service
mainly appealed to German-language newspapers in Brazil, as Havas offered more words and achieved far greater circulation.[87] This changed with
the Nazis' significant funding increase for Transocean in the later 1930s. By
1935, Transocean offered a free service to some papers in São Paolo that they
reproduced under the heading "Spécial" or SI (Service International).[88]

To ensure more transmissions from Germany, the Nazis significantly improved wireless and radio through the Rehmate and Zeesen stations. They
constructed a large radio tower at Rehmate for the summer Olympics of
1936.[89] They also improved the range of Zeesen, a shortwave broadcasting
station just south of Berlin. By 1938, David Sarnoff—head of the Radio Corporation of America (RCA) and founder of the National Broadcasting
Company (NBC)—believed that "with excellent engineering and astute publicity technique this giant station [Zeesen] has become the most potent
agency for the dissemination of political doctrine that the world has known."[90]

By 1933, Transocean news reached Uruguay, Chile, Columbia, Venezuela,
and Mexico. In 1938–1939, Transocean broadcast 9.5 hours daily in German, 9
hours in English, 2 in French, and 18 in Spanish, showing the importance of
the South American market. After the war began, Transocean swiftly increased to broadcasting 70 hours daily through multiple transmitters: 16

hours in German, 22 in English, and 32 in Spanish.[91] By 1940, the service reached into the provinces in Argentina, Brazil, and Uruguay.

Transocean's success ebbed as the United States escalated pressure. Peru and Cuba ordered Transocean to shut down its offices in 1940 for spreading news designed "to harm democratic institutions."[92] Mexico, Ecuador, and Columbia followed suit in 1941. Brazil, Bolivia, and Uruguay declared war on Germany after the Pan-American Conference with the United States in Rio de Janeiro in January 1942. Consequently, they shut down any receipt of Transocean. This was a particularly heavy blow in Brazil, where 79 Brazilian newspapers printed 30,000 reports monthly in 1940 and 20 radio stations also picked up Transocean.[93]

Only Argentina and Chile remained. In Chile, Transocean had created a subsidiary called Pach. Pach pretended to be Chilean and provided its news to provincial papers free of charge. Transocean bulletins were also distributed through German radio, Radio Hucke, which the British ambassador to Chile thought was "probably the best radio station in Santiago" and which could be easily heard around the country.[94] The British believed that they had "a press advantage, while the Germans are far ahead of us as far as the radio is concerned."[95] Chilean newspapers printed Transocean interviews and news in December 1942, but the Transocean office was shut in January 1943.[96]

Argentina remained loyal to Transocean longest. Reuters constantly worried about the service and considered extending its services to Latin America in conjunction with the Ministry of Information and the BBC.[97] The Argentine news agency ANDI only stopped receiving Transocean in December 1944, when Allied bombing had effectively destroyed Nazi radio capacity. This was nearly a year after Argentina had officially broken off relations with Germany in January 1944.

Not all Transocean news was widely published. The nature of the news mattered. A more overtly propagandistic Christmas report of 1942 appeared in only four newspapers in Buenos Aires, one of which was the German *La Plata Zeitung*. Meanwhile, official declarations, interviews, and in-depth reporting about the war appeared in all Argentine press. This included items like news of the assassination in Algeria in December 1942 of Admiral Jean-François Darlan, minister of the interior, defense, and foreign affairs in the Vichy government.[98]

Transocean's technical capacities and personnel also seemed to lag behind the Americans. In 1938 Transocean had fewer than twenty staff in Buenos

Aires, while the AP had around two hundred. The AP transmitted more than 12,000 words of a speech given by Hitler before the Reichstag on February 20, 1938. Transocean only supplied 3,000. No South American newspaper wanted to publish a Hitler speech verbatim: "It is a question of prestige," noted a British informant in a secret document, that Transocean "should be able to supply the <u>best</u> version of any Hitler speech."[99]

Within South American countries themselves, it is unclear how far Transocean's news affected attitudes toward the Nazi regime and the Axis powers. These attitudes depended greatly on the individual country's circumstances and domestic politics. While Nazi takeover of German institutions did not particularly succeed in Brazil, it worked in Chile.[100] In Argentina, at most 5 percent of German citizens living there became Nazi Party members.[101] The owners of the liberal German-language newspaper *Argentinisches Tageblatt* refused to convert it to a Nazi mouthpiece.[102] Still, Germans had used Transocean as a political tool to compete with the top players in South America—France and the United States. By the time of its trial in July 1941, Transocean made Americans fear that they might lose a war of words against Germany in arenas far from the physical battlefield. The same fear played out in different ways in East Asia.

A Dangerous Element for the Interests of Peace: Transocean in East Asia

Unlike the relatively large German-speaking population in South America, there were barely any German speakers in East Asia. Only around five hundred lived in Shanghai in the 1930s. But Transocean's news to East Asia made foreign governments highly suspicious. As early as 1935, TASS, the Soviet news agency, warned that Transocean represented "a dangerous element for the interests of peace between the USSR and other powers, particularly in the Far East."[103] Agence Havas, Reuters, and United Press along with Japanese news agencies all battled with Transocean for column space, particularly in China.

Like South America, East Asia became important because German elites feared that the lack of news from Germany undermined German political and economic influence. Transocean initially built on German contact with the Dutch during World War I, including Telefunken's attempt to build a wireless tower in Java (see Chapter 2). Transocean signed a contract with a

Dutch agency in 1922 to send news to Dutch ships and the Dutch East Indies. Newspapers in the British Straits Settlements also printed thirty to forty Transocean telegrams daily from the mid-1920s until 1934.[104] Transocean signed a contract with the Japanese news agency, Nippon Denpō Tsūshinsha (Dentsū, Japan Telegraphic News Agency), in September 1919 to exchange news. In 1926, however, the Japanese Telegraph Administration refused to take Transocean's special service from Berlin at anything other than an appointed time and for a much higher price. The government had set up a news agency syndicate, Nippon Shimbun Rengōsha (Associated Press of Japan, Rengō), and hoped to kill competition by excluding Transocean from Japan.[105] Transocean had to combine radio and cables, which proved more expensive. The German Postal Ministry subsidized two-thirds of the costs of sending news from Nauen. Japanese customers paid the rest.[106]

Transocean transferred its focus to China in 1926.[107] Transocean's representative in Asia, Joseph Plaut, found himself working against the growing success of United Press. Like Associated Press, United Press had greatly increased its investment and presence in East Asia during the 1920s, leaving Plaut with the impression that the United States wanted to achieve "mastery of the news field all over the world." Plaut asked for more investment to ensure that Transocean could broadcast four times daily to East Asia rather than once. Transocean also needed to report a few headline stories a week: reporting more news was an "existential question." It would enable Transocean to "disguise" any Foreign Office propaganda "through neutral, real 'news'."[108] Plaut even used the English word "news" in his original German report. The German word "Nachrichten" did not imply impartiality.

In China, Transocean succeeded by playing the anti-imperial card. Germany had possessed its own colony in China—Qingdao—until World War I. China had also been a major destination for German exports. Ironically, losing Qingdao helped Weimar Germany in its relationship with China. Germans now interacted with the Chinese "as non-colonialist equals" and were thus "more welcome in many business and political circles than other Westerners," according to historian Rana Mitter.[109] During the Weimar Republic and in the first years of the Nazi period, there was strong and growing trade between Germany and China as well as German support and training for Chiang Kai-shek's Chinese Republican Army.[110]

News followed a trajectory similar to those of trade and military training. After the May Fourth Movement of 1919, Chinese intellectuals came to support the idea of "news communication sovereignty." China had failed to influence the Versailles Peace Conference, they believed, because it had not recognized how communications could change the outcome. These intellectuals lamented that China lacked its own news agency to send news abroad. Men like Zhao Meng, a Chinese journalist employed by AP and then Reuters, believed that a Chinese news agency would counter the biased foreign news agencies that controlled news from China.[111] "While China may be an independent nation," Zhao declared in 1931, "its publicity channels abroad are in the hands of foreign news agencies and newspapers."[112] China needed its own news agency.

The Chinese government thus established a national news agency in 1927, called Kuomin. In 1928, Transocean became Kuomin's international partner for anti-imperial and technological reasons. Reuters had been the main agency in China up to 1927, as British and Danish cable companies held exclusive rights to control international telegraphy from China.[113] The Chinese now wished to avoid Reuters, which they deemed an imperial agency.[114] Transocean's news also arrived faster because of wireless. While Reuters news mostly arrived by cable, Transocean news was sent by longwave from Nauen to the Chinese government's wireless station in Shanghai. The broadcasts were to happen over shortwave, once Nauen's technology allowed in 1929.[115]

The Kuomin-Transocean partnership was somewhat concealed because Chinese news agencies served as intermediaries. The Chinese Ministry of Foreign Affairs delegated Da Zhong (Ta Chung) news agency to disseminate Transocean news from Shanghai to the rest of China. The Asiatic News Agency distributed Transocean news in Beijing and Tianjin, generally in English.[116] Some newspapers printed the news in a column labeled "German wireless." Some labeled it "Transocean Kuo Min Wireless Service." Others distributed the news throughout the newspaper or printed it under the name of the Chinese news agency that supplied it. These myriad labeling practices make it hard to track the spread of Transocean news. It is easier to trace fellow journalists' reactions; these are particularly important because newspapers were a key source for politicians as well as the public.

Foreign language newspapers were particularly important in countries like China, where foreign correspondents frequently did not speak the language. Conversely, Chinese newspapers generally had no correspondents abroad and relied on news agencies to supply foreign news. Just after becoming leader of the Republic of China in 1928, Chiang Kai-shek noted in a telegram to all newspapers in December 1929: "The press is the proper channel and organ for the expression of opinion. It represents public opinion."[117] Chinese officials used newspapers as evidence for international and national public opinion and sought to control them to create compliant citizens.

For O. M. Green, the British editor of *North China Daily News* from 1911 to 1930, wireless "brought changes which cannot but be viewed with misgiving." He warned in 1933 that "Shanghai, the chief centre for distribution for China, has become a vast whispering gallery for the nations."[118] The amount of foreign news printed in Chinese newspapers had increased from just one column prior to World War I to four or five by the late 1920s. While cable companies could restrict access, governments could send propaganda over wireless with impunity. This had unleashed a flood of news to Shanghai: 3,500 words daily from Havas, 2,000 from Transocean, many items from Japan's news agencies, as well as the Soviet Union's TASS and occasionally even Italy. Green worried about the radio tower that Telefunken was erecting in China and feared that the inundation of government-subsidized services would shut out "genuine news-selling organisations," like Reuters.[119]

In 1927, Reuters feared that Transocean along with United Press would become "a serious competitor to agency services" in East Asia.[120] Reuters relied on cables, finding them the best means to ensure that their news reached only subscribers, rather than illicit listeners. After the 1928 contract between Transocean and Kuomin, however, the British ensured that its wireless also reached China. By 1930, almost all Reuters agents in China had wireless receivers.

News agencies attracted great attention from American politicians too. Men as high up as Henry Stimson, newly appointed secretary of state, congratulated the United Press on opening a bureau in China in March 1929, declaring that the agency would "perform a new public service of national importance."[121] Plaut believed that the introduction of Transocean's service had led to increased competition between Reuters, AP, and UP in Shanghai for news share.[122]

The German government hoped that Transocean's news would increase trade with China. The French, at least, agreed, bemoaning that Chinese imports of German goods had doubled from 1913 to 1927.[123] The Havas representative in Shanghai, Jean Fontenoy, tried to copy both Transocean's use of wireless and its cooperation with a Chinese news agency. From April 1930, Havas sent four press communiqués daily by shortwave from Pontoise, northwest of Paris. Fontenoy also signed a contract with the Chinese Information Agency, Chang Chou, in September 1930.[124] The contract proved ineffective, as Havas's contract with Reuters technically forbade it to distribute financial news and compete with Reuters in China. Plus nowhere in China could initially receive transmissions from Pontoise. Newspapers complained about the tardy and inappropriate news items that generally arrived later than a Reuters cable or Transocean wireless.[125] Speed was "the [main] virtue of an agency," wrote Fontenoy to his superiors in Paris. French news always came in third or fourth place after Reuters, United Press, and Kuomin-Transocean.[126]

Fontenoy despaired so greatly that in February 1931, he merely recommended asking Transocean to moderate its polemics about France, rather than fighting Transocean's official relationship with the Chinese government.[127] Still, Havas did modify its contract with Reuters to allow both to supply news to China. Transocean also pushed Havas to switch wholesale to wireless: by 1934, 99.5 percent of Havas news reached French receivers in China over wireless.[128]

The strength of different news agencies varied within China. By 1932, Transocean, Havas, Reuters, and United Press competed on fairly even terms in Beijing; all four supplied between 1,032 and 1,216 items to the *Peking Chronicle* over one six-month period. Reuters supplied the most, Havas the least. The situation differed dramatically in Tianjin, where Havas and Reuters dominated the Chinese and foreign newspaper markets. Only 2,007 Transocean items appeared in foreign papers, compared to 5,188 Havas and 4,228 Reuters items.[129]

After 1933, the Nazi government retained the focus on China, but dramatically increased the number of Transocean journalists and broadcasts. In April 1933, the Nazis recalled the sole Transocean representative in Asia, Joseph Plaut. He was Jewish. Plaut's indispensability rapidly became clear, however. In September 1933, he was allowed to fulfill the end of his contract, but on a domestic rather than foreign salary. There is no record of Plaut's fate, though he worked for Transocean as late as March 1934.[130] Transocean vastly expanded its personnel from just Plaut to thirty-six editors in China by 1940. Branches opened in places like Beijing in 1934 and Nanjing in 1936.[131]

Other Nazi media efforts in China found limited success.[132] But Transocean's cooperation with Chinese news agencies aggravated international news relations. The Chiang Kai-shek regime's Central News Agency entered into a relationship with Transocean in late 1934. This allowed Transocean to undermine Havas and Reuters, which had signed contracts with Central News Agency in 1933 and 1932, respectively.[133] The agreement allowed

Central News to distribute Transocean in English and Chinese everywhere in China except Shanghai, where Transocean retained its alliance with Kuomin.[134] Transocean supplied its news to Central News Agency and Kuomin for free: political influence was more important than profit.[135] From 1934, Transocean sent its news directly to newspapers in multiple Chinese cities like Beijing, Nanjing, Tianjin, and Dairen.[136]

Kuomin also developed an alliance with United Press. This combination of German and American sources allowed it to cover much of the globe, though UP appeared more in English-language than Chinese-language newspapers.[137] In the mid-1930s, both Havas and Reuters maintained their considerable lead over Kuomin and Transocean.[138] Perhaps ignorant of Transocean's relationship with Kuomin, a new Havas representative in 1938 claimed that newspapers did not take Transocean voluntarily "for its propagandistic character is too marked, the English defective and the journalistic presentation unkempt."[139] The Havas assessment belied the reality that by summer 1939, forty-four newspapers in China and Chinese radio subscribed to Transocean directly, over and above its agreements with Kuomin and Central News.[140]

The quality of Transocean's news improved when a competent journalist, Hans Melchers, became manager of East Asian operations in November 1937. Politics in Europe also created more interest in German news and the German perspective. As the Sudetenland crisis heated up in 1938, more Chinese papers printed Transocean. The trend continued in 1939. Although still lagging behind Reuters and Havas, Chinese newspapers in Shanghai printed 2,648 characters of Transocean news in August 1939 compared to 1,817 in June 1939.[141] By 1940, Transocean was one of China's leading news agencies and delivered news to twenty radio stations.

In many ways, the East Asian front of World War II began before the European. The start of the Second Sino-Japanese War in 1937 came hot on the heels of the Japanese invasion of Manchuria in 1931. From 1940 until the end of World War II, China was roughly divided into two spheres with two separate governments: the Japanese-occupied area with a government in Nanjing and the Chinese led by Chiang Kai-shek with a government in Chongqing. Melchers insisted throughout the war that Transocean report on both regimes. He even secured interviews with Chiang Kai-shek and other important members of the Chongqing government in summer 1939.[142] Melchers claimed after the war that objectivity had constantly guided his work.[143]

Transocean's news gathering did not follow the politics of the war. After World War II began in Europe, there was almost total silence about Japan in Nazi press conferences.[144] Behind the scenes, Transocean's contact with Japan and Japanese-occupied areas was extensive. It continued to cooperate with the Kuomintang even after Germany and the Kuomintang had broken off diplomatic relations in 1941. In July 1941, Germany officially recognized Wang Jingwei's puppet government in Nanjing as the legitimate Chinese government. Chiang Kai-shek's government in Chongqing then declared war on Germany on December 9, 1941. After Germany recognized Wang Jingwei's government, the Transocean representative left Chongqing. Nevertheless, Transocean continued to disseminate news to Chongqing. At that point, Transocean supplied the second-largest amount of news to Chongqing behind United Press, but ahead of Reuters and Havas. The official news agency in Chongqing, Central News Agency, continued to receive Transocean over wireless; Transocean engaged a Chinese representative to translate its news. In April 1942, Central Daily News printed 192 Reuters articles, 276 from United Press, and 108 from Transocean—a rather large quantity for an enemy news agency.[145]

Simultaneously, Transocean expanded to Japanese-occupied China; it was the exception to Japan's protective news policies. When Japan first occupied cities in China from 1937, it forbade foreign news agencies from operating there. The Japanese were keen to control news after their experiences with British and American news agencies. Japan had long despised its subjugated status as a colonial territory on the world map of Western news agencies. Japan was one of the main territories that sparked the AP's decision to leave the news agency cartel in 1933–1934.[146] Furthermore, the Japanese government wished to achieve equal status for its news agency. In a move paralleling the creation of the DNB, the government merged the two main Japanese agencies, Rengō and Dentsū, to found Dōmei Tsūshinsha (Allied News Agency) in 1935–1936 as an umbrella agency. Dōmei served as the government's official agency and broadcast news over radio, increasing its range to occupied territories once World War II broke out.[147] Despite its smaller reach, Dōmei insisted in contracts with Havas on equality and reciprocity.[148]

After the Japanese installation of Wang Jingwei's puppet government in 1940, Transocean reestablished an office in Nanjing. In mid-1940, only Dōmei and Transocean had signed contracts with the official Nanjing news agency, Central Press Service (previously called China News Agency).[149] Reuters and United Press were not allowed to reenter, even prior to Pearl

Harbor. In 1941, Central Press Service printed 12,554 Transocean items and only 5,003 Dōmei items.[150] On the anniversary of reopening its office in Nanjing, Hans Melchers even received the Gold Medal of the Nanjing Government from Wang Jingwei personally.[151]

Outside Nanjing, the Chinese- and foreign-language press in Japanese-occupied China continued to print more Transocean news than any other news agency. From December 1941 to early 1943, Transocean remained the most-printed news agency in all major cities: Shanghai, Hankou, Tsingtao, Beijing, Tianjin, Nanjing, and Changchun in Manchuria.[152] Only thereafter did Dōmei become the leading news agency in Hankou, Nanjing Province, and Beijing. Despite the turning tide of the war in Europe, Transocean maintained its leading position elsewhere in China. Transocean even reached an agreement with one Tokyo newspaper, *Mainichi Shimbun,* giving the paper the right to receive Transocean news.[153]

The situation was radically different in territory that Japan conquered after Pearl Harbor. The Japanese had developed grand plans for "hegemonic regionalism" long before 1941, though these became increasingly nationalist in tenor over the 1930s. Japanese leaders conceived of regional dominance of East Asia and the Pacific as a "Greater East Asia Co-Prosperity Sphere." Countries within the "Greater East Asia Co-Prosperity Sphere" needed to be subdued and controlled. Japanese leaders created complex and ambitious plans for new communications networks and a vast system of cables and wireless to cover newly acquired territories.[154] After Pearl Harbor, Japanese forces swiftly swept through East Asia and the Pacific, conquering Singapore in February 1942, Indonesia in March 1942, and the Philippines in April 1942, before the Allies began their first major military offensive at Guadalcanal in August 1942.

In general, the Japanese exerted far stricter control over news in newly conquered Southeast Asian territories than in China. Transocean had broadcast services from Singapore to Manila, Colombo, Jakarta, Bangkok, and Hong Kong from 1927.[155] By the late 1930s, British officials were so concerned about Transocean activity in British colonies like Hong Kong that they refused Transocean access to Singapore.[156] After December 1941, news dissemination in Japanese-conquered territories became considerably more difficult. A report of May 1943 noted that while Transocean had previously concentrated on counteracting enemy propaganda, "now it has become our task to establish ourselves and to eke out an appropriate space for German news in East Asia in spite of considering all Japanese plans and wishes."[157]

Cooperation with the Japanese increased Transocean's news supply problems. The Japanese hoped that German news would simply cede to Dōmei. Transocean representatives were willing to work with Japan, but refused to allow Japan to monopolize news. Transocean wanted the East Asian press to present the German point of view directly from German sources.

Despite these difficulties, Transocean retained a dominant position in much of Japanese-occupied territory. Transocean's reach in Southeast Asia had been extensive by the late 1930s. The Thai Department of Posts and Telegraphs distributed 107 pages of Transocean wireless news daily in February 1938, compared to 51 pages from the Japanese news agency Rengō and only 35 pages from the British wireless station at Rugby. German wireless was more technically reliable than Rugby, and Transocean sent five times as much news as the British. Sir Josiah Crosby, head of the UK legation to Thailand, minced no words in condemning the "relative inferiority" of the British service. "I trust that I shall not cause offence," he concluded in his lengthy report to then foreign secretary Anthony Eden in 1938, "if I say that in this business of national propaganda it is as though we were being bombarded by our opponents with heavy cannon and were returning fire with what is not very much better than a pop-gun."[158]

After the Thai and Japanese governments signed a mutual offensive-defensive pact in late December 1941, the Japanese gained full access to Thai military facilities as well as transport and communications networks. The Japanese used this to create a second layer of censorship over and above Thai measures. Although Thai newspapers swiftly suffered under paper shortages, they began to rely on Transocean more after December 1941; the Thai alliance with the Japanese meant that they could no longer use Reuters news after British entry into the war in Asia. Thai newspapers printed far less Dōmei news than Transocean as late as September 1942, the last figures available.[159]

Transocean had sent a representative to French Indochina in mid-1941, as Japan now controlled northern Indochina and Germany had conquered France in May 1940. Transocean reached an agreement with ARIP, the local news agency that had previously worked solely with Havas. Dōmei entered French Indochina in 1942, but newspapers in Hanoi still printed Transocean news at about the same rate as Dōmei.[160] The Philippines and Dutch East Indies were the main exception to Japanese tolerance of German news. After the Japanese conquests of 1942, the Japanese removed the Transocean representative from the Philippines and allowed no foreign news representatives, presumably as the Philippines were so close to the front. Japan guarded Hong Kong and the Dutch East Indies with similar vigilance.

Allied bombing ended Transocean's connections to Asia. By 1943, bombing was hobbling wireless infrastructure in Germany. As the war progressed, news agency employees were increasingly deployed in other, more immediately relevant fields. By September 1944, only 43 domestic employees of Transocean and its European subsidiary, Europapress, remained of the 419 from just a year before. The agencies stopped sending news at the end of World War II. Transocean was officially dissolved in 1957, after a short-lived attempt to revive it in 1951–1952.[161]

On April 23, 1945, DNB correspondent Alfred Lückenhaus sent his last telegram from Beijing to Berlin. It was "an inconsequential routine report, which held absolutely no meaning for a city closed in by crowds of enemy armies," remembered Lückenhaus ten years later.[162] The connection with Berlin broke off soon after he had sent his final message. Lückenhaus and all other German foreign correspondents learned about the end of the war through Reuters reports and Allied radio. American intelligence officers placed journalists under special scrutiny in late 1945. A report in April 1946 claimed that the Nazis maintained "a powerful German propaganda machine" in China throughout World War II and that most of the propaganda agencies "served as cover for intelligence agents."[163]

Along with the other five hundred German residents in Beijing, Lückenhaus was expelled from China and left by ship for Europe in June 1946.[164] In Shanghai, meanwhile, American military officers prosecuted Nazi news agency correspondents and journalists under charges of espionage. The men were convicted and sent to Landsberg prison in Germany before being released in 1955. An appeal found that their conviction had happened in an extraterritorial space, making it null and void.[165]

Conclusion

The Nazis achieved unprecedented reach with Transocean. Transocean built on thirty years of work on wireless and news agencies. Just like Hugenberg, Schwedler, and Mantler, Goebbels and Ribbentrop believed in the power of news agencies to propagate a German cause. All thought that Transocean's news offered a path to world-power status, though they differed in their vision of what that would mean.

News could not cover up the reality of the war. But it did convince certain journalists, politicians, and intelligence agencies that German influence over regions like East Asia and Latin America far outstripped its military and economic sway. They built on strategies and infrastructure from Imperial Germany and the Weimar Republic to make Transocean's news the leading source in surprising places like Japanese-occupied China. Although the Japanese and German spheres may have been militarily separate during World War II, divided along the seventieth meridian of longitude, East Asia featured prominently in Nazis' international vision of news and propaganda. The British, French, and Americans began to take Transocean seriously, perhaps too seriously, in South America. It was not always clear how many readers or listeners were "converted" to the Nazi cause by news. Still, elites were convinced that the news mattered. News too played its part in the total war of the twentieth century.

CONCLUSION

Karl Bücher—the founder of the first Institute for Newspaper Science in Germany—concluded in 1926 that most people did not know how news really worked. Just a few levers controlled "the sprawling newspaper network" around the world. It was easy for "a strong hand" to gain control over those levers and acquire "an incalculable influence on public opinion—to the blessing or curse of the people, as the case may be." Ignorance offered an opportunity for those who controlled the levers of news agencies. Many editors of small newspapers took news agency material because it was cheap or free, "without even having the slightest idea of whom they are serving with that material."[1] Media scholar Otto Groth agreed, noting in 1928 that "controlling newspaper material at its origin and procurement enables even stronger and more comprehensive influence on public opinion than purchasing and investing in newspapers."[2]

Groth and Bücher were right. Networks behind the news shaped information far more consistently and consequentially than any single newspaper. Our fixation on bustling newsrooms and journalists has obscured the key people and processes behind the scenes. Journalists and newsrooms could only bustle with news because of political, economic, and technological institutions and infrastructures. Political networks meant access to information, favorable regulation, and subsidies. News also relied on business mechanisms of cartels and vertical integration. Finally, new communications technologies like wireless offered ways to bypass older networks.

News agencies are one way to trace these dynamics because they inter-twine institutions, infrastructures, and information. News agencies had formed the key bottleneck in the supply chain of news since the mid-nineteenth century. The structure of news agencies "ranks among one of the most difficult theoretical and practical teachings on newspapers," wrote German newspaper editor Hans Kapfinger in 1932.[3] Their entanglement in political and economic institutions made them hard to understand both in 1932 and now. But that complexity also made them a source of power.

Many German elites besides Groth, Bücher, and Kapfinger saw the im-portance of networks behind the news. Communications was not just "soft power" and cultural diplomacy. Politicians, industrialists, military generals, journalists, and businessmen believed communications could be translated into hard political, economic, and military gains. They used private and public mechanisms both to control the news business and to exploit it for wider aims.

Domestically, politicians such as Prince Maximilian von Baden or Carl Severing clung to the semiofficial Wolff news agency as the swiftest and most reliable method to calm and control a German population during the Weimar Republic. Others like Hans von Bredow hoped that a financial news agency, Eildienst, could soothe economic woes. Alfred Hugenberg tried to use the right-wing news agency Telegraph Union to promote economic nationalism. The news agency consensus united disparate elites in the conviction that these companies could achieve political, economic, and cultural aims outside the realm of communications.

This conviction made communications a core element of German foreign policy too. Starting around 1900, elites increasingly saw Germany as an international and imperial rather than a continental power. A global Ger-many needed a news empire to match its new political, economic, and mili-tary ambitions. World War I seemed to confirm that modern warfare was as much about information as infantry. German chancellor from 1909 to 1917, Theobald von Bethmann Hollweg, believed Germany had lost the war partly because it failed to find an "offensive rallying cry" and to "make a global case [for itself]."[4] Many Germans thought that Reuters and Havas had manipu-lated global news to garner international support for the Entente. Leading Nazis drew the lesson that a world war could only be won with weapons *and* words. They used one news agency founded in 1913, Transocean, to fight that battle in regions like South America and East Asia.

Technology also played a crucial role in the news agency consensus. Wire-less enabled Germans to transcend the boundaries set by cables and cartels.

It could undermine cartel structures by sending news furtively to British ships in the case of Transocean or to German communities in Eastern Europe and the Baltic states in the case of the Telegraph Union. Wireless invisibly subverted British, French, and American control of news abroad. The Nazi emphasis on wireless and radio built on decades of German enthusiasm about how new communications technologies could change the international balance of power.

The year 1945 spelled the end of this news agency consensus in Germany. Allied bombs in the last years of World War II had destroyed the physical infrastructure of wireless. Allied occupation sought to transform German attitudes to news. News agencies still existed, but their function changed drastically in the two Germanies after the war.

Information management formed a central part of Allied occupation policies: media seemed the most powerful method to reeducate the German population. The Americans, British, French, and Soviets confiscated all means of communications immediately after occupying a particular area. For a few months, Germans received information only from Allied army group newspapers. In mid-1945, the Soviets and then the Americans began to license newspapers.[5] The license period ended in September 1949. By then, there were 156 daily newspapers in the Western zones. This included almost all the publications that would later become West Germany's major newspapers, like *Die Welt* and *Süddeutsche Zeitung*.

Historians have claimed that one of the Allies' greatest successes was reorganizing German media.[6] News agencies seemed the most obvious example of a clean break—or *Stunde Null* (Zero Hour)—after 1945.[7] Each occupying power created a news agency in its zone. The Soviets allowed the creation of Allgemeiner Deutscher Nachrichtendienst (ADN, General German News Service) in October 1946, which became the state news agency of East Germany. After the three Western zones merged to create West Germany in May 1949, the three news agencies in the Western zones followed suit and created the dpa (Deutsche Presse-Agentur, German Press Agency) in August 1949. The dpa followed the Associated Press's cooperative business model: it is owned by newspapers and operated for newspapers. Its first message in 1949 presented an apparent triumph of Anglo-American norms of journalism, stating that the agency would maintain "objective news and independence from all state, party political, and economic interest groups."[8]

Still, 1945 was not as clean a break as it initially seemed. Outward appearances covered continuities of personnel and cultural norms.[9] Transocean's representative in East Asia during World War II, Hans Melchers, worked as managing director of the news agency in the British zone, the DPD, and then as the first managing director of dpa from 1949 to 1950. Maximilian Besserer von Thalfingen, who had served on the boards of Telegraph Union and the DNB, became managing director of the dpa in the early 1950s.[10]

News agencies also continued to cooperate internationally. The dpa cooperated with foreign agencies to become the dominant supplier of international news in its domestic market. It initially exchanged news with Reuters, International News Service (INS) and, until 1971, with United Press International, the American news agency created from the merger of the United Press and the INS in 1958. The dpa has remained the main news agency in Germany. Internationally, it is firmly second-tier behind Reuters, Associated Press, and Agence France-Presse (AFP).

Nevertheless, the role of news and news agencies changed dramatically within West German politics. Rather than use news agencies, the first postwar West German chancellor, Konrad Adenauer, and his successors used West Germany's economic weight and political integration into the European community and NATO to achieve German diplomatic goals. Adenauer tried, but failed, to create a central Ministry of Information. Instead, he forged close, personal relationships with particular journalists, cultivating direct contact at his *Teegespräche* (tea talks) over and above more professional and regulated interactions.[11] Still, the *Spiegel* affair of 1962 showed that journalists would now speak truth to power. Several journalists and editors of the newsmagazine *Der Spiegel* were arrested and accused of treason for publishing details of a Defense Ministry document. Defense Minister Franz Josef Strauss lost his position over instigating the arrests. When the Federal Constitutional Court of Germany declined to put the journalists on trial for their actions in 1966, it was a clear turning point for democratic and politically independent journalism in postwar West Germany.

The dpa appears not to have registered significantly on chancellors' radars nor did they seek to use it as a political or economic tool. Despite continuities across 1945, this was a remarkable transformation. Elites no longer saw news agencies as a way to change international opinion about Germany. Rather, West Germany succeeded by integrating itself into American and European structures such as NATO and the European Economic Community. The exigencies of the Cold War, West German economic success, and involvement in international organizations were far more important than any news from Germany.

Meanwhile, radio and news agencies remained central to international politics. Radio broadcasting and jamming across the Iron Curtain continued throughout the Cold War.[12] News also became a source of North–South tension. A UNESCO study of 1953 criticized Anglo-American dominance of global media, particularly by news agencies like Reuters and Associated Press.[13] In 1980, the MacBride Report, commissioned by UNESCO, condemned the "harmful disparities both between countries and within them."[14] The report called for a New World Information and Communication Order (NWICO) that would democratize mass media. The United States and Great Britain reacted angrily to the report's implications of media imperialism. They withdrew in protest from UNESCO: the United States in 1984, rejoining in 2003, Britain in 1985, rejoining in 1997. (In October 2017, the United States announced plans to withdraw again, effective December 31, 2018, over what the State Department called UNESCO's "continuing anti-Israel bias."[15])

Al Jazeera's emergence as a TV network in the 2000s seemed to answer UNESCO's call for more non-Western media, particularly during the "Al Jazeera moment" of the Arab Spring in 2011.[16] In fact, the Qatari state-subsidized Al Jazeera was the harbinger of a new era when many more states would again use international media for national purposes. China's Xinhua news agency and TV channel CCTV (China Central Television) supply news to many countries around the world. Meanwhile, RT (Russia Today), supported by Vladimir Putin's Russia, and the Internet Research Agency have used new technologies of social media and the internet to project international prowess.

The history in this book offers no easy lessons. Perhaps there are only ever cautionary tales. The first cautionary tale is about the mutually sustaining relationship between media and democracy. Democratic institutions do not necessarily create critical and independent media or vice versa.[17] During the Weimar Republic, a free press could not protect democracy. At times, the raucous media even unintentionally undermined the political system by making it appear scandal-ridden and irredeemable. Conversely, state interventions in media could not protect democracy. In the late 1920s and early 1930s, bureaucrats and politicians like Hans von Bredow and Heinrich Brüning thought state supervision of radio content and state ownership of Wolff would deescalate political tensions. They only made it easier for the Nazis to control the media once they came to power. At the same time, the hidden split in news provision between the right-wing Telegraph Union and semiofficial Wolff undermined attempts to create a unified base of facts and narratives about life in Weimar Germany. The vast majority of news consumers, however, had no idea that their news differed from anybody else's. In both the past and the present, the networks and businesses behind the news influenced news consumption and democratic discourse far more than we have often recognized.

The history of news agencies supplies a second cautionary tale about money in the media. It is surprisingly hard to make money from news.[18] The post–World War II period was the exception rather than the rule. In the second half of the twentieth century, newspaper ownership seemed like a license to print money. Newspapers averaged annual returns of 12 percent in the United States. Some newspapers generated profits of 30 percent. In comparison, grocery store profits were in the 2 percent range and department stores around 4 percent.[19] In nonexceptional periods, when profits are hard to come by, companies become more reliant on the state or more susceptible to outside control. The problem of profits has long made news firms likelier to participate in business arrangements like cartels and monopolies as well as more open to outside influences.

A third cautionary tale is that those outside influences can be both national and international. Media environments have never been hermetically sealed within the borders of nation-states.[20] In the modern age, the internationalism was concealed behind national newspapers, radio, and TV channels. But international news supply networks always lay behind the news that consumers received. German news agencies are just one example of how information flowed across borders and how elites have long sought to manipulate those flows. The history of news from Germany also suggests that countries feeling encircled or internationally weak may use communications as a way out. They may seek more national sovereignty by influencing international affairs through news.

A fourth cautionary tale is about communications technology. The media theorist Marshall McLuhan famously wrote that "the medium is the message."[21] Technology does shape the message. But political and economic aims for content shaped technological innovation too. Technology is inherently neither good nor bad. It is how we use it that matters. Utopian visions that communications can create world peace are destined for failure. That is not because of the technology. It is because of human nature.

A fifth and final cautionary tale is about assessing the influence of news. Many equated published opinion with public opinion and thought that controlling news supply would enable them to control public opinion. But news agencies could not and did not provide a panacea. Nor could their representations erase realities on the ground. Friedrich von Payer, German vice-chancellor for the last year of World War I, reflected later that "in 1918 the mood of the German people was a very decisive factor, and one can exert official control over mood perhaps temporarily, but not in the long run and certainly not to order."[22] It is hard to measure the exact influence of the media in the present, let alone in the past. The problem was that elites believed that news had enormous influence (without sufficient evidence) and made decisions accordingly. Reality could matter less than elite interpretations of those realities.[23] Communications and information are important parts of history that we need to take seriously. But we should not overestimate their influence. Sometimes communications mattered a great deal; sometimes they did not. Modern history is full of "exorbitant expectations" about the media that the media cannot fulfill.[24]

Prominent American political theorist and journalist Walter Lippmann expressed a surprisingly similar opinion to Friedrich von Payer. In his writings in the 1920s, Lippmann tried to adapt theories about liberal citizenship and the press to the realities of the postwar world. "The newspapers are regarded by democrats as a panacea for their defects," wrote Lippmann.[25] The problem for Lippmann was that newspapers were placed on a pedestal with no foundation. Readers were expected to know something about everything so that they could become informed voters; the press was supposed to provide that knowledge. These assumptions misunderstood readers and misunderstood the press. Readers did not just consume information from a naive position of ignorance. Rather, they interpreted the news through their own belief systems.

In *Public Opinion*—a book published in 1922 that helped to usher in serious scholarship on the media—Lippmann introduced the current meaning of "stereotypes" to explain how we create "pictures in our heads" of the world around us. Stereotypes, wrote Lippmann, were not just shortcuts to help people to understand society. They were "the projection upon the world of our own sense of our own value, our own position and our own rights."[26] It was a mistake to think that news operated in a vacuum and could change opinions instantaneously. The newspaper provided information that people would slot into their preexisting understandings of the universe.

Flawed assumptions about readers produced a flawed expectation of the press. This expectation, Lippmann believed, mistakenly portrayed "the single reader as theoretically omnicompetent, and puts upon the press the burden of accomplishing whatever representative government, industrial organization, and diplomacy have failed to accomplish. Acting upon everyone for thirty minutes in twenty-four hours, the press is asked to create a mystical force called Public Opinion that will take up the slack in public institutions. The press has often mistakenly pretended that it could do just that." It was an inherently impossible task. The press could not substitute for good government, business, and diplomacy. News could not, and still cannot, paper over lived experience. The press, Lippmann cautioned, was "no substitute for institutions."[27] Institutions mattered just as much in interwar Germany as they did in the United States, though their relative strengths led to very different political outcomes.

Lippmann was right that people were not as easily manipulated as many feared. But they were also not immune to influence. The effects of news were not always predictable and they remain difficult to isolate today. What is clear is that citizens could not form opinions on events that they did not even know had happened. What was suppressed or filtered mattered just as much as what was printed. Control over information supply and infrastructure provided that type of power.

Beyond what citizens thought or believed, what often mattered more was what elites thought that citizens wanted. When elites no longer believed in upholding democratic institutions, a free press alone could not stop a democracy's disintegration. Democracy can die in full daylight, and has done before.

LIST OF ABBREVIATIONS

AAK   Archiv der Akademie der Künste (Archive of the Academy of Arts), Berlin

AAN   Archiwum Akt Nowych (Archive of Modern Records), Warsaw

AG   Aktiengesellschaft (Joint Stock Company)

AN   Archives Nationales (National Archives), Paris

ANA   Amtliche Nachrichtenstelle (Official News Office, Austrian News Agency)

AP   Associated Press

APCA   Associated Press Corporate Archives, New York

BA MA   Bundesarchiv Militärarchiv (Federal Archive, Military Archive), Freiburg

BArch   Bundesarchiv (Federal Archive), Berlin-Lichterfelde

BArchK   Bundesarchiv (Federal Archive), Koblenz

BT   British Telecom Archives, London

DHD   Deutscher Handelsdienst (German Trade Service)

DIHT   Deutscher Industrie- und Handelstag (German Association of Industry and Trade)

DNB   Deutsches Nachrichtenbüro (German News Office)

DNVP   Deutschnationale Volkspartei (German National People's Party)

DVP   Deutsche Volkspartei (German People's Party)

FARA   Foreign Agents Registration Act

GmbH   Gesellschaft mit beschränkter Haftung (Limited Liability Company)

GStA PK   Geheimes Staatsarchiv Preußischer Kulturbesitz (Secret State Archive of Prussian Cultural Heritage), Berlin

HUAC   House Un-American Activities Committee
IfZ   Institut für Zeitungsforschung (Institute for Newspaper Research), Dortmund
KPD   Kommunistische Partei Deutschlands (Communist Party of Germany)
LNA   League of Nations Archive, Geneva
MSZ   Ministerstwo Spraw Zagranicznych (Ministry of Foreign Affairs), Poland
NARA   National Archives and Records Administration, Washington, DC
NL   Nachlass (Private Papers)
NSDAP Nationalsozialistische Deutsche Arbeiterpartei (National Socialist German Workers Party or Nazi Party)
ÖStA   Österreichisches Staatsarchiv (Austrian State Archive), Vienna
PA AA Politisches Archiv des Auswärtigen Amtes (Political Archive of the Foreign Office), Berlin
PAT   Polska Agencja Telegraficzna (Polish Telegraph Agency)
RA   Reuters Archive, London
RMA   Royal Mail Archive, London
RMVP   Reichsministerium für Volksaufklärung und Propaganda (Reich Ministry for Public Enlightenment and Propaganda)
SPD   Sozialdemokratische Partei Deutschlands (Social Democratic Party of Germany)
TASS   Telegrafnoe agentstvo Sovetskogo Soiuza (Telegraph Agency of the Soviet Union)
TNA   The National Archives, London
TU   Telegraphen-Union (Telegraph Union)
UP   United Press
USPD   Unabhängige Sozialdemokratische Partei Deutschlands (Independent Social Democratic Party of Germany)
VDZV   Verein Deutscher Zeitungs-Verleger (Association of German Newspaper Publishers)
WAC   BBC Written Archive Centre, Reading
WTB   Wolff's Telegraphisches Bureau (alternative contemporary spellings include Wolff's Telegraphisches Büro, Wolffs Telegraphen Bureau, Wolff'sche Telegraphen-Bureau)

NOTES

Introduction

1. MI5 confidential report on Transocean, 1936, The National Archives, London, KV3/100.
2. Minutes of the seventh plenary assembly of Agences Alliées (European news agencies allied in a cartel), Strbské-Pleso, Czechoslovakia, June 16–25, 1935, Archives Nationales, Paris, 5AR/473. Translations in this book are by the author, unless otherwise indicated.
3. Andrew Pettegree, *The Invention of News: How the World Came to Know about Itself* (New Haven, CT: Yale University Press, 2014); Will Slauter, "The Rise of the Newspaper," in Richard R. John and Jonathan Silberstein-Loeb, eds., *Making News: The Political Economy of Journalism in Britain and America from the Glorious Revolution to the Internet* (Oxford: Oxford University Press, 2015), 19–46.
4. Oliver Boyd-Barrett and Terhi Rantanen, eds., "The Globalization of News," in *The Globalization of News* (London: Sage, 1998), 6.
5. Karl Bücher, *Gesammelte Aufsätze zur Zeitungskunde* (Tübingen: H. Laupp, 1926), 36.
6. On geoeconomics, see Hans Kundnani, *The Paradox of German Power* (London: Hurst, 2014).
7. Terhi Rantanen, *When News Was New* (Chichester: Wiley-Blackwell, 2009). Communications scholars often think about this question in terms of "news values." For the most recent work, see Tony Harcup and Deidre O'Neill, "What Is News? News Value Revisited (Again)," *Journalism Studies* 18, no. 12 (2017): 1470–1488. On the related concept of information, see John Seely Brown and Paul Duguid, *The Social Life of Information* (Boston: Harvard

Business School Press, 2002); Paul N. Edwards et al., "Historical Perspectives on the Circulation of Information," *American Historical Review* 116, no. 5 (2011): 1393–1435.

8. Philipp Gassert and Christine von Hodenberg, "Media: Government versus Market," in Christof Mauch and Kiran Klaus Patel, eds., *The United States and Germany during the Twentieth Century: Competition and Convergence* (New York: Cambridge University Press, 2010), 227–245; Heidi J. S. Tworek and John Maxwell Hamilton, "The Natural History of the News: An Epigenetic Study," *Journalism: Theory, Critique, Practice* 18, no. 4 (2017): 391–407.

9. See "The Conscience of Society: Max Weber on Journalism and Responsibility," in Hanno Hardt, *Social Theories of the Press: Constituents of Communication Research, 1840s to 1920s,* 2nd ed. (Lanham, MD: Rowman and Littlefield, 2001), 127–142.

10. The word *Nachricht* emerged in the seventeenth century, meaning "Mittheilung zum Darnachrichten." *Deutsches Wörterbuch von Jacob Grimm und Wilhelm Grimm,* vol. 13 (Leipzig: Hirzel Verlag, 1889), col. 103.

11. Some, like Mahatma Gandhi, also fought for alternatives within the British and American systems. Isabel Hofmeyr, *Gandhi's Printing Press: Experiments in Slow Reading* (Cambridge, MA: Harvard University Press, 2013).

12. Joseph Nye, *Soft Power: The Means to Success in World Politics* (New York: Public Affairs, 2004).

13. David Blackbourn, "Germany and the Birth of the Modern World, 1780–1820" (2012), accessed August 3, 2018, https://www.ghi-dc.org/fileadmin/user_upload/GHI_Washington/Publications/Bulletin51/009_bu51.pdf; Ulrike Strasser, "A Case of Empire Envy? German Jesuits Meet an Asian Mystic in Spanish America," *Journal of Global History* 2, no. 1 (2007): 23–40.

14. Sebastian Conrad, "Transnational Germany," in James N. Retallack, ed., *Imperial Germany, 1871–1918* (Oxford: Oxford University Press, 2008), 237. Sebastian Conrad, *Globalisation and the Nation in Imperial Germany,* trans. Sorcha O'Hagan (Cambridge: Cambridge University Press, 2010).

15. Markus Krajewski, *Restlosigkeit: Weltprojekte um 1900* (Frankfurt am Main: Fischer Taschenbuch Verlag, 2006). I use the concept of "world" because it was the term most used by Germans at the time. However, Germans privileged particular parts of the globe as the "world" they wished to reach. I use the term "international" because it conveys the central role of the nation-state in this story. Internationalism could be liberal, fascist, Communist, etc. See Glenda Sluga and Patricia Clavin, eds., *Internationalisms: A Twentieth-Century History* (Cambridge: Cambridge University Press, 2016). There is a lively historiographical debate about global vs. world vs. transnational vs. international history. Some see the global as "an interpretive framework," e.g., Tony Ballantyne and Antoinette Burton, "Empires and the Reach of the Global," in Emily Rosenberg, ed., *A World Connecting, 1870–1945* (Cambridge, MA: Harvard University Press, 2012), 301. Others have

emphasized how local and national contexts shaped reactions to global developments. Vanessa Ogle, *The Global Transformation of Time: 1870–1950* (Cambridge, MA: Harvard University Press, 2015). Critics of global history believe it privileges connections over disjuncture. Jeremy Adelman, "Is Global History Still Possible or Has It Had Its Moment?" *Aeon* (2017), accessed February 25, 2018, https://aeon.co/essays/is-global-history-still-possible-or-has-it-had-its-moment. For an overview and defense of global history, see Richard Drayton and David Motadel, "Discussion: The Futures of Global History," *Journal of Global History* 13, no. 1 (2018): 1–21.

16. John Pizer, *The Idea of World Literature: History and Pedagogical Practice* (Baton Rouge: Louisiana State University Press, 2006).

17. Quinn Slobodian, "How to See the World Economy: Statistics, Maps, and Schumpeter's Camera in the First Age of Globalization," *Journal of Global History* 10, no. 2 (2015): 307–332; Quinn Slobodian, *Globalists: The End of Empire and the Birth of Neoliberalism* (Cambridge, MA: Harvard University Press, 2018); Cornelius Torp, *Die Herausforderung der Globalisierung: Wirtschaft und Politik in Deutschland 1860–1914* (Göttingen: Vandenhoeck & Ruprecht, 2005).

18. Heidi Tworek, "Der Weltverkehr und die Ausbreitung des Kapitalismus um 1900," *Themenportal Europäische Geschichte* (2015), accessed August 3, 2018, http://www.europa.clio-online.de/essay/id/artikel-3795.

19. German historians have long disputed how to characterize the complex domestic political system of Imperial Germany: strong control vested in the monarch and his chosen cabinet combined with an elected parliament and bureaucracy that could check the monarch's power as well as an increasingly vibrant democratic culture. For an overview of the debate, see Matthew Fitzpatrick, *Purging the Empire: Mass Expulsions in Germany, 1871–1918* (Oxford: Oxford University Press, 2015), 5–8. On democratic culture, see Margaret Lavinia Anderson, *Practicing Democracy: Elections and Political Culture in Imperial Germany* (Princeton, NJ: Princeton University Press, 2000). The German system was also highly federal; Prussia was by far the largest state. On Prussian democracy, see Hedwig Richter, *Moderne Wahlen: Eine Geschichte der Demokratie in Preußen und den USA im 19. Jahrhundert* (Hamburg: Hamburger Edition, 2017). On Prussia, see Christopher Clark, *Iron Kingdom: The Rise and Downfall of Prussia, 1600–1947* (Cambridge, MA: Harvard University Press, 2006). On democracy after 1918, see Tim B. Müller and Adam Tooze, eds., *Normalität und Fragilität: Demokratie nach dem Ersten Weltkrieg* (Hamburg: Hamburger Edition, 2015).

20. Cornelius Klee, "Transocean," in Jürgen Wilke, ed., *Telegraphenbüros und Nachrichtenagenturen in Deutschland: Untersuchungen zu ihrer Geschichte bis 1949* (Munich: K. G. Saur, 1991), 191.

21. Sven Beckert, *Empire of Cotton: A Global History* (New York: Knopf, 2014).

22. Ian Milligan, "Illusionary Order: Online Databases, Optical Character Recognition, and Canadian History, 1997–2010," *Canadian Historical Review* 94, no. 4 (2013): 540–569.

23. Otto Groth, *Die Zeitung: Ein System der Zeitungskunde* (Mannheim: J. Bensheimer, 1928), 1:166.

24. Pierre Bourdieu, *Language and Symbolic Power*, ed. John B. Thompson (Cambridge: Polity, 1991). The classic work on speech act theory is J. L. Austin, *How to Do Things with Words* (Cambridge, MA: Harvard University Press, 1975). For an overview of political science approaches to institutions, see Orfeo Fioretos, Tulia Falleti, and Adam Sheingate, eds., *The Oxford Handbook of Historical Institutionalism* (Oxford: Oxford University Press, 2016).

25. On how journalistic forms and conventions like interviews create "performative power," see Marcel Broersma, "Journalism as Performative Discourse: The Importance of Form and Style in Journalism," in Verica Rupar, ed., *Journalism and Meaning-Making: Reading the Newspaper* (Cresskill, NJ: Hampton Press, 2010), 15–35.

26. Michael Palmer, "What Makes News," in Boyd-Barrett and Rantanen, *The Globalization of News*, ch. 11.

27. E. Kensinger and Daniel Schacter, "Amygdala Activity is Associated with the Successful Encoding of Item, But Not Source, Information for Positive and Negative Stimuli," *Journal of Neuroscience* 26, no. 9 (2006): 2564–2570. Less than half of readers remember the news outlet where they read a story. More people could remember how they found a story: 67 percent could remember which social media platform they used to find a story. Digital News Report, Reuters Institute for the Study of Journalism (June 22, 2017), accessed August 14, 2018, https://reutersinstitute.politics.ox.ac.uk/sites/default/files/Digital%20News%20Report%202017%20web_0.pdf.

28. This is known in communications literature as the "third-person effect." While a news item might not influence the mass audience it addressed, it could trigger reactions by invoking uninvolved "third persons" who believed in the power of the message W. Phillips Davison, "The Third-Person Effect in Communication," *Public Opinion Quarterly* 47, no. 1 (1983): 1–15.

29. Frank Bösch, *Öffentliche Geheimnisse: Skandale, Politik und Medien in Deutschland und Großbritannien 1880–1914* (Munich: Oldenbourg, 2009); Dominik Geppert, *Pressekriege: Öffentlichkeit und Diplomatie in den deutsch-britischen Beziehungen (1896–1912)* (Munich: Oldenbourg, 2007); Jörg Requate, *Journalismus als Beruf: Entstehung und Entwicklung des Journalistenberufs im 19. Jahrhundert: Deutschland im internationalen Vergleich* (Göttingen: Vandenhoeck & Ruprecht, 1995).

30. Peter Fritzsche, *Reading Berlin 1900* (Cambridge, MA: Harvard University Press, 1996). Work on the press often focuses on cities, most obviously because the first mass newspapers and most newspaper innovations emerged in urban environments. See, e.g., Karl Christian Führer, *Medienmetropole*

Hamburg: Mediale Öffentlichkeiten 1930–1960 (Munich: Dölling und Galitz Verlag, 2008); Julia Guarneri, *Newsprint Metropolis: City Papers and the Making of Modern Americans* (Chicago: University of Chicago Press, 2017).

31. David Ciarlo, *Advertising Empire: Race and Visual Culture in Imperial Germany* (Cambridge, MA: Harvard University Press, 2011).

32. Bernhard Fulda, *Press and Politics in the Weimar Republic* (Oxford: Oxford University Press, 2009); Corey Ross, *Media and the Making of Modern Germany: Mass Communications, Society, and Politics from the Empire to the Third Reich* (Oxford: Oxford University Press, 2008); Corey Ross, "Writing the Media into History: Recent Works on the History of Mass Communications in Germany," *German History* 26, no. 2 (2008): 299–313.

33. Much modern communications history focuses on one country or only uses sources in English. Even works integrating both the UK and the United States are rare. Michele Hilmes, *Network Nations: A Transnational History of British and American Broadcasting* (New York: Routledge, 2012); John and Silberstein-Loeb, eds., *Making News*. Scholars have paid significant attention to the imperial dimensions of communications, particularly for the British Empire. See, e.g., Christopher Bayly, *Empire and Information: Intelligence Gathering and Social Communication in India, 1780–1870* (Cambridge: Cambridge University Press, 1996); Amelia Bonea, *The News of Empire: Telegraphy, Journalism, and the Politics of Reporting in Colonial India, c. 1830–1900* (Oxford: Oxford University Press, 2016); Duncan Bell, "Dissolving Distance: Technology, Space, and Empire in British Political Thought, 1770–1900," *Journal of Modern History* 77, no. 3 (2005): 523–562; Simon Potter, *News and the British World: The Emergence of an Imperial Press System, 1876–1922* (Oxford: Clarendon, 2003); Simon Potter, *Broadcasting Empire: the BBC and the British World, 1922–1970* (Oxford: Oxford University Press, 2012).

34. Benedict Anderson, *Imagined Communities: Reflections on the Origin and Spread of Nationalism*, rev. ed. (London: Verso, 1991).

35. Charles S. Maier, *Once within Borders: Territories of Power, Wealth, and Belonging since 1500* (Cambridge, MA: Harvard University Press, 2016), 301n8.

36. The national and the international were inseparable, partly because their underpinnings—nationalism and internationalism—were "twinned liberal ideologies." Glenda Sluga, *Internationalism in the Age of Nationalism* (Philadelphia: University of Pennsylvania Press, 2013), 3. For a political science perspective on how "hegemonic shocks" in international structures affected national regimes, see Seva Gunitsky, *Aftershocks: Great Powers and Domestic Reforms in the Twentieth Century* (Princeton, NJ: Princeton University Press, 2017).

37. In the 1990s, sociologist Anthony Giddens called the "pooling of knowledge represented by 'news'" an essential condition for the globalization of modernity, while Arjun Appadurai classified "mediascapes" as one of five

dimensions of global flows. Anthony Giddens, *The Consequences of Modernity* (Stanford, CA: Stanford University Press, 1990), 78; Arjun Appadurai, "Disjuncture and Difference in the Global Cultural Economy," *Public Culture* 2, no. 2 (1990): 6. See also Armand Mattelart, *Networking the World, 1794–2000* (Minneapolis: University of Minnesota Press, 2000).

38. Friedrich Blanck, *Der deutsche Nachrichtenmarkt* (Heidelberg: Universitäts-Buchdruckerei von J. Hörning, 1910), 4.

39. The corresponding German terms are *drahtlose Telegraphie* and *drahtloser Funkspruch*. *Funkspruch* referred to the spark (*Funke*) required for early wireless technology.

40. Richard R. John, "Bringing Political Economy Back In," *Enterprise & Society* 9, no. 3 (2008): 488–489. On applying political economy to global communications, see Richard R. John and Heidi J. S. Tworek, "Global Communications," in Teresa da Silva Lopes, Christina Lubinski, and Heidi J. S. Tworek, eds., *The Routledge Companion to the Makers of Global Business* (New York: Routledge, 2019).

41. Most cartels last around five to seven years. Service cartels like the news agency arrangement are rather neglected. Most work focuses on commodities and transportation, e.g., Dominique Barjot, ed., *International Cartels Revisited (1880–1980)* (Caen: Éditions-Diffusion du Lys, 1994); Jeffrey R. Fear, "Cartels," in Geoffrey Jones and Jonathan Zeitlin, eds., *The Oxford Handbook of Business History* (Oxford: Oxford University Press, 2009), 268–292; Peter Z. Grossman, ed., *How Cartels Endure and How They Fail: Studies of Industrial Collusion* (Cheltenham: Edward Elgar, 2004); Debora L. Spar, *The Cooperative Edge: The Internal Politics of International Cartels* (Ithaca, NY: Cornell University Press, 1994).

42. Infrastructure history has blossomed in recent years. See, e.g., Paul Edwards et al., "Introduction: An Agenda for Infrastructure Studies," *Journal of the Association for Information Systems* 10, no. 5 (2009): 364–374; Jo Guldi, *Roads to Power: Britain Invents the Infrastructure State* (Cambridge, MA: Harvard University Press, 2012); Per Högselius, Arne Kaijser, and Erik van der Vleuten, *Europe's Infrastructure Transition: Economy, War, Nature* (London: Palgrave Macmillan, 2016); Richard R. John, "Recasting the Information Infrastructure for the Industrial Age," in Alfred D. Chandler Jr. and James W. Cortada, eds., *A Nation Transformed by Information: How Information Has Shaped the United States from Colonial Times to the Present* (New York: Oxford University Press, 2000): 55–105; Christopher F. Jones, *Routes of Power: Energy and Modern America* (Cambridge, MA: Harvard University Press, 2014); Johan Schot and Vincent Lagendijk, "Technocratic Internationalism in the Interwar Years: Building Europe on Motorways and Electricity Networks," *Journal of Modern European History* 6, no. 2 (2008): 196–217; Thomas J. Misa and Johan Schot, "Inventing Europe: Technology and the Hidden Integration of Europe," *History and Technology* 21, no. 1 (2005): 1–19; Peter Shulman, "Ben Franklin's Ghost: World Peace, American

Slavery, and the Global Politics of Information before the Universal Postal Union," *Journal of Global History* 10, no. 2 (2015): 212–234.

43. Steven Topik and Allan Wells, "Commodity Chains in a Global Economy," in Emily S. Rosenberg, ed., *A World Connecting: 1870–1945* (Cambridge, MA: Belknap Press of Harvard University Press, 2012), 595. See also Emily S. Rosenberg, *Transnational Currents in a Shrinking World: 1870–1945* (Cambridge, MA: Harvard University Press, 2014). For a historiographical overview of telegraphy, see Heidi J. S. Tworek and Simone M. Müller, "'The Telegraph and the Bank': On the Interdependence of Global Communications and Capitalism, 1866–1914," *Journal of Global History* 10, no. 2 (2015): 260–263; Simone M. Müller, "From Cabling the Atlantic to Wiring the World: A Review Essay on the 150th Anniversary of the Atlantic Telegraph Cable of 1866," *Technology & Culture* 57, no. 3 (2016): 507–526.

44. In the German versions, it is a dachshund rather than a cat. The attribution to Einstein seems apocryphal, but is widespread. Albert Einstein, *The Ultimate Quotable Einstein* (Princeton, NJ: Princeton University Press, 2010), 474.

45. On studying technology embedded in systems, see the classic Thomas Hughes, *Networks of Power: Electrification in Western Society, 1880–1930* (Baltimore, MD: Johns Hopkins University Press, 1983).

46. David Edgerton, "From Innovation to Use: Ten Eclectic Theses on the Historiography of Technology," *History and Technology* 16, no. 2 (1999): 111–136; David Edgerton, *The Shock of the Old: Technology and Global History since 1900* (London: Profile Books, 2006); Simone Müller and Heidi J. S. Tworek, "Imagined Use as a Category of Analysis: New Approaches to the History of Technology," *History and Technology: An International Journal* 32, no. 2 (2016): 105–119. Edgerton built on the SCOT (Social Construction of Technology) approach that explores the sociological, systems, and actor-network aspects of technology. On SCOT and communications, see Gabriele Balbi, "Studying the Social History of Telecommunications," *Media History* 15, no. 1 (2009): 85–101. German media theorists have also long focused on the role of technology. Friedrich A. Kittler, *Discourse Networks 1800/1900* (Stanford, CA: Stanford University Press, 1990); Siegfried Zielinski, *Archäologie der Medien: Zur Tiefenzeit des technischen Hörens and Sehens* (Reinbek bei Hamburg: Rowohlt, 2002); Habbo Knoch and Daniel Morat, eds., *Kommunikation als Beobachtung: Medienwandel und Gesellschafts-bilder, 1880–1960* (Munich: W. Fink, 2003).

47. Wilhelm Schwedler, *Die Nachricht im Weltverkehr: Kritische Bemerkungen über das internationale Nachrichtenwesen vor und nach dem Weltkriege* (Berlin: Deutsche Verlagsgesellschaft für Politik und Geschichte, 1922), 128.

48. Alastair Pinkerton and Klaus Dodds, "Radio Geopolitics: Broadcasting, Listening and the Struggle for Acoustic Spaces," *Progress in Human Geography* 33, no. 1 (2009): 19.

49. On the general neglect of wireless telegraphy, see Timothy Campbell, *Wireless Writing in the Age of Marconi* (Minneapolis: University of Minnesota

Press, 2006), ix–xi. There are exceptions, particularly articles on wireless newspapers. Noah Arceneaux, "The Ecology of Wireless Newspapers: Publishing on Islands and Ships, 1899–1913," *Journalism & Mass Communication Quarterly* 91, no. 3 (2014): 562–577; Roland Wenzlhuemer, "The Ship, the Media, and the World: Conceptualizing Connections in Global History," *Journal of Global History* 11, no. 2 (2016): 163–186. Balbi and Natale have argued that radio experienced a "double birth" of wireless and then spoken radio. Gabriele Balbi and Simone Natale, "The Double Birth of Wireless: Italian Radio Amateurs and the Interpretative Flexibility of New Media," *Journal of Radio and Audio Media* 22, no. 1 (2015): 26–41. For a technological history of wireless, see Sungook Hong, *Wireless: From Marconi's Black-Box to the Audion* (Cambridge, MA: MIT Press, 2001). Scholarship on German wireless has concentrated on the pre-1918 period, e.g., Michael Friedewald, "The Beginnings of Radio Communication in Germany, 1897–1918," *Journal of Radio Studies* 7, no. 2 (2000): 441–463; Reinhard Klein-Arendt, *Kamina ruft Nauen! Die Funkstellen in den deutschen Kolonien 1904–1918* (Cologne: W. Herbst, 1996); Sebastian Mantei, *Von der Sandbüchse zum Post-und Telegraphenland: Der Aufbau des Kommunikationsnetzwerks in Deutsch-Südwestafrika (1884–1915)* (Windhoek: Namibia Wissenschaftliche Gesellschaft, 2007).

50. Heather Ellis, "Marconi, Masculinity and the Heroic Age of Science: Wireless Telegraphy at the British Association Meeting at Dover in 1899," *History and Technology* 32, no. 2 (2016): 120–136; Marc Raboy, *Marconi: The Man Who Networked the World* (New York: Oxford University Press, 2016). On how rivalries around wireless patents helped to create the notion of the lone inventor, see Stathis Arapostathis and Graeme Gooday, *Patently Contestable: Electrical Technologies and Inventor Identities on Trial in Britain* (Cambridge, MA: MIT Press, 2013), ch. 6.

51. Accessed February 25, 2018, https://www.nobelprize.org/nobel_prizes /physics/laureates/1909.

52. The pathbreaking work in the *Sonderweg* debate is David Blackbourn and Geoff Eley, *The Peculiarities of German History: Bourgeois Society and Politics in Nineteenth-Century Germany* (Oxford: Oxford University Press, 1984). On the difficulty of defining "German history," though only in the European context, see the classic James Sheehan, "What Is German History? Reflections on the Role of the Nation in German History and Historiography," *Journal of Modern History* 53, no. 1 (1981): 1–23. Helmut Walser Smith suggests that historians move beyond the *Sonderweg* debate to "emphasize the embeddedness and the impact of German history in and on wider developments, and render these qualities as the central organizing principles of modern German history." Helmut Walser Smith, ed., *The Oxford Handbook of Modern German History* (New York: Oxford University Press, 2011), 1.

53. For example, Shelley Baranowski, *Nazi Empire: German Colonialism and Imperialism from Bismarck to Hitler* (Cambridge: Cambridge University Press, 2010); Vejas Liulevicius, *War Land on the Eastern Front: Culture, National*

Identity and German Occupation in World War I (Cambridge: Cambridge University Press, 2000). On German colonialism, see Sebastian Conrad, *German Colonialism: A Short History*, trans. Sorcha O'Hagan (Cambridge: Cambridge University Press, 2012); Bradley Naranch and Geoff Eley, eds., *German Colonialism in a Global Age* (Durham, NC: Duke University Press, 2014).

54. Daniel Bessner, *Democracy in Exile: Hans Speier and the Rise of the Defense Intellectual* (Ithaca, NY: Cornell University Press, 2018); Udi Greenberg, *The Weimar Century: German Émigrés and the Ideological Foundations of the Cold War* (Princeton, NJ: Princeton University Press, 2014); Noah Strote, *Lions and Lambs: Conflict in Weimar and the Creation of Post-Nazi Germany* (New Haven, CT: Yale University Press, 2017); Moritz Föllmer, *Individuality and Modernity in Berlin: Self and Society from Weimar to the Wall* (Cambridge: Cambridge University Press, 2013).

55. For example, Geoffrey Jones, *Multinationals and Global Capitalism: From the Nineteenth to the Twenty-First Century* (Oxford: Oxford University Press, 2005) and the pioneering work of Mira Wilkins, e.g., *The Emergence of Multinational Enterprise: American Business Abroad from the Colonial Era to 1914* (Cambridge, MA: Harvard University Press, 1970). For the latest work, see da Silva Lopes, Lubinski, and Tworek, eds., *The Routledge Companion to the Makers of Global Business*.

56. Geoffrey Jones and Christina Lubinski, "Managing Political Risk in Global Business: Beiersdorf, 1914–1990," *Enterprise and Society* 13, no. 1 (2012): 85–119.

57. Bernhard Rieger, *Technology and the Culture of Modernity in Britain and Germany, 1890–1945* (Cambridge: Cambridge University Press, 2005), 18. The main overview history of German media from the late nineteenth century to 1945 explicitly omits technology. Ross, *Media and the Making of Modern Germany*.

1. The News Agency Consensus

1. Gottfried Traub, *Erinnerungen: Wie ich das "Zweite Reich" erlebte: Tagebuch-notizen aus der Hitlerzeit* (Stuttgart: E. Traub, 1998), 279.

2. Ernst Heerdegen, *Der Nachrichtendienst der Presse* (Leipzig: Emmanuel Reinicke, 1920), 41.

3. Yrjö Kaukiainen, "Shrinking the World: Improvements in the Speed of Information Transmission, c. 1820–1870," *European Review of Economic History* 5, no. 1 (2001): 1–28.

4. Daniel Headrick, *The Invisible Weapon: Telecommunications and International Politics, 1851–1945* (New York: Oxford University Press, 1991); Simone Müller, *Wiring the World: The Social and Cultural Creation of Global Telegraph Networks* (New York: Columbia University Press, 2016); Roland Wenzl-huemer, *Connecting the Nineteenth-Century World: The Telegraph and Global-ization* (Cambridge: Cambridge University Press, 2012).

5. On news agency business models, see Gerben Bakker, "Trading Facts: Arrow's Fundamental Paradox and the Origins of Global News Networks,"

in Peter Putnis, Chandrika Kaul, and Jürgen Wilke, eds., *International Communication and Global News Networks: Historical Perspectives* (New York: Hampton Press, 2011), 9–54; Heidi J. S. Tworek, "Political and Economic News in the Age of Multinationals," *Business History Review* 89, no. 3 (2015): 447–474.

6. N. Hansen, "Depeschenbureaus und internationales Nachrichtenwesen," *Weltwirtschaftliches Archiv* 3, no. 1 (1914): 80.

7. On cartel agencies, see Dieter Basse, *Wolff's Telegraphisches Bureau: 1849 bis 1933: Agenturpublizistik zwischen Politik und Wirtschaft* (Munich: K. G. Saur, 1991); Esperança Bielsa, "The Pivotal Role of News Agencies in the Context of Globalization: A Historical Approach," *Global Networks* 8, no. 3 (2008): 347–366; Pierre Frédérix, *Un siècle de chasse aux nouvelles: de l'agence d'information Havas à l'Agence France-Presse (1835–1957)* (Paris: Flammarion, 1959); Antoine Lefébure, *Havas: Les arcanes du pouvoir* (Paris: B. Grasset, 1992); Alexander Nalbach, "'Poisoned at the Source'? Telegraphic News Services and Big Business in the Nineteenth Century," *Business History Review* 77, no. 4 (2003): 577–610; Volker Barth, "The Formation of Global News Agencies, 1859–1914," in W. Boyd Rayward, ed., *Information beyond Borders: International Cultural and Intellectual Exchange in the Belle Époque* (Farnham: Ashgate, 2014), 35–48; Terhi Rantanen, "Foreign Dependence and Domestic Monopoly: The European News Cartel and U.S. Associated Presses, 1861–1932," *Media History* 12, no. 1 (2006): 19–35; Donald Read, *The Power of News: The History of Reuters,* 2nd ed. (Oxford: Oxford University Press, 1999); Jonathan Silberstein-Loeb, *The International Distribution of News: The Associated Press, Press Association, and Reuters, 1848–1947* (Cambridge: Cambridge University Press, 2014).

8. This interaction between smaller and cartel agencies created "bi-directional dependency." Terhi Rantanen, *Mr. Howard Goes to South America: The United Press Associations and Foreign Expansion* (Bloomington: School of Journalism, Indiana University, 1992), 4.

9. Starting in 1900, Wolff paid Reuter and Havas 22,500 marks annually, rather than a percentage of profits. This was an increase of 10,000 marks, but Reuters and Havas no longer held the right to see Wolff's accounts.

10. Basse, *Wolff's Telegraphisches Bureau,* 210–212.

11. Board of Directors meeting, September 30, 1930, Associated Press Corporate Archives, Kent Cooper Collection, Box 23, Folder 9, 4.

12. Cited in Jeffrey Fear, *Organizing Control: August Thyssen and the Construction of German Corporate Management* (Cambridge, MA: Harvard University Press, 2005), 238.

13. Hansen, "Depeschenbureaus und internationales Nachrichtenwesen," 78.

14. Clemens Wurm, "Politik und Wirtschaft in den internationalen Beziehungen: Internationale Kartelle, Außenpolitik und weltwirtschaftliche Beziehungen, 1919–1939," in Clemens Wurm, ed., *Internationale Kartelle und Außenpolitik: Beiträge zur Zwischenkriegszeit* (Stuttgart: Franz Steiner, 1989), 9–10.

15. Fear, *Organizing Control,* 247.

16. Hansen, "Depeschenbureaus und internationales Nachrichtenwesen," 94.

17. Max Garr, *Die wirtschaftlichen Grundlagen des modernen Zeitungswesens* (Vienna: F. Deuticke, 1912), 29.

18. Paul F. Douglass, Karl Bömer, and Emil Dovifat, "The Press as a Factor in International Relations," *Annals of the American Academy of Political and Social Science* 162 (1932): 268.

19. Ludwig Salomon, *Geschichte des deutschen Zeitungswesens: Von den ersten Anfängen bis zur Wiederaufrichtung des Deutschen Reiches* (Aalen: Scientia, 1973, orig. publ. 1906), 3:558.

20. Emil Sehling, "6/IV: Gesetz über das Telegraphenwesen des Deutschen Reiches," *Die civilrechtlichen Gesetze des Deutschen Reiches* (Leipzig: Veit, 1902), 200.

21. Peter Winzen, *Das Kaiserreich am Abgrund: Die Daily-Telegraph-Affäre und das Hale-Interview von 1908: Darstellung und Dokumentation* (Stuttgart: Franz Steiner, 2002), 125n2.

22. Fritz Stern, *Gold and Iron: Bismarck, Bleichröder, and the Building of the German Empire* (New York: Knopf, 1977), 266.

23. Hans Morf, *Die Drahtberichterstattung im modernen Zeitungswesen* (Bern: Stämpfli, 1912), 74.

24. Hermann Diez, *Das Zeitungswesen* (Leipzig: B. G. Teubner, 1910), 89. Diez also published a version in 1919.

25. Silberstein-Loeb, *The International Distribution of News,* 165.

26. Basse, *Wolff's Telegraphisches Bureau,* 65–90; Michael Palmer, "L'Agence Havas et Bismarck: l'échec de la triple alliance télégraphique (1887–1889)," *Revue d'histoire diplomatique* 90 (1976): 321–357.

27. Matthias Lau, *Pressepolitik als Chance: Staatliche Öffentlichkeitsarbeit in den Ländern der Weimarer Republik* (Stuttgart: Franz Steiner, 2003).

28. On the Berlin conference, see Steven Press, *Rogue Empires: Contracts and Conmen in Europe's Scramble for Africa* (Cambridge, MA: Harvard University Press, 2017).

29. Bernhard von Bülow, "A Place in the Sun," *Stenographische Berichte über die Verhandlungen des Reichstags IX* LP, 5th session, vol. 1, (Berlin, 1898). Translated by Adam Blauhut, accessed July 15, 2017, http://germanhistorydocs .ghi-dc.org/pdf/eng/607_Buelow_Place%20in%20the%20Sun_111.pdf.

30. Sebastian Conrad, "Transnational Germany," in James Retallack, ed., *Imperial Germany, 1871–1918* (Oxford: Oxford University Press, 2008), 219–42.

31. Calculated from Stephen Broadberry and Mark Harrison, "The Economics of World War I: A Comparative Quantitative Analysis." Working Paper, 2005, p. 25, accessed September 27, 2017, www2.warwick.ac.uk/fac/soc /economics/staff/mharrison/papers/wwitoronto2.pdf.

32. David Ciarlo, *Advertising Empire: Race and Visual Culture in Imperial Germany* (Cambridge, MA: Harvard University Press, 2011).

33. John Phillip Short, *Magic Lantern Empire: Colonialism and Society in Germany* (Ithaca, NY: Cornell University Press, 2012).

34. Patrick Bernhard, "Borrowing from Mussolini: Nazi Germany's Colonial Aspirations in the Shadow of Italian Expansionism," *Journal of Imperial and Commonwealth History* 41, no. 4 (2013): 621.

35. Sebastian Conrad, *German Colonialism: A Short History*, trans Sorcha O'Hagan (Cambridge: Cambridge University Press, 2012); Bradley Naranch and Geoff Eley, eds., *German Colonialism in a Global Age* (Durham, NC: Duke University Press, 2014); Britta Schilling, *Postcolonial Germany: Memories of Empire in a Decolonized Nation* (Oxford: Oxford University Press, 2014).

36. Cited in Dirk Bönker, "Global Politics and Germany's Destiny 'from an East Asian Perspective': Alfred von Tirpitz and the Making of Wilhelmine Navalism," *Central European History* 46, no. 1 (2013): 95.

37. Kristin Kopp, *Germany's Wild East: Constructing Poland as Colonial Space* (Ann Arbor: University of Michigan Press, 2012); Vejas Liulevicius, *The German Myth of the East: 1800 to the Present* (Oxford: Oxford University Press, 2009); Philipp Ther, "Deutsche Geschichte als imperial Geschichte: Polen, slawophone Minderheiten und das Kaiserreich als kontinentales Empire," in Sebastian Conrad and Jürgen Osterhammel, eds., *Das Kaiserreich transnational: Deutschland in der Welt 1871–1914* (Göttingen: Vanderhoeck & Ruprecht, 2006), 129–148.

38. Halford Mackinder, "The Geographical Pivot of History," *Geographical Journal* 23, no. 4 (1904): 421–437.

39. Halford Mackinder, *Democratic Ideals and Reality: A Study in the Politics of Reconstruction* (London: Constable & Company, 1919).

40. Paul Rohrbach, *Der deutsche Gedanke in der Welt* (Düsseldorf: K. R. Langewiesche, 1912). Citation from English translation, *German World Policies* (London: Macmillan, 1915), 218.

41. Rohrbach, *German World Policies*, 216. Rohrbach would produce many suggestions on improving news supply to bolster German power abroad well into the Weimar Republic. For a biography, see Horst Bieber, *Paul Rohrbach: Ein konservativer Publizist und Kritiker der Weimarer Republik* (Munich-Pullach: Verlag Dokumentation, 1972).

42. Dominik Geppert, *Pressekriege: Öffentlichkeit und Diplomatie in den deutsch-britischen Beziehungen (1896–1912)* (Munich: Oldenbourg, 2007), 80.

43. Letter from Heinrich Schnee to Imperial Colonial Office, July 12, 1913, Bundesarchiv Berlin-Lichterfelde (henceforth BArch) R1001/2696, 229–232.

44. Geppert, *Pressekriege*, 222–227.

45. Max Wittwer, *Das deutsche Zeitungswesen in seiner neueren Entwicklung: Beiträge zur Geschichte des deutschen Zeitungswesens* (Halle: Kaemmerer, 1914), 42; Morf, *Die Drahtberichterstattung im modernen Zeitungswesen*, 75–76.

46. Winzen, *Das Kaiserreich am Abgrund*, 115–117, 125; Frank Bösch, *Öffentliche Geheimnisse: Skandale, Politik und Medien in Deutschland und Großbritan-*

nien 1880–1914 (Munich: Oldenbourg, 2009), 406–419; Martin Kohlrausch, *Der Monarch im Skandal: Die Logik der Massenmedien und die Transformation der wilhelminischen Monarchie* (Berlin: Akademie Verlag, 2005), 243–301. On cooperation between Bülow, Hammann, and Mantler, see Nathan Orgill, "'Three and a Half Men': The Bülow-Hammann System of Public Relations before the First World War" (PhD diss., University of Michigan, 2009).

47. Cited in Martin Mayer, *Geheime Diplomatie und öffentliche Meinung: Die Parlamente in Frankreich, Deutschland und Großbritannien und die erste Marokkokrise 1904–1906* (Düsseldorf: Droste, 2002), 311. On press politics in the Foreign Office, see Martin Wroblewski, *Moralische Eroberungen als Instrumente der Diplomatie: Die Informations- und Pressepolitik des Auswärtigen Amts 1902–1914* (Göttingen: V&R Unipress, 2016).

48. Cited in Geppert, *Pressekriege,* 80.

49. Letter from Mantler to Hammann, January 16, 1908, cited in Heinz Alfred Gemeinhardt, *Deutsche und österreichische Pressepolitik während der bosnischen Krise 1908/09* (Husum: Matthiesen, 1980), 37.

50. Geppert, *Pressekriege,* 86–87.

51. Report by Ludwig Asch to Hammann, May 6, 1912, Politisches Archiv des Auswärtigen Amtes, Berlin (henceforth PA AA) R1646.

52. Heerdegen, *Der Nachrichtendienst der Presse,* 54–56.

53. For example, Max Roscher, "Über das Wesen und die Bedingungen des internationalen Nachrichtenverkehrs," *Weltwirtschaftliches Archiv* 3, no. 1 (1914): 37–59.

54. Calculated from Arthur Lewis, "The Rate of Growth of World Trade, 1830–1973," in Sven Grassman and Erik Lundberg, eds., *The World Economic Order: Past and Prospects* (New York: St. Martin's Press, 1981), 11–74.

55. Cornelius Torp, "The Coalition of 'Rye and Iron' under the Pressure of Globalization: A Reinterpretation of Germany's Political Economy before 1914," *Central European History* 43, no. 3 (2010): 401–427.

56. Cited in Rudolf Rotheit, *Die Friedensbedingungen der deutschen Presse: Los von Reuter und Havas!* (Berlin: Puttkammer & Mühlbrecht, 1915), 13.

57. Dankwart Guratzsch, *Macht durch Organisation: Die Grundlegung des Hugenbergschen Presseimperiums* (Düsseldorf: Bertelsmann Universitätsverlag, 1974), 110.

58. Hansen, "Depeschenbureaus und internationales Nachrichtenwesen," 95.

59. *Deutsche Presse* 28, July 1914.

60. For example, Garr, *Die wirtschaftlichen Grundlagen des modernen Zeitungswesens,* 29. For the same view in 1928: Otto Groth, *Die Zeitung: Ein System der Zeitungskunde* (Mannheim: J. Bensheimer, 1928), 1:487.

61. Transcript of 197th session of the Reichstag, January 22, 1914, BArch R1501/114179, 273. Reply to Dr. Werner from Vice-Chancellor and Secretary of the Interior, Clemens von Delbrück, January 23, 1914, BArch R1501/114179, 276.

62. David Oels and Ute Schneider, eds., „Der ganze Verlag ist einfach eine Bonbonniere": Ullstein in der ersten Hälfte des 20. Jahrhunderts (Berlin: De Gruyter, 2015); Elisabeth Kraus, Die Familie Mosse: Deutsch-jüdisches Bürgertum im 19. und 20. Jahrhundert (Munich: C. H. Beck, 1999).

63. Kurt Koszyk, Zwischen Kaiserreich und Diktatur: Die sozialdemokratische Presse von 1914 bis 1933 (Heidelberg: Quelle & Meyer, 1958), 188.

64. On the Kulturkampf, Rebecca Ayako Bennette, Fighting for the Soul of Germany: The Catholic Struggle for Inclusion after Unification (Cambridge, MA: Harvard University Press, 2012).

65. Rudolf Stöber, Deutsche Pressegeschichte: Einführung, Systematik, Glossar (Konstanz: UVK-Medien, 2000), 209. On the rise of mass media, see Corey Ross, Media and the Making of Modern Germany: Mass Communications, Society, and Politics from the Empire to the Third Reich (Oxford: Oxford University Press, 2008), 11–34. On paper, see Heidi J. S. Tworek, "The Death of News? The Problem of Paper in the Weimar Republic," Central European History 50, no. 3 (2017): 328–346.

66. See Peter Fritzsche, Reading Berlin 1900 (Cambridge, MA: Harvard University Press, 1996).

67. Jochen Hung, "'Der deutschen Jugend!': The Newspaper Tempo and the Generational Discourse of the Weimar Republic," in Jochen Hung, Godela Weiss-Sussex, and Geoff Wilkes, eds., Beyond Glitter and Doom: The Contingency of the Weimar Republic (Munich: Iudicium, 2012), 105–118.

68. Richard Evans, The Coming of the Third Reich (London: Allen Lane, 2003), 120. On newspapers in the Weimar Republic, see Bernhard Fulda, Press and Politics in the Weimar Republic (Oxford: Oxford University Press, 2009), ch. 1.

69. Jochen Hung, "'Bad' Politics and 'Good' Culture: New Approaches to the History of the Weimar Republic," Central European History 49, no. 3–4 (2016): 441–453.

70. Hjalmar Schacht, "Statistische Untersuchung über die Presse Deutschlands," Jahrbuch für Nationalökonomie und Statistik 15 (1898): 517.

71. Wittwer, Das deutsche Zeitungswesen, 14, 20.

72. On smaller agencies, see Jianming He, Die Nachrichtenagenturen in Deutschland: Geschichte und Gegenwart (Frankfurt am Main: Peter Lang, 1996), 89–110; Christine Wunderlich, "Telegraphische Nachrichtenbüros in Deutschland bis zum Ersten Weltkrieg," in Jürgen Wilke, ed., Telegraphenbüros und Nachrichtenagenturen in Deutschland: Untersuchungen zu ihrer Geschichte bis 1949 (Munich: K. G. Saur, 1991), 23–86.

73. Groth, Die Zeitung 1:475.

74. Geheimes Staatsarchiv Preußischer Kulturbesitz, Berlin (henceforth GStA PK) I. HA Rep. 77 tit. 949 11a, 17.

75. Franz Reuter and Otto Meynen, Die deutsche Zeitung: Wesen und Wertung (Munich: Duncker & Humblot, 1928), 167. On layout and presentation, see

David Machin and Sarah Niblock, "Branding Newspapers," *Journalism Studies* 9, no. 2 (2008): 244–259.

76. Wittwer, *Das deutsche Zeitungswesen*, 42.

77. *Handbuch der Weltpresse* (1932), cited in Daniel Gossel, *Medien und Politik in Deutschland und den USA: Kontrolle, Konflikt und Kooperation vom 18. bis zum frühen 20. Jahrhundert* (Stuttgart: Franz Steiner, 2010), 267.

78. Morf, *Die Drahtberichterstattung im modernen Zeitungswesen*, 51–55. For the dates when Wolff's branches opened, see *Vom 75. Geburtstag des W.T.B. den 27. November 1924* (Berlin, 1924), 10–11.

79. Arno Meyer, *Die Organisation des Nachrichtendienstes der Presse: Eine Untersuchung über die Einwirkungen des Gesetzes der Massenproduktion auf die Ausgestaltung des Inhalts der Zeitungen* (Libau: D. Meyer, 1926), 78.

80. Friedrich Winkin, *Der Nachrichtenschnellverkehr im Dienste von Presse und Wirtschaft* (Leipzig: H. Buske, 1934), 45.

81. On journalism's emergence as a profession, see Jörg Requate, *Journalismus als Beruf: Entstehung und Entwicklung des Journalistenberufs im 19. Jahrhundert: Deutschland im internationalen Vergleich* (Göttingen: Vandenhoeck & Ruprecht, 1995); James Retallack, *The German Right, 1860–1920: Political Limits of the Authoritarian Imagination* (Toronto: University of Toronto Press, 2006), ch. 7.

82. Albert Krebs, *The Infancy of Nazism: The Memoirs of Ex-Gauleiter Albert Krebs, 1923–1933*, trans. William Sheridan Allen (New York: New Viewpoints, 1976), 102.

83. Arthur Koestler, *Arrow in the Blue: The First Volume of an Autobiography, 1905–31* (London: Hutchinson, 1983), 226.

84. Joachim Rings, *Amerikanische Nachrichtenagenturen* (Limburg an der Lahn: Limburger Vereinsdruckerei, 1936), 10.

85. Louis Lochner, "Hinter den Kulissen der amerikanischen Berichterstattung," *Deutsche Presse* Sonderdruck 7/9 (1931).

86. Koestler, *Arrow in the Blue*, 225.

87. Rings, *Amerikanische Nachrichtenagenturen*, 11.

88. Klaus Wernecke, "Nachrichtenagenturen und Provinzpresse in der Weimarer Republik," *Zeitschrift für Geschichtswissenschaft* 48, no. 4 (2000): 331; Jürgen Wilke, "Die telegraphischen Depeschen des Wolff'schen Telegraphischen Büros (WTB)," *Publizistik* 49, no. 2 (2004): 128.

89. Heidi J. S. Tworek, "Journalistic Statesmanship: Protecting the Press in Weimar Germany and Abroad," *German History* 32, no. 4 (2014), 559–578. On reprinting in the United States, see Ryan Cordell, "Reprinting, Circulation, and the Network Author in Antebellum Newspapers," *American Literary History* 27, no. 3 (2015): 417–445.

90. W. Phillips Davison, "The Third-Person Effect in Communication," *Public Opinion Quarterly* 47, no. 1 (1983): 1–15.

91. Richard J. Evans, ed., *Kneipengespräche im Kaiserreich: Die Stimmungsberichte der Hamburger Politischen Polizei 1892–1914* (Reinbek bei Hamburg: Rowohlt, 1989).

92. Ian Kershaw, *Popular Opinion and Political Dissent in the Third Reich: Bavaria 1933–1945*, 2nd rev. ed. (Oxford: Clarendon Press, 2002).

93. Michael Warner, *Publics and Counterpublics* (New York: Zone, 2002).

94. William Mackinnon, *On the Rise, Progress, and Present State of Public Opinion in Great Britain and Other Parts of the World* (London: William Clowes, 1828), 15. On researching "public opinion," see Karl Christian Führer, Kurt Hickethier, and Axel Schildt, "Öffentlichkeit—Medien—Geschichte: Konzepte der modernen Öffentlichkeiten und Zugänge zu ihrer Erforschung," *Archiv für Sozialgeschichte* 41 (2001): 1–38.

95. Cited in Menahem Blondheim, "'Public Sentiment Is Everything': The Union's Public Communications Strategy and the Bogus Proclamation of 1864," *Journal of American History* 89, no. 3 (2002): 869.

96. Maximilian von Baden, *The Memoirs of Prince Max of Baden* (New York: Charles Scribner's Sons, 1928), 2:250–251.

97. Deliberations of the Inner War Cabinet, November 7, 1918, printed in Charles Burton Burdick and Ralph Haswell Lutz, eds., *The Political Institutions of the German Revolution, 1918–1919* (New York: F. A. Praeger, 1966), 35.

98. Foreign Office Understate Secretary Dr. Eduard David, Meeting with newspaper publishers, November 13, 1918, BArch R705/22, 80–81.

99. On the phrase, see Jack Shafer, "Who Said It First?" *Slate*, August 30, 2010, accessed August 3, 2018, http://www.slate.com/id/2265540/.

100. Daniel Hucker, "International History and the Study of Public Opinion: Towards Methodological Clarity," *International History Review* 34, no. 4 (2012): 775–794. On Wilson, see Erez Manela, *The Wilsonian Moment: Self-Determination and the International Origins of Anticolonial Nationalism* (Oxford: Oxford University Press, 2007). On media and foreign policy, see Frank Bösch and Peter Hoeres, eds., *Außenpolitik im Medienzeitalter: Vom späten 19. Jahrhundert bis zur Gegenwart* (Göttingen: Wallstein, 2013).

101. Heidi J. S. Tworek, "Peace through Truth? The Press and Moral Disarmament through the League of Nations," *Medien & Zeit* 25, no. 4 (2010): 16–28.

102. See speech by Max Weber, *Verhandlungen des ersten deutschen Soziologentages: Vom 19.–22. Oktober 1910* (Tübingen: J.C.B. Mohr (P. Siebeck), 1911), 39–62 and speech by Max Weber, *Verhandlungen des zweiten deutschen Soziologentages: Vom 20.–22. Oktober 1912* (Tübingen: J.C.B. Mohr (P. Siebeck), 1913), 75–79. On Weber and media, see Siegfried Weischenberg, *Max Weber und die Entzauberung der Medienwelt: Theorien und Querelen—eine andere Fachgeschichte* (Wiesbaden: VS Verlag, 2012). On the development of *Zeitungswissenschaft*, see Stefanie Averbeck, *Kommunikation als Prozess: Soziologische Perspektiven in der Zeitungswissenschaft, 1927–1934* (Münster: Lit, 1999).

103. Wittwer, *Das deutsche Zeitungswesen*, 86.

104. Wilhelm Bauer, *Die öffentliche Meinung und ihre geschichtlichen Grundlagen* (Tübingen: J. C. B. Mohr (P. Siebeck), 1914), 309–310.

105. Ferdinand Tönnies, *Kritik der öffentlichen Meinung* (Berlin: J. Springer, 1922).

106. Karl Bücher, *Gesammelte Aufsätze zur Zeitungskunde* (Tübingen: H. Laupp, 1926), 52.

107. Groth, *Die Zeitung,* 2:226–228.

108. Mark Crispin Miller, "Introduction," in Edward L. Bernays, *Propaganda* (Brooklyn: Ig, 2005), 11–13. On interwar Germany, see Jeffrey Verhey, "Some Lessons of the War: The Discourse on the Propaganda and Public Opinion in Germany in the 1920s," in Bernd Hüppauf, ed., *War, Violence, and the Modern Condition* (Berlin: Walter de Gruyter, 1997), 99–118. For a contemporary philosophical take, see Jason Stanley, *How Propaganda Works* (Princeton, NJ: Princeton University Press, 2015).

109. Paul Rühlmann, *Kulturpropaganda: Grundsätzliche Darlegungen und Aus-landsbeobachtungen* (Charlottenburg: Deutsche Verlagsgesellschaft für Politik und Geschichte m. b. h., 1919).

110. November 4, 1920, PA AA R121096, 84.

111. Arthur Ponsonby, *Falsehood in War-Time: Containing an Assortment of Lies Circulated throughout the Nations during the Great War* (London: G. Allen & Unwin, 1928). On contemporary British attitudes, see Mark Hampton, *Visions of the Press in Britain, 1850–1950* (Urbana: University of Illinois Press, 2004), ch. 5.

112. Wilhelm Schwedler, *Die Nachricht im Weltverkehr: Kritische Bemerkungen über das internationale Nachrichtenwesen vor und nach dem Weltkriege* (Berlin: Deutsche Verlagsgesellschaft für Politik und Geschichte, 1922), viii.

113. Bernays, *Propaganda,* 163.

114. Walter Aub, "Der Fall Hugenberg," *Die Weltbühne* 22 (1926): 287. On *Die Weltbühne,* see István Deák, *Weimar Germany's Left-Wing Intellectuals: A Political History of the Weltbühne and Its Circle* (Berkeley: University of California Press, 1968).

115. Speech to Economic Association, July 1, 1927, Bundesarchiv Koblenz, Nachlass Hugenberg, N1231/113, 91.

116. Corey Ross, "Mass Politics and the Techniques of Leadership: The Promise and Perils of Propaganda in Weimar Germany," *German History* 24, no. 2 (2006): 185.

117. *Meyers Lexikon,* 1939, quoted in Stefan Krings, *Hitlers Pressechef: Otto Dietrich (1897–1952): Eine Biographie* (Göttingen: Wallstein, 2010), 243.

118. Aristotle Kallis, *Nazi Propaganda and the Second World War* (Basingstoke: Palgrave Macmillan, 2005), 4.

119. Quoted in Jeffrey Herf, *The Jewish Enemy: Nazi Propaganda during World War II and the Holocaust* (Cambridge, MA: Harvard University Press, 2006), 20.

120. Joseph Goebbels, "Nachrichtenpolitik," June 6, 1941, reprinted in Bernd Sösemann and Marius Lange, eds., *Propaganda: Medien und Öffentlichkeit in der NS-Diktatur: Eine Dokumentation und Edition von Gesetzen, Führerbe-fehlen und sonstigen Anordnungen sowie propagandistischen Bild- und Textüber-lieferungen im kommunikationshistorischen Kontext und in der Wahrnehmung des Publikums* (Stuttgart: Franz Steiner, 2011), 770.

121. Stefanie Averbeck, "Die Emigration der Zeitungswissenschaft nach 1933 und der Verlust sozialwissenschaftlicher Perspektiven in Deutschland," *Publizistik* 46, no. 1 (2001): 1–19.

122. Robert Brunhuber, *Das moderne Zeitungswesen (System der Zeitungslehre)* (Leipzig: G. J. Göschen, 1907), 104.

123. Jürgen Habermas, *Der Strukturwandel der Öffentlichkeit: Untersuchungen zu einer Kategorie der bürgerlichen Gesellschaft* (Frankfurt am Main: Suhrkamp, 1962). Jürgen Habermas, *The Structural Transformation of the Public Sphere: An Inquiry into a Category of Bourgeois Society,* trans. Thomas Burger (Cambridge, MA: MIT Press, 1989).

124. Habermas, *The Structural Transformation of the Public Sphere,* 187.

125. Craig Calhoun, ed., *Habermas and the Public Sphere* (Cambridge, MA: MIT Press, 1992).

126. Hansen, "Depeschenbureaus und internationales Nachrichtenwesen," 80.

127. Collected in GStA PK I. HA Rep. 89, Nr. 687–693 and I. HA Rep. 77 tit. 946 Nr. 28a.

128. Wedekind, *Fürsten-Korrespondenz,* March 30, 1914, GStA PK I. HA Rep. 89, Nr. 693.

129. Walter Zechlin, *Pressechef bei Ebert, Hindenburg und Kopf: Erlebnisse eines Pressechefs und Diplomaten* (Hannover: Schlüter, 1956), 106. Zechlin was chief press officer from 1926 to 1932.

130. Papers of Heinrich Brüning. Journals, Manuscripts, and Personal Papers, ca. 1930–1970. Tageszettel 1/1/31–10/7/31 in Box 1. HUG(FP) 93.35. Harvard University Archives. Thanks to James McSpadden for pointing this out.

131. Chief press officer Zechlin met every morning with Hindenburg, who liked Zechlin's "amusing manner" so much that he sent the Social Democrat as legate to Mexico in early 1933. Alfred Lückenhaus, *Von draußen gesehen: Bericht eines deutschen Auslandskorrespondenten aus Großbritannien, den Vereinigten Staaten von Amerika, Japan, China, 1924 bis 1945* (Düsseldorf: Robert Kämmerer, 1955), 58.

132. Anke te Heesen, *The Newspaper Clipping: A Modern Paper Object* (Manchester: Manchester University Press, 2014, orig. publ. in German 2006).

133. André Uzulis, "DNB: Darf Nichts Bringen—Eine Nachrichtenagentur im Dritten Reich," in Christoph Studt, ed., *"Diener des Staates" oder "Widerstand zwischen den Zeilen"? Die Rolle der Presse im "Dritten Reich"* (Berlin: LIT, 2007), 111.

134. Gideon Reuveni, *Reading Germany: Literature and Consumer Culture in Germany before 1933,* trans. Ruth Morris (New York: Berghahn Books, 2006). On censorship and sexuality, see Laurie Marhoefer, *Sex and the Weimar Republic: German Homosexual Emancipation and the Rise of the Nazis* (Toronto: University of Toronto Press, 2015).

135. Frank Bösch, "Zeitungsberichte im Alltagsgespräch: Mediennutzung, Medienwirkung und Kommunikation im Kaiserreich," *Publizistik* 49, no. 3 (2004): 319–336.

136. Fulda, *Press and Politics in the Weimar Republic,* ch. 4.

137. Rudolf Seyffert, *Allgemeine Werbelehre* (Stuttgart: C. E. Poeschel, 1929), 388–392. For a similar survey, see Hans Blinde, *Die Zeitung im Dienste der Reklame* (Frankfurt an der Oder: Trowitzsch & Sohn, 1931), 64–65.

138. The next lowest percentage was for agricultural workers, 44.4 percent of whom read nonpolitical local papers.

139. Brunhuber, *Das moderne Zeitungswesen*, 102.

2. A World Wireless Network

1. Sean McMeekin, *The Berlin-Baghdad Express: The Ottoman Empire and Germany's Bid for World Power* (Cambridge, MA: Harvard University Press, 2010).

2. Letter from Helmuth von Moltke the Younger to War Ministry, January 23, 1908, Bundesarchiv, Berlin-Lichterfelde (henceforth BArch) R1001/7184, 7–8.

3. Report from chief of the army general staff to Colonial Office, July 1911, BArch R1001/7198, 26.

4. Report from German consulate in Sydney, July 26, 1911, and report from German Foreign Office, October 31, 1911, BArch R1001/7198, 37–38 and 50–51.

5. Letter from Telefunken to German Colonial Office, November 18, 1911, BArch R1001/7198, 61–62.

6. Simone M. Müller, *Wiring the World: The Social and Cultural Creation of Global Telegraph Networks* (New York: Columbia University Press, 2016), ch. 2.

7. Simone Müller, "Beyond the Means of 99 Percent of the Population: Business Interests, State Intervention, and Submarine Telegraphy," *Journal of Policy History* 27, no. 3 (2015): 439–464.

8. Heidi J. S. Tworek and Simone M. Müller, "'The Telegraph and the Bank': On the Interdependence of Global Communications and Capitalism, 1866–1914," *Journal of Global History* 10, no. 2 (2015): 270–272.

9. Anton Huurdeman, *The Worldwide History of Telecommunications* (Hoboken, NJ: Wiley, 2003), 308.

10. For example, Thomas Lenschau, *Das Weltkabelnetz* (Halle: Gebauer-Schwetschke, 1903); Max Röscher, "Das Weltkabelnetz," *Archiv für Post und Telegraphie* 12 (1914): 373–389.

11. BArch R1001/2693, 75–76 and BArch R1001/2696, 9.

12. Letter from Heinrich Schnee to Imperial Colonial Office, July 12, 1913, BArch R1001/2696, 229–232.

13. Letter from Schnee to Colonial Office, November 23, 1911, BArch R1001/2695, 197.

14. BArch R1001/2696, 9. Wolff's bill to the Colonial Office in October 1913 was 3,917 marks, for example. BArch R1001/2696, 252.

15. BArch R1001/2696, 278.

16. Steffen Bender, *Der Burenkrieg und die deutschsprachige Presse: Wahrnehmung und Deutung zwischen Bureneuphorie und Anglophobie, 1899–1902* (Paderborn: Schöningh, 2009).

17. Letter from Victor von Podbielski to Chancellor Bernhard von Bülow, October 12, 1900, BArch R901/16340, cited in Martin Wroblewski, *Moralische Eroberungen als Instrumente der Diplomatie: Die Informations- und Pressepolitik des Auswärtigen Amts 1902–1914* (Göttingen: V&R Unipress, 2016), 10.

18. Pascal Griset, *Entreprise, technologie et souveraineté: les télécommunications transatlantiques de la France, XIXe–XXe siècles* (Paris: Editions rive droite, 1996).

19. Dominik Geppert, *Pressekriege: Öffentlichkeit und Diplomatie in den deutsch-britischen Beziehungen (1896–1912)* (Munich: Oldenbourg, 2007), 82–84; Daniel Headrick, *The Invisible Weapon: Telecommunications and International Politics, 1851–1945* (New York: Oxford University Press, 1991), chs. 5–6; Daniel Headrick and Pascal Griset, "Submarine Telegraph Cables: Business and Politics, 1838–1939," *Business History Review* 75, no. 3 (2001): 567.

20. Daqing Yang, *Technology of Empire: Telecommunications and Japanese Expansion in Asia, 1883–1945* (Cambridge, MA: Harvard University Asia Center, 2010).

21. Röscher, "Das Weltkabelnetz," 383.

22. On ships, see Dirk Bönker, *Militarism in a Global Age: Naval Ambitions in Germany and the United States before World War I* (Ithaca, NY: Cornell University Press, 2012); Jan Rüger, *The Great Naval Game: Britain and Germany in the Age of Empire* (Cambridge: Cambridge University Press, 2007).

23. On the military use of wireless, see Frederik Nebeker, *Dawn of the Electronic Age: Electrical Technologies in the Shaping of the Modern World, 1914 to 1945* (Hoboken, NJ: Wiley, 2009), ch. 1. On the technological development of wireless, see Sungook Hong, *Wireless: From Marconi's Black-box to the Audion* (Cambridge, MA: MIT Press, 2001).

24. Michael Friedewald, "The Beginnings of Radio Communication in Germany, 1897–1918," *Journal of Radio Studies* 7, no. 2 (2000): 459. See also Michael Friedewald, *Die "tönenden Funken": Geschichte eines frühen drahtlosen Kommunikationssystems 1905–1914* (Berlin: GNT Verlag, 1999); Michael Friedewald, "Telefunken undder deutsche Schiffsfunk, 1903–1914," *Zeitschrift für Unternehmensgeschichte* 46, no. 1 (2001): 27–57.

25. BArch R4702/122, 82.

26. June 28, 1906. Reichsgesetzblatt Nr. 37, 843. Located in BArch R1001/7200, 4.

27. See letters in BArch R1001/7199.

28. October 11, 1912, *Hansard*, column 680. See Stathis Arapostathis and Graeme Gooday, *Patently Contestable: Electrical Technologies and Inventor Identities on Trial in Britain* (Cambridge, MA: MIT Press, 2013), ch. 6.

29. Winseck and Pike assert that the major communications companies cooperated from 1860 to 1930 rather than engaging in imperial competition. Dwayne Winseck and Robert Pike, *Communication and Empire: Media, Markets, and Globalization, 1860–1930* (Durham, NC: Duke University Press, 2007). Yet this ignores the German government's subsidies of Telefunken and German attempts to undermine cooperation.

30. The National Archives, London (henceforth TNA), ADM 116/1409.

31. TNA T 1/11971/25592 and CO 323/716.

32. See Reinhard Klein-Arendt, *Kamina ruft Nauen! Die Funkstellen in den deutschen Kolonien 1904–1918* (Cologne: W. Herbst, 1996); Sebastian Mantei, *Von der Sandbüchse zum Post- und Telegraphenland: Der Aufbau des Kommunikationsnetzwerks in Deutsch-Südwestafrika (1884–1915)* (Windhoek: Namibia Wissenschaftliche Gesellschaft, 2007).

33. Jeffrey Verhey, *The Spirit of 1914: Militarism, Myth and Mobilization in Germany* (Cambridge: Cambridge University Press, 2000).

34. For example, Peter Putnis, "Share 999: British Government Control of Reuters during World War I," *Media History* 14, no. 2 (2008): 141–165.

35. BArch R43I/1507. On the naval news office, see Wilhelm Deist, *Flottenpolitik und Flottenpropaganda: Das Nachrichtenbureau des Reichsmarineamtes 1897–1914* (Stuttgart: Deutsche Verlagsanstalt, 1976).

36. See Martin Creutz, *Die Pressepolitik der kaiserlichen Regierung während des Ersten Weltkriegs: Die Exekutive, die Journalisten und der Teufelskreis der Berichterstattung* (Frankfurt am Main: Peter Lang, 1996); Kurt Koszyk, *Deutsche Pressepolitik im Ersten Weltkrieg* (Düsseldorf: Droste, 1968); Anne Schmidt, *Belehrung, Propaganda, Vertrauensarbeit: Zum Wandel amtlicher Kommunikationspolitik in Deutschland, 1914–1918* (Essen: Klartext, 2006); David Welch, *Germany, Propaganda and Total War, 1914–1918: The Sins of Omission* (London: Athlone, 2000).

37. Jürgen Wilke, *Presseanweisungen im zwanzigsten Jahrhundert: Erster Weltkrieg, Drittes Reich, DDR* (Cologne: Böhlau, 2007), 51.

38. "Oberzensurstelle: Kommunikationsüberwachende Vorschriften des Jahres 1917," printed in Heinz Dietrich Fischer, ed., *Pressekonzentration und Zensurpraxis im Ersten Weltkrieg: Texte und Quellen* (Berlin: V. Spiess, 1973), 272.

39. Letter from Verein Deutscher Zeitungs-Verleger (henceforth VDZV) to *Vossische Zeitung*, published in the evening edition of December 23, 1915, found in BArch R1501/114192, 8. Wolff claimed that it had exercised no monopoly on war news since August/September 1914, when the Deputy General Staff agreed to provide its news to two other smaller agencies, Telegraph Union, and the VDZV news bureau. Letter from Wolff to Reichstag steering committee, January 14, 1916, BArch R1501/114192, 3.

40. Geheimes Staatsarchiv Preußischer Kulturbesitz, Berlin (henceforth GStA PK) I. HA Rep. 77 tit. 945 Nr. 45, 81. VDZV claimed that 1,500 newspapers could not afford Wolff's service, as it was so expensive. Letter from VDZV

to Naval Office, September 11, 1916, Bundesarchiv Militärarchiv, Freiburg (henceforth BA MA) RM3/9941, 52.

41. Letter from Interior Minister Friedrich Wilhelm von Loebell to district administrators in Sigmaringen, April 19, 1915, GStA PK, I. HA Rep. 77 tit. 949 11a, 11.

42. For example, Rudolf Rotheit, *Die Friedensbedingungen der deutschen Presse: Los von Reuter und Havas!* (Berlin: Puttkammer & Mühlbrecht, 1915).

43. Ute Daniel, "Informelle Kommunikation und Propaganda in der deutschen Kriegsgesellschaft," in Siegfried Quandt and Horst Schichtel, eds., *Der Erste Weltkrieg als Kommunikationsereignis* (Gießen: Köhler, 1993), 76–94.

44. Count Kuno von Westarp question in Reichstag, January 17, 1916, BArch R1501/114192, 10.

45. Politisches Archiv des Auswärtigen Amtes, Berlin (henceforth PA AA) R122206.

46. *Des deutschen Michels Bilderbuch, 1896–1921* (Munich: Simplicissimus-Verlag, 1921), 86.

47. Jonathan Reed Winkler, "Information Warfare in World War I," *Journal of Military History* 73, no. 3 (2009): 858.

48. Heidi Evans, "'The Path to Freedom'? Transocean and German Wireless Telegraphy, 1914–1922," *Historical Social Research* 35, no. 1 (2010): 219.

49. Letter from von Kühlmann to Bethmann Hollweg, March 27, 1917 and previous letter exchanges between Ottoman and German war ministries since mid-1915, BArch R1001/7193, 35–42.

50. Reinhard Koch to State Secretary of the Foreign Office, June 15, 1916, BArch R1001/7192a, 68.

51. Strictly confidential letter from Lieutenant Dr. Karl von Lösch to Foreign Secretary Arthur Zimmermann, January 27, 1917, PA AA R120956.

52. David Paull Nickles, *Under the Wire: How the Telegraph Changed Diplomacy* (Cambridge, MA: Harvard University Press, 2003), ch. 6.

53. Captain Schlee from German Embassy in Istanbul, February 26, 1917, BArch R1001/7193, 42.

54. Dirk Bönker, "Global Politics and Germany's Destiny 'from an East Asian Perspective': Alfred von Tirpitz and the Making of Wilhelmine Navalism," *Central European History* 46, no. 1 (2013): 95.

55. Secret letter from War Minister Hermann von Stein to Chancellor Theobald von Bethmann Hollweg and Foreign Office, January 16, 1917, BArch R1001/7192a, 183.

56. Meeting on the creation of a world wireless network for the German empire, November 23, 1916, BArch R1001/7192a, 148–153.

57. Telefunken plan to erect wireless receiver stations, December 7, 1916, BArch R1001/7192a, 174–177.

58. November 30, 1916, article in *New York Times,* forwarded by Telefunken to Imperial Post Office on January 5, 1916, BArch R1001/7192a, 24.

59. Telefunken report to Colonial Office, January 12, 1917, BArch R1001/7192a, 188.

60. Meetings and plans from Telefunken, December 1916, BArch R1001/7192a, 167–179.

61. Secret letter from von Stein to Bethmann Hollweg and Foreign Office, January 16, 1917, BArch R1001/7192a, 184.

62. Hew Strachan, *The First World War* (New York: Viking, 2004), 205–207.

63. Meeting in Imperial Post Office, October 25, 1918, BArch R1001/7195, 39.

64. Secret letter from Telefunken to Imperial Post Office, April 7, 1917, BArch R1001/7193, 19–22.

65. On Hollandsch Nieuwsbureau, see Nicole Eversdijk, *Kultur als politisches Werbemittel: Ein Beitrag zur deutschen kultur- und pressepolitischen Arbeit in den Niederlanden während des Ersten Weltkrieges* (Münster: Waxmann, 2010), 184–200.

66. PA AA R122220.

67. BA MA RM3/9805, 48. On Deutscher Überseedienst (DÜD), see Dankwart Guratzsch, *Macht durch Organisation: Die Grundlegung des Hugenbergschen Presseimperiums* (Düsseldorf: Bertelsmann Universitäts-verlag, 1974), 232–243.

68. Theodor Schuchart, *Die deutsche Außenhandelsförderung unter besonderer Berücksichtigung des Wirtschaftsnachrichtenwesens*, 2nd rev. ed. (Berlin: L. Simion, 1918), 129.

69. May 28, 1915, working committee meeting, BArch R901/57866, 75.

70. See Jürgen Wilke, "Deutsche Auslandspropaganda im Ersten Weltkrieg: Die Zentralstelle für Auslandsdienst," in *Pressepolitik und Propaganda: Historische Studien vom Vormärz bis zum Kalten Krieg* (Cologne: Böhlau, 1997), 79–124. Transocean was the only agency sending out news via wireless overseas.

71. Letter from Transocean employee, Claussen, to Bernstorff, October 25, 1915, PA AA R121099.

72. In a letter to Bethmann Hollweg on April 3, 1916, Bernstorff suggested that the WTB representative in New York, Herr Klaeßig, should add U.S. news. BArch R901/57868, 322. On Bernstorff in the United States, see Reinhard Dörries, *Imperial Challenge: Ambassador Count Bernstorff and German-American Relations, 1908–1917* (Chapel Hill: University of North Carolina Press, 1989).

73. For example, Thomas Boghardt, *The Zimmermann Telegram: Intelligence, Diplomacy, and America's Entry into World War I* (Annapolis: Naval Institute Press, 2012); Niall Ferguson, *The Pity of War* (New York: Basic Books, 1999), ch. 8; Winkler, "Information Warfare in World War I." Works on German propaganda in the United States only mention Transocean or wireless in passing: Chad Fulwider, *German Propaganda and U.S. Neutrality in World War I* (Columbia, MO: University of Missouri Press, 2016), 71; Johannes Reiling, *Deutschland, Safe for Democracy? Deutsch-amerikanische Beziehungen aus dem Tätigkeitsbereich Heinrich F. Alberts, kaiserlicher Geheimrat in Amerika, Erster Staatssekretär der Reichskanzlei der Weimarer Republik, Reichsminister,*

Betreuer der Ford-Gesellschaften im Herrschaftsgebiet des Dritten Reiches 1914 bis 1945 (Stuttgart: Franz Steiner, 1997), 172–173.

74. Chris Capozzola et al., "Interchange: World War I," *Journal of American History* 102, no. 2 (2015): 474.

75. Other names included: "thousand-word service" and "the German wireless."

76. Letter from Hammann to Bethmann Hollweg, November 26, 1916, BA MA RM3/9805, 17–18.

77. This draws from my database of newspaper articles printing Transocean in the United States. I sourced newspapers from Newspaper Archive, Chronicling America, Utah Digital Newspapers, ProQuest, and the Brooklyn Eagle database. The latest work on American newspapers and the outbreak of World War I only used twenty-five daily and Sunday newspapers as well as five national journals. All came from major cities. Phillips Payson O'Brien, "The American Press, Public, and the Reaction to the Outbreak of the First World War," *Diplomatic History* 37, no. 3 (2013): 446–475.

78. Jonathan Reed Winkler, *Nexus: Strategic Communications and American Security in World War I* (Cambridge, MA: Harvard University Press, 2008).

79. Report by Berlin correspondent F. Sacchi, *Corriere della Sera*, November 11, 1915, found in BArch R901/57872, 7.

80. Letter from German embassy in Sofia to Foreign Ministry, October 4, 1917, BArch R901/57861, 45.

81. BArch R8047 provides details of Transocean's operations in Bulgaria.

82. Strictly confidential letter from Alfred von Oberndorff to Chancellor Georg von Hertling, September 20, 1918, BArch R901/57861, 84.

83. Report on Transocean by Hammann, December 8, 1916, PA AA R121103.

84. Letter from Hammann to Bethmann Hollweg, November 26, 1916, BA MA RM3/9805, 17.

85. The initial 2,723 words of news on December 5, 1916 were cut to 1,400 by shortening some items and postponing news on the Reichsbank to the next day. Report from Hammann on Transocean and 1000-word service, December 8, 1916. PA AA R121103.

86. Paul von Schwabach, head of Bleichröder Bank since 1900, resisted the merger as he believed that Transocean merely represented heavy industry. PA AA R122220. Oberndorff supported a merger. Letter from Oberndorff to Hertling, September 20, 1918, BArch R901/57861, 85. See Dieter Basse, *Wolff's Telegraphisches Bureau 1849 bis 1933: Agenturpublizistik zwischen Politik und Wirtschaft* (Munich: K. G. Saur, 1991), 169–186.

87. PA AA R122220.

88. Report on German propaganda, October 30, 1916, TNA INF 1/715.

89. Shellen Wu, "The Search for Coal in the Age of Empires: Ferdinand von Richthofen's Odyssey in China, 1860–1920," *American Historical Review* 119, no. 2 (2014): 339–363.

90. Strachan, *The First World War,* 73–75.
91. Letter from Telefunken to Imperial Post Office, August 29, 1916, BArch R1001/7192a, 122–123.
92. Letter to Telefunken from Colonial Office, November 15, 1916, BArch R1001/7192a, 142.
93. Secret meeting in Imperial Post Office on plans to erect wireless stations in China, March 17, 1917, BArch R1001/7193, 3–8.
94. BArch R1001/7193, 3–8.
95. Letters from Telefunken to Imperial Post Office, April 1917, BArch R1001/7193, 13–16, 45–48.
96. BArch R1001/7193, 30.
97. Letter from Telefunken to Imperial Post Office and Colonial Office, May 15, 1917, BArch R1001/7193, 69.
98. Larsen described his censorship evasion strategies in letters to his sister (June 18, 1917) and brother (July 25, 1917), BArch R1001/7193, 172 and 182.
99. Letter from BArch R1001/7193, 176–177.
100. Monthly report from Telefunken to Colonial Office, January 9, 1918, BArch R1001/7193, 270.
101. Article cited in letter from Telefunken to Colonial Office, December 22, 1917, BArch R1001/7193, 254.
102. Meeting in Imperial Post Office, February 8, 1918, BArch R1001/7193, 327.
103. Telefunken also transferred the operation of Nauen to the new subsidiary, Deutscher Überseeverkehr AG. Secret letter from Telefunken to Imperial Post Office, December 3, 1917, BArch R1001/7193, 241. The company had 10 million marks of share capital. BArch R1001/7193, 404.
104. Letter from Telefunken to Imperial Post Office, March 28, 1918, BArch R1001/7193, 388–390.
105. Monthly report from Drahtloser Überseeverkehr (Telefunken's subsidiary), April 20, 1918, BArch R1001/7194, 18–19.
106. Letter from Drahtloser Überseeverkehr, May 3, 1918, BArch R1001/7194, 27.
107. TNA FO 233/255.
108. For example, TNA MT10/1314/11 and T1/11971/25592.
109. TNA T1/12269/988.
110. BArch R1001/7194, 253.
111. Drahtloser Überseeverkehr to Post Office, October 31, 1918, BArch R1001/7195, 11–26.
112. Contract between Federal Postal Ministry and Telefunken, April–May 1919, BArch R1001/7195, 160–165.
113. Article 197, Treaty of Versailles, June 28, 1919, accessed August 14, 2018, http://avalon.law.yale.edu/imt/partv.asp.
114. Suggestions collected in PA AA R120955 and R120956 and GStA PK I. HA Rep. 77 tit. 949 11a.
115. For example, Georg Huber, *Die französische Propaganda im Weltkrieg gegen Deutschland 1914 bis 1918* (Munich: Dr. F. A. Pfeiffer, 1928), 14.

116. For example, Ludolf Gottschalk von dem Knesebeck, *Die Wahrheit über den Propagandafeldzug und Deutschlands Zusammenbruch: Der Kampf der Publizistik im Weltkrieg* (Munich: Selbstverlag des Verfassers, 1927).

117. Paul Eltzbacher, *Die Presse als Werkzeug der auswärtigen Politik* (Jena: E. Diederich, 1918), 57–58.

118. Letter from War Ministry to Chancellery, February 5, 1918, BArch R43/1569, 48.

3. Revolution, Representation, and Reality

1. Prince Maximilian of Baden, *The Memoirs of Prince Max of Baden* (New York: Charles Scribner's Sons, 1928), 2:353. I cross-referenced von Baden's statements with other sources and use this memoir with all due care concerning its political bent and complex authorial history. See Wolfram Pyta, "Die Kunst des rechtzeitigen Thronverzichts," in Bernd Sösemann and Patrick Merziger, eds., *Geschichte, Öffentlichkeit, Kommunikation* (Stuttgart: Franz Steiner, 2010), 369.

2. Translation from Sebastian Haffner, *Failure of a Revolution: Germany 1918–1919* (Chicago: Banner Press, 1986), 74–75.

3. Scholars remained preoccupied with political questions about the SPD and councils. See, e.g., Heinrich August Winkler, ed., *Weimar im Widerstreit: Deutungen der ersten deutschen Republik im geteilten Deutschland* (Munich: Oldenbourg, 2002).

4. Alexander Gallus, ed., *Die vergessene Revolution von 1918/19* (Göttingen: Vandenhoeck & Ruprecht, 2010).

5. Mark Jones, *Founding Weimar: Violence and the German Revolution of 1918–1919* (Cambridge: Cambridge University Press, 2016); Hedwig Richter and Kerstin Wolff, eds., *Frauenwahlrecht: Demokratisierung der Demokratie in Deutschland und Europa* (Hamburg: Hamburger Edition, 2018). Two recent overviews are: Joachim Käppner, *1918—Aufstand für die Freiheit: Die Revolution der Besonnenen* (Munich: Piper Verlag, 2017); Wolfgang Niess, *Die Revolution von 1918/19: Der wahre Beginn unserer Demokratie* (Berlin: Europa Verlag, 2017).

6. Eric Weitz, "Weimar Germany and Its Histories," *Central European History* 43, no. 4 (2010): 589.

7. The declaration of November 1918 was a performative speech act, meaning a "discursive practice that enacts or produces that which it names." Judith Butler, *Bodies That Matter: On the Discursive Limits of "Sex"* (New York: Routledge, 1993), 13. On how social institutions give validity to speech acts, see Pierre Bourdieu, *Language and Symbolic Power*, ed. John B. Thompson (Cambridge: Polity, 1991).

8. Brian Klaas, "Why Coups Fail," *Foreign Affairs*, July 17, 2016, accessed July 15, 2017, https://www.foreignaffairs.com/articles/turkey/2016-07-17/why -coups-fail. Political science work on coups tends to begin after 1945. For example, Naunihal Singh, *Seizing Power: The Strategic Logic of Military Coups*

(Baltimore: Johns Hopkins University Press, 2014). For a critique of this chronology, see Danny Orbach, "The Not-So-Secret Ingredients of Military Coups," *War on the Rocks,* July 27, 2017, accessed August 1, 2017, https://warontherocks.com/2017/07/the-not-so-secret-ingredients-of-military-coups/?mc_cid=e400363a5f&mc_eid=99cb73d25b.

9. Mary Sarotte, *The Collapse: The Accidental Opening of the Berlin Wall* (New York: Basic Books, 2014). On the fall of the Berlin Wall as a media event, see Julia Sonnevend, *Stories without Borders: The Berlin Wall and the Making of a Global Iconic Event* (New York: Oxford University Press, 2016).

10. John Röhl, *Wilhelm II: Der Weg in den Abgrund, 1900–1941,* 2nd ed. (Munich: Beck, 2009), 1242.

11. Röhl, *Wilhelm II,* 1244.

12. Von Baden, *The Memoirs of Prince Max of Baden,* 2:350.

13. Haffner, *Failure of a Revolution,* 74.

14. Von Baden, *The Memoirs of Prince Max of Baden,* 2:367.

15. Revolutionaries occupied the key Berlin telephone exchanges in the early afternoon, stopping calls. Werner Conze et al., eds., *Quellen zur Geschichte des Parlamentarismus und der politischen Parteien: Die Regierung der Volksbeauftragten 1918/19* (Düsseldorf: Droste, 1969), 6:19.

16. Von Baden, *The Memoirs of Prince Max of Baden,* 2:353.

17. Von Baden, *The Memoirs of Prince Max of Baden,* 2:352.

18. Theodor Wolff, *Tagebücher 1914–1919: Der Erste Weltkrieg und die Entstehung der Weimarer Republik,* ed. Bernd Sösemann (Boppard am Rhein: Harald Boldt Verlag, 1984), 647.

19. Hermann Ullstein, *The Rise and Fall of the House of Ullstein* (New York: Simon and Schuster, 1943), 151–153. For the front page of *B.Z. am Mittag,* see, accessed November 19, 2013, http://www.dhm.de/lemo/objekte/pict/kg_037_1/.

20. On Ebert's ambivalence concerning the abdication, see Lothar Machtan, *Die Abdankung: Wie Deutschlands gekrönte Häupter aus der Geschichte fielen* (Berlin: Propyläen, 2008), 228–235.

21. Conrad Haussmann and Walter Simons, "Record on the meeting between the SPD deputation and the Imperial Chancellor Prince Max von Baden," written on the evening of November 9, in Bundesarchiv, Berlin-Lichterfelde (henceforth BArch) R43I/2746, reprinted in Susanne Miller, Heinrich Potthoff, and Erich Matthias, eds., *Quellen zur Geschichte des Parlamentarismus und der politischen Parteien: Die Regierung der Volksbeauftragten 1918/1919* (Düsseldorf: Droste, 1969), 6/I:3–6.

22. According to the memoirs of a lieutenant present at Spa that day. Alfred Niemann, *Kaiser und Revolution: Die entscheidenden Ereignisse im Großen Hauptquartier* (Berlin: Scherl, 1922), 139–140. This must have happened after 12:35 P.M., as the sheet also stated that Ebert had become chancellor.

23. Haffner, *Failure of a Revolution,* 77; Niemann, *Kaiser und Revolution,* 140.

24. I surveyed thirty-one newspapers for the evening of November 9 and morning of November 10, including major Berlin and regional newspapers as

well as smaller publications. The *Vossische Zeitung* did not print the notice, though it subscribed to Wolff. It almost certainly printed an extra on November 9, as the newspaper I found was from November 10.

25. Of the newspapers surveyed, only a few made it their headline, such as the *Hannoverscher Kurier* or *Tägliche Rundschau*. Others, like the *Kölnische Zeitung*, buried it on the front page in the bottom right-hand corner.

26. Printed in Eberhard Buchner, ed., *Revolutionsdokumente: Die deutsche Revolution in der Darstellung der zeitgenössischen Presse* (Berlin: Deutsche Verlagsgesellschaft für Politik und Geschichte, 1921), 127.

27. Philipp Scheidemann, *Memoiren eines Sozialdemokraten* (Dresden: C. Reissner, 1928), 310–312.

28. Two cofounders of the Spartacists, Hermann Duncker (1874–1960) and Ernst Meyer (1887–1930), former editor of the SPD paper *Vorwärts* and later chief editor of *Die Rote Fahne* in 1921, headed the group.

29. *Die Rote Fahne: Zentralorgan des Spartakusbundes* (Berlin: Scherl, 1918).

30. Manfred Brauneck, *Die Rote Fahne: Kritik, Theorie, Feuilleton, 1918–1933* (Munich: Fink, 1973), 10–11.

31. Kurt Koszyk, *Deutsche Presse, 1914–1945* (Berlin: Colloquium Verlag, 1972), 26–32.

32. C. Jung, *Paradiesvögel: Erinnerungen* (Hamburg: Nautilus / Nemo Press, 1987), 64.

33. Jung, *Paradiesvögel*, 64.

34. Erich Kuttner, *Von Kiel bis Berlin: Der Siegeszug der deutschen Revolution* (Berlin: Verlag für Sozialwissenschaft, 1918), 29.

35. Wilhelm Carlé, *Weltanschauung und Presse: Eine soziologische Untersuchung* (Leipzig: C. H. Hirschfeld, 1931). On Carlé's work, see Stefanie Averbeck, *Kommunikation als Prozess: Soziologische Perspektiven in der Zeitungswissenschaft, 1927–1934* (Münster: Lit, 1999), ch. 6.

36. Buchner, *Revolutionsdokumente*, 136.

37. Quoted in Bart de Cort and Kurt Schilde, *Was ich will, soll Tat werden: Erich Kuttner 1887–1942: Ein Leben für Freiheit und Recht* (Berlin: Edition Hentrich, 1990), 36.

38. The italics are in the original. Georg Ledebour and Prussian Landgericht, Berlin, *Der Ledebour-Prozess; Gesamtdarstellung des Prozesses gegen Ledebour wegen Aufruhr etc. vor dem Beschworenengericht Berlin-Mitte vom 19. Mai bis 23. Juni 1919* (Berlin: Verlagsgenossenschaft Freiheit, 1919), 129.

39. *Kölnische Zeitung*, November 9, printed in Buchner, *Revolutionsdokumente*, 118–119.

40. BArch R705 / 24, 37.

41. Message printed in John Riddell, ed., *The German Revolution and the Debate on Soviet Power: Documents, 1918–1919* (New York: Pathfinder Press, 1986), 59–60.

42. Protocol printed in Riddell, *The German Revolution*, 68.

43. Report on the takeover of Nauen, written on November 13, 1918, BArch R705 / 24, 43.

44. BArch R705/24, 35.

45. Winfried Lerg, *Die Entstehung des Rundfunks in Deutschland: Herkunft und Entwicklung eines publizistischen Mittels* (Frankfurt am Main: J. Knecht, 1965), 49.

46. Messages were collected in BArch R705/24.

47. Report on the takeover of Nauen, November 13, 1918, BArch R705/24, 43.

48. Daily report, Berlin, November 12, 1918, BArch R705/43, 5. A few news items were still censored if deemed likely to cause unrest, such as items about food supplies in Cologne.

49. Daniel Gilfillan, *Pieces of Sound: German Experimental Radio* (Minneapolis: University of Minnesota Press, 2009), 31.

50. Anthony McElligott, *Rethinking the Weimar Republic: Authority and Authoritarianism, 1916–1936* (London: Bloomsbury, 2014), 28–33.

51. Both articles printed in Buchner, *Revolutionsdokumente*, 376.

52. The meeting was ostensibly called to discuss the events of December 6, when a group of officers had attempted to arrest members of the Executive Committee and declare Ebert president of the republic. Heinrich August Winkler, *Von der Revolution zur Stabilisierung: Arbeiter und Arbeiterbewegung in der Weimarer Republik 1918 bis 1924* (Berlin: Dietz, 1984), 97–98.

53. Protocol of meeting between Executive Committee and Committee of People's Deputies, December 7, 1918, printed in Gerhard Engel, Bärbel Holtz, and Ingo Materna, eds., *Groß-Berliner Arbeiter- und Soldatenräte in der Revolution 1918/1919: Dokumente der Vollversammlungen und des Vollzugsrates: Vom Ausbruch der Revolution bis zum 1. Reichsrätekongress* (Berlin: Akademie Verlag, 1993), 618.

54. Politisches Archiv des Auswärtigen Amtes, Berlin (henceforth PA AA) R121101, December 4, 1918, 116.

55. Winfried Lerg, *Rundfunkpolitik in der Weimarer Republik* (Munich: Deutscher Taschenbuch Verlag, 1980), 45.

56. See Winkler, *Von der Revolution zur Stabilisierung,* ch. 2; Jones, *Founding Weimar,* 174–177.

57. See Jung, *Paradiesvögel,* 67.

58. Draft agreement, June 19, 1924, Archiv der Akademie der Künste, Berlin, Franz Jung Archive 173.

59. Cort and Schilde, *Was ich will, soll Tat werden,* 38; Maximilian Ingenthron, „*Falls nur die Sache siegt": Erich Kuttner (1887–1942), Publizist und Politiker* (Mannheim: Palatium, 2000), 161–167.

60. Gerhard Engel et al., eds., *Groß-Berliner Arbeiter- und Soldatenräte in der Revolution 1918/19: Dokumente der Vollversammlungen und des Vollzugsrates: Vom I. Reichsrätekongress bis zum Generalstreikbeschluss am 3. März 1919* (Berlin: Akademie Verlag, 1997), 215n11.

61. Haffner, *Failure of a Revolution,* 129.

62. Announcements printed in Wilhelm Stahl, ed., *Schulthess' europäischer Geschichtskalender 1918* (Nördlingen: C. H. Beck, 1919), 1:11–12.

63. On bureaucrats, see Ulrich Kluge, *Die deutsche Revolution 1918/1919: Staat, Politik und Gesellschaft zwischen Weltkrieg und Kapp-Putsch* (Frankfurt am Main: Suhrkamp, 1985), 70–81.

64. BArch R43I/2469, 140.

65. Letter from Chief Press Officer Friedrich Heilbron to State Secretary in Reich Chancellery, September 3, 1920, BArch R43I/2469, 139.

66. Niall Ferguson, *The Pity of War* (New York: Basic Books, 1999), 241–246.

67. Telegram sent from Robert Farber to Konstantin Fehrenbach on April 9, 1920, reprinted in *Zeitungs-Verlag* 21, no. 16 (April 16, 1920): 554. On the paper crisis, see Heidi J. S. Tworek, "The Death of News? The Problem of Paper in the Weimar Republic," *Central European History* 50, no. 3 (2017): 328–346.

68. BArch R43I/2526, 69.

69. Letter from War Ministry, February 5, 1918, BArch R43/1569, 48.

70. Bourdieu, *Language and Symbolic Power*, editor's introduction, 23.

71. September 20, 1919, PA AA R121429.

72. Letter of March 2, 1919, PA AA R122207.

73. Letter of March 2, 1919, PA AA R122207.

74. Agreement between Reuter and Wolff. Reuters Archive 1/8715519, LN246, December 1919.

75. Letter from Finance Minister Joseph Wirth, August 7, 1920, BArch R43I/2469, 134–135.

76. Letter to the Chancellery, November 21, 1918, PA AA, R122128.

77. Second provisional consultation on the question of paying reimbursements to Wolff Telegraph Bureau, Reich Chancellery, July 16, 1919, BArch R1001/4709, 89.

78. Kluge, *Die deutsche Revolution*, 79–80.

79. BArch R43I/2526, 106. On demands for payment, see also the letter from Wolff to Chief Press Officer Ulrich Rauscher, February 25, 1920, BArch R43I/2526, 51–52; BArch R43I/2473, 79.

80. Replies in BArch R43I/2526, 29–48, 64–68, 94–95.

81. Letter from Finance Minister Joseph Wirth, August 7, 1920, BArch R43I/2469, 134–135.

82. PA AA R122207.

83. Mantler used the French phrase "douce violence." Provisional consultation on the question of paying reimbursements to Wolff Telegraph Bureau, Reich Chancellery, Saturday, July 5, 1919, BArch R1001/4709, 77–81.

84. July 5, 1919, BArch R1001/4709, 80.

85. July 5, 1919, BArch R1001/4709, 80.

86. PA AA R122207.

87. Wolff had already reached this form of agreement with some ministries, like the War Food Office in 1917. BArch R1001/4709, 75 and 86. See also second provisional consultation on the question of paying reimbursements to Wolff Telegraph Bureau, Reich Chancellery, July 16, 1919, BArch R1001/4709, 84–89.

88. Letter from Heilbron to the Chancellery, September 3, 1920, R43I/2469, 138.
89. General draft of contract with Wolff, November 20, 1919, BArch R43I/2526, 233–234.
90. Letter from Finance Minister Matthias Erzberger to the Chancellery, August 31, 1919, BArch R43I/2526, 200.
91. PA AA R122209.
92. The standard account remains Johannes Erger, *Der Kapp-Lüttwitz-Putsch: Ein Beitrag zur deutschen Innenpolitik 1919/20* (Düsseldorf: Droste, 1967).
93. Quoted in H. W. Koch, *Der deutsche Bürgerkrieg: Eine Geschichte der deutschen und österreichischen Freikorps, 1918–1923* (Berlin: Ullstein, 1978), 192. Captain of Köpenick refers to Friedrich Wilhelm Voigt (1849–1922), who posed as a Prussian military officer in 1906. It inspired several plays, including Carl Zuckmayer's in 1931 and here implies that Kapp was a temporary imposter.
94. Wolff Managing Director Heinrich Mantler's note on WTB's role in the Kapp Putsch, September 5, 1921, BArch R43I/2527, 29.
95. Mantler's note on the Kapp Putsch, September 5, 1921, BArch R43I/2527, 30.
96. Printed in Erwin Könnemann and Gerhard Schulze, eds., *Der Kapp-Lüttwitz-Ludendorff-Putsch: Dokumente* (Munich: Olzog, 2002), 142.
97. "Regierungsprogramm," WTB evening edition (March 13, 1920), printed in Könnemann and Schulze, *Der Kapp-Lüttwitz-Ludendorff-Putsch*, 142–144.
98. Mantler's note on the Kapp Putsch, September 5, 1921, BArch R43I/2527, 30, and "In eigener Sache," WTB Nr. 583, April 4, 1920, in BArch R3301/2011, 74.
99. Kuno Friedrich Westarp, *Konservative Politik im Übergang vom Kaiserreich zur Weimarer Republik*, ed. Friedrich Hiller von Gaertringen, Karl J. Mayer, and Reinhold Weber (Düsseldorf: Droste, 2001), 214.
100. Karl Brammer, *Fünf Tage Militärdiktatur: Dokumente zur Gegenrevolution, unter Verwendung amtlichen Materials* (Berlin: Verlag für Politik und Wirtschaft, 1920), 33.
101. Brammer, *Fünf Tage Militärdiktatur*, 34.
102. Winkler, *Von der Revolution zur Stabilisierung*, 302.
103. For the leaflets, see Könnemann and Schulze, *Der Kapp-Lüttwitz-Ludendorff-Putsch*, 145, 155–156.
104. Strike notice printed in Erwin Könnemann, Brigitte Berthold, and Gerhard Schulze, eds., *Arbeiterklasse siegt über Kapp und Lüttwitz* (Glashütten/Taunus: D. Auvermann, 1971), 136–137.
105. PA AA R122207.
106. For Wolff's notices of March 15–17, see Könnemann, Berthold, and Schulze, *Arbeiterklasse siegt*, 154–155; Könnemann and Schulze, *Der Kapp-Lüttwitz-Ludendorff-Putsch*, 237–240.
107. Brammer, *Fünf Tage Militärdiktatur*, 36.
108. Emergency notice printed in Könnemann and Schulze, *Der Kapp-Lüttwitz-Ludendorff-Putsch*, 240.
109. Mantler later claimed that he had announced Wolff's refusal to disseminate more Kapp messages in a press conference on the morning of March 17, after

receiving several patently false items on March 16. This happened before he knew that the Kapp government would collapse. Mantler's note on the Kapp Putsch, September 5, 1921, BArch R43I/2527, 30.

110. Notice printed in Könnemann, Berthold, and Schulze, *Arbeiterklasse siegt*, 168.

111. Stahl, *Schulthess' europäischer Geschichtskalender 1920* (1920), 1:55.

112. WTB emergency early edition, March 18, 1920, printed in Könnemann, Berthold, and Schulze, *Arbeiterklasse siegt*, 170.

113. See Erhard Lucas, *Märzrevolution im Ruhrgebiet*, 3 vols. (Frankfurt am Main: März Verlag, 1970); George J. Eliasberg, *Der Ruhrkrieg von 1920* (Bonn-Bad Godesberg: Verlag Neue Gesellschaft, 1974).

114. Letter from Ludendorff to Kapp, October 28, 1920, printed in Erwin Könnemann, "Kapps Vorbereitung auf einen Prozess, der nie stattfand: Dokumente aus seinem Nachlass," *Zeitschrift für Geschichtswissenschaft* 43 (1995), 714.

115. Max Bauer, *Der 13. März 1920* (Munich: M. Riehn, 1920), 18.

116. Letter from Finance Minister Joseph Wirth, August 7, 1920, BArch R43I/2469, 134–135.

117. For example, September 3, 1920, BArch R43I/2469, 138–140.

118. BArch R1501/114192, 20–21.

119. Letter of July 30, 1920, PA AA R122204.

120. PA AA R122203.

121. Johannes Leicht, *Heinrich Claß 1868–1953: Die politische Biographie eines Alldeutschen* (Paderborn: Ferdinand Schöningh, 2012), 281.

122. Erwin Könnemann, "Umsturzpläne der Alldeutschen im Jahre 1919 und ihre Haltung zum Kapp-Putsch," *Zeitschrift für Geschichtswissenschaft* 38, no. 5 (1990): 440.

123. Essay in *Die Weltbühne*, March 25, 1920, printed in Kurt Tucholsky, *Gesammelte Werke*, ed. Mary Gerold-Tucholsky and Fritz Joachim Raddatz (Reinbek bei Hamburg: Rowohlt, 1975), 2:298.

124. Article reprinted in *Zeitungs-Verlag* 21, Nr. 15, April 9, 1920, column 520–521.

125. "Seinen Mantler nach dem Wind hängen" became a standard joke among the left-wing press. Dieter Basse, *Wolff's Telegraphisches Bureau: Agenturpublizistik zwischen Politik und Wirtschaft 1849 bis 1933* (Munich: K. G. Saur, 1991), 213. See Koszyk, *Deutsche Presse, 1914–1945*, 52–55.

126. "In eigener Sache," WTB Nr. 583, BArch R3301/2011, 74.

127. PA AA R122207.

128. "In eigener Sache," WTB Nr. 583, BArch R3301/2011, 74. Also printed in *Zeitungs-Verlag*, 21, Nr. 15, April 9, 1920, column 522. Wolff issued another similar denial in Wolff's afternoon edition, Nr. 646, April 13, 1920, in response to further accusations by *Die Freiheit*. Basse, *Wolff's Telegraphisches Bureau*, 311n4.

129. PA AA R122207 and BArch R43I/2527, 29.

130. Mantler's note on the Kapp Putsch, September 5, 1921, BArch R43I/2527, 30.

131. "Michel: Nanu, was habe ich da über Nacht für eine Kapp' bekommen?" *Kladderadatsch* (March 28, 1920), 177.
132. Collected in PA AA, R121430.
133. Winkler, *Von der Revolution zur Stabilisierung,* 337.

4. The Father of Radio and Economic News in Europe

1. Joseph Goebbels, "Der Rundfunk als achte Großmacht," *Signale der neuen Zeit: 25 ausgewählte Reden von Dr. Joseph Goebbels,* 8th ed. (Munich: Zentralverlag der NSDAP, 1940), 199.
2. Peter Fritzsche, *A Nation of Fliers: German Aviation and the Popular Imagination* (Cambridge, MA: Harvard University Press, 1992).
3. Goebbels, "Der Rundfunk als achte Großmacht," 203.
4. See Gerald Feldman, *The Great Disorder: Politics, Economics, and Society in the German Inflation, 1914–1924* (New York: Oxford University Press, 1993); Michael Geyer, *Verkehrte Welt: Revolution, Inflation und Moderne, München 1914–1924* (Göttingen: Vandenhoeck & Ruprecht, 1998); Frederick Taylor, *The Downfall of Money: Germany's Hyperinflation and the Destruction of the Middle Class* (New York: Bloomsbury, 2013). For an argument against views that inflation stabilized Germany, see Niall Ferguson, *Paper and Iron: Hamburg Business and German Politics in the Era of Inflation, 1897–1927* (Cambridge: Cambridge University Press, 1995).
5. David Cameron and Anthony Heywood, "Germany, Russia and Locarno: The German-Soviet Trade Treaty of 12 October 1925," in Gaynor Johnson, ed., *Locarno Revisited: European Diplomacy, 1920–1929* (London: Routledge, 2004), 123.
6. Stephen Gross, *Export Empire: German Soft Power in Southeastern Europe, 1890–1945* (Cambridge: Cambridge University Press, 2015). The term *Mitteleuropa* stems from Friedrich Naumann, *Mitteleuropa* (Berlin: G. Reimer, 1915). It implies a Pan-Germanist approach to Central and Eastern Europe that underlay Eildienst / Europradio's dissemination of economic news. On the term, see John Boyer, "Some Reflections on the Problem of Austria, Germany, and Mitteleuropa," *Central European History* 22, no. 3 / 4 (1989): 301–315; P. Bugge, "The Use of the Middle: Mitteleuropa vs. Srední Evropa," *European Review of History* 6, no. 1 (1999): 15–35.
7. The Foreign Trade Office fell under Department X, Foreign Trade, which was dissolved in October 1921 and its functions distributed among other departments, in particular the News Offices for Foreign Trade and the Foreign Office's Domestic District Offices. Politisches Archiv des Auswärtigen Amtes, Berlin (henceforth PA AA) R97669.
8. Ernst Ludwig Voss, *Beiträge zur Klimatologie der südlichen Staaten von Brasilien* (Gotha: J. Perthes, 1903); Ernst Ludwig Voss, *Die Niederschlagsverhältnisse von Südamerika* (Gotha: J. Perthes, 1907).

9. The news was sent by the main telegraph office in Berlin under the keyword "Dahaste" (Deutsche Außenhandelsstelle) in Morse code on longwave through Königswusterhausen.

10. Roselius provided the capital for Eildienst and also chaired the administrative council for the Foreign Office's district branches for export and its news offices for foreign trade. Winfried Lerg, *Rundfunkpolitik in der Weimarer Republik* (Munich: Deutscher Taschenbuchverlag, 1980), 55–56. On Roselius, though not Eildienst, see S. Jonathan Wiesen, *Creating the Nazi Marketplace: Commerce and Consumption in the Third Reich* (New York: Cambridge University Press, 2010), 104–117.

11. Alexander Pohlmann, *Außenwirtschaftlicher Nachrichten- und Auskunftsdienst: Eine etwas verzwickte Geschichte* (Wiesbaden: Koehler & Hennemann, 1982), 19.

12. Various state ministries, particularly the Economics and Foreign Ministries, worked with DIHT after 1918 to disseminate economic news to improve foreign trade. Founded in 1861, DIHT grew far closer to the state after 1918. The various initiatives included a newspaper, *Industrie- und Handelszeitung* (IHZ), to disseminate nonconfidential economic information, and federal news offices to disseminate confidential economic information. Bundesarchiv, Berlin-Lichterfelde (henceforth BArch) R11/1305, 243. The Foreign Office bought IHZ from the Stinnes company effective from December 1925 and gave the shares to the Eildienst fiduciary committee for administration. On IHZ, see Kurt Koszyk, *Deutsche Presse, 1914–1945* (Berlin: Colloquium Verlag, 1972), 108–109; Pohlmann, *Außenwirtschaftlicher Nachrichten- und Auskunftsdienst*, 21–23.

13. On Bredow's role in World War I, see Chapter 2.

14. Speech at socialist economic conference, Berlin, December 1918, Deutsches Rundfunkarchiv, Nachlass Bredow, 617.

15. The Neue Deutsche Kabelgesellschaft was founded in January 1922 to lay and operate a cable from Emden to New York via the Azores. This private company had a contract with the Commercial Cable Company, but received secret subsidies from the German government. Letter from Hans Bredow to Reich Chancellery, January 28, 1922, BArch R43I/1996, 111–112. The continuously loaded cable between Germany and the Azores was completed in 1926 and connected with the Western Union cable to New York.

16. A 1908 amendment classed radio stations as telegraphic and under Federal Telegraph Administration control.

17. Hertha Stohl, *Der drahtlose Nachrichtendienst für Wirtschaft und Politik: Seine Entwicklung und Organisation in Deutschland* (PhD diss., Friedrich-Wilhelms-Universität Berlin, 1931), 17–19.

18. Ministerial meeting, May 16, 1922, BArch R43I/1999, 195–196.

19. Sykes Committee, *Broadcasting Committee Report* (London: HMSO, 1923), 15. On early British and American radio, see Michael Stamm, "Broadcasting News in the Interwar Period," in Richard R. John and Jonathan Silberstein-

Loeb, eds., *Making News: The Political Economy of Journalism in Britain and America from the Glorious Revolution to the Internet* (Oxford: Oxford University Press, 2015), 133–163.

20. Hans von Bredow, *Im Banne der Ätherwellen [Festschrift zum 75. Geburtstag des Verfassers am 26. November 1954]* (Stuttgart: Mundus-Verlag, 1960), 2:164.

21. The minimum monthly subscription was 75 marks or 15 Reichsmarks after the 1924 currency stabilization. Heinz Pohle, *Der Rundfunk als Instrument der Politik: Zur Geschichte des deutschen Rundfunks von 1923/38* (Hamburg: Verlag Hans Bredow-Institut, 1955), 25n15.

22. Meeting of Federal Radio Commission, June 9, 1922, PA AA R121096, 186–187. Eildienst also intended to protect the news from unauthorized listeners through coding the news and changing the key fairly often.

23. Meeting of Federal Radio Commission, June 25, 1923, BArch R3301/2098, 44.

24. Eildienst broadcast register of September 1924, Österreichisches Staatsarchiv (henceforth ÖStA) I/6e/168/V/1a. Creating statistics and numbers, of course, carries its own biases. Theodore M. Porter, *Trust in Numbers: The Pursuit of Objectivity in Science and Public Life* (Princeton, NJ: Princeton University Press, 1995).

25. By 1925, Eildienst reps were in Amsterdam, Antwerp, Belgrade, Berne, Copenhagen, London, Milan, New York, Oslo, Paris, Prague, Sofia, Stockholm, Warsaw, Vienna, Zagreb, and Zurich. BArch R1501/114232, 108–110.

26. Berlin, Cologne, Amsterdam, Paris, London, Zurich-Geneva, Milan, Vienna, New York, Rio de Janeiro. Milan and Vienna only sent an official report once daily, while all other exchanges sent news at least five times daily.

27. "Unser wirtschaftlicher Nachrichtendienst," *Zeitungs-Verlag* Nr. 46, November 18, 1921, column 1599.

28. Letter from VDZV to Foreign Office, August 18, 1922, PA AA R122203.

29. "Monopol und Geschäft. Die Eildienst GmbH und die Presse," December 8, 1923, *Berliner Tageblatt.*

30. "Das Monopol der Eildienst-GmbH," May 31, 1924, *Deutsche Tageszeitung,* Nr. 354.

31. Postal Ministry memo on radio, June 1925, BArch R1501/114232, 108.

32. Press conference of June 12, 1924, BArch R1501/114218. At a previous press conference on June 3, the government had refused to clarify questions about Eildienst's attempts to create a monopoly.

33. Speech by Hans Bredow at the Main Assembly of the Deutsche Weltwirtschaftliche Gesellschaft, June 17, 1921, cited in Bredow, *Im Banne der Ätherwellen,* 2:165. Financial news had long played a key role in stock market speculation. See Will Slauter, "Forward-Looking Statements: News and Speculation in the Age of the American Revolution," *Journal of Modern History* 81, no. 4 (2009): 759–792.

34. A postwar work agreed that the Eildienst service from April 1922 was "a blessing to the whole economy." Hans Bausch, *Der Rundfunk im politischen Kräftespiel der Weimarer Republik 1923–1933* (Tübingen: Mohr, 1956), 14.

35. See Alex Preda, *Information, Knowledge, and Economic Life: An Introduction to the Sociology of Markets* (Oxford: Oxford University Press, 2009), ch. 4. On technology and economic sociology, see T. J. Pinch and Richard Swedberg, eds., *Living in a Material World: Economic Sociology Meets Science and Technology Studies* (Cambridge, MA: MIT Press, 2008).

36. Hannah Catherine Davies, "Spreading Fear, Communicating Trust: Writing Letters and Telegrams during the Panic of 1873," *History & Technology* 32, no. 2 (2016): 159–177.

37. Meeting of Federal Radio Commission, June 25, 1923, BArch R3301/2098, 45. All figures are from this source.

38. BArch R3301/2098, 97. On statistics in the Weimar Republic, see J. Adam Tooze, *Statistics and the German State, 1900–1945: The Making of Modern Economic Knowledge* (Cambridge: Cambridge University Press, 2001), chs. 2–4.

39. DÜD emerged when the industrialists split from the government over Transocean. Industrialists remained very involved in government supplies of economic news. Hugenberg was deputy chairman of Deutscher Wirtschaftsdienst in 1922.

40. Pohlmann, *Außenwirtschaftlicher Nachrichten- und Auskunftsdienst,* 23–25.

41. Foreign Office report to DIHT, March 1926, BArch R11/1308, 6. A conflicting report stated that the Foreign Office finally bought the Deutscher Überseedienst, part of Deutscher Wirtschaftsdienst, at cost in January 1928. BArch R11/1303, 80.

42. BArch R11/1306, 242. These suggestions for reform appear throughout the files of the DIHT, BArch R11.

43. Foreign Office report to DIHT, March 1926, BArch R11/1308, 7. The Foreign Office and Economic Ministry thus planned in June 1928 for regional news offices to disseminate more trade policy news. BArch R11/1305, 9.

44. Geoffrey Jones and Christina Lubinski, "Managing Political Risk in Global Business: Beiersdorf 1914–1990," *Enterprise and Society* 13, no. 1 (2012): 85–119.

45. See "Außenpolitik im Zeichen des Dawes-Plans," in Günter Abramowski, ed., *Die Kabinette Marx I und II. Band 1: 30.11.1923–3.6.1924* (1973), http://www.bundesarchiv.de/aktenreichskanzlei/1919-1933/0000/ma1/ma11p/kap1_1/para2_4.html. On interwar trade policy, see Robert Spaulding, *Osthandel and Ostpolitik: German Foreign Trade Policies in Eastern Europe from Bismarck to Adenauer* (Providence: Berghahn Books, 1997), chs. 3–6.

46. The Czech bureau paid 500 gold francs monthly for the service. ÖStA I/6e/168/V/1a.

47. Archives Nationales, Paris (henceforth AN) 5AR/179.

48. On the interwar German rediscovery of economic *Mitteleuropa,* see Jürgen Elvert, *Mitteleuropa! Deutsche Pläne zur europäischen Neuordnung (1918–1945)* (Stuttgart: Franz Steiner, 1999), 97–111.

49. January 1928, BArch R43I/2000, 181.
50. December 23, 1920, PA AA R121107, 33.
51. The agency changed name to Amtliche Nachrichtenstelle (ANA) on January 1, 1922, upon incorporation into the state. See Edith Dörfler and Wolfgang Pensold, *Die Macht der Nachricht: Die Geschichte der Nachrichtenagenturen in Österreich* (Vienna: Molden, 2001).
52. ÖStA I/6e/168/V/1a. RAVAG was founded in 1924 as the official Austrian radio broadcaster.
53. Contract between ANA and Europradio, May 16, 1924, ÖStA I/6e/168/V/1a.
54. On *Mitteleuropa* as an economic realm, see Peter Theiner, "Mitteleuropa-Pläne im wilhelminischen Deutschland" in Helmut Berding, ed., *Wirtschaftliche und politische Integration in Europa im 19. und 20. Jahrhundert* (Göttingen: Vandenhoeck & Ruprecht, 1984), 128–148, and Peter Krüger, "Die Ansätze zu einer europäischen Wirtschaftsgemeinschaft in Deutschland nach dem Ersten Weltkrieg," in Berding, ed., *Wirtschaftliche und politische Integration,* 149–168.
55. Caveat: Wilke only investigated the first three weeks in December every ten years from 1849 in one newspaper. Also the percentage printed may not correlate with the percentage sent by Wolff. Jürgen Wilke, "Die telegraphischen Depeschen des Wolff'schen Telegraphischen Büros (WTB)," *Publizistik* 49, no. 2 (2004): 130.
56. Under the Reichsmark, the Eildienst monthly subscription came to 75 marks. Subscribers paid 350–500 marks for initial installation of the wireless apparatus. Memo on economic news, 1925, BArch R1501/114232, 110.
57. January 24, 1924, PA AA R121097, 52–53.
58. PA AA R118735. The Special Economic Section in the Foreign Office reiterated that Eildienst was not intended for the press, but interested parties, otherwise it would have cooperated with the Press Department. Eildienst was of course still cooperating with other ministries and receiving benefits through control of receivers and airwaves.
59. Wolff agreed to pay 183 dollars monthly, rather than 50 dollars for Associated Press to send its commercial news as urgent-rate messages. Letter from Mantler, May 31, 1923. Associated Press Corporate Archives, New York, AP02A.3 Box 9, Folder 10.
60. Letter from Wolff to Agences Alliées office in Paris, April 1, 1924, AN 5AR/480.
61. Confidential report of first general conference of Agences Alliées, June 6–11, 1924, Archiwum Akt Nowych, Warsaw, MSZ 7639, 23–24.
62. Report from first Agences Alliées conference, June 1924, Berne, AN 5AR/472, 24. The Swiss news agency also complained about Transradio, a Swiss economic news service founded by Fritz Simon in March 1922. A Marconi company, Transradio used Marconi stations in Zurich and Berne to reach many European countries. Agences Alliées saw this and Eildienst as their two main competitors for economic news. This Transradio was *not* the

Telefunken subsidiary of Transradio AG that operated Nauen from 1919 to 1931 and was the first to introduce duplex transmission.

63. AN 5AR/408.

64. "Carnet de la TSF," *Le Matin,* December 27, 1924.

65. Article of December 1924, *Th. S. F.,* found in AN 5AR/179. A similar article appeared in *Revue juridique internationale de la radioélectricité,* no. 4 (October–December 1924).

66. Royal Mail Archives, POST 33/711.

67. Reuters began to send general news to Europe through wireless in 1929 once it could use the shortwave station at Leafield. John Entwisle, "Myths: Dancing to a Different Tune," *The Baron. Connecting the Dots for Reuters People Past and Present,* accessed November 1, 2011, http://www.thebaron .info/cecilfleetwoodmay.html. See also Donald Read, *The Power of News: The History of Reuters,* 2nd ed. (Oxford: Oxford University Press, 1999), 168.

68. Danish news agency, Ritzau, letter to Reuters, July 2, 1925, AN 5AR/179.

69. Jonathan Silberstein-Loeb, *The International Distribution of News: The Associated Press, Press Association, and Reuters, 1848–1947* (Cambridge: Cambridge University Press, 2014), 188.

70. Jeffrey Fear, "Cartels," in Geoffrey Jones and Jonathan Zeitlin, eds., *The Oxford Handbook of Business History* (Oxford: Oxford University Press, 2009), 285.

71. Meeting in Vienna, May 7–10, AN 5AR/179^1. (Note: The superscript number at the end of this note indicates the stack or bound book of papers within an archival box: "179^1" means box 179, stack 1.)

72. Commission of Seven meeting at Rigi-Kaltbad, February 22–24, 1926, AN 5AR/472.

73. AN 5AR/179.

74. The Agences Alliées attempt to fold Swiss Transradio into its cooperative framework failed. It continued to broadcast in Denmark, Poland, Yugoslavia, Turkey, Greece, Italy, Austria, Switzerland, Spain, and Egypt. Rawitzki had volunteered to negotiate with Transradio in 1926. Sixth ordinary assembly of Agences Alliées, minutes in German, Norway, June 1938, AN 5AR/473, 14.

75. Second conference of Agences Alliées permanent committee, Montana-Vermala, February 13–16, 1928, AN 5AR/473, 26.

76. In 1929, Rawitzki again suggested that Reuters, Havas, and Europradio set up a syndicate with a central office, where each would own a third. AN 5AR/179.

77. Pohlmann, *Außenwirtschaftlicher Nachrichten- und Auskunftsdienst,* 20.

78. Report to Foreign Trade Offices from the Federal Office for Foreign Trade, October 24, 1933, BArch R11/1298. Its full name was: Deutscher Kursfunk GmbH, Betriebsgemeinschaft des Handelsdiensts der CTC Wolff's Telegraphisches Bureau GmbH und des Eildiensts für amtliche und private Handelsnachrichten GmbH.

79. BArch R1501/114236, 135.
80. PA AA R122204. Rawitzki had been one of the initial directors of Eildienst and sat on its first board.
81. Pohlmann, *Außenwirtschaftlicher Nachrichten- und Auskunftsdienst*, 21.
82. Bredow, *Im Banne der Ätherwellen*, 2:167. One scholar noted that Eildienst had a "historical pilot function," but did not delve further. Lerg, *Rundfunkpolitik in der Weimarer Republik*, 56. The few who mention Eildienst cite Lerg as their source.
83. Kate Lacey, *Feminine Frequencies: Gender, German Radio, and the Public Sphere, 1923–1945* (Ann Arbor: University of Michigan Press, 1996), 34.
84. For a comparison of early American, British, and German radio policy, see Heidi J. S. Tworek, "The Savior of the Nation? Regulating Radio in the Interwar Period," *Journal of Policy History* 27, no. 3 (2015): 465–491.
85. Lacey, *Feminine Frequencies*, 30.
86. Bredow, *Im Banne der Ätherwellen*, 2:205–206.
87. Postal Ministry memo on the radio, June 1925, BArch R1501/114232, 64.
88. Bredow, *Im Banne der Ätherwellen*, 2:215.
89. Lacey, *Feminine Frequencies*, 31. On regional broadcasting companies, see Konrad Dussel, *Hörfunk in Deutschland: Politik, Programm, Publikum (1923–1960)* (Potsdam: Verlag für Berlin-Brandenburg, 2002), 40–55; Karl Christian Führer, *Wirtschaftsgeschichte des Rundfunks in der Weimarer Republik* (Potsdam: Verlag für Berlin-Brandenburg, 1997), 17–35.
90. Peter Dahl, *Radio: Sozialgeschichte des Rundfunks für Sender und Empfänger* (Reinbek bei Hamburg: Rowohlt Taschenbuch Verlag, 1983), 33–34.
91. Bettina Hasselbring, "‚Hier ist die Deutsche Stunde in Bayern': Die Anfänge des Rundfunks (1924–1934)," in Margot Hamm, Bettina Hasselbring, and Michael Henker, eds., *Der Ton, das Bild: Die Bayern und ihr Rundfunk 1924–1949–1999* (Augsburg: Haus der Bayerischen Geschichte, 1999), 51–58; Claudia Marwede-Dengg, *Rundfunk und Rundfunkpolitik in Bayern, 1922–1934* (Altendorf: D. Gräbner, 1981).
92. On RRG's foundation, see Dussel, *Hörfunk in Deutschland*, 48–54.
93. Führer, *Wirtschaftsgeschichte des Rundfunks*, 19.
94. Postal Ministry memo, June 1925, BArch R1501/11432, 56.
95. The Postal Ministry's outgoings far exceeded its incomings in the early 1920s. In 1921, it received a subsidy of 1,244,194 marks. BArch R3301/2098, 101.
96. Bredow, *Im Banne der Ätherwellen*, 2:164.
97. Gabriele Rolfes, *Die Deutsche Welle: Ein politisches Neutrum im Weimarer Staat?* (Frankfurt am Main: Peter Lang, 1992).
98. December 20, 1923, BArch R3301/2098, 67.
99. Kurt Häntzschel, quoted in Lacey, *Feminine Frequencies*, 33.
100. Ernst Heilmann, cited in Lerg, *Rundfunkpolitik in der Weimarer Republik*, 84.
101. Dussel, *Hörfunk in Deutschland*, 43.
102. Meeting of the Federal Radio Commission, June 25, 1923, BArch R3301/2098, 43.

103. For applications, see BArch R43I/1999, 227.
104. Letter from Foreign Office to Reich Chancellery, March 17, 1924, BArch R43I/1999, 232. By contrast, the Radio Commission was happy for news services over the telephone to expand considerably, presumably because it was a point-to-point technology like the telegraph. Meeting of Federal Radio Commission, June 25, 1923, BArch R3301/2098, 46.
105. BArch R1501/114232, 49.
106. March 1926, BArch R1501/114236, 88. Each regional radio company could decide which news services it would receive. Several companies did not take Wolff or TU news as they found them too costly. Others received news for free from local newspapers, like Mitteldeutscher Rundfunk AG. BArch R1501/114236, 61–63.
107. BArch 1501/114236, 222.
108. Sykes Committee, *Broadcasting Committee Report*, 6.
109. Lerg, *Rundfunkpolitik in der Weimarer Republik*, ch. 4.
110. Karl Christian Führer, "Auf dem Weg zur Massenkultur? Kino und Rundfunk in der Weimarer Republik," *Historische Zeitschrift* 262 (1996): 776.
111. Lerg, *Rundfunkpolitik in der Weimarer Republik*, ch. 7; Corey Ross, *Media and the Making of Modern Germany: Mass Communications, Society, and Politics from the Empire to the Third Reich* (Oxford: Oxford University Press, 2008), 279–281. On the relative unimportance of radio for Nazi electoral success, see Maja Adena et al., "Radio and the Rise of the Nazis in Prewar Germany," *The Quarterly Journal of Economics* 130, no. 4 (2015): 1885–1939.
112. Carl Schmitt, "Further Development of the Total State," February 1933, trans. Simone Draghici, accessed August 1, 2017, https://www.counter-currents.com/2013/07/further-development-of-the-total-state-in-germany.
113. Carl Schmitt, *Verfassungslehre* (Berlin: Duncker & Humblot, 1954, orig. publ. 1928), 168.
114. Schmitt, "Further Development of the Total State."
115. Goebbels, "Der Rundfunk als achte Großmacht," 197.
116. Carolyn Birdsall, *Nazi Soundscapes: Sound, Technology and Urban Space in Germany, 1933–1945* (Amsterdam: Amsterdam University Press, 2012).
117. Hans Sarkowicz, "Das Radio im Dienst der nationalsozialistischen Propaganda," in Bernd Heidenreich and Sönke Neitzel, eds., *Medien im Nationalsozialismus* (Paderborn: Ferdinand Schöningh, 2010), 209.
118. Goebbels, "Der Rundfunk als achte Großmacht," 198.
119. Goebbels, "Der Rundfunk als achte Großmacht," 204.

5: Cultural Diplomacy in Istanbul

1. Letter from Hermann von Ritgen to Käte Witt, June 24, 1927, Politisches Archiv des Auswärtigen Amtes, Berlin (henceforth PA AA) R122198.
2. All quotations from letter from Käte Witt to Foreign Office, June 30, 1927, PA AA R122198.
3. See David Reynolds, "International History, the Cultural Turn and the Diplomatic Twitch," *Cultural & Social History* 3, no. 1 (2006), 75–91. On soft

power, see Joseph S. Nye, *Soft Power: The Means to Success in World Politics* (New York: Public Affairs, 2004).

4. Michael David-Fox, *Showcasing the Great Experiment: Cultural Diplomacy and Western Visitors to the Soviet Union, 1921–1941* (Oxford: Oxford University Press, 2012), 14.

5. Richard Langhorne and Keith Hamilton, *The Practice of Diplomacy: Its Evolution, Theory, and Administration,* 2nd ed. (London: Routledge, 2011), 177; David-Fox, *Showcasing the Great Experiment;* Frank Ninkovich, *The Diplomacy of Ideas: US Foreign Policy and Cultural Relations, 1938–1950* (Cambridge: Cambridge University Press, 1981); Frank Trommler, *Kulturmacht ohne Kompass: Deutsche auswärtige Kulturbeziehungen im 20. Jahrhundert* (Cologne: Böhlau, 2014).

6. Akira Iriye, *Cultural Internationalism and World Order* (Baltimore: Johns Hopkins University Press, 1997), 100–101.

7. For the same point in pre-1914 press policy, see Martin Wroblewski, *Moralische Eroberungen als Instrumente der Diplomatie: Die Informations- und Pressepolitik des Auswärtigen Amts 1902–1914* (Göttingen: V&R Unipress, 2016), 325.

8. Walther Heide, *Diplomatie und Presse: Vortrag* (Cologne: Gilde-Verlag, 1930), 19.

9. Tomoko Akami, "The Emergence of International Public Opinion and the Origins of Public Diplomacy in Japan in the Inter-War Period," *Hague Journal of Diplomacy* 3 (2008): 99–128.

10. PA AA Nachlass Nadolny 107. Nadolny headed Ebert's presidential office in 1919–1920, was German legate in Stockholm from 1921 to 1924, then ambassador to Turkey from 1924 to 1932. He led the German delegation to the Geneva disarmament conference in 1932–1933, became ambassador to Moscow in 1933 for eight months before resigning and retiring to his estates until after 1945, when he campaigned for German reunification.

11. Letter from Nadolny to Albert von Baligand of the Press Department, July 18, 1927, PA AA R122198.

12. Telegram from Baligand to Nadolny, PA AA R122198.

13. Irmgard Farah, *Die deutsche Pressepolitik und Propagandatätigkeit im osmanischen Reich von 1908–1918 unter besonderer Berücksichtigung des "Osmanischen Lloyd"* (Beirut: Franz Steiner, 1993).

14. S. Chase Gummer, "The Politics of Sympathy: German Turcophilism and the Ottoman Empire in the Age of the Mass Media, 1871–1914" (PhD diss., Georgetown University, 2010).

15. Hans von Huyn, *Tragedy of Errors: The Chronicle of a European,* trans. Countess Nora Wydenbruck (London: Hutchinson & Co., 1939), 144.

16. Dominik Geppert, *Pressekriege: Öffentlichkeit und Diplomatie in den deutsch-britischen Beziehungen (1896–1912)* (Munich: Oldenbourg, 2007); Sonja Hillerich, *Deutsche Auslandskorrespondenten im 19. Jahrhundert: Die Entstehung einer transnationalen journalistischen Berufskultur* (Berlin: De Gruyter Oldenbourg, 2018). On American foreign correspondents, see John Maxwell

Hamilton, *Journalism's Roving Eye: A History of American Foreign Reporting* (Baton Rouge: Louisiana State University Press, 2011).

17. PA AA R557.

18. Friedrich Dahlhaus, *Möglichkeiten und Grenzen auswärtiger Kultur- und Pressepolitik dargestellt am Beispiel der deutsch-türkischen Beziehungen 1914–1928* (Frankfurt am Main: Peter Lang, 1990), 231–238; Michael Kunczik, *Geschichte der Öffentlichkeitsarbeit in Deutschland* (Cologne: Böhlau, 1997), 148–153.

19. Orhan Koloğlu, *Havas-Reuter'den Anadolu Ajansı'na* (Ankara: ÇGD Yayınları, 1994), 41–45. Thanks to Jesse Howell and Cemal Kafadar for their help with Turkish.

20. Letter from Wolff to Foreign Office, August 26, 1924, Bundesarchiv, Berlin-Lichterfelde (henceforth BArch) R901/57865, 59–60.

21. Report to Foreign Office, June 1925, PA AA Botschaft Ankara 787.

22. Contract between Reuters, Havas, and Agence d'Anatolie, January 14, 1925, Archives Nationales, Paris, 5AR/412, Article 1, Paragraph 10. The contract was extended to five years in March 1926 and was renewed in 1931.

23. PA AA R122207.

24. Report on Wolff, January 14, 1929, PA AA R122204.

25. Letter from Nadolny to the Foreign Office, September 26, 1924, BArch R901/57865, 67.

26. Letter from Nadolny to the Foreign Office, October 20, 1924, BArch R901/57865, 81.

27. Telegram from Nadolny to the Foreign Office, August 20, 1924, BArch R901/57865, 54.

28. Letter from Wolff to Ritgen, April 3, 1925, BArch R901/57865, 122.

29. Recommendation, November 23, 1923, PA AA Pers Presse 722.

30. Hans Jürgen Müller, *Auswärtige Pressepolitik und Propaganda zwischen Ruhrkampf und Locarno (1923–1925): Eine Untersuchung über die Rolle der Öffentlichkeit in der Außenpolitik Stresemanns* (Frankfurt am Main: Peter Lang, 1991).

31. Peter Bauer, *Die Organisation der amtlichen Pressepolitik in der Weimarer Zeit (Vereinigte Presseabteilung der Reichsregierung und des Auswärtigen Amtes)* (Berlin: s.n., 1962), 35–37.

32. Kurt Doß, *Das deutsche Auswärtige Amt im Übergang vom Kaiserreich zur Weimarer Republik: Die Schülersche Reform* (Düsseldorf: Droste, 1977); William Young, *German Diplomatic Relations, 1871–1945: The Wilhelmstrasse and the Formulation of Foreign Policy* (Lincoln, NE: iUniverse, 2006), 152–158.

33. Dr. Karl Spieker, chief press officer from 1923 to 1925, cited in Markus Schöneberger, *Diplomatie im Dialog: Ein Jahrhundert Informationspolitik des Auswärtigen Amtes* (Munich: Olzog, 1981), 44.

34. Dr. Otto Kiep, chief press officer from 1925 to 1926, *Zeitung und Zeit. Festschrift des Zeitungs-Verlags zur Hauptversammlung des VDZV zu Köln am 27. Juni 1926*, found in BArch R1501/144226, 16.

35. Letter from Nadolny to Press Department, August 10, 1925, PA AA R122198.
36. Letter from Nadolny to Press Department, August 11, 1925, BArch R901/57865, 125.
37. PA AA R122198.
38. Letter from Ritgen to Press Department, May 1927, PA AA R122198.
39. Letter from Foreign Office to Ritgen, November 25, 1925, PA AA R122198.
40. Letter from Ritgen to Press Department, May 1927, PA AA R122198.
41. The correspondent was named Wertheimer. PA AA Botschaft Paris 684b.
42. Huyn also worked as press attaché in the German embassy in Warsaw from 1927.
43. Huyn, *Tragedy of Errors*, 141.
44. Kurt Doß, *Zwischen Weimar und Warschau: Ulrich Rauscher, Deutscher Gesandter in Polen, 1922–1930: Eine politische Biographie* (Düsseldorf: Droste, 1984).
45. Wilhelm H. Schröder, "Kollektive Biographik: Grundauswertung des BIOSOP-Projektes," last modified November 20, 2009, accessed February 24, 2018, http://www.bioparl.de. Among SPD candidates, 14 percent described themselves as journalists in 1912, as opposed to 2 percent in other parties. Alex Hall, *Scandal, Sensation, and Social Democracy: The SPD Press and Wilhelmine Germany, 1890–1914* (Cambridge: Cambridge University Press, 1977), 32–33.
46. Letter from Wolff to Ritgen, December 30, 1926, PA AA Botschaft Ankara 787.
47. Letter from Ritgen to Press Department, October 1926, PA AA R122198.
48. Huyn, *Tragedy of Errors*, 91–93.
49. Hartwig Gebhardt, *Mir fehlt eben ein anständiger Beruf: Leben und Arbeit des Auslandskorrespondenten Hans Tröbst (1891–1939): Materialien zur Sozial- und Kulturgeschichte des deutschen Journalismus im 20. Jahrhundert* (Bremen: Edition Lumière, 2007).
50. See Dahlhaus, *Möglichkeiten und Grenzen auswärtiger Kultur- und Presse- politik*, 255–261.
51. Rudolf Nadolny, *Mein Beitrag: Erinnerungen eines Botschafters des Deutschen Reiches* (Cologne: DME-Verlag, 1985), 182.
52. Letter from Ritgen to Press Department, May 1927, PA AA R122198.
53. Memorandum on *Türkische Post* by Ritgen, n.d. but probably mid- to late 1927, PA AA R122199.
54. Pressa represented one of Germany's most important efforts at cultural diplomacy through the press in the Weimar period. As mayor of Cologne, Konrad Adenauer was heavily involved in the exhibition. BArch R43I/2481. See Jeremy Anysley, "Pressa Cologne, 1928: Exhibitions and Publication Design in the Weimar Period," *Design Issues* 10, no. 3 (1994): 53–76.
55. This was to be known as Presse Orientale or Omar service. PA AA R122197.
56. Hans Tröbst's first contract as a foreign correspondent in 1927 paid 6,000 Reichsmarks annually, though he received extra money from his officer's

pension and writing articles for various newspapers, which brought his salary almost to the level of a lawyer. Gebhardt, *Mir fehlt eben ein anständiger Beruf,* 202. Salaries for foreign correspondents varied tremendously and could be paid as a fixed monthly salary, per contribution, or a combination of both. For comparison, section editors of German newspapers received an average annual income of 6,948 Reichsmarks in 1927. Otto Groth, *Die Zeitung: Ein System der Zeitungskunde* (Mannheim: J. Bensheimer, 1930), 4:108.

57. PA AA R122198. German archival sources refer to pounds as "gold pounds," because the British had reintroduced the gold standard in 1925. 84 pounds a month would be approximately 71,000 U.S. dollars a year in 2018. Calculated on August 10, 2018 using the simple Purchasing Power Calculator from https://measuringworth.com.

58. Letter to Press Department from Ritgen, October 1926, PA AA R122198.

59. There was one correspondent in Istanbul, Copenhagen, Geneva, Madrid, Moscow, Oslo, Rome, Warsaw, Vienna, and Washington, DC, with two in London and Paris. The amount of salary covered varied from a third to full coverage, as for Istanbul, Copenhagen, Moscow, Rome, and Washington, DC. Report on Wolff, January 14, 1929, PA AA R122204.

60. Müller, *Auswärtige Pressepolitik und Propaganda,* 52n136.

61. Müller, *Auswärtige Pressepolitik und Propaganda,* 65–69.

62. Edgar Stern-Rubarth, *Die Propaganda als politisches Instrument* (Berlin: Trowitsch, 1921), 1.

63. Bundesarchiv Koblenz, NL Stern-Rubarth N1541.

64. Letter by Chief Press Officer Walter Zechlin, January 16, 1929, PA AA R122204.

65. Many correspondents worked for several papers, while all Wolff's employees just worked for the agency except its representatives in Prague and Brussels. For comparison, the *Frankfurter Zeitung* had 20 correspondents abroad in 19 cities, 22 correspondents in 19 cities wrote for the *Berliner Tageblatt,* while 17 wrote for the *Hamburger Fremdenblatt.* Calculated from *Jahrbuch der Tagespresse,* 3rd ed. (Berlin: Carl Duncker Verlag, 1930), 391–404.

66. Peter de Mendelssohn, *Zeitungsstadt Berlin: Menschen und Mächte in der Geschichte der deutschen Presse* (Frankfurt am Main: Ullstein, 1959), 287–288.

67. PA AA R122198.

68. Draft contract between Wolff and Ritgen in agreement with Press Department, June 1927, PA AA R122198, §4. The contract also stipulated that Ritgen could use his spare time to write for other German newspapers after prior agreement with the Foreign Office, the German embassy in Turkey, and Mantler.

69. PA AA R122200.

70. Report to Foreign Office, June 1925, PA AA Botschaft Ankara 787.

71. Letter from Nadolny to Foreign Office, November 1926, BArch R901/57865, 160. Letter from Wolff, December 30, 1926, PA AA Botschaft Ankara 787.

72. Letter from Wolff to Ritgen, December 30, 1926, PA AA Botschaft Ankara 787.

73. Agence d'Anatolie received annual government subsidies and substantially expanded its base of correspondents by 1927. PA AA Botschaft Ankara 787.

74. February 27, 1928, BArch R901/57863, 201.

75. Report from Nadolny to Foreign Office, May 11, 1931, BArch R901/57865, 254–255.

76. PA AA R122205a. Schmidt-Dumont became attaché for the Balkans and Central Asia in 1934. PA AA Botschaft Ankara 791. In 1938, he became attaché for the German legations in Teheran and Baghdad and the consulate in Beirut. PA AA Botschaft Ankara 160.

77. Letter from Wolff to Foreign Office, May 28, 1931, BArch R901/57865, 257.

78. Letter from Press Department, coordinated with Wolff, to Nadolny, September 14, 1931, BArch R901/57865, 259.

79. Letter from Walter Zechlin to Wolff managing director Hermann Diez, April 11, 1932, BArch R901/57865, 279.

80. PA AA Botschaft Ankara 791.

81. Letter from Ritgen to the Press Department, October 17, 1927, PA AA R122199.

82. Letter from Diez to Press Department, early 1928, PA AA R122199. Otto Ritgen became one of the three men leading Telegraph Union's news service in 1930. Letter from Telgraph Union to Press Department, October 1, 1930, PA AA R122188.

83. Letter from Ritgen to Zechlin, April 1, 1928, PA AA R122199.

84. Letter from Ritgen to Zechlin, April 1, 1928, PA AA R122199.

85. *Milliet, Echo de Turquie* in Istanbul, *Hakimiet i Millie* in Ankara, and *Mokattam* in Cairo. Upon Nadolny's request, Ritgen began to write weekly articles for *République* and *Djumhuriet* as well in March 1929, for which the Press Department raised his salary to 350 marks monthly. PA AA R122199.

86. Letter from Ritgen to Aufklärungs-Ausschuss Hamburg, July 1929, PA AA R122199.

87. After the experience with Ritgen in 1931, Zechlin relaxed the condition that only full-time journalists could attend. PA AA R122199. There were several associations for correspondents for foreign press: Verein der ausländischen Presse, Verband der Auslandspresse, as well as Verband ausländischer Pressevertreter.

88. Ritgen replaced Wolff's representative, Wilhelm von Hahn, who had taken over in January 1934 from Wilhelm von dem Hagen, who had been in Vienna since 1910. Österreichisches Staatsarchiv, Vienna (henceforth ÖStA) I/6e/176/V-5.

89. ÖStA I/6e/176/V-5.

90. Letter from Franz von Papen, August 26, 1936, BArch R55/204, 300.

91. BArch R55/204, 339.

92. PA AA Personalakten 12389 and 12390 (Ritgen).

93. Nadolny, *Mein Beitrag,* 185–186.

94. Walter Zechlin, *Pressechef bei Ebert, Hindenburg und Kopf: Erlebnisse eines Pressechefs und Diplomaten* (Hanover: Schlüter, 1956), 5.

95. Heide, *Diplomatie und Presse,* 19.

96. Letter from Ritgen to Zechlin, April 1, 1928, PA AA R122199.

97. Wolff's director Diez's phrase at a meeting to renew treaties in London in February 1932. Letter from Roderick Jones to Havas Director André Meynot, February 17, 1933. Reuters Archive 1/869623, LN45.

98. Letter from Havas correspondent in Berlin to central office, February 3, 1927, Archives Nationales, Paris, 5AR/180.

6: False News and Economic Nationalism

1. Letter from Chief Press Officer Mironov, Soviet embassy, to Chief Press Officer Zechlin, April 16, 1926, Politisches Archiv des Auswärtigen Amtes, Berlin (henceforth PA AA) R122186.

2. Otto Groth, *Die Zeitung: Ein System der Zeitungskunde* (Mannheim: J. Bensheimer, 1928), 1:527–528.

3. Bundesarchiv Koblenz (henceforth BArchK) Nachlass (henceforth NL) Hugenberg N1231/269, 20. Some claimed that Telegraph Union did not receive the most subsidies, but rather two closely allied companies: Patria Literarischer Verlag and Dammert-Verlag. The distinction seems arbitrary, as the three offered their products together. Letter from Heribert Fröchte to Arthur Rawitzki, November 2, 1929, PA AA R122188.

4. Alfred Hugenberg, "Parteien und Parlamentarismus," *Der Tag,* January 9, 1926, in Alfred Hugenberg, *Streiflichter aus Vergangenheit und Gegenwart,* 2nd ed. (Berlin: A. Scherl, 1927), 83.

5. Modris Eksteins, *The Limits of Reason: The German Democratic Press and the Collapse of Weimar Democracy* (London: Oxford University Press, 1975), 80. For the latest in the extensive DNVP literature, see Barry Jackisch, *The Pan-German League and Radical Nationalist Politics in Interwar Germany, 1918–1939* (Farnham: Ashgate, 2012), ch. 6; Larry Eugene Jones, ed., *The German Right in the Weimar Republic: Studies in the History of German Conservatism, Nationalism, and Antisemitism* (New York: Berghahn Books, 2016); Thomas Mergel, "Das Scheitern des deutschen Tory-Konservatismus: Die Umformung der DNVP zu einer rechtsradikalen Partei 1928–1932," *Historische Zeitschrift* 276 (2003): 323–368; Philipp Nielsen, "Verantwortung und Kompromiss: Die Deutschnationalen auf der Suche nach einer konservativen Demokratie," in Tim B. Müller and Adam Tooze, eds., *Normalität und Fragilität: Democratie nach dem Ersten Weltkrieg* (Hamburg: Hamburger Edition, 2015), 294–314; Maik Ohnezeit, *Zwischen „schärfster Opposition" und dem „Willen zur Macht": Die Deutschnationale Volkspartei (DNVP) in der Weimarer Republik 1918–1928* (Düsseldorf: Droste, 2011); Daniel Ziblatt, *Conservative Parties and the Birth of Democracy* (Cambridge: Cambridge University Press, 2017), chs. 8–9.

6. Ziblatt, *Conservative Parties and the Birth of Democracy*, 308. For a summary of the vast literature on Hugenberg's media empire, see Daniel Gossel, *Medien und Politik in Deutschland und den USA: Kontrolle, Konflikt und Kooperation vom 18. bis zum frühen 20. Jahrhundert* (Stuttgart: Franz Steiner, 2010), 245–295. For an account of TU based only on German archives, see Martin Neitemeier, "Die Telegraphen-Union," in Jürgen Wilke, ed., *Telegraphenbüros und Nachrichtenagenturen in Deutschland: Untersuchungen zu ihrer Geschichte bis 1949* (Munich: K. G. Saur, 1991), 87–134.

7. Memorandum on the necessity of retaining two big news agencies in Germany, May 1933, BArchK NL Hugenberg N1231/39, 2.

8. Report from December 1922 on the Prussian Landtag, Bundesarchiv Berlin-Lichterfelde (henceforth BArch) R1501/114228, 27.

9. Bernhard Fulda, "Die Politik der ‚Unpolitischen': Boulevard- und Massenpresse in den zwanziger und dreißiger Jahren," in Norbert Frei and Frank Bösch, eds., *Medialisierung und Demokratie im 20. Jahrhundert* (Göttingen: Wallstein, 2006), 48–72.

10. *Deutsche Allgemeine Zeitung* Nr. 164, April 9, 1926, for example, printed the notice verbatim and then wrote one sentence acknowledging the embassy's ignorance of the attack.

11. "Im Netze Hugenbergs," *Vossische Zeitung*, November 24, 1926.

12. Louis Hirschs Telegraphisches Büro OHG; Herold Depeschenbüro GmbH; Deutscher Telegraph, Dr. Rudolf Dammert GmbH; Presse-Centrale Depeschenagentur. Richard Schenkel Depeschenagentur, a Hirsch agency, also merged into Telegraph Union. By 1926, Telegraph Union had twenty-nine branches.

13. Dieter Basse, *Wolff's Telegraphisches Bureau: 1849 bis 1933: Agenturpublizistik zwischen Politik und Wirtschaft* (Munich: K. G. Saur, 1991), 187–191.

14. "Im Netze Hugenbergs," *Vossische Zeitung*, November 24, 1926.

15. Gossel, *Medien und Politik in Deutschland und den USA*, 261–262.

16. Jörg Requate, "Medienmacht und Politik. Die politischen Ambitionen großer Zeitungsunternehmer: Hearst, Northcliffe, Beaverbrook und Hugenberg im Vergleich," *Archiv für Sozialgeschichte* 41 (2001): 79–95.

17. Jeffrey Fear, *Organizing Control: August Thyssen and the Construction of German Corporate Management* (Cambridge, MA: Harvard University Press, 2005), 253.

18. Gerd Meier, *Zwischen Milieu und Markt: Tageszeitungen in Ostwestfalen, 1920–1970* (Paderborn: F. Schöningh, 1999), 65; Klaus Wernecke, "Die Provinzpresse am Ende der Weimarer Republik," in Hartwig Gebhardt, ed., *Presse und Geschichte II: Neue Beiträge zur historischen Kommunikationsforschung* (Munich: K. G. Saur, 1987), 365–404.

19. BArchK NL Hugenberg N1231/172. Three hundred newspapers folded due to hyperinflation. Groth, *Die Zeitung*, 1:207.

20. Letter from Stinnes to Hugenberg, October 11, 1920, BArchK NL Hugenberg N1231/27, 423.

21. For a biography, see Gerald Feldman, *Hugo Stinnes: Biographie eines Industriellen, 1870–1924,* trans. Karl Heinz Silber (Munich: C. H. Beck, 1998).

22. Paul Baumert, "Die Entstehung des deutschen Journalismus in sozialgeschictlicher Betrachtung" (PhD diss., University of Berlin, 1928), 96.

23. ALA broke new ground by conducting consumer analysis. Dirk Reinhardt, *Von der Reklame zum Marketing: Geschichte der Wirtschaftswerbung in Deutschland* (Berlin: Akademie Verlag, 1993), 110–116. On advertising, see David Ciarlo, *Advertising Empire: Race and Visual Culture in Imperial Germany* (Cambridge, MA: Harvard University Press, 2011); Corey Ross, "Mass Politics and the Techniques of Leadership: The Promise and Perils of Propaganda in Weimar Germany," *German History* 24, no. 2 (2006): 192–194; Corey Ross, "Visions of Prosperity: The Americanization of Advertising in Interwar Germany," in Pamela Swett, S. Jonathan Wiesen, and Jonathan Zatlin, eds., *Selling Modernity: Advertising in Twentieth-Century Germany* (Durham, NC: Duke University Press, 2007), 52–77.

24. Groth, *Die Zeitung,* 1:475.

25. Eksteins, *The Limits of Reason,* 79, 83.

26. Max Grünbeck, "Die Deutsche Presse in der Weltwirtschaftskrise," *Zeitungswissenschaft* 6 (1931): 388.

27. Letter from Mironov to Zechlin, April 16, 1926, PA AA R122186.

28. Walter Aub, "Der Fall Hugenberg," *Die Weltbühne* 22 (1926): 289.

29. On China, letter from German Legation to Peking to Press Department, March 12, 1929, PA AA R122188. On German attitudes to Russia and the Soviet Union, see James Casteel, *Russia in the German Global Imaginary: Imperial Visions and Utopian Desires, 1905–1941* (Pittsburgh: University of Pittsburgh Press, 2016).

30. Printed in *Vorwärts,* Nr. 167, April 10, 1926.

31. Fritz von Twardowski, November 16, 1929, PA AA R122213.

32. WTB Notice, November 10, 1929, found in PA AA R122213.

33. "Sowjetrussische Dementis," Asien-Osteuropa-Dienst, Nr. 95, April 9, 1926, located in PA AA R122186. Thanks to Greg Afinogenov for help with conventions in Russian transliteration.

34. "Was ist Wahrheit? TU: Beloborodow ist angeschossen.—WTB: Ich darf dementieren." *Vorwärts,* Nr. 167, April 10, 1926.

35. "Die Lügenagentur Telunion," *Die Rote Fahne,* April 11, 1926.

36. David Cameron and Anthony Heywood, "Germany, Russia and Locarno: The German-Soviet Trade Treaty of 12 October 1925," in Gaynor Johnson, ed., *Locarno Revisited: European Diplomacy, 1920–1929* (London: Routledge, 2004), 122–145.

37. Letter from Mironov to Zechlin, April 16, 1926, PA AA R122186.

38. "Locarno," *Berliner Lokal-Anzeiger,* November 15, 1925, in Hugenberg, *Streiflichter aus Vergangenheit und Gegenwart,* 88.

39. Alfred Hugenberg, "Mehr Wille zur Tat," in Max Weiß, ed., *Der nationale Wille. Werden und Wirken der Deutschnationalen Volkspartei 1918–28* (Essen: Deutsche Vertriebsstelle Rhein und Ruhr, 1928), 268.

40. Hugenberg, *Streiflichter aus Vergangenheit und Gegenwart,* 55.

41. Speech to Economic Association, July 1, 1927, BArchK NL Hugenberg N1231/113, 90.

42. Letter from Heribert Fröchte to Arthur Rawitzki of Kursfunk, November 2, 1929, PA AA R122188.

43. PA AA R122186.

44. Dr. Bosenick, Meeting on Telegraph Union Economic Radio Service, October 7, 1927, PA AA R122187.

45. Councilor Hoffmann, PA AA R122187.

46. Meeting on Telegraph Union, October 7, 1927, BArch R43I/2000, 178.

47. *Zeitungs-Verlag* was the weekly journal for VDZV (Association of German Newspaper Publishers), founded in 1894. Five front pages advertised Telegraph Union between August 28 and October 10, 1924, alone. Two other smaller news agencies used radio: Sozialdemokratischer Parlamentsdienst and Nachrichtenbüro VDZV. VDZV and Wolff jointly owned the latter, which disseminated supplementary services.

48. Thomas Mergel, "Propaganda in der Kultur des Schauens: Visuelle Politik in der Weimarer Republik," in Wolfgang Hardtwig, ed., *Ordnungen in der Krise: Zur politischen Kulturgeschichte Deutschlands 1900–1933* (Munich: Oldenbourg, 2007), 531–560.

49. Press Department report by Meyer-Heydenagen, April 19, 1926, PA AA R122186.

50. "Was Sowjet-Dementis wert sind," Telegraph Union Nr. 220, April 21, 1926, found in PA AA R122186.

51. Letter from Mironov to Zechlin, April 16, 1926, PA AA R122186.

52. Rantanen found contracts between ROSTA (renamed TASS in 1925) and both TU and Wolff from 1922 in Russian archives. Terhi Rantanen, *Howard Interviews Stalin: How the AP, UP, and TASS Smashed the International News Cartel* (Bloomington: School of Journalism, Indiana University, 1994), 14.

53. Second conference of Agences Alliées permanent committee in Montala-Vermala, February 13–16, 1928, Archives Nationales, Paris (henceforth AN) 5AR/473, 15.

54. Press Department report, April 19, 1926, PA AA R122186.

55. Letter from Telegraph Union to Wilhelm Stein, German embassy press officer in Warsaw, December 23, 1925, PA AA R122186.

56. Press Department report by Meyer-Heydenagen, April 19, 1926, PA AA R122186.

57. Press Department report on meeting with Telegraph Union editor in chief Steinfurth, April 28, 1926, PA AA R122186.

58. Joseph B. Phillips, "Signer of Czar's Death Warrant Seized as an Anti-Soviet Plotter," *New York Herald Tribune,* January 27, 1937, 1 and 13. Thanks to Terry Martin for his help on trying to verify this story.

59. Manfred Hildermeier, "Germany and the Soviet Union," in Eduard Mühle, ed., *Germany and the European East in the Twentieth Century* (Oxford: Berg, 2003), 29–44.

60. Also known as the Treaty of Berlin, it was ratified on June 29, 1926, and renewed by an additional protocol on June 24, 1931, which was ratified on May 5, 1933.

61. Röllinghoff worked in Moscow until his retirement in 1935. PA AA R122200.

62. Letter from Zechlin to Diez, January 1929, PA AA R122200.

63. For example, the *Leipziger Tageblatt* agreed to pay for 4,500 words a month from United Press in 1924. Arno Meyer, *Die Organisation des Nachrichtendienstes der Presse: Eine Untersuchung über die Einwirkungen des Gesetzes der Massenproduktion auf die Ausgestaltung des Inhalts der Zeitungen* (Libau: D. Meyer, 1926), 75.

64. Letter from Mironov to Zechlin, April 27, 1926, PA AA R122186.

65. "Lügenfabrikation über die UdSSR," *Die Rote Fahne*, April 18, 1926.

66. Report from Wolff to Agences Alliées headquarters, September 21, 1927, AN 5AR/175.

67. Lisa Fazio et al., "Knowledge Does Not Protect Against Illusory Truth," *Journal of Experimental Psychology* 144, no. 5 (2015): 993–1002; Stephen Lewandowsky et al., "Memory for Fact, Fiction, and Misinformation: The Iraq War from 2003," *Psychological Science* 16, no. 3 (2005): 190–195.

68. Brendan Nyhan and Jason Reifler, "When Corrections Fail: The Persistence of Political Misperceptions," *Political Behavior* 32, no. 2 (2010): 303–330.

69. Brendan Nyhan, Ethan Porter, Jason Reifler, and Thomas Wood, "Taking Corrections Literally but Not Seriously? The Effects of Information on Factual Beliefs and Candidate Favorability," June 29, 2017, accessed August 1, 2017, https://ssrn.com/abstract=2995128.

70. The Foreign Office received the report from Dr. Karl Johann von Voss, general manager of Ost-Express, a news service founded in 1919 to supply Germans with news from Eastern Europe, the Baltics, and the Soviet Union. The service had a special relationship to the Press Department, even negotiating with Wolff to exchange news on Eastern Europe in 1932. The Nazis expanded Ost-Express to include East Asia. PA AA R122184 and R122185.

71. On the interwar conflict over Vilnius/Wilno, see Timothy Snyder, *The Reconstruction of Nations: Poland, Ukraine, Lithuania, Belarus, 1569–1999* (New Haven, CT: Yale University Press, 2003), ch. 3.

72. Telegraph Union report from Kaunas, July 28, 1928, found in PA AA R122187.

73. For example, *Berliner Börsen-Zeitung, Kreuzzeitung, Germania, Hamburgischer Correspondent, Braunschweiger Neueste Nachrichten* on July 29, 1928. Clippings located in PA AA R122187.

74. *Der Abend: Spätausgabe der Vorwärts,* Nr. 364, August 3, 1928, 1.

75. *Jüdische Stimme,* July 26, 1928.

76. "Chinesische Zustände," in *Tägliche Rundschau*, October 13, 1926, found in BArch R55/21069, 35. On Germans' interwar views of the East, see Vejas

Liulevicius, *The German Myth of the East, 1800 to the Present* (Oxford: Oxford University Press, 2009), ch. 6.

77. Dr. Karl Voss, Ost-Express, in letter to Press Department, July 31, 1928, PA AA R122187. On German attitudes to Poland, see Kristin Kopp, *Germany's Wild East: Constructing Poland as Colonial Space* (Ann Arbor: University of Michigan Press, 2012).

78. For example, report from German legation in Bucharest, April 19, 1926, PA AA R122186.

79. Letter from Rauscher to Press Department, May 1, 1930, PA AA R122188.

80. Letter from Aschmann to Bernstorff, December 23, 1932, PA AA R122188.

81. Peter Fischer, *Die deutsche Publizistik als Faktor der deutsch-polnischen Beziehungen 1919–1939* (Wiesbaden: O. Harrassowitz, 1991), 89.

82. Letter from Werner von Heimburg, Scherl Paris representative, January 5, 1932, PA AA Botschaft Paris 685a.

83. Letter from Ernst von Mensenkampff to Legation Counselor Rießer, March 19, 1932, PA AA Botschaft Paris 685a.

84. Letter from German Ambassador in Paris Leopold von Hoesch to the Press Department, January 13, 1930. PA AA R122213.

85. Letter to Hermann Diez, March 1932, PA AA R122214.

86. Confidential minutes of Agences Alliées conference in Warsaw, May 23–27, 1927, AN 5AR/464.

87. Letter to Press Department, March 12, 1929, PA AA R122188.

88. Around 1,600 newspapers received Telegraph Union in Germany and German-speaking areas. Ludwig Bernhard, *Der Hugenberg-Konzern: Psychologie und Technik einer Großorganisation der Presse* (Berlin: Springer, 1928), 89. Around 1,350 newspapers took TU in Germany in 1932. Hans Kapfinger, "Das Nachrichtenwesen," in Johann Wilhelm Naumann, ed., *Die Presse und der Katholik: Anklage und Rechtfertigung: Handbuch für Vortrag und Unterricht* (Augsburg: Haas & Grabherr, 1932), 191.

89. On the politics of cartography, see Guntram Henrik Herb, *Under the Map of Germany: Nationalism and Propaganda 1918–1945* (London: Routledge, 1996); Michael Heffernan, "The Cartography of the Fourth Estate: Mapping the New Imperialism in British and French Newspapers, 1875–1925," in James R. Akerman, ed., *The Imperial Map: Cartography and the Mastery of Empire* (Chicago: University of Chicago Press, 2009), 261–300.

90. On ANA, see Edith Dörfler and Wolfgang Pensold, *Die Macht der Nachricht: Die Geschichte der Nachrichtenagenturen in Österreich* (Vienna: Molden, 2001).

91. Letter from Wolff to ANA, July 26, 1927, Österreichisches Staatsarchiv, Vienna (henceforth ÖStA) I/6e/165/V-5.

92. Anson Rabinbach, *The Crisis of Austrian Socialism: From Red Vienna to Civil War, 1927–1934* (Chicago: University of Chicago Press, 1983), 33.

93. Reuters and Havas signed a contract with the Austrian news agency in December 1919 that allowed the agency to sign its own contracts with Wolff

and Eastern European agencies. The contract was renewed with minor modifications in 1929 and 1934. AN 5AR/419.

94. Confidential information from ANA, August 1927; letter from Wolff to ANA, July 26, 1927, ÖStA I/6e/165/V-5.

95. Letter from ANA to Wolff, August 8, 1927, ÖStA I/6e/165/V-5.

96. Letter from Wolff to ANA, March 19, 1926, ÖStA I/6e/176/V-5.

97. On German and Austrian support for a democratic Germany that included Austria, see Erin Hochman, *Imagining a Greater Germany: Republican Nationalism and the Idea of Anschluss* (Ithaca, NY: Cornell University Press, 2016).

98. Report from January 28, 1930, BArch R43I/2482, 80–81. The German government ended payments in March 1930.

99. *Neuer Wiener Journal, Wiener Neueste Nachrichten, Der Tag, Wiener Allgemeine Zeitung.* Clippings found in PA AA R122187.

100. Letter from Mantler to Zechlin, November 22, 1926, PA AA R122186.

101. ANA in confidential letter from German legation in Vienna, October 25, 1928, PA AA R122187.

102. Letter from *Salzburger Volksblatt* to ANA, December 29, 1927, ÖStA I/6e/172, V-1A.

103. Heidi J. S. Tworek, "The Creation of European News: News Agency Cooperation in Interwar Europe," *Journalism Studies* 14, no. 5 (2013), 730–742.

104. Meyer, *Die Organisation des Nachrichtendienstes der Presse*, 82.

105. Minutes, Agences Alliées permanent committee first meeting in Puidoux-Chexbres, August 31–September 2, 1927, AN 5AR/473, 9–10.

106. The Polish government even ordered a Polish translation of Ludwig Bernhard's book on Hugenberg (*Der Hugenberg-Konzern*) after publication in 1928. Archiwum Akt Nowych (henceforth AAN) Ambasada RP w Berlinie 2345.

107. PAT agreed to pay Reuters and Havas 30,000 francs annually for the news. Contract of December 15, 1921, AN 5AR/419, 4–5. The contract was renewed with minor changes in 1926, 1932, and 1935. On PAT, see Andrzej Notkowski, *Prasa w systemie propagandy rządowej w Polsce 1926–1939: Studium techniki władzy* (Łódź: Państwowe Wydawnictwo Naukowe, 1987), 240–263; Eugeniusz Rudziński, *Informacyjne agencje prasowe w Polsce 1926–1939* (Warsaw: Państwowe Wydawnictwo Naukowe, 1970), chs. 2 and 5.

108. Letter from German Ambassador in Warsaw Ulrich Rauscher to Zechlin, September 26, 1925, PA AA R122186.

109. Letter from Post and Telegraph Ministry, December 21, 1928, AAN Konsulat Generalny RP w Berlinie 87, 14–15. These measures followed the first agreement on mutual nonaggression in the sphere of radio between Poland and Germany in October 1927. This was renewed in March 1931.

110. AAN MSZ 7666, 47.

111. December 15, 1933, AAN MSZ 7666, 77–78.

112. Letter from Wolff representative in Vienna, Wilhelm von dem Hagen, to Press Department, March 30, 1931, PA AA R122188.
113. Namely *Prager Tagblatt* and *Bohemia* in September 1926. PA AA R122186.
114. PA AA R122188.
115. Bernhard, *Der Hugenberg-Konzern*, 89–90.
116. Bernhard, *Der Hugenberg-Konzern*, 90.
117. Gossel, *Medien und Politik*, 291; Bernhard Fulda, *Press and Politics in the Weimar Republic* (Oxford: Oxford University Press, 2009), 143–146.

7: The Limits of Communications

1. Peter Theodor Koch, DNB's first news sheet to subscribers, January 2, 1934, Archives Nationales, Paris (henceforth AN) 5AR/177. Koch had previously worked for Wolff since 1924. He had strong relations with Reuters and Havas correspondents, a little too close for some Nazi officials in 1936 who reprimanded him for watching the opening of the 1936 Olympics in the Reuters box. He was not fired, but effectively demoted to a post in Copenhagen in October 1936. Bundesarchiv Berlin-Lichterfelde (henceforth BArch) R55/204, 326.
2. Letter from Dr. Rudolf Dammert to Foreign Office, September 23, 1929, Politisches Archiv des Auswärtigen Amtes, Berlin (henceforth PA AA) R122227.
3. Letter from director of Universum-Verlagsanstalt to Press Department, August 28, 1930, PA AA R122227.
4. Note that the survey did not examine stock market and economic news. Admiral a. D. Paul Behncke, *Der deutsche Zeitungsdienst und das Überseeausland* (Berlin: Walter de Gruyter & Co., 1930), booklet found in PA AA R121432.
5. Klaus Wernecke, "Nachrichtenagenturen und Provinzpresse in der Weimarer Republik," *Zeitschrift für Geschichtswissenschaft* 48, no. 4 (2000): 332.
6. Hans Kapfinger, "Das Nachrichtenwesen," in Johann Wilhelm Naumann, ed., *Die Presse und der Katholik: Anklage und Rechtfertigung: Handbuch für Vortrag und Unterricht* (Augsburg: Haas & Grabherr, 1932), 190.
7. Erich Schairer, "Alfred Hugenberg," (first published in 1929), translated and reproduced in Anton Kaes, Martin Jay, and Edward Dimendberg, eds., *The Weimar Republic Sourcebook* (Berkeley: University of California Press, 1994), 74.
8. Markus Schöneberger, *Diplomatie im Dialog: Ein Jahrhundert Informationspolitik des Auswärtigen Amtes* (Munich: Olzog, 1981), 86–87.
9. Requests from 1921 to 1926 in PA AA R122186 and R122187. Wolff's Diez and Mantler were often consulted and advised against granting privileges to Telegraph Union.
10. Letter from *Osnabrücker Zeitung*, April 20, 1926, to Press Department, PA AA R122195, 5.
11. The gathering was called "Politischer Abend für die deutsche Presse." Schöneberger, *Diplomatie im Dialog*, 54.

12. For example, press conference of July 15, 1926, PA AA R121592.
13. Letter from Mantler to Press Department, November 14, 1925, PA AA R122186. For similar complaints up to 1933, see PA AA R122188.
14. The budget had been 636,000 Reichsmarks in 1925. Hans Jürgen Müller, *Auswärtige Pressepolitik und Propaganda zwischen Ruhrkampf und Locarno (1923–1925): Eine Untersuchung über die Rolle der Öffentlichkeit in der Außenpolitik Stresemanns* (Frankfurt am Main: Peter Lang, 1991), 68.
15. Director of Federal Statistical Office, November 29, 1926, PA AA R122186.
16. PA AA R122187.
17. Confidential letter from Dr. Fritz von Twardowski to Ministry of the Reichswehr, May 1927, PA AA R122195, 29. Twardowski later served as chief spokesperson for the West German government from 1950 to 1952.
18. Letter, May 1927, PA AA R122195, 29.
19. Meeting between Zechlin, von Twardowski, and Albert von Baligand of the Press Department and editors Gesell and Belian of Telegraph Union, January 26, 1928, PA AA R122187.
20. See PA AA R122214.
21. BArch R43I/2479, 87–91.
22. Interdepartmental meeting on ticker, June 26, 1930, BArch R43I/2479, 197–203.
23. Letter from State Secretary Dr. Pünder in Reich Chancellery, October 30, 1929, BArch R43I/2479, 97.
24. Report by Zechlin, July 4, 1930, BArch R43I/2479, 220.
25. Bernhard Fulda, *Press and Politics in the Weimar Republic* (Oxford: Oxford University Press, 2009), 62–63; Klaus Petersen, *Zensur in der Weimarer Republik* (Stuttgart: J. B. Metzler, 1995), pt. 3.
26. *Berliner Lokal-Anzeiger, Der Tag,* and *Berliner Illustrierte Nachtausgabe.* BArch R43I/2468, 54. It is, however, a myth that press coverage by Hugenberg papers and Telegraph Union propelled Hitler to prominence. Fulda, *Press and Politics in the Weimar Republic,* 143–146.
27. Letter from Finance Ministry to Interior Ministry, December 20, 1929, BArch R43I/2468, 53.
28. Letter from Finance Minister Paul Moldenhauer to Severing and other ministers, April 10, 1930, BArch R43I/2468, 72.
29. Severing on the Interior Ministry decision, December 30, 1929, BArch R43I/2468, 55. Some Prussian state officials agreed; e.g., Dr. Corsing. November 15, 1929, BArch R43I/2468, 33–36.
30. The compensation claim against the Prussian state reached court in January 1934. Unsurprisingly, the judgment of February 1932 was overturned. The Prussian state paid all court costs as well as compensation of 50,000 Reichsmarks. January 31, 1934, Bundesarchiv Koblenz (henceforth BArchK) Nachlass (henceforth NL) Hugenberg N1231/576, 99.
31. Letter from Interior Minister Wilhelm von Gayl to federal and Prussian ministers, June 24, 1932, BArch R43I/2468, 153.

32. It needed subsidies of 30,000 Reichsmarks in the first year. Wolff proposal, March 11, 1931, PA AA R122227.

33. The electoral funds from the Interior Ministry would cover the costs. Notice to all ministers, August 19, 1930, BArch R43I/2468, 87–90.

34. Daniel Gossel, *Medien und Politik in Deutschland und den USA: Kontrolle, Konflikt und Kooperation vom 18. bis zum frühen 20. Jahrhundert* (Stuttgart: Franz Steiner, 2010), 271.

35. BArchK NL Hugenberg, N 1231/274, 12.

36. Letter from Diez to Wolff's representative in Paris, Emil Wertheimer, January 11, 1930, PA AA R122213.

37. PA AA R122204. Mantler claimed to the Associated Press that Wolff had earned 9 percent on a capital stock of 800,000 marks in 1925. Elmer Rogers Reports on Foreign News Agencies, 1926, Associated Press Corporate Archives, New York, AP02.3 Box 10, folder 1, 3.

38. The Foreign Office reduced its subsidies to Wolff from 400,000 Reichsmarks in 1928 to 266,000 Reichsmarks. PA AA R122204.

39. Contract of February 2, 1921, described in letter from Dr. Solmssen, chairman of the board of Deutsch-Atlantische Telegraphengesellschaft (DAT), December 19, 1930, BArch R43I/1997, 21.

40. The American Radio Corporation already held 3 million Reichsmarks of shares in Transradio, giving it a veto. Report by Postal Ministry working committee, January 15, 1931, BArch R43I/1997, 107. German industry, principally represented by Solmssen and Wilhelm Cuno, saw global cartels as the best means to secure Germany's place in global communications. Solmssen also wanted Transradio and DAT to merge as the only way for DAT to remain profitable. However, the Entente Commission had forced the Postal Ministry to make overseas radio private, which it had never wanted, as it believed that the state should control overseas radio traffic.

41. The Postal Ministry had already collected 17 million of the 28 million needed to take over Transradio. It borrowed the rest from the Finance Ministry, thinking that annual savings would soon pay for the 7 million Reichsmarks still needed to buy Transradio equipment. Report by Postal Ministry working committee, January 15, 1931, BArch R43I/1997, 108.

42. Hitler's speeches had surprisingly little impact on Nazi electoral success. Peter Selb and Simon Munzert, "Examining a Most Likely Case for Strong Campaign Effects: Hitler's Speeches and the Rise of the Nazi Party, 1927–1933," *American Political Science Review* (forthcoming). Preprint accessed August 1, 2018, https://osf.io/preprints/socarxiv/t75p3. The Nazi Party was generally more successful in areas with right-wing, neutral, or bourgeois press. On how the press influenced Nazi voters, see Jürgen Falter, *Hitlers Wähler* (Munich: Beck, 1991), 325–329.

43. Roger Griffin, *The Nature of Fascism* (London: Pinter, 1991), 93–111.

44. Österreichisches Staatsarchiv, Vienna (henceforth ÖStA) I/6e/174/V-5.

45. Schöneberger, *Diplomatie im Dialog*, 113.

46. Jürgen Reitz, "Das Deutsche Nachrichtenbüro," in Jürgen Wilke, ed., *Telegraphenbüros und Nachrichtenagenturen in Deutschland: Untersuchungen zu ihrer Geschichte bis 1949* (Munich: K. G. Saur, 1991), 214.

47. ÖStA I/6e/176/V-5.

48. Letter from Paul Ravoux to Havas headquarters in Paris, August 23, 1933, AN 5AR/181². (Note: The superscript number at the end of this note indicates the stack or bound book of papers within an archival box: "181²" means box 181, stack 2.)

49. PA AA R122196, 43.

50. André Uzulis, *Nachrichtenagenturen im Nationalsozialismus: Propagandain-strumente und Mittel der Presselenkung* (Frankfurt am Main: Peter Lang, 1995), 245–248.

51. Letter from Ravoux to Havas headquarters, June 22, 1933, AN 5AR/181².

52. For three instances in September/October 1933, see Hans Bohrmann, ed., *NS-Presseanweisungen der Vorkriegszeit: Edition und Dokumentation* (Munich: Saur, 1984), 1933, 1:115, 126, 180.

53. Report on events in Germany, November 29, 1933, ÖStA I/6e/174/V-5.

54. Strictly confidential report by Otto Mejer, October 19, 1933. BArch R34/Kleine Erweiterung (Kl. Erw.) 640, 2–9.

55. BArch R34/Kl. Erw. 640, 85; BArch R55/827.

56. Report on events in Germany, November 16, 1933, ÖStA I/6e/174/V-5.

57. Calculated from entries located in BArch R55/24.

58. BArch R55/204, 265.

59. September 23, 1939, BArch R55/204, 286.

60. Otto Mejer, letter on the history of German news agencies, 1856–1945, 1956, BArch R34/Kl. Erw. 640, 79.

61. Letter from Wolff to ANA, December 9, 1933, ÖStA I/6e/174/V-5.

62. Report on events in Germany, November 16, 1933, ÖStA I/6e/174/V-5.

63. AN 5AR/488.

64. Letter from Reich Office for Foreign Trade to Foreign Office, January 12, 1935, PA AA R122196, 80–81.

65. Uzulis, *Nachrichtenagenturen im Nationalsozialismus*, 106–107.

66. Three-Party Treaty, March 15, 1934. The treaty was effective from July 1, 1934, until December 31, 1937, with automatic renewal if no party terminated the contract prior to June 30, 1937. Diez had tried to negotiate for this in 1932. Diez had also tried unsuccessfully to negotiate with Reuters to remove Reuters's right to disseminate German news in its wireless services. Reuters Archive, London, 1/869623, LN45.

67. Letter from Mejer to Propaganda Ministry, October 11, 1934, PA AA R122196, 68–69.

68. AN 5AR/182².

69. On foreign correspondents in Nazi Germany, see Martin Herzer, *Auslands-korrespondenten und auswärtige Pressepolitik im Dritten Reich* (Cologne: Böhlau, 2012).

70. Peter Longerich, *Propagandisten im Krieg: Die Presseabteilung des Auswärtigen Amtes unter Ribbentrop* (Munich: Oldenbourg, 1987).

71. Aristotle Kallis, *Nazi Propaganda and the Second World War* (Basingstoke: Palgrave Macmillan, 2005), 8.

72. Dietrich asserted greater control in 1942, by transferring ownership of DNB, Transocean, and Europapress into a new trustee company, Telos Verwaltungsgesellschaft mbH. This was meant to optimize control over the three agencies and occurred simultaneously to the Transocean-Europapress merger, though the agencies continued to compete and drain money. Cornelius Klee, "Transocean," in Wilke, *Telegraphenbüros und Nachrichtenagenturen*, 204–210.

73. Klee, "Transocean," 246–264.

74. André Uzulis, "DNB: Darf Nichts Bringen—Eine Nachrichtenagentur im Dritten Reich," in Christoph Studt, ed., *"Diener des Staates" oder "Widerstand zwischen den Zeilen"? Die Rolle der Presse im "Dritten Reich"* (Berlin: LIT, 2007), 109. DNB also used foreign radio news. From mid-1940, the Foreign Office centralized this in "Sonderdienst Seehaus."

75. Norman Domeier, "Geheime Fotos: Die Kooperation von Associated Press und NS-Regime (1942–1945)," *Zeithistorische Forschungen* 14, no. 2 (2017): 199–230; Harriet Scharnberg, "Das A und P der Propaganda: Associated Press und die nationalsozialistische Bildpublizistik," *Zeithistorische Forschungen* 13, no. 1 (2016): 11–37. The AP responded with its own report on its actions in Nazi Germany in May 2017, https://www.ap.org/about/history/ap -in-germany-1933-1945/.

76. For details on Hellschreiber and the Hell system, accessed January 9, 2017, https://www.nonstopsystems.com/radio/hellschreiber.htm#top-of -page.

77. Uzulis, *Nachrichtenagenturen im Nationalsozialismus*, 211–214.

78. PA AA R122196, 287–288. The percentages for the seventeenth agency in Bucharest are not listed.

79. BBC Written Archives Centre, Reading, R28/86.

80. Philip M. Taylor, *Munitions of the Mind: A History of Propaganda from the Ancient World to the Present Day*, 3rd ed. (Manchester: Manchester University Press, 2003), 225.

81. The other colors were: yellow (permission to publish nonverbatim); red (confidential background information for journalists not to be published); blue (strictly confidential background information for editors in chief, high-level civil servants, and important members of the Nazi Party).

82. Reitz, "Das DNB," 229.

83. Horst Pöttker, "Journalismus als Politik: Eine explorative Analyse von NS-Presseanweisungen der Vorkriegszeit," *Publizistik* 51, no. 2 (2006): 168–182.

84. David Welch, *The Third Reich: Politics and Propaganda* (New York: Routledge, 1989), 39. On press directives, see Jürgen Wilke, *Presseanweisungen im zwanzigsten Jahrhundert: Erster Weltkrieg, Drittes Reich, DDR* (Cologne: Böhlau, 2007), 115–255.

85. Emil Dovifat, *Zeitungslehre I*, 2nd rev. ed. (Berlin: Walter de Gruyter & Co., 1944), 78.

86. Calculated from table in Reitz, "Das DNB," 230.

87. The Nazis did retain some smaller agencies for two reasons. First, they served different publics from the DNB, such as religious groups. Second, they disguised Nazi control over the DNB. In 1939, there were 407 members of the Reichsverband deutscher Korrespondenz- und Nachrichtenbüros. Doris Kohlmann-Viand, *NS-Pressepolitik im Zweiten Weltkrieg: Die "vertraulichen Informationen" als Mittel der Presselenkung* (Munich: Saur, 1991), 109.

88. Willi Weber, "Die kommentierte Auslandsnachricht: Eine Notwendigkeit für die Provinzpresse," *Deutsche Presse* 25 (1934): 4.

89. Gabriele Toepser-Ziegert, "Einführung," in Bohrmann, ed., *NS-Presseanweisungen der Vorkriegszeit*, 1:122.

90. Fritz Sänger, *Politik der Täuschungen: Missbrauch der Presse im Dritten Reich: Weisungen, Informationen, Notizen, 1933–1939* (Vienna: Europaverlag, 1975), 42. Newspapers were still allowed to subscribe to the American agencies United Press and International News Service, which only larger newspapers could afford.

91. Quoted in Richard Evans, *The Third Reich in Power, 1933–1939* (New York: Penguin Press, 2005), 147.

92. Corey Ross, *Media and the Making of Modern Germany: Mass Communications, Society, and Politics from the Empire to the Third Reich* (Oxford: Oxford University Press, 2008), 298–301.

93. Annual report for Cautio, 1936, BArch R55/827, 74.

94. Ross, *Media and the Making of Modern Germany*, 333. Germans also saw news at cinemas.

95. Gerhard Eckert, *Der Rundfunk als Führungsmittel* (Heidelberg: K. Vowinckel, 1941), 49.

96. Michael Hensle, *Rundfunkverbrechen: Das Hören von "Feindsendern" im Nationalsozialismus* (Berlin: Metropol, 2003).

97. Ian Kershaw, *Popular Opinion and Political Dissent in the Third Reich: Bavaria 1933–1945*, 2nd rev. ed. (Oxford: Clarendon Press, 2002); David Welch, "Nazi Propaganda and the Volksgemeinschaft: Constructing a People's Community," *Journal of Contemporary History* 39, no. 2 (2004): 213–238.

98. Peter Fritzsche, *An Iron Wind: Europe under Hitler* (New York: Basic Books, 2016), 14.

99. The station's archive was destroyed after the war so no transcripts remain. Johanna Lutteroth, "Deckung, Deckung, Schmutz," *Spiegel Online*, October 24, 2013, accessed February 27, 2018, http://einestages.spiegel.de/s/tb/29658/soldatensender-calais-britischer-radiosender-im-zweiten-weltkrieg.html.

100. Uzulis, *Nachrichtenagenturen im Nationalsozialismus*, 214–217.

101. Modris Eksteins, *The Limits of Reason: The German Democratic Press and the Collapse of Weimar Democracy* (London: Oxford University Press, 1975), 71.

102. Dirk Blasius, *Weimars Ende: Bürgerkrieg und Politik 1930–1933* (Göttingen: Vandenhoeck & Ruprecht, 2005), 12. The latest overview work in the

voluminous literature on the end of the Weimar Republic is Benjamin Carter Hett, *The Death of Democracy: Hitler's Rise to Power and the Downfall of the Weimar Republic* (New York: Henry Holt and Company, 2018).

8: The World War of Words

1. Edward Bliss Jr., *Now the News: The Story of Broadcast Journalism* (New York: Columbia University Press, 1991), 155. Thanks to Michael Socolow for reminding me of this.
2. Columbia Broadcasting System, *From D-Day through Victory in Europe: The Eye-Witness Story as Told by War Correspondents on the Air* (New York, 1945), 12.
3. Nicholas O'Shaughnessy, *Selling Hitler: Propaganda and the Nazi Brand* (London: Hurst, 2016). On advertising in the Third Reich, see Pamela Swett, *Selling under the Swastika: Advertising and Commercial Culture in Nazi Germany* (Stanford, CA: Stanford University Press, 2013).
4. MI5 confidential report on Transocean, 1936, The National Archives, London (henceforth TNA) KV3/100.
5. TNA INF1/715.
6. Wilhelm Schwedler, *Die Nachricht im Weltverkehr: Kritische Bemerkungen über das internationale Nachrichtenwesen vor und nach dem Weltkriege* (Berlin: Deutsche Verlagsgesellschaft für Politik und Geschichte, 1922), x.
7. Schwedler, *Die Nachricht im Weltverkehr,* 128.
8. On Northcliffe, see J. Lee Thompson, *Northcliffe: Press Baron in Politics, 1865–1922* (London: John Murray, 2000).
9. Bundesarchiv, Berlin-Lichterfelde (henceforth BArch) R3301/2098, 98.
10. "Far East Dangers; Incessant German Propaganda; Lord Northcliffe's Warning," *The Times,* January 3, 1922, 10.
11. "Propaganda by Wireless. German 'News' Mischief. Nauen and its Children. A Week's Test," *The Times,* January 17, 1922, 11. See also "Wireless News for the World," *The Times,* February 21, 1922, 11.
12. Letter from Legate von Schön in Beijing to Walter Zechlin, April 2, 1925, BArch R901/57684, 120.
13. Letter from Wilhelm Solf, German ambassador in Tokyo, to the Foreign Office, January 12, 1922, BArch R901/57662, 85. Transocean often used cover agencies to spread its news. Transocean's wireless service had operated in China since September 1921. It was disseminated by a Chinese contact, Mitchell Chang, under the name "Asiatic News Agency, Chinese Wireless Service, Berlin resp. Nauen" in English or "Deutsch-chinesische Telegramm Agentur" in German.
14. BArch R901/57662, 169.
15. *Hansard,* March 6, 1922, vol. 151, col. 835.
16. British Parliamentary Debate, July 21, 1921, British Telecom Archives (henceforth BT), POST 30/1530B.

17. July 21, 1921, BT POST 30/1530B. All foreign and some Chinese newspapers apparently printed the House of Commons question on Transocean verbatim without commentary. Letter from German embassy in Beijing to the Foreign Office, March 25, 1922, BArch R901/57662, 215.

18. Daniel Headrick, *The Invisible Weapon: Telecommunications and International Politics, 1851–1945* (New York: Oxford University Press, 1991), 132.

19. Letter from Reuters to General Post Office, October 24, 1923, BT POST 33/1499.

20. Letter exchange between British embassy in Berlin and Foreign Office, May 1924, Politisches Archiv des Auswärtigen Amtes, Berlin (henceforth PA AA) R121097, 108–115.

21. PA AA R122203.

22. Richard Evans, *The Coming of the Third Reich* (London: Allen Lane, 2003), 459.

23. Schwedler, May 27, 1933, BArch R901/60792, 134.

24. Subsidies reached 6 million Reichsmarks by 1941. Cornelius Klee, "Transocean," in Jürgen Wilke, ed., *Telegraphenbüros und Nachrichtenagenturen in Deutschland: Untersuchungen zu ihrer Geschichte bis 1949* (Munich: K. G. Saur, 1991), 190.

25. Christian Taaks, *Federführung für die Nation ohne Vorbehalt? Deutsche Medien in China während der Zeit des Nationalsozialismus* (Stuttgart: Franz Steiner, 2009), 136.

26. Report on Transocean, March 11, 1933, BArch R901/60792, 104.

27. N.d., presumably 1939, quoted in André Uzulis, *Nachrichtenagenturen im Nationalsozialismus: Propagandainstrumente und Mittel der Presselenkung* (Frankfurt am Main: Peter Lang, 1995), 227.

28. Taaks, *Deutsche Medien in China,* 136.

29. BArch R901/60792. On the Middle East (without mentioning Transocean), see Jeffrey Herf, *Nazi Propaganda for the Arab World* (New Haven, CT: Yale University Press, 2009); David Motadel, *Islam and Nazi Germany's War* (Cambridge, MA: Harvard University Press, 2014); Francis Nicosia, *Nazi Germany and the Arab World* (New York: Cambridge University Press, 2015).

30. Secret letter from C. W. Dixon, Dominions Office, to Liddell, November 1937, TNA KV3/100.

31. Secret letter to C. R. Price, Dominions Office, November 30, 1937, TNA KV3/100.

32. "British News Abroad. Memorandum by the Secretary of State for Foreign Affairs, Anthony Eden," Secret, December 8, 1937, TNA CAB24/273, 2.

33. Quoted in Richard Langhorne and Keith Hamilton, *The Practice of Diplomacy: Its Evolution, Theory, and Administration,* 2nd ed. (London: Routledge, 2011), 181. Significant changes did occur prior to 1938. See Norbert Frei et al., *Das Amt und die Vergangenheit: Deutsche Diplomaten im Dritten Reich und in der Bundesrepublik,* 2nd ed. (Munich: Karl Blessing Verlag, 2010), 51–132.

34. On Goebbels-Ribbentrop conflicts, see Peter Longerich, *Propagandisten im Krieg: Die Presseabteilung des Auswärtigen Amtes unter Ribbentrop* (Munich: Oldenbourg, 1987), 126–148.

35. Alfred Naujoks, Nuremberg Trial Proceedings, vol. 4, 24th Day, December 20, 1945, Morning Session, 242. Accessed January 22, 2018, http://avalon.law.yale.edu/imt/12-20-45.asp.

36. Letter from Edmund Fürholzer in Shanghai to Transocean, February 14, 1936, BArch R901/57687, 219.

37. Uzulis, *Nachrichtenagenturen im Nationalsozialismus,* 221.

38. Press Directive, July 25, 1940, Jürgen Hagemann, *Die Presselenkung im Dritten Reich* (Bonn: Bouvier, 1970), 81.

39. Otto Mejer, seventh plenary assembly of Agences Alliées, Strbské-Pleso, Tatra Mountains, June 1935, Archives Nationales, Paris (henceforth AN) 5AR/473. Another participant at the conference claimed that Transocean was unknown in Europe except in Spain.

40. Increased Nazi spending expanded Europapress beyond Europe, encroaching on Transocean territory. The two agencies formally merged on March 26, 1943, to save costs. Uzulis, *Nachrichtenagenturen im Nationalsozialismus,* 93–104. The Spanish official news agency, Efe, received Transocean after the Spanish Civil War. Transocean tried to enter Greece, Portugal, and Cyprus in the mid-1930s. List of subscribers, April 13, 1934, BArch R901/57671, 78–81. Transocean's photos were highly successful. In 1940, Brazilian newspapers printed 500–1,500 photos monthly; Shanghai newspapers printed 300–450.

41. On the DNB in China, see Taaks, *Deutsche Medien in China,* 125–134. By the mid-1930s, the DNB had correspondents in Tokyo, Shanghai, Nanjing, and Beijing, as well as Manchuria, once Japan invaded.

42. Schwedler, May 27, 1933, BArch R901/60792, 134.

43. Walter Hagemann, *Publizistik im Dritten Reich: Ein Beitrag zur Methodik der Massenführung* (Hamburg: Hansischer Gildenverlag, 1948), 235–236.

44. Hugo Fernández Artucio, *The Nazi Underground in South America* (New York: Farrar & Rinehart, 1942), 92.

45. National Archives and Records Administration II, Washington, DC (henceforth NARA), RG59, Box C248; C302, 862.20211; Box C358, 862.20251/89; Box 5587, 862.20210.

46. The trial records and letters are located at NARA RG60, Box 116, File 39–51–1017.

47. See Max Paul Friedman, *Nazis and Good Neighbors: The United States Campaign against the Germans of Latin America in World War II* (Cambridge: Cambridge University Press, 2003); Michaela Hönicke Moore, *Know Your Enemy: The American Debate on Nazism, 1933–1945* (Cambridge: Cambridge University Press, 2010); Uwe Lübken, *Bedrohliche Nähe: Die USA und die nationalsozialistische Herausforderung in Lateinamerika, 1937–1945* (Stuttgart: Franz Steiner, 2004).

48. Accessed February 26, 2018, http://legisworks.org/congress/75/publaw-583.pdf.

49. Letter from German embassy in Washington, DC, to Foreign Office, October 17, 1938, PA AA R105013.

50. The summary of HUAC's findings appears in *Special Committee on Un-American Activities. House of Representatives 76th Congress 3rd Session on H. Res. 282. Appendix II* (Washington, DC, 1940), 969–1053.

51. Accessed February 26, 2018, https://archive.org/details/investigation ofu194102unit.

52. Joe Alex Morris, *Deadline Every Minute: The Story of the United Press* (Garden City, NY: Doubleday, 1957), 236.

53. See http://legisworks.org/congress/75/publaw-583.pdf.

54. Speculation in Hagemann, *Die Presselenkung im Dritten Reich*, 317n105.

55. The trial records and letters are located at NARA, RG60, Box 116, File 39–51–1017.

56. Cited in Robert William Desmond, *Tides of War: World News Reporting, 1931–1945* (Iowa City: University of Iowa Press, 1984), 157.

57. Fernández Artucio, *The Nazi Underground in South America*, 92–104.

58. Norman Domeier, "Geheime Fotos: Die Kooperation von Associated Press und NS-Regime (1942–1945)," *Zeithistorische Forschungen* 14, no. 2 (2017): 199–230; Harriet Scharnberg, "Das A und P der Propaganda: Associated Press und die nationalsozialistische Bildpublizistik," *Zeithistorische Forschungen* 13, no. 1 (2016): 11–37. The AP responded with its own report in May 2017. Accessed March 14, 2018, https://www.ap.org/about/history/ap-in-germany-1933-1945.

59. Klee, "Transocean," 193.

60. Frauke Pieper, *Der deutsche Auslandsrundfunk: Historische Entwicklung, verfassungsrechtliche Stellung, Funktionsbereich, Organisation und Finanzierung* (Munich: C. H. Beck, 2000), 17, 21.

61. H. J. P. Bergmeier and Rainer Lotz, *Hitler's Airwaves: The Inside Story of Nazi Radio Broadcasting and Propaganda Swing* (New Haven, CT: Yale University Press, 1997); Stanley Newcourt-Nowordworski, *Black Propaganda in the Second World War* (Stroud: Sutton, 2005).

62. PA AA PersAkte 17077 Zapp.

63. Dies committee report, December 28, 1939, found in PA AA R105014.

64. Letter from German embassy in Washington, DC, to Foreign Office, January 26, 1940, PA AA R105014.

65. Ronald Newton, *The "Nazi Menace" in Argentina, 1931–1947* (Stanford, CA: Stanford University Press, 1992), 91.

66. Dankwart Guratzsch, *Macht durch Organisation: Die Grundlegung des Hugenbergschen Presseimperiums* (Düsseldorf: Bertelsmann Universitätsverlag, 1974), 228.

67. Stefan Rinke, *„Der letzte freie Kontinent": Deutsche Lateinamerikapolitik im Zeichen transnationaler Beziehungen, 1918–1933* (Stuttgart: Heinz, 1996), 287.

68. Rhoda Desbordes, "Representing 'Informal Empire' in the Nineteenth Century: Reuters in South America at the Time of the War of the Pacific, 1879–83," *Media History* 14, no. 2 (2008): 121–139. On cable competition to South America, see Jill Hills, *The Struggle for Control of Global Communica-*

tion: The Formative Century (Urbana: University of Illinois Press, 2002), ch. 5; Dwayne Winseck and Robert Pike, *Communication and Empire: Media, Markets, and Globalization, 1860–1930* (Durham, NC: Duke University Press, 2007), 61–91.

69. Article 1, Contract between Havas and AP, November 16, 1918, AN 5AR/416. On the AP's growing reach, see Gene Allen, "Catching up with the Competition: The International Expansion of Associated Press, 1920–1945," *Journalism Studies* 17, no. 6 (2016): 747–762.

70. Contract between AP and Havas, September 4, 1935, AN 5AR/416.

71. Transradio was to own 65 percent, Transocean 35 percent. Transocean would cover salaries as well as fees for sending the news from Nauen. The company was to deliver four hundred words for free daily to newspapers. BArch R901/57676, 304.

72. Emil Rotscheidt and Erich Quäck, "Transradio," in *25 Jahre Telefunken: Festschrift der Telefunken-Gesellschaft 1903–1928* (Berlin: W. Simon, 1928), 199. On Germans in Argentina, see Benjamin Bryce, *To Belong in Buenos Aires: Germans, Argentines, and the Rise of a Pluralist Society* (Stanford, CA: Stanford University Press, 2018).

73. Even here, the government competed with Telegraph Union, which worked with the Chamber of Trade to send news to South America. Telegraph Union's representative, Dr. Belian, negotiated with the head of radio in the Argentine Navy, Captain Orlandini, to take the Telegraph Union service from Nauen, though this did not occur. BArch R901/57678, 136–147.

74. Letter from Bagel to Transocean, March 1, 1927, BArch R901/57678, 269.

75. Letter from Sir Eric Drummond to Wilhelm Schwedler, May 28, 1931, BArch R901/57664, 215. League of Nations Archive C.348.M.161.1934.VIII.

76. Rotscheidt and Quäck, "Transradio," 201. On shortwave, see Daniel Headrick, "Shortwave Radio and its Impact on International Telecommunications between the Wars," *History & Technology* 11 (1994): 21–32.

77. Pascal Griset, *Entreprise, technologie et souveraineté: les télécommunications transatlantiques de la France, XIXe–XXe siècles* (Paris: Editions rive droite, 1996), 406. For French-American rivalry, see 401–424.

78. Report from Havas office in Buenos Aires, June 17, 1930, AN 5AR/205.

79. Klee, "Transocean," 177.

80. Havas increased from 25,000 words monthly on average in 1927 to 50,000 by 1929. Report from Havas office in Buenos Aires, June 17, 1930, AN 5AR/205.

81. AN 5AR/205.

82. Havas central office to representative Delalot in Buenos Aires, January 22, 1931, AN 5AR/41². (Note: The superscript number at the end of this note indicates the stack or bound book of papers within an archival box: "41²" means box 41, stack 2.)

83. February 1938, AN 5AR/213.

84. James Cane, *The Fourth Enemy: Journalism and Power in the Making of Peronist Argentina, 1930–1955* (University Park: Pennsylvania State University Press, 2012), 132.

85. Rotscheidt and Quäck, "Transradio," 199.

86. March 1932 report on Agencia Brasileira, AN 5AR/41³.

87. Havas telegraphed around four thousand words daily to Brazil in 1929. AN 5AR/205.

88. Letter from Agence Havas representative in Rio to Havas headquarters, May 11, 1935, AN 5AR/410.

89. Michael Socolow, *Six Minutes in Berlin: Broadcast Spectacle and Rowing Gold at the Nazi Olympics* (Urbana: University of Illinois Press, 2016).

90. "The American System of Broadcasting and Its Function in the Preservation of Democracy," address by David Sarnoff, April 28, 1938, summarized in Howard S. LeRoy, "Treaty Regulation of International Radio and Short Wave Broadcasting," *American Journal of International Law* 32, no. 4 (1938): 731.

91. Klee, "Transocean," 191.

92. Quoted in Klee, "Transocean," 198.

93. Klee, "Transocean," 199.

94. "Report on German, Italian and Japanese propaganda," sent by airmail from HM Ambassador at Santiago to Principal Secretary of State for Foreign Affairs, April 22, 1941, TNA FO371/25889.

95. Note on front of file, April 1941, TNA FO371/25889.

96. BArch R901/58399, 74.

97. Letter from Reuters to BBC, October 21, 1942, BBC WAC R28/153.

98. BArch R901/58399, 72–74.

99. "Still Larger German News Service to South America," secret, April 21, 1938, TNA KV 3/100.

100. Peter Veit and Olaf Gaudig, *Hakenkreuz über Südamerika: Ideologie, Politik, Militär* (Berlin: Wissenschaftlicher Verlag Berlin, 2004), 78–82; Peter Veit and Olaf Gaudig, *Der Widerschein des Nazismus: Das Bild des Nationalsozial-ismus in der deutschsprachigen Presse Argentiniens, Brasiliens und Chiles 1932–1945* (Berlin: Wissenschaftlicher Verlag, 1997).

101. Jürgen Müller, "Entwicklung und Aktivitäten der NSDAP in Argentinien, 1931–1945," in Holger M. Meding, ed., *Nationalsozialismus und Argentinien: Beziehungen, Einflüsse und Nachwirkungen* (Frankfurt am Main: Peter Lang, 1995), 69.

102. Sebastian Schoepp, *Das „Argentinische Tageblatt" 1933 bis 1945: Ein Forum der antinationalsozialistischen Emigration* (Berlin: Wissenschaftlicher Verlag, 1996).

103. Minutes of seventh plenary assembly of Agences Alliées conferences, Strbské-Pleso, Czechoslovakia, June 16–25, 1935, AN 5AR/473.

104. Klee, "Transocean," 181. Transradio had direct radio traffic with the Philippines and Dutch East Indies.

105. This is what Joseph Plaut believed. Letter from Plaut to Foreign Office, April 15, 1926, BArch R901/57685, 60.

106. BArch R901/57685, 136.

107. PA AA R122217.

108. Report by Plaut, May 10, 1927, BArch R901/57685, 278.

109. Rana Mitter, *China's War with Japan, 1937–1945: The Struggle for Survival* (Harmondsworth: Penguin, 2014), 162–163.

110. See William Kirby, *Germany and Republican China* (Stanford, CA: Stanford University Press, 1984).

111. Sheng-Chi Shu, "Managing International News-Agency Relations under the Guomindang: China's Central News Agency, Zhao Minheng, and Reuters, 1931–1945," *Frontiers of History in China* 10, no. 4 (2015): 624–625.

112. Paper presented at the fourth biennial conference of the China branch of the Institute of Pacific Relations, Hangzhou, October–November 1931. Cited in Shu, "Managing International News-Agency Relations," 595.

113. See Winseck and Pike, *Communication and Empire*, ch. 4; Erik Baark, *Lightning Wires: The Telegraph and China's Technological Modernization, 1860–1890* (Westport, CT: Greenwood Press, 1997).

114. Jean Fontenoy, Havas's representative in Shanghai, attributed much of Transocean's success to its anti-imperial tone. Letter from Fontenoy to Havas headquarters, November 6, 1930, AN 5AR/310.

115. Agreement between Chinese National Government and Plaut as representative of Transocean, Wolff, and Europapress, October 3, 1928, BArch R901/57686, 148–155. Transocean agreed to send 1,500 words daily.

116. PA AA R122216.

117. Quoted in O. M. Green, *The Organisation of News from the Far East* (London: Royal Institute of International Affairs, Chatham House, 1933), 11. On Chiang Kai-shek and the press, see Parks M. Coble Jr., "Chiang Kai-shek and the anti-Japanese Movement in China: Zou Tao-fen and the National Salvation Association, 1931–1937," *Journal of Asian Studies* 45, no. 2 (1985): 296.

118. Green, *The Organisation of News from the Far East,* 5–6.

119. Green, *The Organisation of News from the Far East,* 5–6.

120. Letter from Reuters to Agences Alliées headquarters in Paris, February 28, 1927, AN 5AR/410.

121. *North China Daily News,* March 5, 1929, in AN 5AR/310.

122. Report by Plaut on 1928–1929, BArch R901/57686, 206–210. On Shanghai media pre-1930, see Rudolf Wagner, "The Role of the Foreign Community in the Chinese Public Sphere," *China Quarterly* 142, no. 2 (1995): 423–443.

123. Chinese imports of German goods rose from 28.3 million taels in 1913 to over 56 million in 1927. AN 5AR/310. A measurement used in custom duties, the Haikwan tael was equivalent to 1,558 Chinese dollars. Gerd Hardach, *The First World War, 1914–1918* (Berkeley: University of California Press, 1977), 264n37. The usual exchange rate was 2 Chinese dollars to 1 U.S. dollar.

124. AN 5AR/310.

125. Letter from *North China Daily News and Herald,* Shanghai to Fontenoy on February 19, 1931, AN 5AR/310.

126. Letters from Fontenoy to Havas headquarters, November 2 and December 16, 1930, AN 5AR/310.

127. Letter from Fontenoy to French consular legate in China, February 4, 1931, AN 5AR/310.

128. Report by Henri Barde, September 5, 1934, AN 5AR/310. Barde replaced Fontenoy in September 1931.

129. Note that United Press was even less successful in the foreign press in Tianjin, supplying only 1,288 items. Table comparing citation of news agency messages by the press, July 16 to December 31, 1932, AN 5AR/310.

130. According to a Press Department letter, asking Plaut to hand over records, March 20, 1934. PA AA R122196, 52.

131. Taaks, *Deutsche Medien in China*, 142–144.

132. Taaks, *Deutsche Medien in China*.

133. AN 5AR/416. Reuters and Havas briefly contemplated creating a joint Chinese news agency in 1928. AN 5AR/314. On Chinese news agencies, see Shu, "Managing International News-Agency Relations under the Guomindang."

134. AN 5AR/311.

135. AN 5AR/410.

136. See statistics in AN 5AR/313^2. I have used present-day appellations for Chinese cities. At the time, they were known as Peking, Nanking, Tientsin, and Dalian.

137. In 1935 at least, according to the Havas representative in Shanghai. AN 5AR/311.

138. In September 1935, the Shanghai press published 2,910 Chinese characters of Havas, 2,918 of Reuters, and 1,776 Kuomin. AN 5AR/311. Transocean fell from 23.2 percent in 1936 to 12.6 percent in 1938. AN 5AR/313^1.

139. Havas representative in Shanghai, Lapine, August 3, 1939, AN 5AR/313^1.

140. Klee, "Transocean," 196.

141. For comparison, in August 1939, Chinese newspapers in Shanghai printed 5,530 characters of Havas news, 2,996 of Reuters, and 1,341 of United Press. AN 5AR/313^1.

142. T. N. Harper and C. A. Bayly, *Forgotten Armies: The Fall of British Asia, 1941–1945* (Cambridge, MA: Harvard University Press, 2005), 137.

143. "Memorandum regarding Transocean," March 10, 1946, summarized in Taaks, *Deutsche Medien in China*, 145.

144. Taaks, *Deutsche Medien in China*, 502.

145. BArch R901/58399, 59–60.

146. Jonathan Silberstein-Loeb, *The International Distribution of News: The Associated Press, Press Association, and Reuters, 1848–1947* (Cambridge: Cambridge University Press, 2014), 291–304; Tomoko Akami, *Japan's News Propaganda and Reuters' News Empire in Northeast Asia* (Dordrecht: Republic of Letters, 2012), 241–276. Ironically, many Japanese ideas about propaganda came from translations of and contact with German thinkers and German

media. Fabian Schäfer, *Public Opinion, Propaganda, Ideology: Theories on the Press and Its Social Function in Interwar Japan, 1918–1937* (Leiden: Brill, 2012).

147. Tomoko Akami, *Soft Power of Japan's Total War State: The Board of Information and Dōmei News Agency in Foreign Policy, 1934–45* (Dordrecht: Republic of Letters, 2014). On Japanese press policies from 1932 to 1945, see Gregory Kasza, *The State and the Mass Media in Japan, 1918–1945* (Berkeley: University of California Press, 1988), 121–231. On Japanese views of propaganda, see Barak Kushner, *The Thought War: Japanese Imperial Propaganda* (Honolulu: University of Hawai'i Press, 2006).

148. Agreement of April 1938 between Dōmei and Agence Havas. Dōmei also agreed to supply direct services to agencies allied with Havas in paragraph 2 of the contract. AN 5AR/312².

149. Shu, "Managing International News-Agency Relations under the Guomindang," 612–616.

150. BArch R901/58399, 56.

151. BArch R901/58399, 56.

152. BArch R901/58399. Reuters continued to provide service to the foreign press under Japanese supervision, but stopped in May 1942. Dōmei then published Reuters news, though how it received the news is unclear. After May 1943, bombing of German archives seems to have destroyed the statistics. On Transocean in Shanghai, see Astrid Freyeisen, *Shanghai und die Politik des Dritten Reiches* (Würzburg: Königshausen & Neumann, 2000), 219–223.

153. BArch R901/58399, 61.

154. See Daqing Yang, *Technology of Empire: Telecommunications and Japanese Expansion in Asia, 1883–1945* (Cambridge, MA: Harvard University Asia Center, 2010).

155. BArch R901/57685.

156. TNA CO273/657/15.

157. BArch R901/58399, 64. Peter de Mendelssohn claimed that the Japanese often used DNB or Transocean items and sent them out through Dōmei without labeling their origins, though he only discussed news in Japan itself. Peter de Mendelssohn, *Japan's Political Warfare* (New York: Routledge, 2011 [1944]), 40–41.

158. Letter from Sir Josiah Crosby, to Anthony Eden, February 9, 1938, TNA CO273/657/15, 25.

159. Report of January 1943, BArch R901/58399, 62–63.

160. BArch R901/58399, 63–64.

161. Klee, "Transocean," 210. For the "official" company history, see "Die Transocean: Ein kurzer Abriss über Entstehung und Werdegang der deutschen Auslands-Agentur: Aufgezeichnet von der Geschäftsleitung. Berlin 1950," Nr. I AK 67/1169, Institut für Zeitungsforschung, Dortmund.

162. Alfred Lückenhaus, *Von draußen gesehen. Bericht eines deutschen Auslandkorrespondenten aus Großbritannien, den Vereinigten Staaten von Amerika, Japan,*

China, 1924 bis 1945 (Düsseldorf: Robert Kämmerer, Verlag für Politische Bildung, 1955), 272.

163. Secret Report, German Propaganda Agents and Organizations in China during World War II, Strategic Services Unit, April 16, 1946, NARA RG226, E182, Box 23, Folder 124. Hans Melchers insisted that Transocean was a private company with no connections to the German government. Statement by Melchers, January 30, 1946, NARA RG226, E182A, Box 16, Folder 123.

164. For detailed lists of repatriated Germans, see NARA RG226, E182, Box 21, Folder 117.

165. NARA RG226, E182, Box 10, Folder 69.

Conclusion

1. Karl Bücher, *Gesammelte Aufsätze zur Zeitungskunde* (Tübingen: H. Laupp, 1926), 36.

2. Otto Groth, *Die Zeitung: Ein System der Zeitungskunde* (Mannheim: J. Bensheimer, 1929), 2:601.

3. Kapfinger edited the *Straubinger Tagblatt*. Hans Kapfinger, "Das Nachrichtenwesen," in Johann Wilhelm Naumann, ed., *Die Presse und der Katholik: Anklage und Rechtfertigung: Handbuch für Vortrag und Unterricht* (Augsburg: Haas & Grabherr, 1932), 188.

4. Theobald von Bethmann Hollweg, *Betrachtungen zum Weltkriege*, ed. Jost Dülffer (Essen: Reimar Hobbing, 1989), 181–182.

5. Jessica Gienow-Hecht, *Transmission Impossible: American Journalism as Cultural Diplomacy in Postwar Germany, 1945–1955* (Baton Rouge: Louisiana State University Press, 1999).

6. Norbert Frei and Johannes Schmitz, *Journalismus im Dritten Reich* (Munich: Beck, 1989), 184.

7. For example, Jürgen Wilke, "Nachrichtenagenturen," in Jürgen Wilke, ed., *Mediengeschichte der Bundesrepublik Deutschland* (Cologne: Böhlau, 1999), 469.

8. Cited in Wilke, "Nachrichtenagenturen," 473.

9. Christina von Hodenberg, *Konsens und Krise: Eine Geschichte der westdeutschen Medienöffentlichkeit, 1945–1973* (Göttingen: Wallstein, 2006), ch. 3.

10. Frei and Schmitz, *Journalismus im Dritten Reich*, 186–196.

11. Matthias Weiss, "Öffentlichkeit als Therapie. Die Medien- und Informationspolitik der Regierung Adenauer zwischen Propaganda und kritischer Aufklärung," in Norbert Frei and Frank Bösch, eds., *Medialisierung und Demokratie im 20. Jahrhundert* (Göttingen: Wallstein, 2006), 73–120.

12. Marsha Siefert, "Radio Diplomacy and the Cold War," *Journal of Communications* 53, no. 2 (2003): 363–73.

13. Francis Williams, *Transmitting World News: A Study of Telecommunications and the Press* (Paris: UNESCO, 1953).

14. *Many Voices, One World: Toward a New, More Just and More Efficient World Information and Communication Order* (London: UNESCO, 1980), 10, http://unesdoc.unesco.org/images/0004/000400/040066eb.pdf. A follow-up

study was published in association with UNESCO in 1992. Oliver Boyd-Barrett and Daya Kishan Thussu, *Contra-flow in Global News: International and Regional News Exchange Mechanisms* (London: J. Libbey, 1992). On NWICO, see Jonas Brendebach, "Towards a New International Communication Order? UNESCO, Development, and 'National Communication Policies' in the 1960s and 1970s," in Jonas Brendebach, Martin Herzer, and Heidi Tworek, eds., *International Organizations and the Media in the Nineteenth and Twentieth Centuries: Exorbitant Expectations* (New York: Routledge, 2018), 158–181.

15. U.S. State Department press release, October 12, 2017. Accessed August 11, 2018, https://www.state.gov/r/pa/prs/ps/2017/10/274748.htm.

16. Schumpeter, "The Al Jazeera Moment," *The Economist,* February 3, 2011. Accessed July 25, 2017, http://www.economist.com/blogs/schumpeter/2011/02/al_jazeera_moment.

17. For similar skepticism, see Corey Ross, "Writing the Media into History: Recent Works on the History of Mass Communications in Germany," *German History* 26, no. 2 (2008): 299–313; Hans-Ulrich Wehler, "Haben kritische Medien die Bundesrepublik stabilisiert?" in Patrick Bahners and Alexander Cammann, eds., *Bundesrepublik und DDR: Die Debatte um Hans-Ulrich Wehlers „Deutsche Gesellschaftsgeschichte"* (Munich: C. H. Beck, 2009), 276.

18. With the same argument for Anglo-American news, see Richard R. John and Jonathan Silberstein-Loeb, eds., *Making News: The Political Economy of Journalism in Britain and America from the Glorious Revolution to the Internet* (Oxford: Oxford University Press, 2015).

19. Robert Picard, "Cash Cows or Entrecôte: Publishing Companies and Disruptive Technologies," *Trends in Communication* 11, no. 2 (2003): 127–136.

20. Some overview histories have implied this. See, e.g., Paul Starr, *The Creation of the Media: Political Origins of Modern Communications* (New York: Basic Books, 2004).

21. Marshall McLuhan, *Understanding Media: The Extensions of Man,* ed. W. Terrence Gordon (Corte Madera, CA: Gingko Press, 2003).

22. Friedrich von Payer, *Von Bethmann Hollweg bis Ebert: Erinnerungen und Bilder* (Frankfurt am Main: Frankfurter Societäts-Druckerei, 1923), 255.

23. Volker Berghahn, *Germany and the Approach of War in 1914* (New York: St. Martin's Press, 1993), 13. On the importance of representation in post–World War I Germany, see Richard Bessel, "Introduction," in Richard Bessel and E. J. Feuchtwanger, eds., *Social Change and Political Development in Weimar Germany* (London: Barnes and Noble, 1981).

24. Jonas Brendebach, Martin Herzer, and Heidi Tworek, "Introduction," in Brendebach, Herzer, and Tworek, eds., *Exorbitant Expectations,* 1–10.

25. Walter Lippmann, *Public Opinion* (Mineola, NY: Dover Publications, 2004, orig. publ. 1922), 17.

26. Lippmann, *Public Opinion,* 52.

27. Lippmann, *Public Opinion,* 196–197.

ARCHIVES CONSULTED

Archival Sources

AUSTRIA

Österreichisches Staatsarchiv, Vienna (ÖStA, Austrian State Archive)

I/6b   Ministerratspräsidium—Presseleitung
I/6e   Telegraphisches-Korrespondenz-Büro/Amtliche Nachrichtenstelle

FRANCE

Archives Nationales, Paris (AN, National Archives)

5AR   Agence Havas

GERMANY

Archiv der Akademie der Künste, Berlin (AAK, Archive of the Academy of Arts)

Nachlass Franz Jung

Bundesarchiv, Berlin-Lichterfelde (BArch, Federal Archive)

Alfred-Ingemar Berndt (files from former Berlin Documentation Center)

Maximilian, Freiherr Besserer von Thalfingen (files from former Berlin Documentation Center)

Otto Dietrich (files from former Berlin Documentation Center)

N2106	Nachlass Otto Hammann
N2195	Nachlass Martin Mohr
NS26	Hauptarchiv der NSDAP
R2	Finanzministerium
R11	Deutscher Industrie- und Handelstag / Reichswirtschaftskammer
R34	Deutsches Nachrichtenbüro
R43	Reichskanzlei
R43I	Alte Reichskanzlei
R43II	Neue Reichskanzlei
R55	Reichsministerium für Volksaufklärung und Propaganda
R114	Eildienst für amtliche und private Handelsnachrichten GmbH
R705	Informationsstelle der Reichsregierung
R901	Auswärtiges Amt
R1001	Reichskolonialamt
R1501	Reichsministerium des Innern
R3001	Justizministerium
R3301	Reichsministerium für Wiederaufbau
R4701	Reichspostministerium
R4702	Reichspostzentralamt
R8047	Transozean, Zweigstelle Sofia

Bundesarchiv, Koblenz (BArchK, Federal Archive)

Kl. Erw. 302	Papiere von Otto Mejer
N1016	Nachlass Bernhard von Bülow
N1053	Nachlass Wilhelm Solf
N1231	Nachlass Alfred Hugenberg
N1541	Nachlass Dr. Edgar Stern-Rubarth
Zsg 105	Sammlung Otto Jung
Zsg 116	Pressedienst-Sammlung DNB
Zsg 135	Presseausschnitt-Sammlung Müller

Bundesarchiv Militärarchiv, Freiburg (BA MA, Federal Archive, Military Archive)

N253	Nachlass Alfred von Tirpitz
RM3	Reichsmarineamt, Nachrichtenbüro

Deutsches Rundfunkarchiv, Frankfurt (DRA, German Broadcasting Archive)

Nachlass Hans von Bredow

Geheimes Staatsarchiv Preußischer Kulturbesitz, Berlin (GStA PK, Secret State Archive of Prussian Cultural Heritage)

I. HA Rep. 77   Ministerium des Innern
I. HA Rep. 84a   Justizministerium
I. HA Rep. 89   Geheimes Zivilkabinett
VI. HA   Familienarchive und Nachlässe (Nachlass Wolfgang Kapp)

Institut für Zeitungsforschung, Dortmund (IfZ, Institute for Newspaper Research)

Nr. I AK 67/1169 Die Transocean. Berlin 1950

Politisches Archiv des Auswärtigen Amtes, Berlin (PA AA, Political Archive of the Foreign Office)

Akten der Außenhandelsstelle des Auswärtigen Amtes (Abteilung X)
Botschaft Ankara/Konstantinopel
Botschaft Buenos Aires
Botschaft Paris
Botschaft Peking
Botschaft Washington DC
Deutschland 126 Nr. 2i (Die Continental-Korrespondenz)
England Politik 12 (England Pressewesen)
Europa Generalia 86 secr. & Nr. 1–4 (Telegraphen-Institute des In- und
    Auslandes)
Gesandtschaft Bern
Geschäftsstelle für die Friedensverhandlungen
Nachlass Rudolf Nadolny
Nachlass Walter Zechlin
Personalakten (Albert Haas, Helmuth Friedrich Wilhelm von dem Hagen,
    Hermann von Ritgen, Manfred Zapp)
Personalakten der Beschäftigten der Presseabteilung (Hermann von Ritgen)
Personalverwaltungsakten Schwell-Liste (Albert Haas)
Politische Abteilung III Politik 11 & 12 (Journalisten, Presse)
Presseabteilung
Rechtsabteilung
Sonderreferat Wirtschaft
Türkei Politik 12 (Türkei Pressewesen)
Vereinigte Staaten von Amerika 11 & 12 (Journalisten und Pressevertreter;
    Pressewesen)

POLAND

Archiwum Akt Nowych, Warsaw (AAN, Archive of Modern Records)

Ambasada RP w Berlinie
Ambasada i Konsulat Generalny w Londynie
Ambasada RP w Paryżu
Ambasada RP w Washingtonie
Konsulat Generalny RP w Berlinie
Konsulat Generalny RP w Monachium
Konsulat Generalny RP w Olsytnie
Konsulat Generalny RP w Szeczinie
Ministerstwo Spraw Zagranicznych (MSZ, Ministry of Foreign Affairs)

SWITZERLAND

League of Nations Archive, Geneva (LNA)

UNITED KINGDOM

BBC Written Archive Centre, Reading (WAC)

R28	News, Reuters Ltd

British Telecom Archives, London (BT)

POST 30/1530B	Wireless Telegraphy in Germany, 1904–1932
POST 33	Post Office: Registered Files, Minuted Papers (General)

The National Archives, London (TNA)

AIR5/548	Scheme by Marconi Ltd. for Wireless Communication throughout the British Empire
ADM116	Admiralty: Record Office: Cases
CAB24	War Cabinet and Cabinet: Memoranda, 1915–1939
CAB37/130	Records of the Cabinet Office: The Failure of German Diplomacy, 1915
CAB37/140	Records of the Cabinet Office: Memo on Global German Communications, 1916
CAB68	Records of the Cabinet Office: German Propaganda, 1940
CO	Records of the Colonial Office, Commonwealth and Foreign and Commonwealth Offices, Empire Marketing Board, and Related Bodies

FO233	Foreign Office: Consulates and Legation, China
FO371	Foreign Office: Political Departments: General Correspondence
FO925/30010	Wireless Map of the World, 1912
FO1056	Control Office for Germany and Austria
HW	Records Created or Inherited by Government Communications Headquarters (GCHQ)
INF1/715	Ministry of Information: Foreign Countries' Propaganda Organisation
MT9	Board of Trade and Ministry of Transport: Marine, Harbours, and Wrecks
MT10	Board of Trade Harbour Department: Correspondence and Papers
KV	Records of the Security Service
T1	Treasury Board Papers and In-Letters
WO32	War Office and Successors: Registered Files
WO208	War Office: Military Operations and Intelligence

Reuters Archive, London (RA)

Royal Mail Archive, London (RMA)

POST 33	Post Office: Registered Files, Minuted Papers (General)

UNITED STATES

Associated Press Corporate Archives, New York, NY (APCA)

Kent Cooper Collection
Subject Files AP02A.3

Harvard University Archives, Cambridge, MA

Heinrich Brüning Papers

National Archives and Records Administration II, Washington, DC (NARA)

RG59	General Records of the Department of State
RG60	Department of Justice
RG226	Office of Strategic Services (OSS)

Newspapers

Chronicling America Database (www.chroniclingamerica.loc.gov)
8-Uhr Abendblatt
Bayerische Staatszeitung
Berliner Blatt
Berliner Börsen-Courier
Berliner Börsenzeitung
Berliner Lokal-Anzeiger
Berliner Morgenpost
Berliner Tageblatt
Berliner Volkszeitung
Daily Mail
Der Reichsbote
Der Tag
Deutsche Tageszeitung
Deutsche Warte
Deutscher Reichsanzeiger
Die Post
Die Rote Fahne
Dresdner Anzeiger
Dresdner Neueste Nachrichten
Dziennik Poznański
Financial Times
Frankfurter Zeitung
Germania
Hamburger Nachrichten
Hannoverscher Kurier
Kölnische Zeitung
Königsberger Hartungsche Zeitung
Le Matin
Magdeburgische Zeitung
München-Augsburger Abendzeitung
Neue Deutsche Presse
Neue Preußische Zeitung (Kreuzzeitung or *Kreuz-Zeitung)*
New York Times
Newspaper Archive Database (https://newspaperarchive.com)
Norddeutsche Allgemeine Zeitung
ProQuest Historical Newspapers Archive
Rheinisch-Westfälische Zeitung
Sächsische Staatszeitung
Stettiner Abendpost
Tägliche Rundschau
The Economist

The Times
Vorwärts
Vossische Zeitung
Weser-Zeitung

Magazines and Periodicals

Deutsche Presse
Hansard
Kladderadatsch
Simplicissimus
Zeitungs-Verlag
Zeitungswissenschaft

LIST OF FIGURES

Figure 1. *Kladderadatsch* Cartoon, March 31, 1917

Figure 2. Map of Wolff's Branches in Germany, *Zeitungswissenschaft,* 1926

Figure 3. *Simplicissimus* Cartoon, September 22, 1914

Figure 4. U.S. Newspapers Printing Transocean Articles, 1915–1917

Figure 5. *Kölnische Zeitung,* Evening Edition, November 9, 1918

Figure 6. *Berliner Tageblatt,* Evening Edition, November 9, 1918

Figure 7. *Kladderadatsch* Cartoon, March 28, 1920

Figure 8. Telegraph Union Advertisement, *Zeitungs-Verlag,* September 5, 1924

Figure 9. Telegraph Union Advertisement, *Zeitungs-Verlag,* October 10, 1924

Figure 10. Telegraph Union Advertisement, *Zeitungs-Verlag,* February 16, 1929

Figure 11. Telegraph Union Advertisement, *Deutsche Presse,* May 24, 1930

Figure 12. Map of Transocean Services, 1933

Figure 13. French Wireless Towers in Buenos Aires, 1933

ACKNOWLEDGMENTS

Networks behind the news are hidden. So too are the networks behind a book. Many kind and brilliant people have helped me to publish these pages. My words of thanks here are only a small token of my gratitude for their generous support.

Charles S. Maier advised me to choose a subject I loved for my first book, because I'd be stuck with it for a decade. As with all his advice, he was completely right. His insights have shaped this work and my academic trajectory more than he perhaps realizes. I am deeply grateful for his counsel, friendship, and adventurous spirit. The idea for this work emerged from work for David Blackbourn, and his comments influenced its conclusion. Niall Ferguson encouraged me to think big and be bold. Joachim Whaley and Martin Ruehl nurtured my interest in German history. Emma Rothschild's encouragement and wise words of wisdom have made a world of difference.

Many dear colleagues and friends read versions of the full manuscript. Simone M. Müller has long been an indispensable partner in so many ventures, an indomitable pillar of support, and an inspiration. Sonja Glaab-Seuken's passion for press history and sharp eye for detail made an enormous difference, from the days when we sat in the archives together right up to the end. Hans Kundnani's comments and moral support helped a great deal. Michael Stamm combines clear thinking about communications with infectious curiosity. Richard R. John's guidance was crucial, his comments astute, and his generosity unparalleled.

My deepest thanks to those who read chapters or extracts, including Michel Ducharme (my introduction guru), Eagle Glassheim (my super-supportive mentor), and John Maxwell Hamilton (who really showed me how to write).

Yuliya Komska's perceptive feedback and enthusiasm were indispensable. Peter Gordon provided shrewd comments and support at crucial moments. James McSpadden's enthusiastic suggestions and archival nuggets much improved this book. Wordsmith Maya Jasanoff devised the first half of my title.

I received useful feedback at dozens of conferences and workshops, including the American Historical Association, Business History Conference, German Studies Association, International Communication Association, the Radio Conference, Society for the History of Technology, Zentrum für Zeithistorische Forschung, Universität Bielefeld, Freie Universität, Justus-Liebig-Universität, Universität Leipzig, Louisiana State University, the Potomac Center for the Study of Modernity, the German Historical Institutes in London and Washington, DC, the Ziegler Speaker Series at the University of British Columbia (UBC), and the Modern European History Workshop and the Center for History and Economics Seminar at Harvard University. In particular, I benefited from suggestions by Tariq Omar Ali, Christopher Buschow, Philip Fileri, Florian Greiner, Pascal Griset, Carla Heelan, Kuba Kabala, Brendan Karch, Léonard Laborie, Hassan Malik, Johan Mathew, Sreemati Mitter, Jürgen Wilke, and Jeremy Yellen. My students at both Harvard and the University of British Columbia sharpened my thinking and reminded me why the history of news matters. The nine undergraduates from History 92r at Harvard in 2015 (and Gabriel Pizzorno) were a particularly intrepid team, whose research on digitized newspapers informed a crucial part of Chapter 2.

Conversations with and help from many others vastly improved this book, including Ann M. Blair, Timothy Cheek, Jesse Howell, Piotr Kosicki, Terry Martin, Vanessa Ogle, Sophus Reinert, Tehila Sasson, Louis and Shirley Shakinovsky, Daniel Lord Smail, and Nikki Usher Layser. I learned so much about German and media history from Jonas Brendebach, Chase Gummer, Martin Herzer, Sam Lebovic, Suzanne Marchand, Chase Richards, Jonathan Silberstein-Loeb, Quinn Slobodian, Annette Vowinckel, and Thomas Weber. I am also grateful to David Armitage, Jason Barcus, Sugata Bose, James T. Kloppenberg, Ian J. Miller, Paul Nolte, Glenda Sluga, Norman Strauss, Nicholas White, and Sir Richard Wilson for their support. Richard Cavell, Lisa Coulthard, Alfred Hermida, T'ai Smith, and Geoffrey Winthrop-Young showed me what great interdisciplinary media studies looks like. Thank you to Katia Bowers, Jeffrey Byrne, John Christopoulos, Michel Ducharme, Kyle Frackman, Eagle Glassheim, Ilinca Iurascu, Steven Lee, Tina Loo, Richard Menkis, Leslie Paris, and Jessica Wang for generously helping me to navigate life at UBC and in Vancouver. I was so lucky to start in the History Department at the same time as David Morton, journalism expert and my marking buddy. Bradley Miller and Joshua Cramer cooked me more than my fair share of delicious meals, saved me from several domestic disasters, and made me laugh.

Many people facilitated my research trips: my dear cousin Ana Stefanović in Geneva, the Kaminiorz family in Recklinghausen, Hannah Callaway in Paris, Iva Gaberova and Dan Burke in London. Iva kept London home; the book was only complete with some paragraphs on Bulgaria for her. Susanne Brück, Dominik Fungipani, and Claudia Streim opened up their houses and hearts to me; David Löwenstein, Kilu von Prince, Linn Friedrichs, and Rudy Hoppe also make Berlin home.

Staff in twenty archives around the world were unfailingly helpful. I am especially indebted to the staff at the Federal Archives in Berlin, Koblenz, and Freiburg, Politisches Archiv des Auswärtigen Amtes, Archiv der Akademie der Künste, and Geheimes Staatsarchiv Preußischer Kulturbesitz in Berlin, as well as Archives Nationales (Paris), Archiwum Akt Nowych (Warsaw), and Österreichisches Staatsarchiv (Vienna). Particular thanks to John Entwisle of the Reuters Archive (London) as well as Valerie Komor and Francesca Pitaro of the Associated Press Corporate Archives (New York). I gratefully acknowledge the generous support for my research provided by Deutscher Akademischer Austauschdienst (DAAD), the Minda de Gunzburg Center for European Studies, the Davis Center for Russian and Eurasian Studies, and the History Department at Harvard University as well as the University of British Columbia and the Herchel Smith Travel Fund, Emmanuel College, Cambridge University. I also thank the staff of the Harvard History Department, especially Laura Johnson and Mary McConnell, who brightened every day at work for three years. I am grateful to Harvard University Press, particularly Andrew Kinney, Stephanie Vyce, and Olivia Woods, for shepherding this project to completion. Thanks to Jonathan Gough, Jonas Stuck, and especially Jonathan Palmer for help with the figures. Ian Beacock kindly assisted with checking the proofs. Portions of Chapter 2 were first published as "How Not to Build a World Wireless Network: German-British Rivalry and Visions of Global Communications in the Early Twentieth Century," *History and Technology* 32, no. 2 (2016): 178–200, and are reprinted here with permission.

Much of this book was revised and completed during fellowships at the Zentrum für Zeithistorische Forschung in Potsdam and the Transatlantic Academy at the German Marshall Fund of the United States in Washington, DC. Special and deeply heartfelt thanks to Frank Bösch, Karen Donfried, and Stephen Szabo for hosting me. It was a delight to spend the year of 2016–2017 with such a smart and supportive cohort of Transatlantic Academy fellows: Frédéric Bozo, Stefan Fröhlich, Wade Jacoby, Harold James, Michael Kimmage,

Hans Kundnani, Yascha Mounk, and Mary Elise Sarotte. I owe an immeasurable debt of gratitude to Mary Elise Sarotte in particular for her unstinting support.

Family has constantly shown me the most important things in life. Nada and Richard Johnn cheered and encouraged me. Wiesława, Stefan, Jadwiga, and Monica Tworek supported me with love. I am beyond blessed that Connie Eysenck and Didier Godat opened their house to me in Washington, DC; they along with Adrien Godat, Lisa Johnson, and Eve Eysenck Godat made DC my home in 2016–2017. All my grandparents lived through the turmoil of twentieth-century Europe. Their travails started my fascination with history. Eva and Milorad Taušanović, my maternal grandparents, inspired me with their bravery, kindness, and astonishing facility with languages. My paternal grandparents, Hans and Sybil Eysenck, remain my models for successful and bold academics.

Finally, Lilly and Gary Evans are parental paragons. They have always supported and encouraged my projects, going above and beyond countless times to help me. I only hope they know how much their generosity and love mean to me. Michael Tworek shaped this piece of work in multiple ways, from teaching me Polish to believing in me. He has endured my obsession with news with good grace and humor, encouraging me in this endeavor with his time and love. It is to him and my parents that I dedicate this book.

INDEX

Page numbers followed by *f,* n or nn indicate figures or notes.

8-Uhr-Abendblatt, 77

Adenauer, Konrad, 227, 277n54
Adorno, Theodor, 40
Advertising, 9, 15, 22, 24, 30, 42–43, 84,
  87; Telegraph Union and, 145, 147, 152,
  153*f,* 160–163, 162*f,* 171–175, 172*f,* 174*f*
Africa, German colonies in, 23, 24, 26,
  46–51, 55, 185, 201. *See also* South Africa
Agence Bulgare, 62
Agence d'Anatolie, 125–126, 130, 132,
  135–136, 279n73
Agence France-Presse (AFP), 22, 227
Agence Havas, 11, 18–20, 22, 62, 86,
  110–112, 140, 165, 187, 188, 244n9,
  272n76, 285n93; Brazil and, 211, 298n87;
  China and, 213, 216–219, 300n133;
  cultural diplomacy and, 135, 137; DNB
  and, 187, 188, 190, 191, 287n1; Eildienst
  and, 109–112; German imperial
  ambitions and, 26; Havasian, 111–112;
  PAT and, 166, 286n107; South
  America and, 28, 208–211; Telegraph
  Union and, 156, 165; Transocean and,
  201, 205, 208, 209–210, 211, 213,

216–219, 221; Turkey and, 125–126, 132,
  135; wireless and, 210, Wolff and, 137,
  140, 285n93; World War I and, 61, 62,
  208, 225
Agences Alliées, 110–112, 165, 166, 184,
  187, 272n74. *See also* Cartels, news
  agencies and
Agence Télégraphique Suisse, 110
Agencia Brasileira, 211
Agencia Noticiosa Argentina (ANDI),
  210–212
Agencja Telegraficzna Express, 167
Albrecht, Gustav, 185
Alekseev, Porfiri, 148
Algeciras conference (1906), 26
Al Jazeera, 228
Allgemeine Anzeigen (ALA), 145, 147
Allgemeiner Deutscher Nachrichtendi-
  enst (ADN), 226
Allgemeiner Deutscher Verband
  (Pan-German League), 144
Amann, Max, 189, 192
American Federal Telegraph
  Company, 64
American Radio Corporation, 289n40

Amtliche Nachrichtenstelle (ANA, Austrian news agency), 109, 139, 163–165, 271n51, 285n93

Amts-Correspondenz privilege, Wolff and, 21, 84

Anderson, Benedict, 9

Anschluss (annexation of Austria), 139, 191

Anti-Semitism, 29, 39, 69, 73, 93, 130, 170, 183–185, 187, 201, 217

Appadurai, Arjun, 239n37

Arco, Georg von, 57

Argentina, 8, 200, 208–212, 210f, 213

Argentinisches Tageblatt, 213

Asia Eastern Europe Service (AOD), 147–148, 152

Asiatic News Agency, 215, 293n13

Asquith, Herbert, 51

Associated Press (AP), 34, 140, 226–228; DNB and, 187, 188, 190; East Asia and, 214–216, 219; Nazi Germany and, 206, 213; news agency cartel and, 11, 20, 53, 140, 187, 188, 219; South America and, 206, 208, 210–211, 213; Transocean and, 196, 206, 208, 210–211, 213, 214, 216, 219; Wolff and, 20, 217n59

Association of Foreign Press Representatives (Verband ausländischer Pressevertreter), 138, 279n87

Association of German Newspaper Publishers. (Verein Deutscher Zeitungs-Verleger, VDZV), 34, 52, 105, 116, 255nn39–40, 283n47

Association of Industrialists (Bund der Industriellen), 28

Atatürk, Mustafa Kemal, 125

Atlantic Communication Company, 102

Aub, Walter, 39

Audience. *See* Listeners; Public opinion; Readers

Auflagenachrichten, 191–192

August Scherl. *See* Scherl (publisher)

Außenhandelsstelle (Foreign Trade Office), 101, 107, 267n7

Austria, 30, 39, 40, 59, 68, 108–109, 130, 139, 161, 163–165, 167, 186, 191. *See also* Amtliche Nachrichtenstelle

Austria-Hungary, 23. *See also* k. u. k. Korrespondenzbureau

Australia, 19, 28, 47, 48, 55

Authoritarianism, 6, 13, 39, 40, 94, 167. *See also* Nazi Party

Azores, cable laid via, 48, 52, 103, 268n15

Baden, Maximilian von, 37, 70, 72–75, 77, 225

Balkan-Orient-Dienst, 138

Bauer, Gustav, 91, 92

Bauer, Max, 93

Bauer, Otto, 163

Bauer, Wilhelm, 38

Bavaria, 114–115

BBC (British Broadcasting Company/ Corporation), 5, 104, 113, 114, 116–117, 207, 212

Beiersdorf company, 13, 108

Beijing, 58, 66, 161, 199, 215, 217, 218, 220; German residents in, 222

Beloborodov, Aleksandr Grigorievich, 141, 144, 145, 147–152, 154–156

Berlin Alexanderplatz (novel), 31

Berlin–Baghdad railway, 45, 46, 124, 125

Berlin: Die Sinfonie der Großstadt (film), 31

Berliner Lokal-Anzeiger, 77–78, 91, 145, 179

Berliner Tageblatt, 26, 74, 76f, 77, 81, 105, 140, 144, 278n65

Berman, Heinrich, 166–167

Bernays, Edward, 39

Berndt, Alfred-Ingemar, 184–185, 186

Bernhard, Ludwig, 168

Bernstorff, Johann Heinrich von, 60, 257n72

Besserer von Thalfingen, Maximilian, 227

Bethmann Hollweg, Theobald von, 52, 59, 60, 225

Bismarck, Otto von, 5, 21, 22–24, 27, 30, 124, 127

Bleichröder Bank, 21, 29, 144, 181–182, 258n86

Bleichröder, Gerson von, 5, 21, 29

Blitzfunktelegramme (radio telegrams), 107

Bourdieu, Pierre, 8, 85

Braun, Karl Ferdinand, 12, 46

Brazil, 58, 101, 208, 211–212, 213
Bredow, Hans von: Eildienst and, 100–104, 106–108, 113–114, 119, 123, 151, 225; imprisioned by Nazis, 118, 119; spoken radio and, 114–119, 228; Telefunken and, 57, 67–68, 100, 102
Brunhuber, Robert, 40, 44
Brüning, Heinrich, 41, 179, 180, 183, 194, 228
Bücher, Karl, 38, 224, 225
Bulgaria, 60, 61–62, 63, 68, 136, 138, 161
Bülow, Bernhard von, 27
Bund der Industriellen. *See* Association of Industrialists
Burgfrieden, 52
B.Z. am Mittag, 27, 29–30, 74

Cables. *See* Telegraph cables
Cable & Wireless (British company), 182
Carlé, Wilhelm, 78–79
Cartels, news agencies and, 11, 18–23, 26, 29, 41, 84, 86, 110–113, 188, 208, 224, 229, 244n9, 290n66. *See also* Agences Alliées
Catholic Center Party (Zentrum), 30, 83
Cautio Trust, 186
Censorship of news: Germany and, 22, 42, 52, 80, 92, 116, 148, 151, 179, 188–189; Great Britain and, 48–49; Japan and, 221; Russia and, 65–66; United States and, 55, 57, 206
Central News Agency, in China, 217–218, 219
Central Press Service, in China, 219–220
Chamberlain, Austen, 200
Chiang Kai-shek, 214, 215, 217–219
Chicago Herald, 60
Chile, 211–213
China: declaration of war on Germany, 66; DNB and, 131, 203–204, 222; Japanese-occupied, 3, 15, 218–220, 223; news agency cartel and, 20; Telegraph Union and, 147; Transocean and, 15, 196, 199, 203–204, 213–220, 293n13; wireless in, 57, 58, 63–68, 215–218
China Central Television (CCTV), 228

Cinema, 116
Claß, Heinrich, 94
Cohen-Reuß, Max, 81
Colonial Office, German, 24, 46, 48, 50, 51, 52, 55, 57
Colonialism, 6, 20, 49, 50, 55, 58, 219–220; Germany and, 6, 9, 12, 13, 23–26, 45–52, 55–57, 185, 201, 214
Communications. *See* Journalism; News; News agencies; Newspapers; Radio; Wireless telegraphy
Communist Party of Germany (KPD), 31, 77, 149
Companhia Radiotelegrafica Brasileira, 211
Concordia, 164
Continental Korrespondenz, 27–28
Continental-Telegraphen-Compagnie (CTC). *See* Wolff's Telegraphisches Bureau
Cooper, Kent, 20
Coordinator of Inter-American Affairs (CIAA), of U.S., 207
Corriere della Sera, 61
Council of People's Deputies (Rat der Volksbeauftragten), 80–82
Crosby, Josiah, 221
Cultural diplomacy, 122–124; foreign correspondents and, 122–135, 277nn56,57, 278nn65,68; Germany and, 122–140, 278n68; Ritgen and, 121–139, 278n68; in Turkey, 121–140
Czechoslovakia, 160–161, 167–168, 186

Daily Mail, 66, 198, 199
Daily Mirror, 198
Daily Telegraph, 26–27
Dammert, Rudolf, 173
Dammert news agency, 103–104, 144, 173
Darlan, Jean-François, 212
Däumig, Ernst, 92
David-Fox, Michael, 122
Da Zhong news agency, 215
Dehmel, Richard, 89
Delbrück, Schickler & Co., 184

Democracy, 5, 6, 13, 14–15, 30–31, 39, 73, 79, 97, 171, 175, 212, 227; news and, 168–169, 178–183, 228–229; public opinion and, 85, 194, 229–231; radio and, 99–100, 113–115, 183. *See also* Elections; Public opinion; Weimar Republic

Denmark, 49, 65, 67, 111, 164, 272n74

Deutsch-Atlantische Telegraphengesellschaft (DAT), 182–183, 289n40

Deutsche Allgemeine Zeitung, 133

Deutsche Bank, 45

Deutsche Demokratische Partei (DDP), 83

Deutsche Kabelgrammgesellschaft (German Cablegram Company), 27

Deutsche Presse, 173, 174f

Deutscher Handelsdienst (DHD), 150–151, 177

Deutscher Industrie-und Handelstag (DIHT), 107–108, 268n12

Deutscher Kursfunk, 112, 151, 188, 272n78

Deutscher Tickerdienst, 178

Deutscher Überseedienst (DÜD), 59, 107, 198, 270nn39, 41

Deutscher Wirtschaftsdienst, 107, 270nn39,41

Deutsches Nachrichtenbüro (DNB), 42, 109, 131, 170, 183–194, 219, 222, 291nn72,81; anti-Semitism and, 187; creation of, 170, 183–188, 201; domestic news and, 188–194; Hellschreiber and, 190–191, 193; nicknames of, 188, 193; Ritgen and, 139, 279n88; Telegraph Union and, 183–188, 189, 195, 227; Transocean and, 201, 203–204, 207; Turkey and, 137; Wolff and, 183–188, 189, 195

Deutsche Stunde für drahtlose Belehrung und Unterhaltung (German Hour for Wireless Education and Entertainment), 114–115

Deutsche Südwestafrikanische Zeitung, 48

Deutsche Tageszeitung, 91, 106

Deutsche Volkspartei (DVP), 143

Deutsche Zeitung, 77

Deutschnationale Volkspartei (DNVP), 31, 53, 94, 142–143, 180

Deutsch-Niederländische Telegraphengesellschaft, 49

Dietrich, Otto, 184, 185, 189, 291n72

Diez, Hermann, 22, 95, 148, 181, 184, 185, 287n9, 290n66

Diplomacy. *See* Cultural diplomacy; Foreign correspondents: diplomacy and

Döblin, Alfred, 31

Dōmei Tsūshinsha (Allied News Agency), 219; in China, 219–220, 221, 301n152; in Indochina, 221; in Thailand, 221

Domestic politics, Weimar Republic and communications, 171–183, 194. *See also* Democracy; Deutsches Nachrichtenbüro (DNB); Imperial Germany; Kapp Putsch; Revolution of 1918–1919; Telegraph Union; Weimar Republic; Wolff's Telegraphisches Bureau

dpa (Deutsche Presse-Agentur), 226, 227

Drach, Fritz, 82

Dradag (Drahtloser Dienst), 116

Drahtloser Überseeverkehr (Wireless Overseas Traffic), 66–67

Drews, Bill, 37

Drummond, Eric, 209

Dutch colonies, German wireless and, 49, 58, 68, 213–214, 221–222, 298n104

Dutch East Indies (Indonesia), 213–214, 221–222, 298n104. *See also* Java, German wireless and

East Asia, 6, 12, 15, 24, 29, 55, 57, 60, 68, 197, 213–223, 225, 227, 284n70; DNB and, 203–204; Transocean and, 197, 203–204, 213–223. *See also* China; Japan

Eastern and Associated Companies (telegraph), 47

Ebert, Friedrich, 6, 37–38, 42, 70, 74–75, 77, 80–82, 85

Economic nationalism. *See* Hugenberg, Alfred: economic nationalism and; Telegraph Union: economic nationalism and

Economics, news and, 28–29, 44, 100–101, 106–108, 112–113, 119, 123, 150–151, 177. *See also* Exports, news and

Eden, Anthony, 201, 203, 221

Editors Law, 185–186, 192

Eher Verlag, 184, 186, 192, 201

Eichhorn, Emil, 82

Eildienst (Swift Service), 14–15, 35, 68, 126, 152, 178, 184, 188, 268n10, 269nn22,25,26; Austria and, 109; Bredow and, 100–104, 106–108, 109, 113–114, 119–120, 225; democratic and economic aims for, 99–108, 119, 123, 225, 267n6, 268n9; Foreign Office and, 101–102, 105–108, 120, 134, 136, 139, 140; influence on spoken radio, 100, 102, 113–118, 120; news agency cartel and, 108–113, 165; origins of, 100–101; Postal Ministry and, 101–104, 106, 119, 151–152; Telegraph Union and, 151–152; Wolff and, 105, 110–113, 151, 184, 188. *See also* Europradio

Eilvese, wireless tower at, 53, 68, 182, 200

Einstein, Albert, 11, 241n44

Elections, 81, 83, 85, 99, 143, 237n19. *See also* Democracy

Eltzbacher, Paul, 69

Erzberger, Matthias, 89

Espionage, 4, 196, 204–207, 222

Europapress, 59, 62, 204, 222, 291n72, 295n40

Europradio, 108–112. *See also* Eildienst

Evans, Richard J., 201

Exchange Telegraph Company, 142, 161

Exports, news and, 28–29, 53, 54*f*, 100–101, 107–108, 112–113, 119, 123, 142, 150, 177, 197, 216. *See also* Economics, news and

Fake news, 4; faked photographs 59–60, 63. *See also* False news; *Lügenpresse*

False news, 39, 53, 54*f*, 69, 78, 81–82, 85, 92, 95, 152, 199; Nazis and, 188–189, 203; Telegraph Union and, 141, 143, 150, 152, 154–157, 159, 160, 164. *See also* Fake news; *Lügenpresse*

Fascism. *See* Authoritarianism; Nazi Party

Fear, Jeffrey, 111

Federal Broadcasting Commission (Reichsrundfunkkommission), 82

Federal German Press Association (Reichsverband der Deutschen Presse), 116, 138

Federal Radio Company (Reichsrundfunkgesellschaft), 115

Fehrenbach, Konstantin, 84

Fontenoy, Jean, 216–217, 299n114

Foreign Agents Registration Act (FARA), of U.S., 205–206

Foreign correspondents, 3, 32, 85–86, 132, 147, 160, 199, 215, 222, 277n56; anti-Semitism and, 130; diplomacy and, 124–125, 129–130, 132, 160; DNB and, 190; Telegraph Union and, 147, 154–155, 160; Weimar government and, 34–35, 127–130, 134; Wolff and, 122–124, 129, 134. *See also* Journalism; Newspapers

Foreign Office, German, 23, 24, 109, 123, 127–128, 130, 140, 150, 159, 175, 208; Eildienst and, 101–102, 105–106, 107–109, 116, 120, 151, 188; Nazis and, 183–184, 203, 206–207; news subsidies and, 15, 28, 48, 59, 94, 133–134, 148, 176, 182; Ritgen and, 121–122, 124, 129–131, 132, 134–136, 138, 139, 140; Telegraph Union and, 152, 159, 160, 178–179; Transocean and, 39, 59, 62, 136, 200, 203, 206–207, 214; wireless and, 55, 57, 59, 68–69, 82, 120, 200; Wolff and, 29, 53, 85, 87–88, 90, 93–94, 122, 126, 129–131, 133–136, 140, 148, 159, 160, 176, 182. *See also* Press Department

Foreign policy. *See* Foreign Office, German; Press Department; Transocean: German foreign policy and

France, 26, 45, 123; cables and, 49; cultural diplomacy and, 123; empire and, 26, 28, 46, 49, 68, 221; German concerns about control of news, 17, 18, 26–28, 46, 56, 131, 136; newspapers and, 32, 63; Transocean and, 197, 199–200, 209–210, 210*f*, 213, 216–217, 221, 223. *See also* Agence Havas

Frankfurt School, 40
Frankfurter Zeitung, 26, 31, 37, 81, 95, 125, 130, 144, 175, 192–193, 278n65
Freiheit, Die, 78, 266n128
Fuchs, Georg, 78, 82
Fulda, Bernhard, 42
Funkerspuk (phantom radio operators), 80
Fürholzer, Edmund, 203–204

Gayl, Wilhelm von, 180
Generalanzeiger newspapers, 30
General German Trade Union (ADGB), 91
Geopolitik, 25
German American Bund, 205
German Colonial Society, 24
Germania (Argentina), 60
Germania (Germany), 30
Germania (San Salvador), 63
German-Soviet Neutrality and Nonaggression Pact (1926), 141, 149–150, 156, 284n60
Giddens, Anthony, 239n37
Gleiwitz Incident, 203
Globalization: Germany and, 5–6, 17–18, 20–21, 23–24, 28, 45–47, 56–57, 63, 102, 225; history and, 236n15; news and, 1–3, 5–6, 10, 21, 28, 45–47, 225, 228, 239n37
Goebbels, Joseph: DNB news and, 42, 189, 190, 203–204; news and, 6, 191, 192, 206–207; news agencies and, 42, 222; propaganda and, 6, 39–40, 189; radio and, 99, 100, 101, 113, 118, 119; Transocean and, 203–204; Wolff and, 185
Goethe, Johann Wolfgang von, 6
Gontard, Friedrich von, 75
Goschen, Edward, 28
Great Britain: cultural diplomacy and, 123; empire and, 45, 48–49; German concerns about control of news, 1, 2f, 3, 6, 10, 12, 17, 18, 25–28, 48–49, 53, 54f; Hellschreiber and, 191, 193; interception of Zimmerman telegram, 56; MacBride report and, 228; naval power of, 24; newspapers and, 32; submarine cable system of, 3, 6, 14, 19,

47–49, 200; Transocean and, 62–63, 196, 197–203, 223; wireless plans and, 45–46, 197, 200; World War I and, 12, 53, 54f, 198. *See also* Reuters Telegram Company
Green, O. M., 216
Groener, Wilhelm, 85
Gross, Stephen, 100
Groth, Otto, 8, 38, 224, 225

Haas, Albert, 208
Habermas, Jürgen, 40–41
Hagen, Wilhelm von dem, 163, 279n88
Hahn, Wilhelm von, 278n88
Hamburger Echo, 76
Hamburger Fremdenblatt, 175, 278n65
Hamburger Tageblatt, 33–34
Hammann, Otto, 27, 59, 60
Häntzschel, Kurt, 115
Harnisch, Johannes, 91
Haushofer, Karl, 25
Havas. *See* Agence Havas
Havas, Charles, 19
Havasian. *See* Agence Havas
"Heartland theory" (Mackinder), 25
Heerdegen, Ernst, 18
Heide, Walther, 140
Hell, Rudolf, 190
Hellschreiber wireless ticker machine, 137, 190–191, 193
Herold Verlagsanstalt, 184
Hertling, Georg von, 62
Hess, Rudolf, 25, 204
Heydrich, Richard, 203
Hindenburg, Paul von, 42, 90, 99, 118, 180, 185, 252n131
Hitler, Adolf, 99, 143, 183, 203; Hugenberg and, 185; news and, 42, 179, 189, 190, 191, 206, 213, 288n26
Höfle, Anton, 115
Hollandsch Nieuwsbureau, 59
Homeyer, Friedrich von, 201, 204, 210–211
Hoover, J. Edgar, 15, 196, 204–206
Horkheimer, Max, 40
House Un-American Activities Committee (HUAC), of U.S., 205–206, 207

Hugenberg, Alfred, 39, 175, 144, 186, 208, 222; economic nationalism and, 15, 41, 141–145, 150, 169, 225; Hitler and, 179, 185; Kapp Putsch and, 94; media companies owned by, 28, 31, 107, 142–147, 164–165, 173, 181, 270n39; Nazi Party and, 185–186; politics and, 31, 39, 94, 142–145, 150, 169, 175, 178–181; Telegraph Union and, 15, 94, 140–147, 150, 169, 173, 179, 185–186, 225; Transocean and, 59; Wolff and, 144; Young Plan and, 179

Hurd, Percy Angier, 200

Huth company, 103, 114

Huyn, Hans von, 130, 131

I. G. Farben, 193

Imperial Germany (Kaiserreich), 13, 36, 83, 124–125, 130, 170, 179, 223, 237n19; end of, 70–79. *See also* Wilhelm II, Kaiser

Imperialism. *See* Colonialism

Ina-Nachrichtendienst (Ina News Service), 102

Indochina, 221

Industrie-und Handelszeitung (IHZ), 268n12

Information. *See* Journalism; News; News agencies; Newspapers; Radio; Wireless telegraphy

Information warfare. *See* News; News agencies

Infrastructure, 1, 5, 6–16, 45–47, 49, 53, 63, 69, 84, 222–223, 224, 226, 231, 240n42; DNB and, 183, 187, 195; Eildienst and, 99–102, 114–115; Nazis and, 99–101, 203–204, 207–208, 222, 223; Ottoman Empire and, 124, 125. *See also* Eilvese; Königswusterhausen; Nauen; Radio; Railways; Sayville; Telefunken; Telegraph cables; Tuckerton; Wireless telegraphy; Zeesen

Institut für Zeitungskunde (Institute for Newspaper Education), 34, 38, 224

International News Service (INS), 156, 227, 292n90

International Telegraph Union (ITU), 47

Intelligence. *See* Espionage; Journalism; News

Italy, 23, 199, 216, 272n74

Izvestia, 155, 156

Jackson, Robert H., 205

Japan, 63, 67, 123; cables and, 49; news agency cartel and, 20, 26; occupation of China, 3, 15, 218–220, 223; occupation of Southeast Asia, 221–222; Transocean and, 199, 200, 214, 218–221, 301nn152,157

Java, German wireless and, 58, 68, 213. *See also* Dutch East Indies

John, Richard R., 10

Juchacz, Marie, 85

Journalism, 3, 4, 7–8, 34, 35–36, 197, 215, 218, 224–227, 230–231; German attitudes to, 4, 6–7, 9, 11, 15, 30–44, 75, 118, 129–130, 140, 145, 179–181, 195, 224–227; German politicians and, 23, 30, 37–42, 70, 85, 127, 130, 139–140, 175–176, 179–181, 227; Kapp Putsch and, 92, 95; Nazis and, 170–171, 184, 185, 191–192; Telegraph Union and, 181; Wolff and, 85–86, 95, 181. *See also* Cultural diplomacy; Foreign correspondents; News; Newspapers

Jüdische Stimme, 157, 158

Jung, Franz, 78–79, 82

Kaiserreich. *See* Imperial Germany

Kapfinger, Hans, 225

Kapp Putsch, 14, 72, 89–97

Kapp, Wolfgang, 90–97

Kautsky, Karl, 79–80

Kellogg–Briand Pact, 158, 168

Kiep, Otto, 128

Kladderadatsch cartoons, 1, 2f, 4, 5, 95, 96f, 97

Klaas, Brian, 72

Koch, Peter Theodor, 170, 184, 186, 287n1

Koestler, Arthur, 35

Kölnische Zeitung, 71f, 134, 175, 262n25

Königswusterhausen, wireless tower at, 53, 68, 104, 114, 115, 268n9
Kopflose Zeitungen (headless newspapers), 32
Korrespondenzbüros (correspondence bureaus), 32, 86–87
Korrespondenz Gelb (Correspondence Yellow), 87, 93
Kracauer, Siegfried, 30
Kraus, Kristian, 180–181
Krupp, 144, 145, 208
k. u. k. Korrespondenzbureau (Austro-Hungarian news agency), 61–62, 125
Kulturkampf, 30
Kuomin (Chinese news agency), 215–218
Kuttner, Erich, 78–79, 82

Lacey, Kate, 115
Landwirtschaftliche Korrespondenz, 180
Larsen, Sophus, 64–67
Larsz, Franz (Franz Jung pseudonym), 82
Latin America. *See* South America
Latvia, 166
Latvijas telegrafa agentūra (LETA), 166
Law against Filth and Smut, 44
Lazarsfeld, Paul, 40
League of Nations, 38, 123, 154, 201, 209
Lebensraum, 25
Ledebour, Georg, 80–81
Leipziger Neueste Nachrichten, 144
Lewis, Willmott, 205
Liebknecht, Karl, 77, 79, 81, 83, 89
Lincoln, Abraham, 37
Lippmann, Walter, 230–231
Listeners, 105, 118, 167, 193, 196, 216, 223. *See also* Public opinion; Readers
Lithography, 3
Lithuania, 157–159
Lloyd George, David, 200
Locarno treaties, 150, 168
Lochner, Louis, 34–35
Lorenz (company), 103, 114, 178
Lückenhaus, Alfred, 222
Ludendorff, Erich, 69, 90, 93, 94
Lügenpresse (lying press), 170. *See also* Fake news; False news

Lüttwitz, Walther von, 89–90, 92
Luxemburg, Rosa, 78, 83, 89

MacBride Report (UNESCO), 228
Mackinder, Halford, 24–25
Mackinnon, William, 36–37
Mahan, Alfred Thayer, 24, 25, 49
Maier, Charles S., 9–10
Mainichi Shimbun, 220
Maison Wdowinski, 108
Mantler, Heinrich, 27, 83, 87–89, 110, 184, 222, 289n37; Kapp Putsch and, 90–92, 95, 265n109, 266n125; South America and, 208; Telegraph Union and, 165, 166, 176, 287n9
Marconi Company, 46, 50–51, 64, 66, 67, 271n62
Marconi, Guglielmo, 12, 46
Materndienst, 32, 173
Matin, Le, 110–111
McLuhan, Marshall, 229
Media. *See* Cinema; News; News agencies; Newspapers; Radio
Mejer, Otto, 186
Melchers, Hans, 218, 220, 227, 302n163
Mensenkampff, Ernst von, 159–160
Mexico, 56, 57, 58, 211, 212, 252n131
MI5, 197
Middle East, 45–46, 56, 124, 125, 131, 132, 139, 197, 201, 202f. *See also* Ottoman Empire
Mitter, Rana, 214
Moltke, Helmuth von (the Younger), 46
Mosse (publishing company), 29–30, 82
München-Augsburger Abendzeitung, 17, 145
Münchner Neueste Nachrichten, 145
Münzenberg, Willi, 31

Nachricht (news), 4–5, 236n10. *See also* News
Nachrichtenstelle für den Orient (News Office for the Orient), 125
Nachtausgabe, 31, 145
Nadolny, Rudolf, 124, 126, 128–129, 131, 132, 135, 136, 140, 275n10, 279n85

Nauen, wireless tower at, 12, 51, 53, 55–58, 64, 66, 68, 77, 80, 102, 108, 126, 182, 199–200, 209, 214, 215

Naujoks, Alfred, 203

Nazi Party: DNB's creation and staffing, 170–171, 183–188, 201; DNB's reporting, 188–194; espionage and, 204–207, 222; news, propaganda, and press policy of, 15, 36, 39–40, 42, 99, 101, 117–120, 169, 171, 183, 189, 192–197, 201, 203–204, 222, 289n42; radio and, 14, 99, 101, 113, 117–120, 190–191, 197, 203, 211–212, 226; South America and, 210, 213; Telegraph Union's coverage and, 143

Neue Deutsche Kabelgesellschaft, 268n15

Neue Jugend, Die, 78

News, 5, 9–10, 34–44, 230–231, 236n15, 238n27; cautions about, 228–231; definitions of, 4–5; economic news, 100–108, 113, 119, 123, 151, 225; German beliefs about, 4–6, 10, 34–44, 239n37; information warfare and, 1, 3. *See also* Economics, news and; Espionage; Exports, news and; Fake news; False news; Journalism; News agencies; Newspapers; Objectivity; Propaganda; Public opinion; Readers

News agencies, 10, 18–23, 34–43, 224–225; changed role after World War II, 227–228; emergence and reach of, 3–4; German concerns and, 23–29, 44; German fascination with, 8–10, 238n28; newspapers and, 29–35. *See also* Agences Alliées; Cartels, news agencies and; News agency consensus; *specific agencies*

News agency consensus, 4, 17–18, 44, 98, 225–226; defined, 14. *See also* News agencies

Newspapers: censorship and, 178–179; digitized, 7, 60–61; diplomats and, 130–131; Eildienst and, 105–106, 110–112; German colonial and German-language abroad, 48, 59–60, 65, 121, 124, 128, 131, 157–159, 211–213; Hugenberg and, 143–147, 164–165, 175, 179, 186;

Kapp Putsch and, 90–91, 94–95; Nazis and, 170–171, 185–186, 189, 191–195, 201, 204; news agencies and, 29–35, 98, 110–111, 116, 143–144, 147, 156, 159, 161, 166–168, 173–176, 180–182, 191–192, 197, 208–221, 224–226; revolution and, 70, 71f, 74–79, 82–84; as sources, 7, 35; World War I and, 52–53, 59–63, 84, 134; World War II and, 196, 203–204, 206–207, 212–213, 219–221. *See also* Foreign correspondents; Journalism

New World Information and Communication Order (NWICO), 228

New York Herald, 60

New York Herald Tribune, 155

New York Times, 60, 75

Nippon Denpō Tsūshinsha (Dentsū), 214, 219

Nippon Shimbun Rengōsha (Rengō), 214, 219, 221

Norddeutsche Allgemeine Zeitung, 87

Northcliffe, Lord Alfred, 15, 145, 196, 198, 199

Noske, Gustav, 83, 89, 91

Nyhan, Brendan, 157

Oberndorff, Alfred von, 62

Objectivity, 4, 34–35, 128, 139, 154, 166, 226; Nazis and, 39–40, 170, 218

Öffentlichkeit, 41. *See also* Habermas; Public sphere

Olympics (summer 1936), 211, 287n1

Ostasiatischer Lloyd, 20, 60, 65

Ost-Express, 284n70

Ottoman Empire, 26, 45, 55, 124–125. *See also* Middle East

Pach, 212

Papen, Franz von, 139

Payer, Friedrich von, 230

Peking Chronicle, 217

Philippines, 220–222, 298n104

Piłsudski, Józef, 157–159

Plata Zeitung, La, 211, 212

Plaut, Joseph, 214, 216, 217

Podbielski, Victor von, 49

Poincaré, Raymond, 200
Point-to-many technology, 12, 13, 51
Point-to-point technology, 12, 51, 103,
    274n104
Poland, 108, 157–160, 166–167, 203,
    286n106
Police: protests, revolution and, 73, 82,
    163; radio confiscation and, 103–104;
    surveillance and, 36, 42
Political economy, 10–11, 14
Politisch-Parlamentarische Nachrichten, 82
Polska Agencja Telegraficzna (PAT),
    108–109, 112, 166, 286n107
Ponsonby, Arthur, 39
Post Office, British, 104, 111, 200
Postal Ministry, German, 103, 117, 182,
    214; Bredow and, 68, 100, 102, 113, 115,
    119; Eildienst and, 100, 101–106,
    112–113, 115, 120, 151; radio and, 113–115,
    117, 119–120, 151, 164; Telefunken and,
    64, 82, 182; Telegraph Union and,
    151–152, 164; ticker machines and, 178;
    wireless and, 55, 57, 82, 100–106, 198;
    Wolff and, 21, 164, 198
Prensa, La, 200, 209
Press. *See* News; News agencies;
    Newspapers; Radio
Pressa, 132, 137, 277n54
Press Department: creation and
    organization of, 41, 52, 105, 123, 127–128,
    140, 183–184, 203; domestic reporting
    and, 175–177, 179, 183–184; foreign
    correspondents and, 127; Nazi Party
    and, 183–184, 203; Ritgen and, 127–129,
    133, 137–138; Telegraph Union and, 148,
    150, 152, 154–160, 175–177; Wolff and,
    88, 94–95, 97, 123, 126–128, 133–135, 137,
    140, 148, 155–157, 160, 175–177. *See also*
    Foreign Office, German
Propaganda: DNB and domestic, 183,
    188–197; Kapp Putsch and, 93; news
    and, 4, 38–40, 115, 126, 133–134, 138, 201,
    214; World War I and, 4, 38, 52–53,
    59–60, 61f, 69, 125, 198; World War II
    and 196–197, 203–204, 206–207,
    211–213, 219–223. *See also* False news;

Listeners; Public opinion; Propaganda
    Ministry; Readers; Transocean:
    German foreign policy and
Propaganda Ministry (Nazi), 39, 42,
    183–184, 186, 189–190, 203
Prussia, 21–22, 37, 70, 73, 90, 94, 144,
    157–158, 160–161, 179–181, 288n30
Public opinion, 5, 9, 18, 35–43, 69, 129, 140,
    205, 215–216, 224; democracy and, 85,
    194, 229–231; flawed assumptions about,
    9, 18, 229–231; Nazis and, 42, 170–171,
    194; news agencies and, 18, 34, 35–43,
    92, 95, 141, 165, 224; psychology of, 157.
    See also Listeners; Propaganda; Readers
Public Opinion (Lippmann), 230–231
Public sphere (Habermas), 40–41

Radek, Karl, 155
Radio: American, 114, 196, 207; in
    Austria, 164–165; BBC and, 104, 111,
    114, 116–117; in China, 216, 218; Cold
    War and, 228; Czechoslovakia and,
    160–161, 167–168; DNB and, 192;
    Eildienst's influence on, 14–15, 100,
    102, 113–118, 120, 151; German name for,
    114; Goebbels and, 99–101, 118, 119; in
    Japan, 214, 219; manufacturers and,
    103, 114, 178; Nazi Party and, 14–15,
    99–101, 117–119, 190–193, 203, 207,
    211–212, 226; news and, 113–119, 151–152;
    Poland and, 166–167; regulation of, 21,
    79–81, 99–104, 113–118, 183; *Rundfunk*
    and, 114; *Saalfunk* and, 114; in South
    America, 208–212; Telegraph Union
    and, 116–117, 151–152, 155, 160–168, 162f,
    175, 177; Transocean and, 197, 208–212,
    218; wireless and, 11–13, 102–104; Wolff
    and, 33, 116–117, 126, 151–152, 160–161,
    175; World War II and, 193, 196, 203,
    207, 222. *See also* Bredow, Hans von;
    Postal Ministry; Telefunken; Trans-
    radio (German); Voss, Ernst Ludwig;
    Wireless telegraphy
Radio Hucke, 212
Radio-Vekehrs-AG (RAVAG), 109,
    271n52

Railways, 11. *See also* Berlin-Baghdad railway

Ratzel, Friedrich, 25

Rauscher, Ulrich, 130, 159–160

Ravoux, Paul, 188, 190

Rawitzki, Arthur, 111–112, 184–185, 272nn74,76

Razón, La, 209

Readers, 9, 24, 34–44, 149, 157, 230–231; advertising and, 42–43; German beliefs about, 4, 34–44, 143, 179–180, 223, 230; Nazis and, 192–193, 223; news agencies and, 5, 9, 17–18, 32, 34–35, 155, 192, 194, 197; newspapers and, 29–32, 34–44, 84. *See also* Listeners; Propaganda; Public opinion

Redlich, Alexander, 164–165

Rehmate, radio tower at, 211

Reichsanzeiger, 87

Reichsministerium für Volksaufklärung und Propaganda (RMVP). *See* Propaganda Ministry

Reichsverband der Deutschen Presse. *See* Federal German Press Association

Reichszentrale für Heimatdienst, 176

Reich Telegraph Law (1892), 21, 103

Reismann-Grone, Theodor, 145, 185

Reith, John, 113

Reuterian. *See* Reuters Telegram Company

Reuter, Julius, 19, 21

Reuters Telegram Company, 1, 2*f,* 3, 11, 18–23, 28, 48, 61, 86, 187, 225, 227, 228, 244n9; ANA and, 165, 285n93; China and, 213, 215–219, 221; DNB and, 187, 188, 190, 191, 222, 290n66; Eildienst and, 109–112; German imperial ambitions and, 25, 26, 28–29, 48; PAT and, 166, 286n107; Reuterian, 111–112, 200; South Africa and, 201–203; South America and, 208, 212; Telegraph Union and, 165; Turkey and, 125–126, 132; wireless and, 200, 207, 216; Wolff and, 28–29, 48, 86, 110–111, 132, 140, 184, 187; World War I news and, 53, 54*f,* 61, 62, 225; World War II news and, 208, 212, 213, 215–219, 221, 222, 301n52

Revolution of 1918–1919, 70–72, 77–83

Rheinisch-Westfälische Zeitung, 185

Ribbentrop, Joachim von, 189, 203, 222

Richthofen, Ferdinand von, 63

Riefenstahl, Leni, 197

"Ring Combination." *See* Cartels, news agencies and; Agences Alliées

Rings, Joachim, 35

Ritgen, Hermann von, 15, 121–140, 160, 167, 278n68, 279n88

Ritgen, Otto, 137, 138, 186

Rohrbach, Paul, 25, 246n41

Röllinghoff, Wilhelm, 135, 148, 284n61

Roselius, Ludwig, 101–102, 268n10

Rosenberg, Alfred, 189

Ross, Colin, 207, 208

Ross, Corey, 39

Roßmann, Erich, 78–79

Rote Fahne, Die, 78, 149, 152, 262n28

Roth, Joseph, 30–31

RT (Russia Today), 5, 228

Rühlmann, Paul, 39

Rümelin, Eugen, 136

Rundfunk. See Radio

Russian Revolution, 38, 79, 141

Saalfunk plan. *See* Radio

Sacred Office for the Propagation of the Faith, of Catholic Church, 38

Salzburger Volksblatt, 165

Sarnoff, David, 211

Sayville, German wireless tower at, 51, 53, 55, 60, 61*f,* 102

Schabowski, Günther, 72–73

Schacht, Hjalmar, 31, 41, 59, 198

Schairer, Erich, 175

Scheidemann, Philipp, 37, 70, 74, 77

Scherl (publisher), 78, 82, 103, 142, 145, 160, 179–180, 186

Scheüch, Heinrich, 37

Schmidt-Dumont, Dr., 131, 136, 279n76

Schmitt, Carl, 117–118

Schnee, Heinrich, 26, 48

Schüler, Edmund, 127, 130

Schulte, Karl, 201

Schürff, Hans, 165

Schwabach, Paul von, 144, 182, 258n86
Schwarzhörer (illegal listeners), 105
Schwedler, Wilhelm, 12, 39, 68, 198, 201, 204, 222
Schweizerische Depeschenagentur, 61
Seeckt, Hans von, 90
Seipel, Ignaz, 163, 164
Semashko, Nikolai, 148
Severing, Carl, 179–180, 194, 225
Seyffert, Rudolf, 42–43
Shanghai, 57, 66, 215–216, 218, 220, 222, 295n41, 299n114, 300 nn137,138,141; Germans in, 213, 222
Siemens & Halske, 49, 67, 126, 178; rivalry with Anglo-American cable companies, 47
Simon, Fritz, 271n62
Simplicissimus cartoon, 53, 54*f*
Social Democratic Party (SPD), 30, 83, 179, 194; dispute with USPD, 77, 79–81; journalists and, 130, 252n131, 277n45; Kapp Putsch and, 90, 93; revolution of 1918–1919 and, 37, 77–78, 85, 260n3; stab-in-the-back myth and, 69; *Vorwärts* and, 78, 262n28; Wilhelm II's abdication and, 37, 74; Wolff and, 79, 85
Solf, Wilhelm, 75, 80
Sonderweg, 13, 242n52
South Africa, 49, 197, 201–203, 202*f*
South America, 15, 20, 28–29; German immigrants to, 208; Telegraph Union and, 297n73; telegraphy and, 12, 47, 49, 55; Transocean and, 68, 197, 204–213, 223, 225, 297n71
Soviet Union: Beloborodov and, 141, 155; cultural diplomacy and, 122; German information warfare and, 3, 213; occupation of Germany, 194, 226; Russian Revolution's influence on Germany, 79–80; Telegraph Union and, 141–144, 147–157, 166; trade relations with Germany, 141, 149–150, 152, 156; Wolff and, 147–149, 152, 154, 156. *See also* TASS
Spartacists, 77–78, 79, 82, 85, 262n28

Speech act theory, 8, 260n7
Spengler, Oswald, 25
Spiegel, Der, 227
Stab-in-the-back myth *(Dolchstoßlegende),* 69, 90
Stern-Rubarth, Edgar, 133–134
Stimson, Henry, 216
Stinnes, Hugo, 59, 145, 146
Stinnes–Legien agreement, 85
Strauss, Franz Josef, 227
Stresemann, Gustav, 6, 34–35, 59, 71*f,* 127, 134, 164, 176; trade and, 123, 149–150; Transocean and, 68, 198
Submarine telegraph cables. *See* Telegraph cables
Süddeutsche Zeitung, 227
Suriname, 46, 68
Sweden, 65, 92, 110, 206
Symbolic power (Bourdieu), 8, 85
Syndikat Deutscher Überseedienst (German Overseas Service Syndicate), 28, 59
Syndikat für die Auslandsnachrichten (Syndicate for Foreign News), 28
Systempresse, 168, 170

Tag, Der, 145, 179
Tägliche Rundschau, 103, 158–159
TASS (Telegrafnoe agentstvo Sovetskogo Soiuza), 147–148, 154, 155, 156, 213, 216, 283n52
Telefunken, 49–50, 53, 57–58, 60, 103, 114; Bredow and, 57, 100, 102; China and, 63–68, 216; colonial wireless network and, 46–47, 68, 213–214; German government and, 46, 49–50, 57–58, 60, 63–68, 255n29; Java and, 58, 68, 213; Marconi Company and, 46, 50–51; Transocean and, 60, 61*f,* 65, 68, 208–209, 211; world wireless network and, 47–48, 57–58. *See also* Transradio (German)
Telegraph cables, 1, 2*f,* 3, 6, 11–12, 19, 40, 45–53, 54*f,* 107, 225, 268n15; France and, 19, 49; Germany and, 11–12, 21, 45–53, 56–57, 69, 102–103, 173, 178, 182; Great

Britain and, 6, 19, 45–53, 54*f*, 69, 182, 200, 208, 215–216; Japan and, 49, 220; United States and, 47–49, 208; World War I and, 52–53, 54*f*, 69, 190. *See also* Wireless telegraphy

Telegraph Union, 98, 141–144, 146–169, 171–182, 189, 227, 280n3, 283n47; Austria and, 163–165, 186; Beloborodov affair and, 141, 143, 144, 145, 147–152, 154–156; Czechoslovakia and, 160–161, 167–168, 186; DNB and, 183, 185–187, 192, 195; Dradag and, 116, 117; economic nationalism and, 15, 171, 225; integration in Hugenberg's media empire, 39, 142–147, 173; Latvia and, 165–166; Lithuania and, 157–159; Poland and, 157–160, 166–167, 264n70, 286n107; radio and, 151–152, 155, 160, 161–168, 162*f*; Ritgen and, 137, 138; Soviet-German relationship and, 147–157; TASS and, 147–149; Wolff and, 86, 94, 98, 116, 140, 142, 147–149, 151–157, 159–161, 163–166, 168–169, 173, 175, 180–182, 228–229. *See also* Advertising: Telegraph Union and; Hugenberg, Alfred

Telephones, 23, 73–74, 136, 261n15, 274n104; Eildienst and, 103, 105, 126; news dissemination and, 33, 84, 87, 88, 90, 93, 161, 165, 191

Telos Verwaltungsgesellschaft, 291n72

Tempo, 31

Thailand, 221

"Third-person effect," 36, 238n28

Ticker machines and services, 33, 74, 137, 178–179, 190–191, 193. *See also* Hellschreiber wireless ticker machine

Tidningarnas Telegrambyra, 110

Times (London), 124–125, 134, 154, 198, 199, 205

Tirpitz, Alfred von, 6, 24

Tjarks, Hermann, 208, 210–211

Tonn, Günther, 205–206

Tönnies, Ferdinand, 38

Toronto Star, 7

Tractatus telegrams, 61, 87

Transatlantisches Bureau, 28

Transocean, 15, 28, 39, 42, 59–63, 65, 68, 136, 140, 196–223, 202*f*, 225–226, 227; anti-Semitism and, 201, 217; China and, 65, 196, 199, 203–204, 214–220, 293n13; cultural diplomacy and, 136; D-day reporting and, 196; Dutch colonies and, 214; East Asia and, 213–223, 226–227; France and, 200, 209–210, 210*f*, 216–217; German foreign policy and, 15, 196–223, 225; Great Britain and, 62–63, 196–203, 207, 212–213, 216; Japan and, 214, 216, 219–221; radio and, 196, 197, 200, 207, 208–212, 214, 216, 218, 219; South America and, 196, 201–213, 223, 297nn71,73; Soviet Union and, 213; Telefunken and, 208–209; Telos and, 291n72; Thailand and, 221; United States and, 60–61, 61*f*, 196, 204–207, 212, 223; wireless and, 136, 197, 198–201, 203, 208, 209–211, 210*f*, 213, 215–217, 219–222; Wolff and, 62; World War I news and, 59–63, 61*f*, 68, 198; World War II news and, 196–197, 204, 206–207, 211–213, 219–223

Transradio (German), 53, 102, 182, 208–209, 211, 289nn40,41, 297n71, 298n104. *See also* Telefunken

Transradio Internacional Compania Radiotelegrafica, 209

Transradio (Swiss), 271n62, 272n74

Traub, Gottfried, 17

Treaty of Brest-Litovsk, 24

Treaty of Rapallo, 150, 168

Treaty of Saint-Germain, 109

Treaty of Versailles, 68, 89, 100, 108, 113, 123, 179

Tröbst, Hans, 131, 277n56

Trotsky, Leon, 155

Tucholsky, Kurt, 30, 94–95

Tuckerton, wireless tower at, 51

Turkey, 68, 121–140. *See also* Ottoman Empire

Türkische Post, 131–132, 136–138

Ullstein, Leopold, 29–30, 31

Ullstein: publishing company, 29–30, 31, 35, 82, 134; news service, 134

Unabhängige Sozialdemokratische Partei Deutschlands (USPD), 77, 78, 80–82, 92

United Press (UP): agents arrested by Gestapo, 206; Argentina and, 211; China and, 213, 214, 216–219; DNB and, 187; Japan and, 219; merger with INS, 227; Nazi Party and 35, 206, 292n90; South America and, 206, 208, 210, 211; Telegraph Union and, 142, 156, 161, 187; Transocean and, 206, 208, 210, 211, 213, 214, 216–220

United States: cultural diplomacy and, 122–123; Foreign Agents Registration Act of, 205–206; German wireless towers in, 51, 53, 55, 58, 60, 102; HUAC and, 205–206, 207; MacBride report and, 228; Transocean and, 60–61, 61f, 196, 204–207, 212, 216, 223. See also Associated Press; International News Service; United Press

Universum-Film AG (UFA), 145

Van de Woude (Dutch engineer), 57–58, 65

Verband ausländischer Pressevertreter. See Association of Foreign Press Representatives

Verein Deutscher Zeitungs-Verleger (VDZV). See Association of German Newspaper Publishers

Versailles conference, 25, 123, 215. See also Treaty of Versailles

Voice of America (VOA), 207

Voigt, Friedrich Wilhelm, 265n93

Völkischer Beobachter, 201

Volksempfänger (people's receivers), 118

Volksgemeinschaft (people's community), 39, 142, 170, 183

Vorwärts, 31, 78, 81, 82, 149, 157–158, 262n42

Voss, Ernst Ludwig, 101–102, 106, 114–115

Voss, Karl Johann von, 284n70

Vossische Zeitung, 3, 30, 140, 144, 164, 261n24

Wang Jingwei, 219–220

War Press Office. See Press Department

Weber, Max, 4, 38

Weimar Republic: business and, 100, 178, 180–181; China and, 214; democracy and, 15, 30–31, 98, 115–116, 169, 183, 194, 225, 228–229; elections and, 81, 83, 85, 99, 143; founding of, 14, 70–83; hyperinflation during, 84, 97, 100, 107, 108, 119, 146; Kapp Putsch and, 91–93, 97–98; laws and, 44, 178, 179–180; Nazis and, 99, 170, 194–195, 223; newspapers and, 30–31, 38, 42–43, 147; press politics and, 41–42, 44, 128, 170–183, 194, 225, 228–229; radio and, 115–116, 118–119; South America and, 208; Soviet Union and, 149–150; Telegraph Union and, 143, 169–179, 181; Turkey and, 125, 139; Wolff and, 82–89, 97, 171, 173–183; Young Plan and, 179. See also Democracy; Revolution of 1918–1919

Welt, Die, 227

Welt am Abend, 31

Weltbühne, Die (journal), 39

Weltliteratur (world literature), 6

Weltmacht (world power), 6

Weltpolitik (world politics), 6, 24, 51

Weltprojekte (world projects), 6

Weltverkehr (world traffic), 6

Weltwirtschaft (world economy), 6

Werner, Ferdinand, 29

Westarp, Kuno von, 53

Wilhelm II, Kaiser, 6, 14, 24, 41; abdication of, 70–79, 71f, 76f; Burgfrieden and, 52; Daily Telegraph affair and, 26–27; first Moroccan crisis and, 26; German imperial ambitions and, 24, 26–27, 45–46, 124; Middle East and, 45, 124; public opinion and, 37, 41; wireless and, 46, 49

Wilson, Woodrow, 37–38, 65, 73

Winkler, Heinrich August, 97

Wipro (Wirtschaftsstelle der Provinzpresse), 146–147, 181, 186
Wireless telegraphy, 10–13, 103, 198,
225–226, 240n39, 241n49; Bredow and,
100, 102–104, 106–107, 113, 114, 118–119;
in China, 63–68, 215–216, 219; Eildienst
and, 15, 100–107, 109, 110–111, 113, 120;
France and, 209–210, 210f, 216–217;
German domestic control of, 21, 77,
79–82, 100–107, 113, 151–152, 177–178;
German international networks of, 12,
46–47, 49–52, 53–68, 120, 182, 208–211,
221–222; Great Britain and, 45–46,
51–52, 67, 200, 203, 216, 221; Treaty of
Versailles and, 68–69; in Turkey, 123,
126, 136; World War I and, 52–53,
55–69, 125. See also Hellschreiber
wireless ticker machine; Infrastructure;
Marconi; Radio; Telefunken; Transocean, German foreign policy and
Wirth, Joseph, 86
Witt, Käte, 121–122, 124, 129, 135, 138
Wolff, Bernhard, 19, 183
Wolff's Telegraphisches Bureau (WTB),
10–11, 18–23, 28–29, 32–35, 33f, 41, 69,
110, 146–149, 189, 192, 225, 244n9;
anti-Semitism and, 29, 183–185; CTC
and, 21, 181; DNB and, 170, 183–188,
191, 195; Dradag and, 116; Eildienst
and, 105, 110–112, 271nn58,59; German
government ministries and, 29, 48, 50,
53, 82–90, 93–94, 97, 120–137, 140, 144,
148, 160, 168, 171, 175–178, 180–184,
194–195, 228, 229, 277n56, 278nn65,68;
German imperial ambitions and,
25–27, 48; Kaiser's abdication and,
70–79, 71f, 76f; Kapp Putsch and,
89–97; Telegraph Union and, 86, 94,
98, 116, 140, 142, 151–157, 159–161,
163–166, 168–169, 173, 175–178; Trans-

ocean and, 61–62, 198; wireless and, 48,
50, 151, 178, 198–199; World War I news
and, 52–53, 59, 61–62, 255n39,40
Wolff, Theodor, 74
Workers' and Soldiers' Councils, 77–82,
87, 260n3
World War I, 5, 6, 37–38, 56, 125, 190, 198;
cables and, 52, 54f, 56; reporting on, 5,
6, 52–53, 58–62, 69, 225; wireless and,
12, 47, 51–53, 55–69
World War II, 190, 192–193, 225; news
agencies' changed role after, 226–229;
reporting on, 196, 200, 201–203, 208,
212–223, 301nn152,157. See also
Deutsches Nachrichtenbüro (DNB);
Nazi Party

Xinhua news agency, 5, 228

Young Plan, 179

Zaleski, August, 157, 158
Zapp, Manfred, 205–206, 207
Zechlin, Walter, 41, 134, 139–140, 156, 177,
252nn129,131, 279n87
Zeesen, radio tower at, 115, 211
Zeitungsromane (novels serialized in
newspapers), 30–31
Zeitungs-Verlag, 105, 152, 153f, 162f, 172f,
283n47
Zeitungswissenschaft 33f; (newspaper
science) discipline, 38
Zentralfunkleitung (Central Radio
Committee), 80
Zentralstelle für Auslandsdienst
(Central Office for Service Abroad),
59–60
Zhao Meng, 215
Ziblatt, Daniel, 143
Zimmermann, Arthur, 56